Music Through Sources and Documents

Ruth Halle Rowen

Professor of Music
The City College of New York
The Graduate School of the City University of New York

Prentice-Hall, Inc., Englewood Cliffs, New Jersey 07632

Library of Congress Cataloging in Publication Data

ROWEN, RUTH HALLE.
   Music through sources and documents.

   Bibliography: p.
   Includes index.
   1. Music—History and criticism—Sources.
2. Music—Performance—History—Sources. 3. Music—
Theory—History—Sources.
ML160.R88   780'.9   78–2268
ISBN 0–13–608331–5

To Sy, Mary Helen, and Louis
My Sources of Inspiration

© 1979 by Prentice-Hall, Inc., Englewood Cliffs, N.J. 07632

Printed in the United States of America

10 9 8 7 6 5 4 3 2 1

PRENTICE-HALL INTERNATIONAL, INC., *London*
PRENTICE-HALL OF AUSTRALIA PTY. LIMITED, *Sydney*
PRENTICE-HALL OF CANADA, LTD., *Toronto*
PRENTICE-HALL OF INDIA PRIVATE LIMITED, *New Delhi*
PRENTICE-HALL OF JAPAN, INC., *Tokyo*
PRENTICE-HALL OF SOUTHEAST ASIA PTE. LTD., *Singapore*
WHITEHALL BOOKS LIMITED, *Wellington, New Zealand*

Contents

Prelude

Music Through Sources and Documents is an organized sampling of written materials compiled for the purpose of exploring the substance of music in the realm of knowledge. The items, chosen from treatises, letters, archival documents, and books, are involved with aspects of the practice, theory, aesthetics, and criticism of music, examined period by period.

Juxtaposed are the abstract and the concrete, the legendary and the historical, the lofty and the commonplace, the amateur and the professional. As musical truths pass from one generation to another, identifying themselves again and again, they explain elemental phenomena concerning melody, intervals, form, temperament, and instruments. By examining these subjects, as well as others, in their successive stages, we may understand how words like *harmony*, *imitation*, *sonata*, *modulation*, and *symphony* came to have widely differing meanings which are nevertheless compatible.

When we read today about traditional ceremonial music and about the influence of music on the youth of ancient Greece, we may be frustrated by the small amount of music that has actually been preserved. Yet, as we read on into the Middle Ages, the Renaissance, the Baroque Period, the Classical Era, and beyond, we find that ancient descriptive and scholarly writings continue to shape the living practice even though little music from earliest times remains to be heard.

Fortunately, most of the musical styles represented in these pages may be illustrated by an abundance of music. Since the true purpose for reading about music lies in the application of the knowledge thus gained to the music itself, the most desirable way of using these sources and documents is to become acquainted with the kinds of music to which they refer.

The author is deeply indebted to the guides, academic and bibliographical, institutional and individual, oral and written, named and unnamed, which led the way toward the personal discovery of these passages. Special thanks must be given to those who through the years made accessible the resources and services for research at the City College of New York, at the Graduate Center of the City Univerity of New York, at Columbia University, and at the New York Public Library. Furthermore, the author's aspirations and the desire to present these materials to a wide audience have been tuned and tempered to perfection by Norwell F. Therien, Jr., Barbara A. Barr, and Teru Uyeyama.

RUTH HALLE ROWEN
The City College of New York and
The Graduate School of the City University of New York

Abbreviations

GMB   *Geschichte der Musik in Beispielen*, ed. Arnold Schering (Leipzig: Breitkopf & Härtel, 1931; New York: Broude Brothers, 1950)

HAM   *Historical Anthology of Music*, ed. Archibald T. Davison and Willi Apel (Cambridge, Mass.: Harvard University Press, 1950)

HMS   *The History of Music in Sound*, ed. Gerald Abraham (New York: Oxford University Press, with records manufactured by RCA Victor)

LU 1   *Liber Usualis* with introduction and rubrics in English, ed. by the Benedictines of Solesmes (Tournai, New York: Desclée, 1962); modern Gregorian square notation on four-line staff

LU 2   *Liber Usualis Missae et Officii* (Paris, Tournai, Rome: Desclée, 1954); modern round notation on five-line staff

MM   *Masterpieces of Music Before 1750*, ed. Carl Parrish and John F. Ohl (New York: W. W. Norton & Co., Inc., 1951)

MSO   *Music Scores Omnibus*, ed. William J. Starr and George F. Devine (Englewood Cliffs, N.J.: Prentice-Hall, Inc., 1964)

SRMH   *Source Readings in Music History*, ed. Oliver Strunk (New York: W. W. Norton & Co., Inc., 1950)

SSMS   *Study Scores of Musical Styles*, ed. Edward R. Lerner (New York, St. Louis, San Francisco, Toronto, London, Sydney: McGraw-Hill Book Co., 1968)

TEM   *A Treasury of Early Music*, ed., Carl Parrish (New York: W. W. Norton & Co., Inc., 1958)

1

Ancient Mention
of Musical Practices

1.1 THE *BIBLE*

Among the earliest literary sources relating to musical thought and practices in the Near East are the books of the Bible. Scattered throughout the Old and New Testaments are references to musical instruments and the custom of singing hymns and psalms.

The Bible is a compilation of writings gathered together over thousands of years from about the second millennium B.C. As time went on, portions of the Old Testament were translated from literary Hebrew into the native tongues in use during ancient times, such as Samaritan, Syriac, and Aramaic, the latter being the vernacular spoken by the Jews themselves. Later there were translations into Greek and then Latin, causing a variety of rhythmical and pitch inflections for the same verses, depending on the dialect or language in which they were chanted.

The poetic texts, narrations of history, and chronicles of current events that permeate the Bible have inspired composers of every era. Oratorios such as Handel's *Israel in Egypt* (1739), Passions, Requiems like that of Brahms (1857–68), and other large-scale vocal works have been based directly on Biblical texts. Biblical stories have also been used as the inspiration of instrumental "program music" without voice, as for example the Biblical sonatas for keyboard instrument by Johann Kuhnau (1700) and those for violin with nonstandard tuning (*scordatura*) by Heinrich Biber (c. 1670). The Latin *Vulgate* translation of *Psalm 150* made by St. Jerome at the end of the fourth century, as well as verses from Psalms

39 and 40, comprise the text of Igor Stravinsky's *Symphony of Psalms* for voices, two pianos, winds, and lower strings (1930).

The Song of Moses at the Red Sea: *Exodus* 15:1, 18–21*

> Then sang Moses and the children of Israel this song unto the Lord, and spake, saying, I will sing unto the Lord, for he hath triumphed gloriously, the horse and his rider hath he thrown into the sea. . . .
> The Lord shall reign for ever and ever.
> For the horse of Pharaoh went in with his chariots and with his horsemen into the sea, and the Lord brought again the waters of the sea upon them; but the children of Israel went on dry land in the midst of the sea.
> And Miriam the prophetess, the sister of Aaron, took a timbrel in her hand; and all the women went out after her with timbrels and with dances.
> And Miriam answered them, Sing ye to the Lord, for he hath triumphed gloriously; the horse and his rider hath he thrown into the sea.

Musical Instruments in Worship: *Psalm 150*

> Praise ye the Lord. Praise God in his sanctuary: praise him in the firmament of his power.
> Praise him for his mighty acts: praise him according to his excellent greatness.
> Praise him with the sound of the trumpet:[1] praise him with the psaltery [2] and harp.[3]
> Praise him with the timbrel [4] and dance:[5] praise him with stringed instruments [6] and organs.[7]

* *From the King James Version of the* Bible.

1. *Trumpet* is a translation of the Hebrew *shofar*, an instrument made from a ram's horn, used for signalling and for welcoming the New Year. The Greek translation *salpinx* designates an instrument associated mainly with the signals of war. Latin translations are *tuba*, *cornea*, and *buccina*.
2. The Hebrew *nevel* or *nebel*, related to the Greek *nabla*, is a stringed instrument referred to as the *psalterio* in the *Vulgate*. Whereas the Hebrew *nebel* may have had either a gourdlike or loomlike frame for a sound chest, the *psalterio*, according to Greek description in the fifth century A.D., was triangular in shape like the Greek letter delta.
3. The Hebrew word for harp was *kinnor*, translated as *kithara*, spelled with a *k* in Greek and a *c* in Latin. This was the instrument on which David played to soothe Saul. The Greek *kithara* and *barbitos*, as well as the Hebrew *kinnor*, were types of lyre, the latter being a general term for stringed instruments with two wooden sides connected by an arm or crossbar.
4. *Tof*, the generic word for *drum*, was translated into Latin and Greek as *tympanum* or *tympano*. Miriam's *tof* is considered to be a tambourine or timbrel.
5. The word for *dance*, the Hebrew *mahol* meaning *to whirl*, was translated into Greek as *chorostasia*, a festive or choral dance performed in a ring.
6. The Hebrew word for *stringed instruments* was *minnim*, from the idea of division, or the placement of strings on an instrument. In Greek and Latin stringed instruments were designated by the words for strings—*chordais* and *chordis*, respectively.
7. The Hebrew *ugab* or pipe became the Greek and Latin *organo*, whose English

Praise him upon the loud cymbals; praise him upon the high sounding cymbals.[8]

Let everything that hath breath praise the Lord. Praise ye the Lord.

Bibliographical Notes

The relationship between music in the synagogue and church is described in Eric Werner, *The Sacred Bridge* (London: Dennis Dobson; New York: Columbia University Press, 1959) and Alec Robertson, *Christian Music* (New York: Hawthorne Books, 1961).

For further information on instruments from ancient times, see John Stainer, *The Music of the Bible* (London: Novello and Company, Limited, 1914; reprint by Da Capo Press, 1970); Francis W. Galpin, *The Music of the Sumerians and Their Immediate Successors the Babylonians and Assyrians* (Cambridge: Cambridge University Press, 1937; reprint, New York: Da Capo Press, 1970); Curt Sachs, *The History of Musical Instruments* (New York: W. W. Norton & Company, Inc., 1940); Curt Sachs, *Real-Lexikon der Musikinstrumente* (Berlin: Julius Bard, 1913; reprint, New York: Dover Publications, 1964); Sibyl Marcuse, *Musical Instruments, A Comprehensive Dictionary* (New York: Doubleday & Company, Inc., 1964).

1.2 THE CHINESE *CANON OF DOCUMENTS*

Chinese musical thought embraces a mythological period that goes back to 2697 B.C. when Emperor Huang Ti (the Yellow Emperor) instructed his minister to go to the Kwan-lun mountains. There a pitch pipe was to be cut from a particular type of bamboo, of a length to sound the note *huang chung* (yellow bell). This principal tone represented the earth, then viewed as the main element.

Although we do not know the absolute pitch the Chinese assigned to the yellow bell, we may find the relative pitches of the Chinese scale as

---

counterpart, *organ*, has assumed a much more elaborate meaning than the simple pipe it was originally.

8. The cymbals, *tzeltzelim* (Hebrew), *kymbalois* (Greek), or *cymbalis* (Latin), are mentioned twice in *Psalm 150*, each time with a modifying adjective. In Hebrew the cymbals are first described as summoning, or as being heard with a clear tone (*shama*). The corresponding Latin adjective, *benesonantibus*, emphasizes the aspect of resounding or reverberating well. When the word for *cymbal* is repeated, it is modified in Hebrew by the word *teru'ah*—literally, *shout* or *cry*. When the word *teru'ah* was applied to an instrument that was blown, such as the *shofar*, it meant a rapid succession of notes like a tremolo. Perhaps a similar rendition is implied here. The corresponding Greek and Latin words express the idea of proclaiming with joy and jubilation—*alalagmon* and *jubilationis*, respectively.

they did, by constructing a spiral with each succeeding pitch pipe two-thirds the length of the preceding one. Starting on C, the series would be C G D A E.

The tradition of ascribing great significance to the pitch pipes was recorded in the *Shû Ching*, the Canon of Documents of Confucianism shaped by the profound philosopher, Confucius (c. 551–479 B.C.) and his numerous disciples. The passage cited below is from *The Canon of Emperor Shun*. According to tradition, the Emperor constructed a lute or zither with five strings. On this instrument he accompanied himself while singing a song of good conduct, comparing the fine influence of rulers and parents to the genial balm of the south wind.

In addition to bamboo pipes and zithers with silk strings, Chinese instruments included chimes or sounding stones, drums covered with skin, wooden rattles, clay ocarinas, mouth organs shaped from gourds, and metal bells.

The Pitch Pipes and the Sounding Stone:
The Canon of Emperor Shun*

The Emperor said, "Kwei, I appoint you to be Director of Music, and to teach our sons, so that the straightforward shall yet be mild; the gentle, dignified; the strong, not tyrannical; and the impetuous, not arrogant. Poetry is the expression of earnest thought; singing is the prolonged utterance of that expression; the tones accompany that utterance, and they are harmonized themselves by the standard pipes. In this way the eight different kinds of musical instruments can be adjusted so that one shall not take from or interfere with another; and spirits and men are brought into harmony."

Kwei said, "I smite the sounding stone. I gently strike it and the various animals lead on one another to dance."

To his Forester and Minister of Agriculture the Emperor said, "I wish to hear the six pitch pipes, the five tones determined by them, and the eight kinds of musical instruments regulated by them, examining thereby the virtues and defects of government. As the odes that go forth from the court set to music, and as they come in from the people, ordered by these five tones, it is yours to hear them for me. When I am doing wrong, it is yours to hear them for me. When I am doing wrong, it is yours to correct me.

"Also, the masters of music set these tones, and continually make their compositions public, as corrected by themselves. If they become reformed they are to be received and employed; if they do not, let the terrors of punishment overtake them."

Kwei said, "When the sounding stone is tapped or struck with force, and the lutes are strongly swept or gently touched to accompany the singing, the progenitors of the Emperor come to the service, and all the princes show their virtue in giving place to one another. In the court below the hall there

* *From* Sacred Books of the East, *ed. F. Max Muller, Vol. III*, The Texts of Confucianism, *trans. James Legge, 2nd ed. (Oxford: The Clarendon Press, 1899), pp. 44–45, 59, 61–62. Reprinted by permission of the Clarendon Press, Oxford.*

are the pipes and hand drums, which join in at the sound of the rattle and cease at that of the stopper, when the organs and bells take their place. This makes birds and beasts fall moving. When the nine parts of the service, as arranged by the Emperor, have all been performed, the male and female phoenix come with their measured gambolings into the court."

Kwei said, "Oh! when I smite the sounding stone, or gently strike it, the various animals lead on one another to dance, and all the chiefs of the official departments become truly harmonious."

The Emperor composed a song about this, and sang,

> When the members work joyfully,
> The head rises grandly;
> And the duties of all the offices are fully discharged!

> When the head is intelligent,
> The members are good;
> And all affairs will be happily performed!

> When the head is vexatious,
> The members are idle;
> And all affairs will go to ruin!

The Emperor said, "Yes, go and be reverently attentive to your duties."

Bibliographical Notes

For further information on music in the realm of ancient Chinese culture, see J. A. Van Aalst, *Chinese Music* (Shanghai: Inspector General of Customs, 1884; reprint, New York: Paragon Book Reprint Corp., 1964); John Hazedel Levis, *Foundations of Chinese Musical Art* (Peking, 1936; reprint, New York: Paragon, 1964). Also, Kazu Nakaseko of Kyoto, Japan, "Symbolism in Ancient Chinese Music Theory," *Journal of Music Theory*, I, No. 2 (1957), 147–180, contains an extensive bibliography of both primary and secondary sources.

1.3 THE *MAHĀBHĀRATA* AND THE *NĀTYASĀSTRA*

The Indian concept of music is bound not only to the senses but also to the intellect and to spiritual values. A vision of the senses, the natural elements, and all of knowledge housed in an eternal mansion is described in the *Mahābhārata* (Great Tale of the Bharatas), a gigantic poem concerning the rivalry among cousins of a royal Hindu family, written from about the sixth century B.C. The passage quoted here is elucidated through Narada, an offspring of the goddess of learning and inventor of the harp.

Information concerning Hindu musical theory and performance is contained in the *Nātyasāstra* (Principles of Dramatic Art), started about the first century B.C. Here such matters as the origins of song, dance, mime, and sentiment are ascribed to four books of knowledge—the four *Vedas*, interpreted by Brahma, the supreme being. His pupil, Bharata the sage, amalgamated this learning into the creation of what is known as the drama. The authorship of the *Nātyasāstra* itself has been attributed to one of the Bharatas, named Bharata-Muni.

Basic to Indian music theory are the *raga* or pattern of tones in a melody and its *tala* or rhythmic pattern. The tones of a raga octave are identified by the syllables *sa, ri, ga, ma, pa, dha, ni*, derived from the calls and cries of animals and birds. Each raga has characteristic motives or melodic formulas, groups of tones which distinguish it from the other ragas. The octave outlining a raga can also be divided theoretically into twenty-two equal microtones called *srutis*.[9] Although no one actually sings or plays a scale of twenty-two srutis, the interval of a single sruti can be determined in practice by tuning one lute to the mode *sadjagrāma* with its *pa* of four srutis, and another to the mode *madhyamagrāma* starting a fourth above with a *pa* of three srutis.[10] Then the two tones designated as *pa* can easily be shown to diverge by a microtone, the extremely small interval of one sruti. The sruti is thus a derived interval, not one identified with the simplest divisions of a single string (such as the intervals of an octave, fifth, fourth, and third).

The rhythmic pattern, the tala (literally, *palm of the hand*), is measured aurally by the clang of the cymbals and visually by the bodily movement of the dance. The smaller units within this measure are

9. An interval from one syllable to the next is measured in terms of four, three, or two srutis. Each note is designated as occurring on the final sruti of its group. Hence, with a total of twenty-two srutis in the octave, the two basic modes or *grāmas* are measured as follows:

	[d	e	f	g	a	b	c	d]
	sa	ri	ga	ma	pa	dha	ni	sa
sadjagrāma	1234	123	12	1234	1234	123	12	1234

	ma	pa	dha	ni	sa	ri	ga	ma	pa
madhyamagrāma	1234	123	1234	12	1234	123	12	1234	123
	[g	a	b	c	d	e	f	g]	

10. The English orientalist William Jones (1746–1794) explained the relative measurements of *pa* in the 2 basic modes as follows: The two scales are made to coincide by taking a sruti from *pa* and adding it to *dha*. [*On the Musical Modes of the Hindus* (1784) in *The Works of Sir William Jones* (London, 1807), Vol. IV, p. 188.]

counted with the aid of the hand and the fingers. The importance of musical rhythm in relation to speech is so great that sometimes the musical quantity determines the verbal articulation, rather than the other way around. Individual rhythmic syllables are classified as being short, long, or protracted. Thus, the tala has accents of both stress and duration. Because of the monophonic nature of the music, and the fact that the rhythms consist of units that are added together rather than multiplied, there is no limit to the degree of complication, ranging all the way up to twenty-six syllables, and more, to a poetic foot.

The Senses and Learning: The *Mahābhārata**

Narada said, "Listen to me, O child, as I tell you about the assembly house of the Grand-sire, that house which none can describe. Ever contributing to the happiness of those within it, its atmosphere is neither cold nor warm. Hunger and thirst or any kind of uneasiness disappear as soon as one goes there. It seems to be made up of brilliant gems of many kinds. It does not seem to be supported on columns. It knows no deterioration, being eternal. That self-effulgent mansion, by its numerous blazing celestial indications of unrivalled splendor, seems to surpass the moon, the sun, and the fire. Stationed in heaven, it blazes forth as if censuring the maker of the day. In that mansion live Intelligence, Space, Knowledge, Air, Heat, Water, Nature, and Earth; Sound, Touch, Form, Taste, and Scent; the Modes of Nature, and the elemental and prime causes of the world; and all Sciences and branches of learning; Histories and all minor branches of learning; the several branches of the *Vedas;* the seven kinds of speech: Understanding, Patience, Memory, Wisdom, Intelligence, Fame, Forgiveness; the Hymns of the *Samaveda,* the Science of hymns in general, and various kinds of Verses and Songs."

The Materials of Music: The *Nātyasāstra*†

There are four types of musical instrument, as follows: stretched, covered, solid, and hollow. The *stretched* comprises stringed instruments; the *covered* designates the drums; as an example of the *solid* one may mention the cymbals; for the *hollow*, the flute.

Only the stretched and the covered instruments are used in dramatic presentation.

The group of performers centered around the strings comprises the singer and his entourage, the players of the *vipanci* [lute with seven strings], the *vina* [generic name for lute], and the *vamsa* [flute].

*From The Mahābhārata of Krishna-Dwaipayana Vyasa, *trans. Pratap Chandra Roy, 1889, Vol. II, Sect. 11, pp. 32–35.*

† *The portion of the* Nātyasāstra *quoted here was translated from the French of* J. Gosset, *"Contribution à l'Etude de la Musique Hindoue" in* Bibliothèque de la Faculté des Lettres de Lyon *(Paris: Ernest Leroux, 1888), Vol. VI, pp. 53–57. A complete translation of the* Nātyasāstra *into English appears as* A Treatise on Ancient Indian Dramaturgy and Histrionics *ascribed to Bharata-Muni, trans. Manomohan Ghosh, Revised second ed. (Calcutta: Manisha Granthalaya, 1967).*

The group of performers in the drum ensemble play on a drum with two heads of different diameters, a drum with one head, and a drum with a loud sound.

In dramatic performance the scene varies according to the country, and the actors use dialects to portray personages of high, low, or middle station.

Thus, these diverse parts, namely, song, instrumental music, and drama, are joined together as in a circle of fire.

When the genre comprising diverse stretched instruments involves musical tones [svara], rhythm [tala], and words [pada], it is called a concert.

Musical sounds are produced in two ways: with the lute and with the body, according to the indication of the distinctive characters which constitute each of them.

There are two kinds of feet [pada], those bound by the rules of the verse and those which are not.

The tala has twenty-one characteristics: ornamentation, regularity, extension, introduction, cymbal, contact, cycle, accentuation, unit of time, duration, element, shattering, pause, time (of which there are three), poetic meter, limb, dance, measurement by four, hand, finger or toe, and interlude.

Following are the seven tones: sadja, rsabha, gāndhāra, madhyama, pancama, dhāivata, nisāda. They are divided into four categories according to the intervals [srutis] which separate them from each other. These are: the sonant or principal tone, the nearest consonant tone, the similar or assonant tone, and the dissonant tone.

Every sonant is likewise a tonic. Tones separated by an interval of nine or thirteen srutis are consonant. A dissonant tone is an interval of twenty srutis away. Tones which are neither tonics, nor consonant, nor dissonant are called assonant.

There are two modes of the scale: sadjagrāma and madhyamagrāma. The only difference in this respect between them is the fact that the consonants sa and pa of the sadjagrāma are replaced in the madhyamagrāma by pa and ri.[11] Each of the modes contains twenty-two srutis.

Bibliographical Notes

A concise summary of the history of the Indian scale is given in Herbert A. Popley, *The Music of India*, 3rd ed. (New Delhi: Y.M.C.A. Publishing House, 1966). Appendix I of Popley contains an extensive bibliography of works in English dealing with Indian music. Also see Arnold Bake, "The Music of India" in *The New Oxford History of Music*, Vol. I, ed. Egon Wellesz (London: Oxford University Press, 1957), pp. 195–227; and William P. Malm, *Music Cultures of the Pacific, the Near East, and Asia* (Englewood Cliffs, N.J.: Prentice-Hall, Inc., 1967), pp. 67–86.

11. From sa to pa in the sadjagrāma is 13 srutis, a consonance equal to our interval of a fifth. From pa to ri in the madhyamagrāma is also a 13-sruti consonance. However, sa to pa in the madhyamagrāma is only 12 srutis, an assonant interval.

2

Greek Sources for the Attributes of Tone in Performance

2.1 PLATO (c. 428–347 B.C.)

Plato, founder of the Academy in Athens, made an intensive study of the moral properties of music. Unlike his master Socrates (470?–399 B.C.), who did not leave anything in writing for posterity, Plato preserved not only his own teachings but also those of his mentor.

In the *Republic*, speaking through Socrates as the personification of wisdom, with Glaucon as interrogator, Plato envisioned the education suitable for the ideal state. During the discussion he identified the ingredients of song as consisting of the words, the harmony, and the rhythm, a definition which was to become the focal point for the beginning of opera in the seventeenth century. The Greek *armonia*, customarily translated into the English *harmony*, literally means *a fitting together*. In a musical situation it might therefore refer to the relationship of the pitches to one another, or to the tuning of the strings of an instrument in agreement with each other. The frequent analogies between human harmony and musical harmony made by Greek writers are comparable to Chinese and Hindu thought in this regard.

In the *Laws* Plato proposed a practical plan for educating the people around him. A prominent feature of his idea was a school system in which the study of music helped to build character.

The Ingredients of Song: *Republic,* Book 3*

"Then now, my friend," I said, "that part of music or literary education which relates to the story or myth may be considered to be finished; for the matter and manner have both been discussed."

"I think so too," he said.

"Next in order will follow melody and song. Everyone can see already what we ought to say about them, if we are to be consistent with ourselves."

"I fear," said Glaucon, laughing, "that the word 'everyone' hardly includes me, for I cannot at the moment say what they should be; though I may guess."

"At any rate you can tell that a song or ode [*melos*] has three constituents—the words [*logos*], the harmony [*armonia*], and the rhythm [*rythmos*]. May I presuppose that degree of knowledge?"

"Yes," he said. "So much as that you may."

"And as for the words, there will surely be no difference between words which are and which are not set to music; both will conform to the same laws, and these have already been determined by us?"

"Yes."

"And the harmony and rhythm will depend upon the words?"

"Certainly."

Music and Gymnastics: *Laws,* Book 6†

We should appoint directors of music and gymnastics, two kinds of each—of the one kind the business will be education, of the other, the superintendence of contests. In speaking of education, the law means to speak of those who have the care of order and instruction in gymnasia and schools, and of the going to school, and of school buildings for boys and girls. And in speaking of contests, the law refers to the judges of gymnastics and of music. And the same who judge the gymnastic contests of men, shall judge the horses. But in music there shall be one set of judges of solo singing, and of imitation—I mean of rhapsodists, players on the kithara, the aulos and the like, and another who shall judge choral song.

First of all, we must choose directors for the choruses of boys, and men, and maidens, whom they shall follow in the amusement of the dance, and for our other musical arrangements. One director will be enough for the choruses, and he should not be less than 40 years of age. One director will also be enough to introduce the solo singers, and to give judgment on the competitors, and he ought not to be less than 30 years of age. The director and manager of the choruses shall be elected in the following manner: Let any persons who commonly take an interest in such matters go to the meeting, and be fined if they do not go. (The guardians of the law shall judge their fault.) But those who have no interest shall not be compelled. The elector shall propose as director someone who understands music, and he while being scrutinized may be challenged on the one hand by those who say he has no skill, and defended on the other by those who say that he

---

Plato, Republic, *trans. Benjamin Jowett, 1871, Book 3.*

† *Plato*, Laws, *trans. Benjamin Jowett, 1871, Books 6, 7.*

has. Ten are to be elected by vote, and he of the ten who is chosen by lot shall be observed, and lead the choruses for a year according to law. And in like manner the competitor who wins the lot shall be leader of the solo and concert music for that year.

Teaching the Kithara: *Laws,* Book 7

The teacher and the learner ought to use the sounds of the kithara because its notes are pure, the player who teaches and his pupil rendering note for note in unison. But complexity and variation of notes when the strings give one sound and the poet or composer of the melody gives another—also when they make concords and harmonies in which greater and smaller intervals, slow and quick, or high and low notes, are combined—or, again, when they make complex variations of rhythms which they adapt to the notes of the kithara—all that sort of thing is not suited to those who have to acquire a speedy and useful knowledge of music in three years. For opposite principles are confusing, and create difficulty in learning, and our young men should learn quickly, and their mere necessary acquirements are not few or trifling. Let the director of education attend to the principles concerning music which we are laying down. As for the songs and words themselves which the masters of choruses are to teach and the character of them, they are the same which, when applied and adapted to the different festivals, are to benefit cities by affording them innocent amusement.

2.2 PYTHAGORAS (6th cent. B.C.) THROUGH EUCLID AND NICOMACHUS

The Greeks called the science of musical sounds *harmonics*. According to Ptolemy of Alexandria (A.D. 2nd cent.),

Harmonics is the perceptive power of differentiating the height and depth of sounds. Sound, moreover, is the affect or feeling from setting the air in motion. Its first and foremost objective is hearing. Thus the two criteria of harmonics are *hearing* and *reason*. But they differ in that *hearing* judges according to substance and feeling, while *reason* judges according to form and the cause of the feeling, for, generally speaking, the sense is suitable for exploring what is close to it; what is accurate it acquires elsewhere. Reason, however, acquires elsewhere what is close to it and explores what is accurate.

An early explorer of the height and depth of sounds was Pythagoras, who in about 529 B.C., together with his colleagues, examined the mystical properties of numbers. Four, or the tetrad, was particularly fascinating because it enumerated such diverse factors as the sides of a square, the seasons, the elements, the successive ages of man, the cardinal virtues, the opposing vices, and the number of notes in a tetrachord, the latter being the basis of the Greek tonal system.

The doctrines of Pythagoras were preserved, amplified, and enriched by Euclid of Alexandria (fl. 300 B.C.) and Nicomachus of Gerasa, northwest Arabia (fl. A.D. 100), among others. A comparison of the approach to musical numbers reveals Euclid presenting an abstract concept in the *Introduction to the Section of the Canon* and Nicomachus placing the conclusions in a physical setting in the *Handbook of Harmonics*. Even though Euclid knows that a stretched string may be induced to vibrate, he chooses to regard the string as a mathematical straight line, deprived of all of its physical properties other than length. Its color, thickness, and weight, or the force of tension on it, are not taken into account. Nicomachus places this mathematical abstraction in an unsuitable physical setting; the proportions that he allegorically ascribes to weights physically refer to the relative lengths of strings. Although the physical misinterpretation has since been corrected by experiment innumerable times, the importance and charm of the story still persists (see **Appendix 1, Chart 1**).

Vibration and Ratio in Musical Pitch: Euclid*

If all things were at rest, and nothing moved, there would be perfect silence in the world. In such a state of absolute quiescence, nothing would be heard, for motion and percussion must precede sound. Just as the immediate cause of sound is some percussion, the immediate cause of all percussion must be motion. Some vibratory impulses or motions causing a percussion on the ear return with greater speed than others. Consequently they have a greater number of vibrations in a given time, while others are repeated slowly, and consequently are less frequent in a given length of time. The quick returns and greater number of such impulses produce the higher sounds, while the slower, which have fewer oscillations, produce the lower. Hence it follows that if sounds are too high, they may be rendered lower by a diminution of the number of such impulses in a given time, and that sounds which are too low, by adding to the number of their impulses in a given time, may be brought up to the degree of sharpness required.

Musical pitches may be said then to consist of parts, inasmuch as they are capable of being rendered precisely and exactly tunable, either by increasing or diminishing the number of the vibratory motions which excite them. But all things which consist of numerical parts, when compared together, are subject to the ratios of number, so that musical sounds or tones compared together must consequently be in some numerical ratio to each other.

Now of numbers, some are said to be to others in multiplicate or multiple ratio $\left[\text{ such as } \frac{2}{1}, \frac{3}{1}, \frac{4}{1}, \right]$, and some in superparticular ratio $\left[\text{ such as }\right.$

---

*Euclid, Introduction to the Section of the Canon, *trans. Charles Davy (Bury St. Edmund's: J. Rackham, 1787).*

$\frac{3}{2}, \frac{4}{3}, \frac{9}{8}$, with numerator larger than denominator by $1 \Big]$: while the rest are in a ratio which is called superpartient $\Big[$ such as $\frac{5}{3}, \frac{7}{4}, \frac{7}{5}$, with numerator larger than denominator by more than $1 \Big]$. Musical sounds or tones must, therefore, be respectively in one or other of these three ratios. Those which are in multiple and superparticular ratios have the common characteristic that they deal with the numeral 1. Now of musical notes we know that some are consonant and others dissonant, and that consonant sounds unite and mix together, while dissonant sounds do not. This being the case, it is probable that consonant sounds, inasmuch as they unite and mutually blend themselves together, are produced by those ratios which have 1 as a characteristic in common, that is, by those ratios which are either multiple or superparticular.

Discovery of the Proportions of Pitches in an Octave: Nicomachus*

They say that this is the way in which Pythagoras, with the use of strings, discovered the numerical quantity of the distance of a fourth and a fifth, also of their union called the octave, and of the tone placed between the two fourths.

One day he was walking intent in thought, trying to find an infallible aid for the ear, free of error, such as sight possesses in the compass and the ruler, and touch has in the scales, or in the invention of measures. He passed, by divine coincidence, in front of a smith's shop, and heard the iron hammers very distinctly striking on the anvil, giving forth sounds perfectly consonant with each other, except in one combination. He recognized among these sounds the consonances of the octave [*diapason*], the fifth [*diapente*], and the fourth [*diatessaron*]. As for the interval between the fourth and the fifth, he perceived that it was dissonant in itself, but, on the other hand, that it was a complement for making up the larger of these two consonances.

Filled with joy, he entered the smith's shop as if the divinity were supporting his intentions. By means of various experiments he recognized that the difference in weights was caused by the difference in sound—not by the effort of the blacksmiths, nor the shape of the hammers, nor the iron which was being pounded. With great care he made note of the weights of the hammers as accurately as possible. Then he returned home.

He fastened a single beam between the angle formed by two walls, to avoid any variable whereby in any manner whatsoever, the use of several beams each having their own properties might render the proof suspect. He suspended from that beam four strings of the same substance, of equal length, equal thickness, and density, and made each of them support a weight which he fastened at the lower end. Besides, he made the lengths of the strings exactly equal. Then, alternately sounding the strings together two by two, he discovered the above-mentioned consonances, each with its own combination of strings.

*Nicomachus, Enchiridion Harmonices *in Marcus Meibomius*, Antiquae Musicae Auctores Septem Graece et Latine *(Amsterdam: Ludovicus Elzevirius, 1552), pp. 10–14,* 26–27.

He found that the string stretched by the suspension of the greatest weight, compared to that which supported the smallest, had the sound of an octave. The former supported the weight of 12 pounds, the latter, 6. He thus established that the octave is in duple proportion, as shown by the weights themselves. Furthermore, he discovered that the string with the greatest weight, compared with next to the smallest, 8 pounds, sounded the fifth. He established that these were in the sesquialtera proportion, $\frac{3}{2}$, the proportion of the weights to each other. Then he compared those with the other supported weights successively. The largest of the other weights on the strings was 9 pounds, sounding the fourth with the heaviest. He established that it was in the inverse proportion, sesquitertia, $\frac{4}{3}$, and that this same weight with the smallest is sesquialtera, because 9 is in that proportion to 6. Likewise, the string with next to the smallest weight, 8 pounds, was in sesquitertia proportion to 6, and in sesquialtera proportion to 12.

Consequently, the interval between the fifth and the fourth, that is, whereby the consonance of the fifth exceeds the fourth, is confirmed to be in sesquioctava proportion, that is, $\frac{9}{8}$. Furthermore, the union of one with the other in either direction forms the consonance of an octave. In other words, the fifth and the fourth placed conjunctly, has a duple proportion, the union of sesquialtera and sesquitertia in these numbers—12:8:6. Inversely, the union of the fourth and fifth comprises duple proportion, sesquitertia and sesquialtera, with 12:9:6 placed in that order.

After applying his hand and his ear to this study, he ingeniously transferred the general results to the strings on the bridge of an instrument, stretching them high or low proportionately by turning pegs.

2.3 ARISTOTLE (b. 384 B.C.) AND PSEUDO-ARISTOTLE

Aristotle, after joining Plato's Athenian Academy at the age of 18, remained under the master's guidance for twenty years. When Plato died in 347 B.C., Aristotle broke relations with his teacher's successor in order to start his own school, the Lyceum, where the method was based on oral discussions. The students, who walked as they talked with Aristotle between the columns of shade trees, came to be known as the Peripatetics.

The *Problems*, discussions on harmonics which took place at the school, were probably not actually written by Aristotle himself. In contrast, Aristotle was the author of the *Poetics*. His views on imitation and the characteristics of poetry and drama were the basis for Zarlino's ideas on these subjects in the Renaissance (see Section 7.5).

Musical Recognition: *Problems,* Book 19, No. 5*

Why do we listen with greater pleasure to men singing music which we happen to know beforehand, than to music which we do not know? Is it because, when we can recognize the song, the meaning of the composer, like a man hitting the mark, is more evident? This is pleasant to consider. Or is it because it is more pleasant to contemplate than to learn? The reason is that in the one case it is the acquisition of knowledge, but in the other it is using it and a form of recognition. Moreover, what we are accustomed to is always more pleasant than the unfamiliar.

Perception of the Octave: *Problems,* Book 19, Nos. 13–14

Why is it that in the octave the concord of the upper note exists in the lower, but not *vice versa?* Is it because, speaking generally, the sound of both exists in both, but if not so then it exists in the lower note, for it is greater?

Why is it that the difference of an octave may be undetected and appear to be in unison as in the Phoenician lyre and in the human voice? For the sound contained in the upper note is not in unison with the lower, but they are analogous to each other at the octave. Is it because the sounds of the two seem identical by analogy; for analogy in sounds means equality, and equality is unity? Men are deceived in the same way by the sound of pipes.

Perception of the Fifth: *Problems,* Book 19, No. 17

Why does not singing in fifths sound like the octave? Is it because one part of the consonance is not the same as the other, as it is in the case of the octave? For in the case of the octave the low note is in the same position in the low register as the high note in the high register. In this way it is at one and the same time the same and different. But in fourths and fifths this is not so, so that the sound of the octave is not apparent; for it is not the same.

Tuning to A: *Problems,* Book 19, No. 36

Why is it that if the *mese* [the middle or central note, see **Appendix 1,** Chart 2] is touched, the sound of the other strings is spoiled, but if on the other hand the *mese* is still and one of the other strings is touched, only that which is touched is spoiled? Is it because for all the strings *being in tune* means standing in a certain relation to the *mese,* and each one's position is already determined by the *mese?* When the cause of being in tune and that which holds them together is removed, this no longer seems to be the same.

Aristotle, Problems, trans. W. S. Hett (Cambridge, Mass.: Harvard University Press, 1936, 1961), I, 381–3, 385–7, 389, 401. Reprinted by permission of the publishers and THE LOEB CLASSICAL LIBRARY.

When, then, one string is out of tune but the *mese* remains unaltered, naturally that string alone fails; for the others are already in tune.

Imitation: *Poetics**

Epic poetry and tragedy, comedy also and dithyrambic poetry,[1] and the music of the aulos and of the kithara in most of their forms, are all in their general conception modes of imitation. They differ, however, from one another in three respects—the medium, the objects, the manner or mode of imitation being in each case distinct.

For as there are persons who, by conscious art or mere habit, imitate and represent various objects through the medium of color and form or again by the voice; so in the arts above mentioned, taken as a whole, the imitation is produced by *rhythm, language,* or *harmony,* either singly or combined. [Section 2.1]

Thus in the music of the aulos and of the kithara *harmony* and *rhythm* alone are employed, as in other arts, such as that of the shepherd's pipe, which are essentially similar to these. In dancing, *rhythm* alone is used without *harmony;* for even dancing imitates character, emotion, and action, by rhythmical movement.

Tragedy is an imitation of an action that is serious, complete, and of a certain magnitude; in language embellished with each kind of artistic ornament, the several kinds being found in separate parts of the play; in the form of action, not of narrative; through pity and fear effecting the proper purgation of these emotions. By *language embellished* I mean language into which *rhythm, harmony,* and *song* enter. By *the several kinds in separate parts* I mean that some parts are rendered through the medium of verse alone, others again with the aid of song.

Now as tragic imitation implies persons acting, it necessarily follows, in the first place, that spectacular equipment will be a part of tragedy. Next come song and diction, for these are the medium of imitation. By *diction* I mean the mere metrical arrangement of the words. As for *song,* it is a term whose sense everyone understands. . . .

Every tragedy must have six parts which determine its quality, namely: plot, character, diction, thought, spectacle, song. Two of the parts constitute the medium of imitation, one the manner, and three the objects of imitation. And these complete the list. These elements have been employed, we may say, by the poets to a man.

The chorus too should be regarded as one of the actors. It should be an integral part of the whole, and share in the action, in the manner not of Euripides but of Sophocles.[2] As for the later poets, their choral songs per-

---

* *Aristotle,* Poetics, *trans. S. H. Butcher (London: Macmillan & Co., 1895), Chapters 1, 2, 6, 12.*

1. The dithyramb, an impassioned lyric poem intoned by a chorus to aulos accompaniment, was composed in honor of Dionysus, the god of the grape and wine. Hence the music of the aulos depicted ecstatic revelry. Traditionally, the goddess Athena discarded the aulos on seeing her puffy cheeks reflected in the water while playing it, and Apollo punished the satyr Marsyas (Pan) for daring to win a contest on the aulos versus the kithara.
2. Among the plays attributed to Euripides (c. 485–406 B.C.) are: *Alcestis, Medea, Iphigenia among the Tauri, Iphigenia at Aulis,* and *Electra.* Those of Sophocles

tain as little to the subject of the piece as to that of any other tragedy. They are, therefore, sung as mere interludes—a practice first begun by Agathon.[3] Yet what difference is there between introducing such choral interludes, and transferring a speech, or even a whole act, from one play to another?

2.4 ARISTOXENUS (late 4th cent. B.C.)

Aristoxenus, born in Tarentum in southern Italy, placed greater emphasis on the musical ear *(audio)* than on mathematical reason *(ratio)*. He was first taught by his father, Spintharus, a well-known musician acquainted with Socrates. Then Aristoxenus went to Athens, where he was one of the Peripatetics studying with Aristotle.

In his *Harmonics* Aristoxenus discusses the correspondence between pitch and space, the limits of perceptible pitch in the musical gamut, and the recognition of microtones or dieses, intervals smaller than a whole tone. His declaration that it is impossible to perform consecutive dieses may be compared with the improbability of performing consecutive Hindu srutis (Section 1.3) Of extreme importance is Aristoxenus' division of a whole tone into two equal semitones, a concept that has often been cited as the first evidence of equal temperament.

Continuous Motion and Motion by Discrete Intervals*

Our first problem consists in ascertaining the various species of motion. Every voice is capable of change of position, and this change may be either continuous or by disjunct intervals. In continuous change of position the voice seems to the senses to traverse a certain space in such a manner that it does not become stationary at any point, not even at the extremities of its progress—such, at least, is the evidence of our sense-perception—but passes on into silence with unbroken continuity. In the other species, which we designate as motion by distinct intervals, the process seems to be of exactly the opposite nature: the voice in its progress stations itself at one definite pitch, and then again at another, pursuing this process continuously—continuously, that is, in time. As it leaps the distances contained between the successive points of pitch, while it is fixed at, and produces sounds upon, the points themselves, it is said to sing only the latter, and to move by discrete intervals. Both of these descriptions must be regarded in the light of sensuous cognition.

---

* *Aristoxenus*, The Harmonics, *trans. Henry S. Macran (Oxford: The Clarendon Press, 1902), pp. 170–173, 175–176, 180, 185, 193–194. Reprinted by permission of the Clarendon Press, Oxford.*

(496?–406 B.C.) include *Oedipus Rex* and *Antigone*. The plots of both playwrights have been used as the basis of opera and ballet throughout the centuries.
3. Agathon (c. 440–401 B.C.), a tragic poet, was one of Plato's friends. Plato's *Symposium* was to have taken place in Agathon's home.

Whether tone can really move or not, and whether it can become fixed at a definite point of pitch, are questions beyond the scope of the present inquiry, which does not demand the raising of this problem. For whatever the answer may be, it does not affect the distinction between the melodious motion of the voice and its other motions. Disregarding all such problems, we describe the motion of the voice as continuous when it moves in such a way as to seem to the ear not to become stationary at any point of pitch. But when the reverse is the case—when the voice seems to the ear first to come to a standstill on one point of pitch, then to leap over a certain space, and, having done so, to come to a standstill on a second point, and to pursue this alternating process repeatedly—the motion of the voice under these circumstances we describe as motion by intervals. We call the motion of speech continuous motion, because in speaking the voice moves without ever seeming to come to a standstill. The reverse is the case with the other motion, which we designate as motion by intervals in that the voice does seem to become stationary; and when employing this motion one is always said not to speak but to sing.

Perceptible and Imperceptible Pitches

It is evident that the voice must in singing produce the tensions and relaxations inaudibly, and that the points of pitch alone must be audibly enunciated. This is clear from the fact that the voice must pass imperceptibly through the compass of the interval which it traverses in ascending or descending, while the tones that outline the intervals must be clear and stable. Hence it is necessary to discuss tension and relaxation, and in addition height and depth of pitch, and finally pitch in general.

Tension is the continuous transition of the voice from a lower position to a higher, relaxation that from a higher to a lower. Height of pitch is the result of tension, depth the result of relaxation. From a superficial consideration of these questions it might appear surprising that we distinguish four phenomena here instead of two, and in fact it is usual to identify height of pitch with tension, and depth of pitch with relaxation. Hence we may perhaps with advantage observe that the usual view implies a confusion of thought. In doing so we must endeavor to understand, by observing the phenomenon itself, what precisely takes place when in tuning we tighten a string or relax it. All who possess even a slight acquaintance with instruments are aware that in producing tension we raise the string to a higher pitch, and that in relaxing it we lower its pitch. Now, while we are thus raising the pitch of the string, it is obvious that the height of pitch which is to result from the process cannot yet be in existence. Height of pitch will only result when the tension on the string becomes stationary and ceases to change, after having been brought by the process of tension to the point of pitch required, in other words, when the increase of tension has ceased and the tension is constant.

The Compass of Sound

For every musical instrument and for every human voice there is a maximum compass which they cannot exceed, and a minimum interval, less than which they cannot produce. No organ of sound can indefinitely enlarge its range or indefinitely reduce its intervals; in both cases it reaches a limit. Each of these limits must be determined by a reference to that which produces the sound and to that which discriminates it—the voice and the ear, respectively. What the voice cannot produce and the ear cannot discriminate must be excluded from the available and practically possible range of musical sound. In the process of reducing the size of an interval, the voice and the ear seem to fail at the same point. The voice cannot differentiate, nor can the ear discriminate, any interval smaller than the smallest diesis, in order to determine what fraction the interval is of a diesis or of any other of the known intervals [**Appendix 1**, Chart 4]. In the process of extending the size of an interval, the power of the ear may perhaps be considered to stretch beyond that of the voice, though to no very great distance. In any case, whether we are to assume the same limit for voice and ear in both directions, or whether we are to suppose it to be the same in the process of reduction but different in the process of extension, the fact remains that there is a maximum and minimum limit of distance on the line of pitch, either common to voice and ear, or peculiar to each.

Tone, Interval, Scale

Briefly, a tone is the incidence of the voice upon one point of pitch. Whenever the voice is heard to remain stationary on one pitch, we have a tone qualified to take a place in a melody.

An interval, on the other hand, is the distance bounded by two tones which do not have the same pitch.

A scale is to be regarded as the succession of two or more intervals. Here we would ask our hearers to receive these definitions in the right spirit, not with jealous scrutiny of the degree of their exactness. We would ask them to aid us with their intelligent sympathy, and to consider our definition sufficiently instructive when it puts them in the path of understandng the thing defined. To supply a definition which affords an unexceptionable and exhaustive analysis is a difficult task in the case of all fundamental motions, and by no means least difficult in the case of the tone, the interval, and the scale.

Division of a Whole Tone

A whole tone is the difference in compass between the first two concords [the fifth and the fourth], and may be divided by the three lowest denominators, since melody admits half-tones, third-tones, and quarter-tones, while undeniably rejecting any interval less than these. Let us designate the smallest of these intervals (the quarter-tone) as the smallest enharmonic diesis, the next (the third-tone) as the smallest chromatic diesis, and the greatest a semitone.

In inquiring into continuity we must avoid the example set by the harmonists in their condensed diagrams, where they mark as consecutive notes those that are separated from one another by the smallest interval. For so far is the voice from being able to produce twenty-eight consecutive dieses, that it can by no effort produce three dieses in succession. In ascending, after two dieses it can produce nothing less than the complement of the fourth, and that is either eight times the smallest diesis, or falls short of it only by a minute and unmelodic interval. We must direct our eyes to the natural laws of melody and endeavor to discover what intervals the voice is by nature capable of placing in succession in a melodic series.

Construction of Melody

The last section of our science is concerned with the actual construction of melody. For since in the same notes, not different in themselves, we have the choice of numerous melodic forms of every character, it is evident that here we have the practical question of the employment of the notes; and this is what we mean by the construction of melody. The science of harmonics, having traversed the said sections, will find its consummation here.

It is plain that the apprehension of a melody consists in noting with both ear and intellect every distinction as it arises in the successive sounds—successive, for melody, like all branches of music, consists in a successive production. For the apprehension of music depends on these two faculties, sense-perception and memory. For we must perceive the sound that is present, and remember that which is past. In no other way can we follow the phenomena of music.

Bibliographical Notes

For Aristoxenus' role in the recognition of equal temperament see Hermann L. F. Helmholtz, *On the Sensations of Tone as a Physiological Basis for the Theory of Music*, trans. and adapted to the use of music students by Alexander J. Ellis (London: 1875; reprint, New York: Dover Publications, Inc., 1954); J. Murray Barbour, *Tuning and Temperament, A Historical Survey* (East Lansing: Michigan State College Press, 1951; reprint, New York: Da Capo Press, 1972).

2.5 ARISTIDES QUINTILIANUS (A.D. 2nd cent.)

Continuing the line of thought established by Aristoxenus that a whole tone may be divided into two equal semitones enables Aristides Quintilianus to define precisely the enharmonic, chromatic, and diatonic genera. In his treatise entitled *On Music*, Aristides also provides evidence for another invaluable musical concept—namely, the ornamentation of a musical sketch. Elaboration of a basic tonal structure, a process indigenous to organized musical creativity, is the means by which a composer is able to spin his web.

The Art of Musical Ornamentation*

Music is the science of melody [*cantus*] and of those things which pertain to melody. Music may be defined as the theoretical and practical art of performing and organizing melody. In other words, music is the art of decorating in tones and motions, using a theme, suitable for performance, whose structure may be decorated with motions. Therefore, the science is one in which an absolute idea exists, and which does not allow for error. Although music is involved with problems or effects which are subject to all sorts of mutations and variations, we call it the good art, because it corresponds to accurate concepts, not useless pursuits. This is a fact observed by our ancestors and expressed in our discourse.

In order to create a song of value, one must consider melody, rhythm, and performance. In melody, tone must be considered in particular. In rhythm one must consider motion, and in performance, measure (of syllabic quantity). Indeed, the characteristics to be considered in connection with a perfect melody are: motion of tone and sounding body, time, and, above all, rhythm. However, we do not say that the art of decoration is worthless. For it is easy to disparage everything in decoration as being useless. An ornamented presentation with audience participation may be more beautiful, charming, and praiseworthy than the given sketch. The ornaments contribute theoretical and practical aspects to the occasion. When something searches among its parts and divisions, and deals with the explanation of art, they say it is theoretical. However, when it works by itself, producing the song skillfully and beautifully, they call it practical.

The materials of music are tone, and motion of a sounding body. Tone is produced by beating the air, that is, by setting the air in motion. Sounding bodies differ; some define one passion better, others another. For time is measured motion and rest. Indeed, motion is either simple or complex. And there is continuous motion, motion by discrete interval, and motion midway between the two. Continuous tone, therefore, is that which is produced by tension and release, quickly and surreptitiously. A discrete interval has vibrations which are evident, but imperceptible in measurement. Medial motion is a combination of both discrete and continuous motion. Therefore continuous motion differs from discrete. Medial motion is what we do when chanting and reciting. Discrete intervals are those which we perform with any simple tones, and which, when united together, we call melody.

Musical Theory and Practice

All music is said to be either theoretical or practical. And the theoretical is that which is distinguished by the artificial relationship between the head and its parts. It investigates the more remote principles, the natural causes, and the entire concert. The practical, indeed, is that which effects artificial computations and attains the goal. Therefore it is called erudite.

* *Marcus Meibom*, Antiquae musicae auctores septem graece et latine (*Amsterdam: Elzevirius, 1652*), II, 5–8, 18–21.

The theoretical is divided into the natural and the artificial. Under the natural are arithmetic and the comprehensive discussion of everything as a whole. The artificial is in three parts: harmonic, rhythmic, and metric. The practical is divided into a section on usage and one on performance. Usage is subdivided into three types of composition: melodic, rhythmic, and poetic. Performance is also subdivided into three types: instrumental, vocal, and dramatic.

Harmonic theory is divided into seven parts as follows: sounds, intervals, systems, genera, tones, mutations, and melodic construction.

The Enharmonic, Chromatic, and Diatonic Genera

Genus is a certain way of dividing the tetrachord. There are three types of genus: enharmonic, chromatic, and diatonic, which are differentiated by longer or shorter distances between the intervals. Thus the enharmonic is that genus which has the smallest conjunct intervals. The diatonic is the genus that has several whole tones; therefore it is used most extensively in music. The chromatic is that which proceeds by semitones. Just as the realm between white and black is called *color,* so the mean between the other two genera is known as *chromatic.* Each of these genera is sung as follows: The enharmonic, ascending, is composed of a quarter-tone, a quarter-tone, and a double-tone. The descent is the opposite. The chromatic ascends by semitone, semitone, and triple-semitone, and descends the opposite way. The diatonic ascends by semitone, tone, tone, and descends to the contrary. Of these the diatonic is the most natural of all, because it can be sung by everyone, even the unskilled. The chromatic is the most artificial, because it can be modulated only by the highly trained. The enharmonic is the most accurate; it is recognized only by the most experienced musicians. For many it is an impossibility. Whence modulation by the quarter-tone is not accepted because it is an irrational interval which can by no means be sung decisively.

Division of the Tetrachord into Sixty Equal Units

Each of these genera progresses either in conjunct or disjunct motion. The motion is conjunct when it progresses through successive tones. It is disjunct when it is full of leaps. Besides, the motion is either direct, reversed, or combined. It is direct when it goes from the low tones to the high ones. It is reversed when the contrary occurs. It is combined when it changes, like a tetrachord ascending by conjunct motion and descending by disjunct. Again, some genera may be divided into particular entities, others not. The enharmonic, because it consists of the smallest dieses, is indivisible. The chromatic may be divided into as many rational intervals as are found between the semitone and the enharmonic diesis. The third type, namely the diatonic, may be divided into as many rational intervals as are found between the semitone and the tone. Therefore there are three species of chromatic and two species of diatonic genus. In all, with these plus the enharmonic, there are six kinds of motion.

In order to clarify what we have said, we shall make the division in numbers, with the assumption that the tetrachord has sixty units. The *enharmonic* is divided into 6, 6, and 48 by a quarter-tone diesis, quarter-tone diesis, and ditone. The *soft chromatic* is divided into 8, 8, and 44 by third-tone diesis, third-tone diesis, and tri-semitone plus third-tone diesis (36 plus 8). The *sesquialtera chromatic* is divided into 9, 9, and 42 by sesquialtera diesis (9 to 6 in relation to the enharmonic), sesquialtera diesis, and tri-semitone plus quarter-tone diesis (36 plus 6). The *tonal chromatic* is divided into 12, 12, and 36 by 2 incomposite semitones and a tri-semitone. The *soft diatonic* is divided into 12, 18, and 30 by semitone, 3 quarter-tone dieses (3 times 6), and 5 quarter-tone dieses (5 times 6). The *diatonic* contains 12, 24, and 24 by semitone, tone, and tone.

2.6 GAUDENTIUS (A.D. 2nd cent.)

In his *Introduction to Harmonics* the Greek philosopher Gaudentius differentiates between tones that are produced on an instrument and those that are sung. Following in the footsteps of Aristoxenus, Gaudentius describes the general characteristics of discrete intervals in a manner scarcely distinguishable from that of his predecessor. However, in the area of *composite* discrete intervals, Gaudentius makes an important contribution. First of all, he emphasizes the fact that the octave is a union of the perfect fourth and the perfect fifth. This observation is of the greatest consequence for understanding the subsequent construction of the medieval modes with their authentic and plagal divisions of the octave (see **Appendix 1,** Chart 5). The distinction between an octave modal pattern with the fifth below the fourth (authentic) and a pattern with the fifth above the fourth (plagal) is one of the natural wonders of music. Its influence on compositional technique reached a culmination in the tonal fugues of Johann Sebastian Bach. Furthermore, Gaudentius' proclamation that the tritone is neither consonant nor dissonant, but paraphonic, somewhere in between, is also prophetic.

The Attributes of Tone*

Tone is the landing of the voice on a single pitch. Pitch is the stationary position of a tone. Thus, when a tone seems to remain on one pitch, we say that the tone is a sound which may be placed in a melody. Tone has color, pitch, and time value. When the time value is longer, we use more time; and when it is shorter, we perform in less time, so that rhythm seems to come into being here. However, only melodies need be made rhythmical in accordance with the time values of the sounds. The placement of a tone

---

* *Marcus Meibom*, Antiquae musicae auctores septem graece et latine (*Amsterdam: Elzevirius, 1652), I, 2–5, 9–12.

may be high or low. Those which appear in the same place we say are in unison. We also distinguish between high tones and low tones according to their position. Furthermore, color is the difference between tones that seem to have the same position and time value, that is, when a musical sound is uttered on a natural tone and also on one that is similar.

The Greek Lesser and Greater Systems [4]
(see **Appendix 1,** Chart 2)

In the lesser system, which is conjunct, there are three tetrachords, joined together in two places by tones in common, namely, the mese (a) and the hypate meson (E). The proslambanomenos (A) does not belong to any tetrachord. In the greater system, which is called disjunct, there are four tetrachords, of which the Hypaton and Meson are joined together by a common tone, hypate meson (E). But they are disjunct from the rest by the tone which occurs from mese (a) to paramese (b♮).

The combination of the two systems yields a total of twenty-six essential tones, of which eight are common to both systems, up to and including the mese. Consequently there are in all eighteen essential tones with which any song may be performed with the voice or on the tibia or kithara. Generally speaking, these are the tones with which melodic motion may be produced.

Fixed and Mobile Tones

This combination and classification of tones is in the diatonic genus. However, the names of the tones are the same in all the genera, except for the mobile tones. When there is a change of genus, one adds to each mobile tone the qualification suitable for the particular genus, such as enharmonic lychanos, chromatic lychanos, or diatonic lychanos.

Among the concerted tones some are in unison, some are consonant, and some are paraphonic. Those which are in unison do not differ from each other either in depth or height. Consonant tones, when they are produced simultaneously, either by striking or blowing on an instrument, always result in the same musical sound, whether the motion is from the low tones to the high, or the high tones to the low. When, for example, the mixture in the production of the two tones makes it seem as if they are one, then they are said to be consonant. Dissonant tones, when they are produced simultaneously either by striking or blowing on an instrument, never seem to be the same in any part of the musical sound, whether the motion is from low to high or high to low. When they are produced simultaneously, they do

---

4. Chart 2 shows the Greek lesser and greater systems in the diatonic genus. The outer pitches of the tetrachords were fixed and unchangeable in all 3 genera, namely, diatonic, chromatic, and enharmonic. The 2 inner pitches of each tetrachord varied according to the genus. For example, in descending order, the Hypaton tetrachord, outlined by the tones E and B, contains the tones D and C for the diatonic genus, C# and C for the chromatic genus, and C with the quarter-tone below C for the enharmonic genus. In other words, the Hypaton lychanos may be D, C#, or C, depending on the genus. In the text here, to distinguish the names of the tetrachords from those of the notes, the tetrachords are capitalized.

not show any evidence of blending with each other. Paraphonic tones are intermediate between consonance and dissonance. They seem to be close to consonance, as is seen in the tritone from parhypate meson (F) to paramese (b♮) and in the ditone from the diatonic meson (G) to the paramese (b♮).

The Octave as a Perfect Composite Interval

There are six consonances in the perfect system. The first is the fourth [*diatessaron*]. The second is the fifth [*diapente*], which is a whole tone larger than the fourth. Whence some people have defined the interval of a tone as the difference in size between the first two consonances. The third consonance, the octave [*diapason*], is a composite of the other two. For when the fifth is added to the fourth, the outer tones create a consonance. This kind of consonance is called an octave. The fourth consonance is the combination of the octave and the fourth. The fifth consonance is the octave plus the fifth. The sixth consonance is the double octave.

It is possible to conceive of other consonances by combining these with each other. But the instruments would not be able to bear the increased tension. One must have consideration for the strength of the instruments and for the human voice, from which we derive all of the consonances.

Bibliographical Notes

Here Gaudentius is naming the tones according to their positions on an instrument. For an example of the Greek vocal notation in letters, see the "Skolion of Seikilos" in *MSO*, Part 1, p. 1. This song, dated c. 100 B.C., is one of about 20 examples of Greek music that have survived. It is recorded on a pillar of stone found in Asia Minor in 1883. A photograph appears in Curt Sachs, *The Rise of Music in the Ancient World, East and West* (New York: W. W. Norton & Co., Inc., 1943), Plate 8. The text of the song indicates that a person should be happy, since the span of life is short. Seikilos' Song also appears in *GMB*, p. 1, *HAM*, Vol. I, p. 10, and *HMS*, Vol. I, p. 35.

2.7 ATHENAEUS (fl. A.D. 225)

Athenaeus wrote an exhaustive symposium on ancient culture entitled *The Deipnosophists*, whose setting was a fictitious banquet at the house of Laurentius, a Roman nobleman. Athenaeus, born in Egypt at Naucratis, the Canopic Mouth of the Nile, wrote in Greek. References to contemporary personages and to the accomplishments of earlier artists and scholars are abundant to the point that Athenaeus' work becomes a primary source for much information that would otherwise have been lost.

The Water Organ*

Suddenly a noise was heard from one of the neighboring houses. It was very pleasant and agreeable, as if from a water organ. We all turned around towards it, being charmed by the melody. The water organ is a kind of water clock. It cannot therefore be considered a stringed instrument, or one to be played by touching. But perhaps it may be called a wind instrument, because the organ is inflated by the water. For the pipes are plunged down into the water, and when the water is agitated by a youth, as the axles penetrate through the whole organ, the pipes are inflated, and emit a gentle and agreeable sound.

Concerted Music on Lyres and Pipes

But how much better is this water organ than the instrument which is called nabla [see Section 1.1, fn. 2], which Sopater the parodist, in his drama entitled *The Portal*, says is also an invention of the Phoenicians, in the following words:

Nor has the screeching of the Sidonian nabla
Been produced by striking it.

There is also an instrument called the triangle, which Juba mentions in the fourth book of his *Theatrical History*. He says it is an invention of the Syrians, as is also the sambuca, the so-called Phoenician lyre [see Section 1.1, fn. 3]. Juba also says that the Egyptians call the single pipe, the monaulos, an invention of Osiris. They say likewise about the transverse pipe, the plagiaulos, which is called photinx [see Section 1.1, fn. 7].

We know too of some auloi which are half-bored, about which Anacreon says,

What lust has now seized thus upon your mind,
To wish to dance to tender half-bored auloi?

And these pipes are smaller than the perfect pipes. At all events, Aeschylus says, speaking metaphorically, in his *Ixion*,

But very soon the greater swallows up
The lesser and the half-bored pipe.

And these half-bored pipes are the same as those which are called boys' pipes, which they use at banquets, since they are not fit for the games and public shows; for this reason Anacreon called them tender.

And Pratinas the Philasian says that when some hired aulos-players and chorus-dancers were occupying the orchestra, some people were indignant

Athenaeus, The Deipnosophists, *trans. C. D. Yong (London: Henry G. Bohn, 1854), Vol. I, pp. 278–283 [Athenaeus Bk. iv, Chaps. 75–79], Vol. III, pp. 984–987, 989, 1009, 1012–1019 [Athenaeus Bk. vix, Chaps. 9–10, 12, 32, 35–41].*

because the aulos-players did not play in tune to the chorus-singers, as was the national custom, but the choruses instead sang, keeping time to the auloi. And what his opinion and feelings were towards those who did this, Pratinas declares in the following hyporchema [choral song with dance]:

> What noise is this?
> What mean these songs of dancers now?
> What new unseemly fashion
> Has seized upon this stage to Bacchus sacred,
> Now echoing with various noise?

And of the union of auloi with the lyre (for that concert has often been a great delight to us ourselves), Ephippus, in his *Merchandise*, speaks as follows:

> Clearly, O youth, the music of the auloi,
> And that which from the lyre comes, does suit
> Well with our pastimes; for when each resound
> In unison with the feelings of those present,
> Then is the greatest pleasure felt by all.

And the exact meaning of the term *concerted music* is shown by Semus of Delos in the fifth book of his *History of Delos*, where he writes, "But as the term *concert* is not understood by many people, we must speak of it. It is when there is a symphonic contest with aulos and rhythm answering one another."

Chanting the Poems of Homer and Others

Rhapsodists were also present at our entertainments. Larensis delighted in the reciters of Homer to such an extraordinary degree, that one might call Cassander, the king of Macedonia, a trifler in comparison with him.

Chamaeleon, in his essay on Stesichorus, says that not only the poems of Homer, but also those of Hesiod and Archilochus, and also those of Mimnermus and Phocylides, were chanted musically. And Clearchus, in the first book of his treatise on *Riddles* says, "Simonides of Zacynthus used to sit in the theaters on a lofty chair rhapsodizing the verses of Archilochus."

Magadizing [5]

Aemilianus said, "My good friend Masurius, I myself, often, being a lover of music, turn my thoughts to the instrument which is called the magadis,

5. Athenaeus' description of *magadizing*, playing or singing in octaves, may not necessarily refer to the means of tone production, but rather to the reinforced texture of the sound emitted by doubling in octaves. From what he says about men, women, and boys singing in different ranges, and pipes or strings being in different registers, magadizng seems to be a rudimentary polyphony arising by chance from performance in parallel octaves.

and cannot decide whether I am to think that it was a species of aulos or some kind of kithara. For that sweetest of poets, Anacreon, says somewhere or other—

> I hold my magadis and sing,
> Striking loud the twentieth string,
> Leucaspis, as the rapid hour
> Leads you to youth's and beauty's flower.

"But Ion of Chios, in his *Omphale*, speaks of it as if it were a species of aulos, in the following words:

> And let the Lydian magadis-aulos
> Lead the battle-cry.

Masurius replied, "Theophilus the comic poet, in his *Neoptolemus*, uses the verb magadizing, or singing and playing like a magadis, saying,

> It is a knavish trick for a son and a father and a
> mother to magadize, for not one will sing the same melody.

"And Phillis of Delos, in the second book of his *Treatise on Music* says,

> The lyre to which they sang iambic verses, they called
> the iambyca, and the instrument to which they sang
> them in such a manner as to vary the meter a little,
> they called the clepsiambus,[6] while the magadis produced
> the octave, equally in tune for every passage of the singers."

The Triple Kithara

And concerning the instrument called the tripod (this too is a musical instrument), Artemon writes,

> There are many instruments whose existence is uncertain, as, for instance, the tripod of Pythagoras of Zacynthus.[7] Since it was in fashion but a very short time, either because the fingering was exceedingly difficult, or for some other reason, it has escaped the notice of most writers altogether.

> It was used like a triple kithara. Its feet stood on a pedestal which was turned around easily, just like a revolving stool. Strings were stretched along the three intermediate spaces between the legs. Across each space extended an arm with tuning-pegs underneath, to which the strings were

---

6. *Clepsiambus* was derived from the Greek *klepto*, to steal. This concept of metrical variation may be compared with that of the term *tempo rubato*, now used for performing with slight increases or decreases in the speed of the beat, or deviations from the strict meter (see Section 10.2).
7. This is a different Pythagoras from the famous philosopher, Pythagoras of Samos.

attached. And on the top there was the usual vase-shape of the tripod for a sounding-box, with some other ornaments attached to it, all of which gave it a very elegant appearance and a very powerful sound. And in the three spaces Pythagoras put the three modes, Dorian, Lydian, and Phrygian, assigning one mode to each space.

Sitting on a chair made on the same principles of construction, he extended his left hand to hold the instrument, and, while using the plectrum in the other hand, he very easily turned the pedestal with his foot, in order to use whichever side of the instrument he chose to begin with. And, turning to the other side, he continued playing; and then he changed to the third side. So rapidly did the easy movement of the pedestal touched by his foot bring the various sides under his hand, and so rapid was his fingering and execution, that if a person had not seen what was being done, but had judged only by his ear, he would have fancied that he was listening to three kitharas tuned differently.

But this instrument, though it was so greatly admired, after his death soon went out of use.

The Solo Kithara

Now the system of playing the kithara alone was, as Menaechmus informs us, first introduced by Aristonicus of Argos, who was a contemporary of Archilochus, and lived in Corcyra. But Philochorus, in the third book of his *History of Attica* says,

Lysander of Sicyon was the first kitharist to introduce the art of solo instrumental performance, stretching the strings taughtly to a higher pitch, producing a very rich sound, a style which Epigonus was the first to adopt. He did away with the thin, unadorned style current among the solo kitharists by introducing chromatics, iambic meter, magadizing effects, and whistling sounds. He was the first person to alter the character of his instrument while playing. And afterwards, he was the first person to include a group of players around him. And Menaechmus says that Dion of Chios was the first person who ever played on the kithara an ode such as is used at libations to the honor of Bacchus. Timomachus, in his *History of Cyprus*, says that Stesander of Samos further improved his art, and at Delphi was the first person who sang to his kithara the battles narrated in Homer, beginning with the Odyssey. Others say that the first person who ever played amatory strains on his kithara was Amêtor of Eleutherna, who did so in his own city. His descendants are all called Amitores.

3

Roman Sources
for Rhythm and
Musical Articulation

3.1 CICERO (106–43 B.C.)

Discounting the presence or absence of text, the essential ingredients
of melody are tone and rhythm, subjects explored by Latin as well as
Greek authors. The Greek writer Bacchius (A.D. 3rd cent.) summarized
the elements of rhythm as follows:

> What is rhythm? The measurement of time made by a certain constant
> motion. It applies either to words, to melody, or even to the movement of
> the body.
>
> Of how many time-values does it consist? Three.
>
> Which? Short, long, and immeasurable.
>
> What is the short time-value? The smallest value which is not divisible.
>
> What is the long time-value? Double the time-value of the preceding.
>
> What is immeasurable? That which is longer than the short and less than
> the long. When the quantity by which one is smaller or larger cannot be
> evaluated in a simple proportion, it is immeasurable.
>
> How many combinations of time-value are there in rhythm? Four. One
> combines a short with a short, a long with a long, a long with a short, an
> immeasurable with a long.[1]

1. Marcus Meibomius, *Antiquae Musicae Auctores Septem Graece et Latine*, (Am-
telodami: Apud Ludovicum Elzevirium, 1652), pp. 22–24.

Several centuries before the time of Bacchius, the Roman orator and statesman, Marcus Tullius Cicero, himself a student of Greek literature and philosophy, analyzed the measurable and immeasurable aspects of rhythm. Cicero's treatise—entitled *De Oratore*—although mainly directed toward the orator, also takes the musician into account. His concern for the proper projection of the Latin language is of paramount importance to the musician, since the Latin language was dominant in the melodic texts of the Middle Ages.

Music and Oratory*

The ancients imagined in prose a harmony almost like that of poetry. That is, they thought that we ought to adopt a sort of numbers. Musicians, who were also the poets of former ages, contrived verse and song as the ministers of pleasure, so that they might fill the sense of hearing with gratification arising from the numbers of language and the modulation of notes. These two things, therefore (I mean the musical management of the voice, and the harmonious structure of the words) should be transferred, they thought, as far as the strictness of prose will admit, from poetry to oratory.

The largest compass of a period is that which can be rounded off in one breath. This is the boundary set by nature; art has other limits. The beats in the meters of the iamb and the trochee are readily noticeable, as their feet are short. But the numbers [*numeri*] and measures [*modi*] in oratory do not require such sharp-sighted care and diligence as those which must be used by poets. The latter are compelled to formulate the words in a verse in such a way that nothing, even to the least breath, may be shorter or longer than the meter absolutely demands.[2]

All people are moved, not only by words artfully arranged, but also by numbers and the sounds of the voice. How few are those that understand the science of numbers and measures! Yet, if in these the smallest offence be given by an actor, so that any sound is made too short by contraction, or too long by extension, whole theaters burst into exclamations. Does not the same thing also happen with regard to musical notes, that not only whole sets and bands of musicians are turned out by the multitude and the populace for varying one from another, but even single performers for playing out of tune?

---

*Cicero, On Oratory and Orators, *trans. J. S. Watson based on the 1762 trans. of George Barnes (London: George Bell & Sons; New York: The Macmillan Co., 1909), III, xlvii–xlviii, l–li, lvii, lx.*

2. The beats of the meter (*ictus metrici*) were marked by the musician striking the ground with his foot. The shortest metrical feet were the iamb (short–long, 1:2) and the trochee (long–short, 2:1). As the musician lowered his foot, the actor raised his voice. Therefore, the accented or raised syllable was called the *arsis*, and the unaccented syllable was called the *thesis*. Now that musicians associate the accented beat with a lowering of the hand rather than a rise in intensity, and an unaccented beat with a raising of the hand, the downbeat is the *thesis* and the upbeat is the *arsis*.

There is nothing which so naturally affects our minds as numbers and the harmony of sounds, by which we are excited, and inflamed, and soothed, and thrown into a state of languor, and often moved to cheerfulness or sorrow. Their most exquisite power is best suited to poetry and music, and was not, it seems to me, undervalued by our most learned monarch Numa [3] and our ancestors, as the stringed and wind instruments [*fides ac tibiae*] at the sacred banquets and the verses of the Salii sufficiently indicate,[4] but was most cultivated in ancient Greece.

Every emotion of the mind has, by nature, its own peculiar look, tone, and gesture. And the whole frame of a man, his whole countenance, and the sound of his voice reverberate like strings on a musical instrument as they are struck by each successive emotion. For the tones of the voice are like the strings of an instrument, wound up to be responsive to every touch, high–low [*acuta–gravis*], quick–slow [*cita–tarda*], loud–soft [*magna–parva*], while in each of these categories there is a mean. Among these tones, too, are found several other characteristics, smooth–rough [*lene–asperum*], short–long [*contractum–diffusum*], continuous or interrupted breath [*continenti spiritu intermisso*], broken–divided [*fractum–scissum*], diminished–amplified [*attenuatum–inflatum*] by deflection of the tone [*flexo sono*]. For all of these and those that resemble them may be influenced by art and regulation. And they are presented to the orator as colors are to the painter, to produce variety.

The voice doubtless contributes the most to effectiveness and excellence in delivery. Although a full-bodied voice is the chief object of our desire, we must take care of whatever strength of voice we have. On this point, the care of the voice does not concern us here; yet, I personally think we should assist it to the utmost. But it does not seem unsuitable to the purpose of my present remarks to observe that in most things what is most useful is, I know not how, the most becoming. For nothing is more useful for securing power of voice, than the frequent variation of it, nothing more pernicious than an immoderate straining of it without intermission. And what is more adapted to delight the ear, and produce agreeableness of delivery, than change, variety, and alteration of tone? Caius Bracchus, accordingly, used to have a person skillful on the ivory pipe [*fistula*] stand concealed behind him when he made a speech, who was supposed to blow a tone quickly to excite him when he was slack or to restrain him from overexertion.

3.2 VITRUVIUS (1st cent.)

The physical properties of the three genera had been put to practical use by the Roman architect, Marcus Vitruvius Pollio, even before they were summarized in the writings of Aristides and Gaudentius. Vitruvius

---

The word *modus* in reference to rhythm was eventually associated with the rhythmic modes (Section 5.2)

3. Numa Pompilius (715–673 B.C.) was a legendary king of very ancient Rome.

4. The Salii were priests of Mars with whom hymns and dances were associated.

wrote *De Architectura* about 27 B.C., during the time of the rebuilding of Rome under the first Augustus. When designing a site for the theater at the Roman Forum, Vitruvius ingeniously took musical acoustics into account.

In his book Vitruvius includes a chapter on harmonics which admittedly hearkens back to Aristoxenus. An accurate knowledge of harmonics was essential for Vitruvius' plan of building sounding boxes at strategic locations in the theater. So that the reverberation of sound would achieve the most brilliant effect, vases, placed in niches, were tuned to specific tones throughout the Greek musical system, from high to low and low to high, with the lowest tone in the middle. For a small theater Vitruvius prescribed vases tuned to the outer, fixed pitches of the tetrachords; for a larger theater he called not only for a row of vases tuned to harmonic tones but also for rows tuned to chromatic and diatonic tones. Vitruvius made no provision for vases tuned to the enharmonic microtones; he was neither a philosopher nor an experimental scientist exploring the theoretical limits of consonance and dissonance, but rather a practicing architect interested in reinforcing the consonances for the live performer appearing in an actual physical location.

The Site of the Theater*

If the theater is on a hillside, the construction of the foundations will be easier. But if they have to be laid on level or marshy ground, piles and substructures must be used as we have written in the third book concerning the foundations of temples. Above the foundations, the stepped seats ought to be built up from the substructure in stone or marble. . . .

Great care is also to be taken that the place chosen does not deaden the sound, but that the voice can range in it with the utmost clearness. And this can be brought about if a site is chosen where the passage of sound is not hindered. Now the voice is like a flowing breath of air, and is actual when perceived by the sense of hearing. It is moved along innumerable undulations of circles; as when we throw a stone into standing water. Innumerable circular undulations arise spreading from the center as wide as possible. And they extend unless the limited space hinders them, or some obstruction does not allow the directions of the waves to reach the outlets. And so when they are interrupted by obstacles, the first waves flowing back disturb the directions of those which follow. In the same way the voice moves in circular fashion. But while in water the circles move horizontally only, the voice both moves horizontally and rises vertically by stages. Therefore, as in the case with the direction of the waves in water, so with the voice, when no obstacle interrupts the first wave, this in turn does not disturb the second and later waves, but all reach the ears of the top and

* *Vitruvius*, On Architecture, *trans. Frank Granger (Cambridge, Mass.: Harvard University Press, 1962), I, v, Chap. 3, pp. 265–267. Reprinted by permission of the publishers and THE LOEB CLASSICAL LIBRARY.*

bottom rows without echoing. Therefore the ancient architects, following nature's footsteps, traced the voice as it rose, and carried out the ascent of the theater seats. By the rules of mathematics and the method of music, they sought to make the voices from the stage rise more clearly and sweetly to the spectators' ears. For just as organs which have bronze plates as reverberators or horn sounding boards are brought to the clear sound of string instruments, so by the arrangement of theaters in accordance with the science of harmony, the ancients increased the power of the voice.

The Vases of the Theater

According to the mathematical ratios which we are about to propose, construct copper vases in proportion to the size of the theater. Do it in such a way that when they are struck successively they produce the intervals of a fourth, a fifth, and so on through the double octave. These vases are to be placed in niches between the seats of the theater. The vases must not touch the walls or ceiling of the niche; they should be surrounded by empty space. Also, the vases should be placed upside down, with the side facing the stage elevated by wedges at least a half a foot high. And in the lower steps directly in front of the niches, holes two feet long and a half a foot high are left open.

Following is the explanation of the design for the placement of the niches. If the theater is not very large in dimension, plan a horizontal line half way down from the top. On this line are placed thirteen niches separated by twelve equal spaces. The two niches at either end contain vases which sound the tone aa in the manner described above. In the niches second from each end are vases a fourth below, sounding e. The third niches from each end have vases a fourth below, sounding b♮. The fourth niches from each end have vases sounding d. The fifth niches from each end have vases a fourth below, sounding a [*mese*]. The sixth niches from each end have vases a fourth below, sounding E. In the middle is one niche with a vase a fourth below, sounding B♮. With this calculation, the sound, emanating from the stage as if from a central point, spreads out, circulating until it strikes the hollows of the individual vases. This contact incites an increased clarity of tone dependent on the consonant relationship between the sound from the stage and the individual vase.

But if the theater is larger in dimension, its altitude is to be divided into four parts, with three horizontal rows of vases, the first, harmonic, the second, chromatic, and the third, diatonic. In the lowest row, which is the first, are harmonic vases such as those described for the small theater.

This is in accordance with Aristoxenus who, with great vigor and industry established the relationships in music by genus. Anyone who pays attention to these calculations, will find it easier to build fine theaters suited to the natural characteristics of sound and the pleasure of the audience.

Perhaps someone might say that in Rome people build many theaters every year without giving any consideration to these matters. But he would be mistaken, because all public theaters made of wood have several levels of floors whose planks must of necessity resound. Indeed, we may also observe this when listening to performers singing to the cithara. When they wish to sing with a louder tone they turn to the doors of the stage, from which

PITCHES FOR THE ROWS OF VASES
IN VITRUVIUS' THEATERS

center

	1	2	3	4	5	6	7	8	9	10	11	12	13
						5th		5th					
Diatonic (Inner tones of tetrachords)	g	d	c	G	D	A	a	A	D	G	c	d	g
				4th	4th	4th	4th	8ve mese					

					5th			4th					
Chromatic (Inner tones of tetrachords)	f♯	c♯	b♮	F♯	C♯	b♮		b♮	C♯	F♯	b♮	c♯	f♯
		chromatic Synemmenon				para- mese		para- mese		chromatic Synemmenon			
	4th			4th	4th								

Harmonic (Outer tones of tetrachords) Only row in a small theater	aa	e	b♮	d	a	E	B♮	E	a	d	b♮	e	aa
		paramese	mese					mese		paramese			
	4th	4th		4th	4th	4th	4th	4th	4th		4th	4th	

they derive consonant support for the voice. But when theaters are constructed of solid materials, that is, when they are hewn from rock, or built with stones or marble, which cannot resound, then the principles which I have explained should be followed. If someone were to ask in what theater this is done, we would be able to answer, not with theaters in Rome, but in the provinces of Italy and in many Greek cities. And as a model we have Lusius Mummius who demolished the theater at Corinth, transported the copper vases from the spoils to Rome, and dedicated them at the temple of Luna [the moon goddess].

Furthermore, many ingenious architects who have built theaters in small cities, hampered by scant means, have used vases made of pottery chosen for their resonance. By placing the vases according to the computations indicated, they achieved excellent results.

3.3 PRISCIAN (fl. A.D. 500)

The *Institutiones Grammaticae* of Priscianus Caesariensis is a Latin grammar steeped in the teachings of Homer, Plato, and Cicero. Priscian was born in Africa at Caesarea in Mauretania, now the city of Cherchel in Algeria. Eventually he taught at Constantinople.

Priscian's grammar shows the relationship between musical notation and the accents of speech. Even in cases where each minute inflection of the voice cannot be transcribed into written symbols, he believes that there may be some conglomerates of sound which are yet comprehensible. Today, the composer groping for a suitable way to duplicate on paper the image of indefinite pitches, and the folklorist attempting to recapture the essence of a popular song without recording it mechanically, may find comfort in Priscian's understanding of sound. Our contemporary musician realizes that there are many kinds of music for which the written record can be no more than an approximation of what the composer imagines, what the performer presents, or what the listener hears.

Concerning Sound*

Philosophers define sound as the weakest beat of air under one's control really perceptible to the ear, of the kind that comes to the ear in the proper sense. . . . For sound occurs when there is someone actually hearing.

There are four species of sound: articulate, inarticulate, literate, and illiterate. The articulate is that which is joined firmly together, that is to say, connected by some sense of mind, of the sort that is spoken or pronounced. The inarticulate, on the contrary, is that which does not proceed from any affect of the mind. The literate is that which may be written down. The illiterate is that which may not be written down. Therefore certain articulate sounds are composed [inveniuntur] which may be written and understood, such as: Arma virumque cano ["I sing of arms and the man," Virgil's Aeneid].

Some which cannot be written, however, may be understood, such as the hissing and sighs of men. For these sounds, even though they express some meaning by their pronunciations, cannot be written. There are others, however, which although they are written, are still called inarticulate, as they do not mean anything, such as coax [frogs croaking] and cra. Indeed, others, which may neither be written nor understood, are inarticulate and illiterate, such as crepitus [creaking], mugitus [mooing], and the like.

However, we ought to know that these four kinds of sound cause four higher species generally occurring in sound, two for each one alternately combined. Moreover, sound [vox] is just as appropriate for summoning [vocando] as a leader [dux] is for leading [ducendo].

Concerning Accents

A letter is the symbol [nota] of a unit [elementi]. When it is written and it does not reverberate through the voice at all, it is nothing other than a symbol devised for representing the unit. But when it is bellowed forth from the sound of a voice, it becomes an utterance of the unit. As long as it has reason [ratio], the appearance of this thing seems to exist. In fact, percussion from the air corresponds to the beat [ictu] of language, whence sound is formed. In fact, sound is revealed as the body, for if it were not the body the listener's ears would not be touched at all. But when it strikes the ear and ricochets from the unit, it is divided into three parts, namely, height [altitudine], amplitude [latitudine], and duration [longitu-

*Prisciani, Grammatici Caesariensis, Institutionum Grammaticarum in Henrici Keilii II, 5–6. De Accentibus Liber, III, 519–521.

dine]. In fact, a letter has height with regard to pronunciation, fullness with regard to breath, and duration with regard to time. That is to say, it is heard on high, broadly, and at length. Furthermore, the syllables have their own unit which is called production.[5] But there seems to be a difference between the element of a letter and that of a syllable, because the element of a letter is its very pronunciation, and that of a syllable is its production. For what is any element other than the least part of the parts of an articulated sound? Indeed, what remains of the symbol or figure is the element.

Accent is the certain law and rule for raising and lowering the syllable of each and every part of the oration. This makes for the similarity of the elements of letters and syllables, which may also be divided into three parts, acute, grave, and circumflex. The acute accent is therefore devised in order to sharpen or raise the syllable, while the grave is that which depresses or lowers it, and the circumflex is therefore that which lowers and raises. Thus these are among the ten accents which are considered worthy of being designated for this work.[6] The accent *acutus virgula* is directed up from the left to the right, thus: ╱ . The *gravis* descends from the top to the right, thus: ╲ . The *circumflex* note is made from the acutus and the gravis, written thus: ╱╲ . The *longus* is an extended virgula [*virgula iacens*], thus: — . The *brevis* virgula is the lower part of an extended circle, thus: ╰╯ . The *dasia*, which is explained as an aspiration where the letter *h* ought to be placed, is notated with this figure: Ⲅ . The *psile*, which is explained as "dryness," should be used either where there is not enough sound, or where the letter *h* is lacking; this symbol is written: ⅂ .

3.4 BOETHIUS (c. A.D. 490–524)

In the Roman system of education, while the study of rhetoric, along with grammar and logic, belonged to the *Trivium*, the study of music, together with arithmetic, geometry, and astronomy, properly belonged to the *Quadrivium*. However, rhetoricians such as Priscian crossed the *Trivium* barrier to explore such musical factors as tone production, while musical theorists like Boethius often had recourse to logic. One of Boethius' greatest contributions was a demonstration of how to achieve artificial pitches. His determination of the harmonic mean, which divides a larger interval into smaller equal intervals, is a basic method for calculating the temperament of an interval.

Manlius Severinus Boethius was born about four years after the Barbarians invaded Rome. Emperor Constantine, in 326, hoping to protect Christianity from pagan influence, had already moved the seat of the Roman Empire eastward from Rome to Byzantium (to be called Con-

---

5. Guido of Arezzo used a different syllable to identify each of a group of six tones.
6. Many of the accent signs that follow occur in music as single notes and neumes in manuscripts from the ninth century on.

stantinople in his honor). After the following Roman emperors lost
control to the Barbarians, Theodoric the Ostrogoth unified Italy and
made Boethius consul in 510. Boethius, caught in the struggle for power
between Theodoric in the West and Justinian, who was to become
emperor of the Roman Empire in the East, sided with Justinian, a move
that prompted Theodoric to have Boethius executed.

The Three Kinds of Music,
and a Discussion of the Power of Music*

At the beginning of a discussion of music we should consider how many
types of music have been discovered by those who have already studied
the subject. There are three. The first relates to the universe, the second
to human beings, and the third, to instruments, either the cithara or tibiae
or other instruments on which a melody may be played.

As for the first, one can best observe the music of the universe in those
things which one sees in the heaven itself, or in the mixture of the elements,
or in the change of the seasons. For how is it possible for the mechanism
of the sky to move so swiftly through its course in utter silence? And even
though that sound does not reach our ears, which must be the case for a
multitude of reasons, the movement of such great bodies at such an enormous speed could not be totally without sound. This is especially evident,
since the courses of the stars fit together so precisely that it is impossible
to conceive of anything equally well ordered or unified. For some heavenly
bodies travel higher, some lower, and they revolve at precise speeds, so
that through various inequalities a credible plan of courses may be de-
duced. Hence, one cannot deny a credible plan of modulation in this
celestial revolution.

Human music may be understood by delving into one's own personality.
For what is it that unites the contemplative activity of reason with the body,
if not a certain adjustment of low and high tones, as if tempered to produce
a single consonance? What is it, otherwise, that veritably unites among
themselves the parts of the soul which, in the opinion of Aristotle, produce
a union of the rational and the irrational? What, indeed, thoroughly mingles
the elements of the body, or juxtaposes its parts in orderly fashion?

Third is the music which is said to belong to certain instruments. Indeed,
this is produced either by tension, as with strings; or by blowing, as in
tibiae; or by those instruments which are set in motion by water; or by
some sort of percussion, like a hollow bronze vessel struck with a stick,
producing diverse sounds.

The Senses Versus Reason (*Ratio*)

We now make the proposition that we must not trust all judgment to
the senses, even though the origin of this art lies entirely in the sense of

---

*Anicius Manlius Severinus Boethius, De Musica, in Jacques Paul Migne, Patrologiae
Latinae (1844–55), LXIII, Book I, Chaps. 2, 9, 44.

hearing. For if no hearing exists, there can be no discussion at all about tones. On the other hand, hearing to a certain extent retains the origin and change of tones.

Therefore, the utmost perfection in the power of recognition depends on reason which, based on certain rules, never makes a mistake. What more need be said about the error of the senses, since the power of the senses is not the same in all, nor are the senses of an individual always equal. On the other hand, it is pointless to commit to uncertain judgment anything which one truly wants to examine. For this reason the Pythagoreans took a middle path. Although they did not trust all judgment to the ears, certain things were explored by them only with the ears. They measured the consonances themselves by ear. Yet, the distances by which these consonances differed from each other, they did not trust to the ear, whose judgment is not sharp enough, but committed them to the rules of reason [*ratio*]. Thus they made sense subservient to reason, which acted as judge and master. For though the motions of all the arts and of life itself are produced by contact with the senses, yet no certain judgment can be formed about them, no comprehension of the truth can exist, if the authority of reason is lacking. For the mind itself is equally deceived by the smallest and the largest. It can hardly hear the smallest at all because of limitations of perception, and it is often confused by the greatest. Thus with tones, if they are the smallest, the ear has more difficulty in hearing them, if they are the greatest, the ear is deafened by the intensity of the sound.

What a Musician Is

Now let us consider this, that the whole art, and even further, the whole discipline, naturally has a more respected rationale than does a skill executed by the hand and labor of a craftsman. For it is more meaningful and profound to know what someone else does, than to demonstrate oneself what one knows. For physical skill obeys like a servant, while reason commands like a mistress, and unless the hand executes what reason dictates, all is in vain. Thus, how much more effective is the science of music in educating by reason than in demonstrating by work and performance—clearly, as much as the body is surpassed by the mind! Since clearly, a person devoid of reason passes into servitude, reason commands and even leads to integrity. For, unless its command is obeyed, a work devoid of reason will waver. Whence the speculation of reason does not require the practice of execution. Indeed, the works of the hands are nothing, unless led by reason. But how great the glory and merit of reason are, may be understood from this, that the others, so to speak, the physical craftsmen, receive their names, not from the discipline, but rather from the instruments themselves. For the citharist is named from the cithara, the piper from the tibia, and the others from the names of their instruments. But indeed he is a musician who, contemplating rationally, has been attracted to the science of singing, not by the servitude of performances, but by the command of speculation. We see in the construction of buildings as well as in the waging of wars, the opposite designation of the name. For actually, buildings are inscribed and triumphs are celebrated in the names of those by whose command and reason they were initiated, not by the names of those by whose work and service they were completed.

Thus there are three kinds of people who are concerned with the musical art. One kind is concerned with playing instruments, another composes songs, the third judges the performance of instruments and the song. But those who are concerned with instruments, and there squander all of their effort, for example, the citharists, or those who demonstrate their skill on the organ or other musical instruments, are separated from the intellect of musical science, since they are in servitude, as has been said. Nor do they contribute anything to do with reason, since they are totally devoid of speculation. The second group dealing with music is the poets, attracted to song not so much by speculation and reason as by a certain natural instinct. Thus this group is also to be separated from music. The third is that which undertakes the experience of judging, so that it can evaluate the rhythms and cantilena in the song. Since this group is totally concerned with reason and speculation, it is properly regarded as musical. And that man is a musician who, according to speculation or reason appropriate and adaptable to music, possesses the ability to pass judgment on the modes and rhythms, on the types of cantilena and their mixtures, and on the songs of the poets.

3.5 ISIDORE OF SEVILLE (c. 560–636)

The close association of musical performance with the theater is described in the *Etymologies or Origins* of Isidore of Seville. Isidore, whose family probably stemmed from Cartagena on the Mediterranean in southeast Spain, became archbishop of Seville.

He concisely clarifies the distinction between music as the science of harmonics and music as an art. To Isidore music as an art is not infallible, but fanciful. Its creation is so imaginative that it cannot be held within the confines of notation. In addition to the portions of his treatise which he actually labels *music* in the sense of the *Quadrivium*, with its paragraphs describing the intervals, modes, pipes, and lyres, there are sections in which he captures the spirit of the live, unrecorded musical performances of the seventh century, the kind of spirit that the originators of opera tried to recapture a millennium later at the dawn of the Renaissance.

Discipline and Art*

Discipline received its name from studying; whence it may also be called knowledge [*scientia*]. For to "know" is the word meaning to "study," since none of us knows unless he studies. Furthermore, it is called discipline because it is studied fully. . . . Plato and Aristotle attempt to find this dif-

*Isidori Hispalensis Episcopi, Etymologiarum sive Originum libri xx, Bk. I, Sec. i, ii, xviii; Bk. III, Sec. viii, xv; Bk. XVIII, Sec. xlii–li. The entire Latin treatise has been edited by W. M. Lindsay (London: Oxford University Press, 1957).

ference between art and discipline; they say that art is that which can have inconsistencies within itself, but that discipline cannot result in any inconsistencies. For when something is debated in reliable discussion, it is a discipline; when something is treated fancifully and imaginatively, it bears the name of art.

The Seven Liberal Disciplines

There are seven kinds of liberal discipline. The first, grammar, is proficiency in speaking. The second, rhetoric, must be determined according to the brilliance and richness of its eloquence, mostly in public debate. The third, dialectic, also called logic, separates truth from error through the most precise discussion. The fourth, arithmetic, contains the relationships and divisions of the numbers. The fifth, music, consists of songs [*carminibus*] and chants [*cantibus*]. The sixth, geometry, comprises the measurements and dimensions of the earth. The seventh, astronomy, contains the law of the stars.

Music as Sound in Man's Memory

Music is the skill of modulation occurring in tone and chant. It is called music through derivation from the Muses. The Muses were named after the term for "searching," because through them, as the ancients proposed, investigation was made into the influence of songs [*carminum*] and the modulation of the voice. Their sonority, since it pertains to a sense, vanishes as it flows through time, leaving an impression on the memory. Therefore the poets made up the story that the Muses were the daughters of Jove and Memory. For unless the sounds are retained in man's memory, they disappear, because they cannot be written down.

The Theater for Public Performances with Music

The theater is where the stage is set. It has a semicircular shape in which all the people stand while they watch. At first its form was round, just like that of an amphitheater; afterwards the theater was built like half of an amphitheater.

The stage [*scena*] was the place inside the theater constructed like a building with a platform. The platform was called the orchestra. There comedians and tragedians used to sing [*cantabant*]; and actors and mimes used to dance [*saltabant*]. However, what was called stage by the Greeks was built like a dwelling-place. Whence, they used the term "pitching of tents," which was analagous to what was called "the dedication of the tabernacles" among the Hebrews.[7]

Besides, the orchestra was the platform of the stage where a dancer could act, or two could perform together. For there the comedians and

7. The feast of the tabernacles is the Jewish holiday *Succoth*, a time of rejoicing commemorating the booths in which the Israelites lived in the wilderness.

tragedians used to rise to combat with the poets, singing with all kinds of gestures. The stage roles included the tragedians, the comedians, the chorus, the actors, the mimes, and the dancers.

The tragedians are those who make music together [*concinebant*] with time-honored gestures, portraying the grievous misdeeds of the royal family in song as the people watch.

The comedians are those who sing about the actions of the common man with word or gesture, and depict the dishonor of maidens and the affairs of wenches in their stories.

The chorus [*thymelici*] are theatrical musicians who sing accompanied by [*praecanebant*] organs and lyres and citharas. And the said thymelici, because formerly they used to sing in the orchestra while standing on the platform, are called *thymele*.

Actors are those who imitate female gestures while dressing like commonplace women. They portray the stories and active events with dancing. They are called *histriones* either because that style was introduced from Histria [Istria is a province of Italy] or because they portray intricate historic drama as if they were historians.

The mimes were thus called by the Greeks because they were imitators of human actions. They used to have their own narrator who told the story before they performed the play. The plays were prepared by poets in this way to render them highly suitable to the motion of the body.

Moreover, Varro named the dancers [*saltatores*] after Salius the Arcadian, whom Aeneas took with him to Italy, and who was the first to teach the noble Roman youths to dance.[8]

Bibliograhical Note

An English translation of Isidore's section on music in Book III appears in *SRMH*, pp. 93–100.

8. Publius Terentius Varro (1st cent. B.C.) was a Roman poet who wrote an epic called *Argonautica*.

In Book V of the *Aeneid* Virgil describes a race judged by Aeneas in which Salius was a contestant. The race took place in a *circus theatri* (amphitheater). Salius was thwarted from winning by the runner ahead of him who slipped, throwing himself in front of Salius as he felt himself falling, so that his friend might win the race. The gallery, upset by the trickery, favored Salius, whom Aeneas rewarded with the huge hide of an African lion, despite the fact that he did not win.

4

Medieval Chant, Cantilena, and Instrumental Melody

4.1 ST. AUGUSTINE (354–430)

The faculty of retaining sound in the memory is the clue to our ability to follow a musical composition from beginning to end, even though we no longer hear the beginning while we are listening to the end. It is this faculty in its most refined state which enabled Beethoven to compose music when he was totally deaf.

St. Augustine, born in Africa, probably of Roman parents, relates memory to all the senses, including hearing. The musical image he has in mind in his *Confessions* concerns the singing of hymns and psalms in Milan, then the residence of the Western emperors. There Bishop Ambrose, also in touch with the musical practices of the Eastern empire at Constantinople, was composing metrical hymns. The *Te Deum*, a prose hymn, was said to have been composed by St. Ambrose and St. Augustine at the latter's baptism.[1]

---

1. Several different chants for the metrical Ambrosian hymn, *Aeterne Rerum Conditor*, are contained in *HAM*, Vol. I, No. 9. For an example of an Ambrosian psalm see *TEM*, No. 1.

The Singing of Hymns and Psalms in Milan*

When the autumn vacation was over, I notified the people of Milan that they must find another vendor of words for their students; I had difficulty in breathing and the pain in my lungs made me unfit for the duties of a professor.

I wrote to your saintly Ambrose, to tell him of the purpose I now had in mind. The days were all too short, for I was lost in wonder and joy, meditating upon your far-reaching providence for the salvation of the human race. The tears flowed from me when I heard your hymns and canticles, for the sweet singing of your Church moved me deeply. The music surged in my ears, truth seeped into my heart, and my feelings of devotion overflowed, so that the tears streamed down. But they were tears of gladness.

It was not long before this that the Church at Milan had begun to seek comfort and spiritual strength in the practice of singing hymns, in which the faithful united fervently with heart and voice. It was then that the practice of singing hymns and psalms was introduced, in keeping with the usage of the Eastern churches, to revive the flagging spirits of the people. Ever since then the custom has been retained, and the example of Milan has been followed in many other places, in fact in almost every church throughout the world.

Music and Memory

In the memory everything is preserved separately, according to its category. Each is admitted through its own special entrance. For example, light, color, and shape are admitted through the eyes; sound of all kinds through the ears; all sorts of smell through the nostrils; and every kind of taste through the mouth. The sense of touch, which is common to all parts of the body, enables us to distinguish between hard and soft, hot and cold, rough and smooth, heavy and light, and it can be applied to things which are inside the body as well as to those which are outside it. All these sensations are retained in the great storehouse of the memory, which in some indescribable way secretes them in its folds. They can be brought out and called back again when they are needed, but each enters the memory through its own gateway and is retained in it. The things which we sense do not enter the memory themselves, but their images are there ready to present themselves to our thoughts when we recall them.

We may know by which of the senses these images were recorded and laid up in the memory, but who can tell how the images themselves are formed? Even when I am in darkness and in silence I can, if I wish, picture colors in my memory. I can distinguish between any colors that I wish. And while I reflect upon them, sounds do not break in and confuse the images of color, which reached me through the eye. Yet my memory holds sounds as well, though it stores them separately. If I wish, I can summon them too.

*Saint Augustine, Confessions, trans. R. S. Pine-Coffin (Baltimore, Md.: Penguin Books, 1961), Book IX, pp. 189–191, Book X, pp. 214–215. Reprinted by permission of Penguin Books Ltd.

They come forward at once, so that I can sing as much as I want, even though my tongue does not move and my throat utters no sound.[2] And when I recall into my mind this rich reserve of sound, which entered my memory through my ears, the images of color, which are also there in my memory, do not interfere or intrude. In the same way I can recall at will all the other things which my other senses brought into my memory and deposited in it. I can distinguish the scent of lilies from that of violets, even though there is no scent at all in my nostrils, and simply by using my memory I recognize that I like honey better than wine and smooth things better than rough ones, although at that moment I neither taste nor touch anything.

4.2 ST. GREGORY (c. 540–640)
THROUGH JOHN THE DEACON (fl. 870)

About two centuries after a group of chants was associated with the name of St. Ambrose, an even more extensive collection was codified and performed according to the precepts of St. Gregory.

Born into a Roman family that had included a pope in its lineage, Gregory had the background for a position of importance. He became prefect of Rome in 573; this was an imperial office which he held until he decided to quit public life to enter a Benedictine monastery. Because of his earlier experience, he was a likely candidate to go to the imperial court in Constantinople as ambassador of Pope Pelagius II (579–590). There Gregory found Emperor Tiberius II, and then Emperor Maurice, vying with the pope at Rome to set the doctrine of the church. When Gregory himself was elected pope in 590, he was determined to bring the spiritual power back to Rome. His musical accomplishment is described here in the words of John the Deacon, since Gregory wrote little about his activities in this direction. John the Deacon's separation of the style of singing in the territory north of the Alps from that in Rome soon became legendary, to the extent that it was quoted and requoted without benefit of identification of the source.

The Influence of Gregorian Chant
on the Germans and the Gauls*

Then St. Gregory, in the manner of the wisest Solomon, with notes of musical sweetness, most studiously compiled an Antiphonary, a selection exceedingly useful for singers. He also established a school for singers

---

*John the Deacon in Jacques Paul Migne, Patrologiae Latinae, *LXXV*, 90–91.
2. For sound and memory, see Aristoxenus, *Construction of Melody*, Section 2.4.

[*schola cantorum*], which the holy Roman Church to this day operates by the same educational principles. And for the students he built two houses with ample endowments, namely, the one near the steps of the basilica of the blessed Apostle Peter, and the other near the residences of the Lateran patriarchate. From that time until today, his sick bed from which he taught chanting in a reclining position and the very whip with which he threatened the boys, are preserved with appropriate veneration, along with the authentic Antiphonary in which he clearly subdivided the succession of daily prayers by the insertion of an offering before the service.

Elsewhere among the peoples of Europe, quite remarkably, Germans or Gauls were often able to relearn the sweetness of this modulation. Some, so light-headed in the intellect that they were confused about the genuine characteristic of the Gregorian chants, were also so rough by nature that they could not preserve very much at all. The people across the Alps, when they bellow upward with their thundering voices, can never achieve the true sweetness of a recognizable modulation, since the barbaric roughness of their wine-guzzling throats, rather than producing a cantilena gently and beautifully with inflections and repercussions, grates out tones frozen in their tracks, like a wagon confusedly rumbling along steps. And thus, irritating and noisy, it disturbs the intellects of the listeners whom it ought to please.

4.3 CHARLEMAGNE (742–814) THROUGH THE MONK OF ANGOULÊME (11th cent.)

The Roman chant was gaining more widespread acceptance at the time when the civil power of the Frankish King Charlemagne was growing. Intent on achieving religious confirmation for his right to universal rule, Charlemagne decided that the Gallic chant should conform to the Roman. Therefore, in the year 800, when Charlemagne the king was to be crowned Emperor of the West, he chose to go to Rome for Pope Leo III to perform the ceremony.

An account of the life of Charlemagne lies in the archives of the French monastery of Angoulême, which Clovis, King of the Franks, had taken from the Visigoths in 507, and which subsequently was occupied by the Normans in the ninth century. The author of the account, a monk historian of the eleventh century, ascribes to the year 787 the king's desire to reform the Gallican chant in accordance with the true Roman chant of St. Gregory. The Roman chant was heading toward the newer formulation we know of as Gregorian chant today.

Charlemagne's personal involvement with the chant was described by his biographer, the scholar Einhard (c. 770–840), who wrote,

He most diligently improved the method of recitation and of singing to the psalter. For he was extremely well accomplished in both, although he himself neither recited in public nor sang except in a soft voice and with others.

Acceptance of the Roman Chant in Gaul*

And the most pious Charlemagne returned and celebrated Easter at Rome with the apostolic lord. Behold, on the day of the Paschal feast a dispute arose between the Roman and Gallic singers. The Gauls said that they sang better and more beautifully than the Romans. The Romans said that they articulated the cantilenas most expertly since they had been taught by Pope Gregory himself, and accused the Gauls of singing corruptly and destroying the pure cantilena. This dispute came to the attention of His Lordship Charlemagne. Indeed, the Gauls, relying on the favor of Charlemagne, vigorously insulted the Roman singers. The Romans, however, relying on the authority of great instruction, declared that the others were foolish, rustic, and as uneducated as unreasoning animals, and preferred the erudition of St. Gregory to their rusticity.

And when the debate did not end on either side, His Lordship the most pious Charlemagne said to his singers, "Speak freely. Which is purer, and which is better, the living fountain or its streams flowing in the distance?" They all answered in one voice that the fountain as the head and source is the purer; and its streams, the farther away they are from the fountain, are so much the more muddy, filthy, and polluted with impurities.

Then His Lordship Charlemagne said, "Return to the fountain of St. Gregory, since you have manifestly corrupted the ecclesiastical cantilena."

Thereupon, Charlemagne requested from Pope Adrian singers who would correct France in singing. And the pope sent to him Theodore and Benedict, the most learned singers of the Roman church, who had been taught by St. Gregory, and he presented him with the Antiphonal of St. Gregory which he himself had written in Roman notation. Then Charlemagne, turning back to France, sent one singer to the city of Metz, and the other to the city of Soissons, ordering the schoolmasters of all the cities of France to bring the Antiphonals to them for correction and to learn to sing from them. Consequently, the Antiphonals of the Franks, which everyone had marred by adorning or diminishing them arbitrarily, were corrected, and all the singers of France learned the Roman notation which they now call French notation—with the exception that the Franks, with barbaric voices by birth, could not perfectly articulate in song the tremulous or piercing tones, or those which are raised or divided, but broke the sounds in their throats rather than shaping them.

Moreover, the best instruction in singing continued in the city of Metz, and as much as the Roman instruction surpasses that of Metz in the art of cantilena, so much does that of Metz surpass the other schools of the Gauls.

---

*Andreas du Chesne, Historiae Francorum Scriptores (*Lutetiae Parisiorum: Sumptibus Sebastiani Cramoisy Typographi Regij, 1636*), II, 75-76.

Similarly, the Roman singers mentioned above instructed the singers of the Franks in the art of organizing. And Charlemagne once again brought with him from Rome into France masters of grammar and computation, and ordered the study of letters to spread out everywhere. For before the time of Charlemagne there was no study of the liberal arts in Gaul.[3]

4.4 ODO OF CLUNY (879–942)

Odo, the second abbot of the Monastery of Cluny in the eastern part of central France, established extensive reforms in the French monasteries. With the encouragement of the pope, Odo traveled to the Benedictine monasteries of Italy, including Monte Cassino, and the influence of his teaching spread. One of Odo's greatest contributions is the compilation of a *tonary*, a work containing psalm tones, the chant formulas for the eight church modes (see **Appendix 1, Chart 5**).

For each of the eight scale patterns Odo provides a sample melody showing the basic melodic formulas. His instructional text points out the beginning, middle, and end of each melody, thus defining the most elemental musical form. After stating the melodic pattern for the Dorian mode, Odo gives actual chants composed in the mode. Although he goes through this procedure for all eight basic melodic patterns, only the composed chants for the first mode are quoted below.

Intonarium [Tonary]*

Here starts the tonary, diligently tested and arranged by Master Odo, the abbot; tested, properly evaluated, approved, and authenticated by Guido, most holy monk, finest musician: likewise commended most highly as a work necessary for the training of singers honoring the Church, serving God.

---

*Charles-Edmond-Henri de Coussemaker, Scriptorum de musica medii aevi *(Paris: Durand, 1864–1876), II, 117, 142–145.* Quoted from a twelfth-century copy of Odo's manuscript.

3. Another account of this event, by Ekkehard IV (d. 1060), a monk historian at the Monastery of Saint-Gall, assigns the names Petrus and Romanus to the Roman teachers of chant sent to Charlemagne by the Pope. Ekkehard says that Romanus took ill at Saint-Gall (Switzerland) on the way from Italy to France. While Petrus went on to Metz, Romanus received Charlemagne's permission to remain at Saint-Gall, where he founded a singing school based on the authentic Gregorian chant book. (Ekkehard IV, *Casus Sancti Galli* in *Monumenta Germaniae Historia*, Hannover, 1829, II, 102.)

The Monk of Angoulême, who is not as concerned as Ekkehard IV about putting his own monastery to the fore, identifies one authority on Gregorian chant with Metz and the other with Soissons, the location of an abbey where later, in the 12th century, Thomas à Becket, the English church dignitary of Norman background, was to stay during the course of his exile.

The Mode of Intoning the Psalms

The following pattern has been prevalent for the last two-hundred years through the great performances of musical art serving the church of God sincerely and devoutly. How the beginning of the psalm is initiated by the singer, and how it changes may be seen in the *Magnificat*. Indeed it may be seen twice in the *Benedictus*.[4]

Odo of Cluny
The First Mode

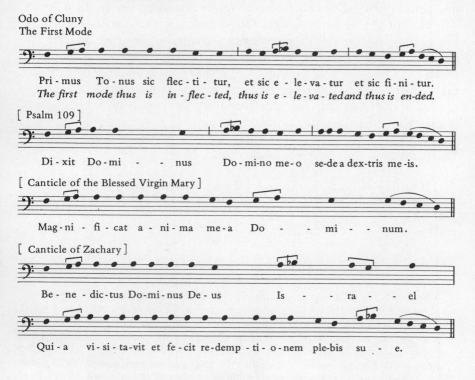

Pri - mus To - nus sic flec - ti - tur, et sic e - le - va - tur et sic fi - ni - tur.
The first mode thus is in - flec - ted, thus is e - le - va - ted and thus is en-ded.

[Psalm 109]

Di - xit Do - mi - - - nus Do - mi-no me - o se-de a dex-tris me -is.

[Canticle of the Blessed Virgin Mary]

Mag - ni - fi - cat a - ni - ma me - a Do - - - mi - - - num.

[Canticle of Zachary]

Be - ne - dic-tus Do-mi - nus De - us Is - - ra - - el

Qui - a vi - si - ta-vit et fe - cit re-demp - ti - o-nem ple-bis su - e.

4.5 AURELIAN OF RÉOME (9th cent.)

The first notation of chant was little more than an indication of accentuation resulting from literary stress or pitch tension. In a ninth-century

---

4. For both the *Magnificat* and the *Benedictus* the melody is to be sung twice.

In the transcription of the musical examples, two-note ascending and descending neumes are indicated by brackets. A three- or four-note descent is indicated by a slur.

Since the melody of the *Magnificat* follows the sample for the second verse, Odo does not have to write it out again, as he does for the *Benedictus*, where the motion (down to F) in the second verse is different from that of the first.

A flat has been indicated above the note b in accordance with the hexachord system (see Guido, Section 4.9), which was prevalent at the time this manuscript was copied.

manuscript from Valenciennes, north of France, Aurelian of Réome uses
rudimentary neumes to identify the endings of a chant in the first authentic mode (Dorian). The work, entitled *The Discipline of Music*, explains
how to hinge the end of the psalm verse to the beginning of the Antiphon,
a procedure necessary for the performance of this type of chant. Basic
to the practice was the alternate singing of the composed Antiphon with
the chanting of successive psalm verses to the appropriate psalm tone.
The text of the lesser doxology, *Gloria Patri, et Filio*, was sung as the
last verse of any psalm. To accommodate the transition from the close of
the psalm verse to the beginning of a particular Antiphon, a choice of
psalm-tone endings was provided. The *different endings* of the mode,
called *varietates* by Aurelian, are now known as *differentiae* or *euouae*
(evovae), the latter term being derived from the vowels of the last words
in the lesser doxology, se*cu*lo*ru*m *a*men.

The Endings for the First Authentic Mode: Chap. X*

The first authentic has several different endings. To be brief, it encompasses three different endings for the introits, the first of which is the Antiphon

$$\text{Gta} \underline{\quad} \diagup ^{--} \cap \cdot \underline{\quad} \; .. \; \nu_{\text{¬}} \underline{\quad}$$

Gaudete in Domino Semper.

The end of the verse goes directly back to the beginning of the antiphon and is identical with it, for it is placed neither up high nor down low.[5]
The second introit is the Antiphon *Justus es Domine*. The end of its verse
is raised up so that it may coincide with the beginning of the antiphon.[6]

---

*Martin Gerber, Scriptores ecclesiastici de musica sacra potissimum (St. Blasien,
1784), I, 42–43, 60. The Valenciennes Manuscript containing the work of Aurelian
is No. 148.*
5. The order of performance is Introit, psalm verse with *differentia*, Introit. In the
case Aurelian is describing, the Introit *Gaudete* starts and ends on d, and the ending
of the Psalm verse is also on d. Following is a possible reconstruction for Aurelian's
heighted neumes, set to the last words of the *Gloria Patri*:

6. The Introit *Justus es Domine* now in use starts with the leap of a fifth from d to
a. Aurelian may be considering a *differentia* leading up to the confinalis, a.

The third is the Antiphon *Suscepimus Deus*. In this, the last syllable of the verse is delayed for a longer time than in the first and second, and the tone is raised up high so that it may be accommodated to the beginning of the introit.

Concerning this matter, the reader may wonder why a single mode of just one kind may have so many different kinds of endings that sometimes the last syllable of the verse is up high, occasionally it is kept down, and very often it is uttered even more deeply, and why in certain modes fewer irregularities of modulations are discovered, as at the end of the verses of these three introits. He who wishes to know the entirety of this science, we send to the music itself, and if he wishes to be involved, he should turn his sights toward the consonance of proportions and the exploration of intervals, and also to the exactitude of mathematics. Then he will be able to know why for one and the same text there may be different patterns of sound, and other things which are too long to tell.

Antiphon, Response, Alleluia: Chap. XX*

The Nocturnal Office consists of antiphons and responses. Reciprocal singing is called antiphonal, because the choirs sing alternately: that is, because the choir that began the antiphon takes it from the other choir to be sung again, imitating in this the Seraphim, concerning whom it is written: *And they cried one to another: Holy, Holy, Holy, Lord, God of Hosts* (Isaiah 6:3). Antiphons were first devised by the Greeks, from whom they took the name, also; but among the Latins their originator was the blessed Ambrose, bishop of Milan, from whom the whole western Church received this custom. Responses, however, were first devised by the Italians, and are called responses because, as one person sang—for it was customary among the ancients for the responses to be sung by soloists—all the rest responded to the singer.

The ceremony of the Mass, on the other hand, consists of antiphons that are called *Introits*, so named because they are sung as the people enter the basilica. The singing of the Introit is prolonged until, in undisturbed order, both the bishop and the other clerical ranks, each according to his dignity, have entered the church and taken their respective positions.

There is also sung a response that is called the *Gradual*, a name applied to it from *gradus* [step], since it was customary for the ancients to stand upon steps when either singing or speaking. Hence, it is said concerning Ezra: *Ezra stood upon the step of wood, which he had made to speak upon* (II Ezra 8:4). Fifteen psalms are called Gradual Psalms, because, as the name indicates, they were sung upon the steps.

The *Alleluia*, however, we took from the Jews, whose language, in fact, it is; it is said to mean praise God, which, in accordance with its dignity, has not been translated into any other language.

Aurelian of Réome, The Discipline of Music (Musica Disciplina), *trans. Joseph Ponte (Colorado Springs: Colorado College Music Press, 1968), Chapter XX, pp. 54–55. Reprinted by permission of the Colorado College Music Press. An excellent bibliography for materials on Aurelian appears on pp. iii–v.*

Bibliographical Notes

For the position of the lesser doxology in relation to the antiphon and psalm see Parrish and Ohl, *Masterpieces of Music Before 1750* (New York: W. W. Norton & Co., Inc., 1951), No. 1.

The modern versions of the chants to which Aurelian refers are contained in the *Liber Usualis*. The Introit *Gaudete in Domino semper* appears in modern Gregorian square notation on a four-line staff in the *Liber Usualis*, with introduction and rubrics in English, edited by the Benedictines of Solesmes (Tournai, New York: Desclée, 1962), p. 334 f. It is transcribed into our customary round notation on a five-line staff in the *Liber Usualis Missae et Officii* (Paris, Tournai, Rome: Desclée, 1954), p. 261 f.

4.6 HUCBALD (c. 840–930)

Hucbald, a Flemish monk, was thoroughly acquainted both with the melodic vagaries of Gregorian chant and with the precision of Greek musical terminology. He was well aware of the difficulties inherent in describing and notating the chant. While the heighted neumes pictured the free flow of the chant as it ascended and descended, they offered little aid to someone who did not have some notion of the melody beforehand. Hucbald sought to reconcile the motion of the chant to the Greek system with its fixed pitches outlining the conjunct and disjunct tetrachords.

Hucbald lived at St. Amand, near Valenciennes, the site of Aurelian's endeavors. Hucbald's uncle, the director of the school of the Abbey of St. Amand, was his first teacher. A rivalry between uncle and nephew flared up over Hucbald's talents as a composer of chant. It subsided when Hucbald's fame spread uncontested through the monasteries and the royal court as well.

In *Concerning Harmonic Practice* (c. 870) Hucbald identifies the tones by establishing their exact locations in the scale. His statement on where to use b♮ and b♭ is disarmingly simple, because he finds each lying comfortably in one of the diatonic tetrachords, as they did in the ancient Greek system (see **Appendix 1**, Chart 2).

Musical Syllables: The Choice Between b♮ and b♭*

Sometimes a melody is infused with one or the other of the two tetrachords. Sometimes it is diverted alternately from one to the other, like when

Martin Gerbert, Scriptores ecclesiastici de musica sacra potissimum *(St. Blasien, 1784), I, 113–114.*

one returns to the *synemmenon* [the tetrachord with b♭] after having left it. An example of this is provided by the Response *Nativitas gloriosae Virginis Mariae*, in which everything proceeds in the *diezeugmenon* [the tetrachord with b♮] from the beginning until one sings *ex stirpe*. But at the third note, on the syllable *pe*, one changes to the *synemmenon* [b♭]. And the entire neume which appears in the name *David* is sung in the *synemmenon*.[7]

Likewise for the Introit *Statuit ei Dominus*—the second note on the syllable *Sta* [a], placed at the distance of a fifth from the first note [d], is tied to the third note above [b♭] by the *synemmenon*, and there is a semitone between these two notes, the second and the third. Now the syllable *Do* is directed toward the *diezeugmenon* [b♮], and the syllable *mi* once more returns down to the *synemmenon* [b♭].[8]

4.7 NOTKER BALBULUS (c. 840–912)

During the ninth century the Monastery of Saint-Gall became the center of musical activity related to the chant. One of the creative monks there, Notker Balbulus (the Stammerer), made an extremely important contribution to the future of musical composition as he sought a solution to the problem of memorizing a long melisma (a musical passage sung to one syllable of text). He composed additional text for the melisma, providing a syllable for each note or neume, and working the insertion into a suitable musical-poetic scheme. The resulting compositions, called sequences, having no place in the book of chants called the *Antiphonal*, were collected as a small appendage to it. Quoted here is the preface to Notker's *Hymn Book* in which he describes this art of composing sequences.

7. A version of the *Nativitas gloriosae* is in the *Liber Usualis* (see Bibliographical Notes, Section 4.5, and *LU 1*, p. 1625, *LU 2*, p. 1506). The chant is in the eighth mode, Hypomixolydian, with the octave range d to d′ and the final on g (see Chart 5, and Odo, Section 4.4). This mode ordinarily has a b♮, and the chant in the *Liber Usualis* does not provide any b♭. However, Hucbald suggests using a b♭ at the end, as in the following example:

ex stir - pe   Da - vid.

8. *Statuit ei Dominus*, in the first authentic mode, appears in the *Liber Usualis* (*LU 1* p. 1182; *LU 2* p. 989) with a leap from a to c on the syllable *Do*, without the b♮ mentioned by Hucbald. Perhaps the b♮, which in effect is a passing tone from a to c, was considered as an unnecessary embellishment in the version in the *Liber*.

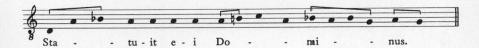

Sta -   - tu - it e - i   Do -   - mi -   - nus.

The Sequence, an Aid to Musical Memory*

In the name of the Lord, here begins Notker's
Hymn Book
This little book contains verses suited to modulation,
So that he who wishes to be in control, may control his breath.

Preface

Hitherto, when I was a young man, I often had to commit to memory extremely long melodies which escaped my shaky memory. I began silently to think about what I might do to retain them. As time went on, it happened that a certain monk from Jumièges, recently sacked by the Normans, came to us, bringing along with him his Antiphonal, in which some verses were measured into sequences.[9] As pleasant as these were to my sight, so were they bitter to my taste. Nevertheless, in imitation of them I began to write *Laudis Deo concinat orbis universus, qui gratis est redemptus*, and further on, *Coluber Adae deceptor*.

When I looked these over with my master Yson, he congratulated me on my enthusiasm, but pointed out my inexperience. He praised what was acceptable, and improved what was less correct saying, "Each individual motion of the cantilena ought to have a single syllable."

On hearing this, I corrected the motions which came on *-ia* until they flowed; however, those on *-le* or *-lu* I neglected to adjust as an impossibility. Yet, afterwards I also understood the latter easily, as the following show: *Dominus in Syna* [10] and *Mater*. And instructed in this way, I soon wrote another one: *Psallat Ecclesia, Mater illibata*.

When I presented these versicles to my master Marcellus, he was delighted. He rolled them up into a scroll and recommended one and another to be sung by the boys.

---

*Liber Hymnorum *(Book of Hymns)*. The title was changed to* Liber Sequentiarum *(Book of Sequences), as it appeared in B. Pez,* Thesaurus Anecdotorum novissimus, *1721. The work appears under the latter title in J. P. Migne,* Patrologiae latinae *(1853),* CXXXI, *1005 ff., from which this source is taken.*

9. The sequence, called *prosa* in France, was worked into the three-part Mass movement, *Alleluia–verse–Alleluia*. Instead of the melismatic repetition of the word *Alleluia* in the third part, a text was troped syllabically to the Alleluia melody of the first part. In the process the original melody was altered extensively. The resulting sequence had a portion of the melody repeated to each pair of added lines, with a single line at the beginning and end. The musical form was abbcc-ddee . . .x.

10. The Alleluia with verse *Dominus in Sina*, together with its sequence by Notker, appears in *HAM*, Vol. I, No. 16.

None of the sequences Notker mentions in this preface are retained in the liturgy today. When the Council of Trent met in 1565, all sequences were abolished with the exception of the *Dies Irae, Lauda Sion, Veni Sancte Spiritus*, and *Victimae Paschali*. The *Stabat Mater* was allowed in 1727.

Bibliographical Notes

See Willi Apel, *Gregorian Chant* (Bloomington: Indiana University Press, 1958) for analyses of the sequences *Coluber Adae deceptor* (p. 457 f.) and *Psallat Ecclesia* (p. 444 ff.)

A sequence was a special kind of trope, an addition to the chant that involved either providing a syllabic text for melismatic chant, inserting decorations within the chant motion, or some combination of both procedures. Although tropes too were banned from the liturgy, some Kyries, such as *Kyrie fons bonitatis*, are still identified by their trope titles (*LU 1*, p. 19). This Kyrie in its liturgical version, juxtaposed with its trope, appears in *MSO*, Part 1, pp. 12–13.

The Alleluia of the Easter Mass, with its verse *Pascha nostrum* and Sequence *Victimae paschali laudes* (*LU 1*, pp. 779 f.) appears in Gregorian notation in *MSO*, Part 1, p. 4. The Dies Irae Sequence (*LU 1*, p. 1810) is in *MSO*, Part 1, p. 10.

4.8 AL FĀRĀBI (870?–950)

In the ninth and tenth centuries Arabic philosophers and scientists translated and commented on the Greek authors Euclid, Ptolemy, and Aristotle, thus helping to preserve these works and transmit them to posterity. In Fārāb, a district of Persia, Aristotle's scholarship was esteemed to the extent that he was called the First Master. The appellation Second Master was conferred on a brilliant young scholar studying there, whose name became synonymous with that of the town. After estimating that he had read the works of Aristotle a hundred times, Al Fārābi humbly admitted that he felt the necessity for continuing to read them over and over again.

In addition to his exploration of cantilena or vocal melody, in his *Book on Music* Al Fārābi considered the performance of melody on an instrument. He established a connection between the Greek tetrachord system (**Appendix 1,** Chart 2) and the tuning of the Arabic Ūd (wood), a kind of lute with a short neck. Basically the Ūd had been tuned in fourths with open strings on g, c, f, and b♭. With the limits of the tetrachords thus set at fixed points, Al Fārābi proceeded to account for the placement of frets on the neck of the instrument, which from a practical standpoint meant the placement of fingers on the string. There is no evidence that there were real, tangible frets on the Ūd at that time. Al Fārābi's measurements were calculated, not for the purpose of instrumental construction, but to accurately define minute intervals of pitch. He did not limit himself to the one-stringed monochord, an instrument devised for experimentation by Pythagoras (Section 2.2), but applied the theory to a multi-stringed instrument currently in use. His fingerings reflected the different genera with their distributions of microtones in specific patterns within the interval of a fourth.[11] Although, by superimposing the genera collectively, he calculated an extended series of microtones within a short distance, he did not intend these pitches to be played successively, any more than did the Greek and Hindu musicians (see Sections 2.4 and 1.3).

Cantilenae in Persia*

Let us explain and briefly illustrate what we mean by *cantilenae*. Some melodies are elusive and difficult to define. Those which are comprehensible have rational pitches and poetic meters from which we may discover the mode of the song and the classification of melodies. But this book does not exhaust the subject of the cantilena, nor does it include everything; for there is a separate book intended for this purpose. This one does not contain any song texts or melodies, since it encompasses all of the concepts of the writers of antiquity as well as current authors. Indeed, this book is directed toward exploring matters pertaining to the poet, or the singer, or the reason for which the song is sung or the melody is created, or to the writing down of certain songs which may be of significant importance, and whose definition may be linked in a suitable way with the definition of cantilena. A cantilena is created as briefly as possible, to the exclusion of superfluous matters and with the condensation of those things which are of little importance. However, it interweaves suitable ornaments and radiance appropriate to it.

Definition of Melody

Let us begin by defining briefly what we understand by "musical art." The term "music" means "melodies." The word "melody" is used sometimes to designate a succession of notes in a fixed order. It may also designate a series of notes somehow joined together and associated with speech sounds. The latter form words signifying ideas, and constitute a phrase which expresses a thought according to the usual rules of language. Melody also has other meanings, but they are not suited to our purpose.

The first meaning is more general than the second, which is like an extension of it. In effect, the first sense concerns notes heard anywhere, pro-

---

Ioanne Godofredo Ludovico Kosegarten, Alii Ispahanensis Liber Cantilenarum Magnus, Ex Codicibus Manu Scriptis Arabice Editus (*Gripesvoldiae: In Libreria Kochiana, 1840*), *pp. 207 ff.*

11. For example, a diatonic genus on the open string g could be performed with the first finger on a, the second finger on b♭', and the fourth finger on c' (leaving the third finger free to play b♮' when needed).

duced by any substance. The second sense, on the contrary, concerns notes susceptible of blending with speech sounds which constitute words signifying an idea, that is to say, vocal sounds which man utters to express his thought and to transmit it to others.

Whatever the differences may be in the two meanings of the word "melody," it includes the elements which make up and fashion song, and those which give it its charm and perfection.

Song, and all that is associated with it, is classified with things which are at the same time sensible, imaginable, and intelligible. Is it one and the same thing which, in song, addresses itself to our senses, our imagination, our intelligence? Or is what is sensible distinct from that which is imaginable? Or further, is song sensible under certain conditions, imaginable and intelligible under others? This question is not specific to song; it is common to all entities of the same kind. In short, the art of music is that which is concerned with melodies and makes them more excellent and perfect.

Practical Music*

An art is musical when it relates to the composition of a musical phrase and its expression, or to the construction of the phrase giving it its form, but without its expression. One gives the name of the art of *practical music* to both, but more frequently to the first. As for the exercise of the faculty which, through the intervention of our hearing, allows us to discern musical phrases, to recognize that one composition is superior to another, to distinguish a harmonious composition from another which is not, one does not call this art. It is rare to meet anyone who is destitute of such discernment; as a matter of fact, we acquire it by practice if it is not innate in us. The third musical art is that which concerns theory. We will treat each of these three aspects of musical art separately; we will then compare them with each other.

That to which the name of the art of practical music refers, is a rational disposition which operates according to a true imagination born in the soul. It gives birth to melodies imagined in a sensible form. The second art to which this name refers is a rational disposition which, acting according to a true image which is formed in the soul, gives birth to melodies in the form of imagery.

A man possesses the art of practical music such as we defined in the first place when he satisfies the two following conditions: first, he must form in his soul one or several images of the musical phrase which he wishes to compose, then he must have an aptitude for regulating the instrument which will produce the impulses from which the musical notes are born. For example, he moves a plectrum, placing it where a sonorous body produces the notes which he needs. The agent of percussion is either the hand of man or the respiratory apparatus which forces the air from the inside of the chest out through the mouth. The hand strikes by itself or with the intervention of a foreign body. The respiratory apparatus, while compressing the air, imparts a sort of impulse. In the first case, instruments of the

---

* *Al Fārābi*, Grand Traité de la Musique, *French trans. by Baron Rodolphe d'Erlanger, in* La Musique Arabe *(Paris: Librairie Orientaliste Paul Geuthner, 1930), I, 6–10, 25, 28.*

lute and kithara families are set in motion; in the second, wind instruments, such as flutes, and the cavities of the larynx, the vocal organs, are set in motion.

Playing a Melody on an Instrument

To fix the place of musical notes on the sonorous bodies, to establish the touches on the lute or on instruments of that species, to determine the place of notes on any instrument whatsoever, is the work of an artisan. As for the voice, it needs a special aptitude to render exactly the notes of a composition already conceived. Experience alone makes it possible to play on an instrument notes determined in advance. It is the artisan who brings to the instrument the qualities necessary for playing fixed notes at fixed points, and it is experience and practice which give the voice the capacity for producing notes which render the conceived melody perceptible to the senses.

Invention of Melody

It is often difficult for someone to compose without the aid of the instrument to which he is accustomed, without being in the surroundings familiar to him, away from the circumstances which he is used to. We know the anecdote of a jeweler, likewise a skillful musician, who could only sing seated while working. A person with that kind of disposition can only understand melodies and imagine them under conditions which please his fancy. On a higher level, talent allows the composer to appreciate his work, to judge whether or not it is refined, discernment being added to the aptitudes already cited. Imagination takes shape in the consonances and dissonances of notes, and in the manner in which one moves the instrument which produces the beats whence the conceived melodies spring into action. Then we are prepared to judge the composition as our imagination presents it to us, but we are not able to explain why we represent it to ourselves thus. This sort of recognition is called knowing that a thing *is what it is*. This level of talent, therefore, allows the recognition of melodies and notes as melodies and notes, but without the knowledge of why they *are what they are*.

When, by virtue of a natural gift or of an acquired experience, one is capable of distinguishing a good melody from a bad one, of recognizing consonant notes and dissonant notes, of combining musical sounds in a manner satisfying to the ear, and of composing the melody which one has conceived, one possesses the practical musical art in its second aspect. One should, for that, be endowed with a very exact ear, with the faculty of perception, and with normal imagination. In other words, one should be able to judge beauty and to listen with taste to that which is not natural to man, and to condemn that which is according to nature. This is what happens to certain individuals endowed with an abnormal ear and imagination. In order for a musician to belong to the category of artists of which we speak, it is sufficient for him to be able to compose music without justifying it, without judging it. Likewise there are musicians endowed in a way that enables them to improvise melodies not planned in their mind. Melody is specified for them only at the moment when it has a sonorous sensation, whether the artist himself has uttered several musical notes or he has heard them expressed by someone else. His art is not inferior to that of the preceding. In short, his dispositions permit him to produce music at the very instant when he composes it, whether he impregnates the ear with humming or with trying some notes on an instrument, but never in any other way. They say that there were musicians whose talent was of that kind, and among the most famous of them they cite Ma'bad of Médine.

Others have a more powerful imagination; their soul shapes the music or the elements which compose it without having to resort to a sonorous sensation, without impregnating the ear. Their desire alone is enough to make the melodies traverse their imagination. However, all do not have this talent to the same degree; some surpass others. Certain people possess it so perfectly that they compose without having to resort to sense-perception. Among others there are weaknesses, and they need, at times to help themselves with sense-perception. This is what they say about Ibn Surayj the Mecquois. When he wanted to compose a chant, he put on a robe covered with small bells whose sonority nearly corresponded to his voice. Then he balanced his shoulders, with his whole body following a certain rhythm, and began to hum. When the cadence of his modulation coincided with the beat of the rhythm which he had chosen, the melody which he had in view was achieved and finally he chanted it.

4.9 GUIDO OF AREZZO (995?–1050)

The most famous teacher-scholar of the eleventh century, Guido of Arezzo, founded a school at the monastery of Pomposa, near Ferrara, Italy, where he avidly sought more efficient ways to teach music. Guido refined the procedure of relating syllables of the chant to pitches, establishing a system of interlocking hexachords in place of the tetrachord system. He also used specific colors for the clef lines of the staff to reinforce the identity of the pitches designated by the clef letters.

Guido was so successful with his methods of instruction that the jealousy of his rivals forced him to leave the monastery at Pomposa for an even more secluded retreat, with the Benedictine monks of Arezzo. There he formulated his thoughts in an open letter to his friend, Monk Michael, and conceived his great commentary, the *Micrologus de Disciplina Artis Musicae* (Details of the Discipline of the Art of Music). The *Micrologus* was copied more often than any other manuscript written during the Middle Ages, and became the basis for prolific, penetrating musical commentary through the eras to come.

Solmization of the Hexachord: Letter to Monk Michael
Concerning an Unfamiliar Melody*

Pope John [XIX (1024–1033)], who now heads the Church of Rome, heard about the fame of our school and how boys learn unfamiliar melodies through our Antiphonal. Greatly astonished, he summoned me to him with three messengers. Accordingly, I went to Rome with the reverend Abbot Grunwald and Peter, Prior of the church of Arezzo, the most learned man of our time.

The Pope was very pleased that I came. He talked to me frequently, inquiring about different things. And he often turned through our Antiphonal as if it were something extraordinary, mulling over the introductory rules. He did not put it down or go away from the place where he was sitting until he found out how to sing a verse of his choice which he had not heard before. Thus, what he could scarcely believe about others, he suddenly realized for himself. . . .

In order to learn a melody which one does not know, most blessed Brother, this is the first thing to do. On the monochord play the notes for each neume according to their letter names. Then by listening to yourself, you will be able to learn just as if you were studying with an actual teacher. But this practice is childish, good certainly for beginners, but very bad for the advanced. For I have seen the wisest men, who, in order to study this art have procured not only Italian, but also Gallic and German, and even Greek teachers. But since they depended on this practice alone, they could not begin to resemble what I call musicians, nor even singers comparable to our juvenile psalmists.

We need not always get the sound of an unfamiliar melody from a man or an instrument, as though we were blind, never proceeding without a guide. On the contrary, we should commit to the depths of our memory the differences and characteristics of the rise and fall of each individual sound. Then you would have the easiest and most valuable means of learning an unfamiliar melody, provided that someone were on hand to teach the student according to our method, not by writing something down, but rather through informal discussion. For, after I began to teach the boys by this method, some of them were easily able to sing an unfamiliar melody within a three-day period, something which could not have been accomplished in many weeks by other methods.

Therefore, if you wish to commit to memory any note or neume [group of notes] so that it will occur to you immediately, wherever you wish, in any song whatsoever, whether familiar or unfamiliar, to the point where you will be able to sing it immediately without hesitation, you should notice the note or neume at the beginning of each important phrase. And, toward memory retention, you should have in mind for each and every note the phrase which begins with that note. As an example take the following melody which I use from beginning to end for teaching the boys.

*Martin Gerbert, Scriptores ecclesiastici de musica sacra potissimum (St. Blasien, 1784), Epistola Guidonis Michaeli Monacho De Ignoto Cantu, II, 44–45; Guidonis Aretini Micrologus, II, 14–18.

Ut que-ant la - xis Re -so-na- re fi - bris Mi - ra ge -sto-rum Fa- mu- li tu - o - rum,
C   D   E   F

Sol - ve pol - lu - ti La - bi - i re - a - tum,San - cte Jo - an - nes.
G   A

Do you see that this melody has six phrases, beginning on six different notes? If you learn the beginning of each phrase well, so that you can begin any phrase you desire immediately, without hesitation, you will easily be able to sing these six notes wherever you see them, according to their characteristics.[12]

On Composing a Melody Competently:
Micrologus

In poetry there are letters and syllables, phrases and feet, and also verses; likewise, in tone there are speech sounds, that is, utterances of which one, two, or three are formed into syllables. And these, alone or in combination constitute a neume, that is, part of a cantilena. One or more phrases make up a division, that is, an appropriate place for exhaling. On this subject, notice that a complete phrase is concisely notated and enunciated, but a syllable is even more concise. The hold [*tenor*], that is, the delay [*mora*] on the final sound, however slight it may be for the syllable, is more extensive for the phrase, and longest for the division.[13] It serves as a sign for these divisions.

12. The vowel sounds, A, E, I, O, U, appear in the hexachord syllables as follows: Ut, rE, mI, fA, sOl, lA. Guido also used the five vowel sounds, apart from their placement in the hexachord, for teaching the students how to sing.
    The text here is the first stanza of the hymn *Ut Queant Laxis*, which has five stanzas in all, each sung to the same melody. It is in the second mode, with finalis on d and reciting tone on f. However, from this melody Guido derived the C hexachord, ut re mi fa sol la / C D E F G a. Using this pattern of steps, he also established hexachords on G and F. Since the hexachord G a b c d e had a b♮, it was called the *hexachordum durum* (hard hexachord). The hexachord F G a b♭ c d, with its b♭, was called the *hexachordum molle* (soft hexachord). The C hexachord, without any b, was known as the *hexachordum naturale* (natural hexachord). See Chart 2.
    The hexachord system as a whole embraced seven interlocking ascending hexachords, starting on the tones Gamma, C, F, G, c, f, and g. Since each hexachord in the gamut had the same pattern of steps, the inherent conflict of b♭ and b♮ occurred between the fourth note of the F hexachord and the third note of the G hexachord.
13. *Mora* is a delay, a prolonging of the tone, which retards the progress of the melody. In the next paragraph Guido uses *morula*, a diminutive of *mora*, while

It is helpful to clap to the cantilena in metrical feet. Some notes have a duration [*morula*] twice as long or twice as short as the others. Or else, some notes have a tremulous duration, that is, a variable length which is sometimes indicated by a horizontal mark [*virgula*] added to the letter.[14] And the distribution of neumes should be stipulated with the greatest care, so that, whether neumes are produced either by a repetition of the same tone, or by a combination of two or more tones, they are nevertheless always united in one of two ways, either as a group of tones or as a ratio of time values. They are sometimes in the proportion of one to one, sometimes two or three to one, and still other times are in the *sesquialtera* (three to two) or *sesquitertia* (four to three) proportion.[15]

The musician kindles the song in his imagination with these divisions, just as the poet creates the verse with feet, except that the musician does not restrain himself with so much adherence to rule, because this art constantly permutates the placement of tones with rational diversity. Even though we do not often understand this rationality, we still regard as rational that by which the mind, in which reason exists, is pleased. But this and matters of this kind are easier to present orally than in writing.

It is proper, therefore, that the melodic phrases [*distinctiones*][16] of the verses be equal in duration, that they sometimes be repeated, or that they otherwise be varied by a slight mutation. And when several phrases are paired, having melodies not too different, sometimes they are altered by means of the modes, or they are constructed so that they ascend and descend in like manner. Also, it is proper for a reciprocal neume to return by the same path by which it had come, even retracking the same footprints. Likewise, when a neume produces an ambitus or outline leaping downward from the high notes [*acutis*], another moves upward from below, answering from the low notes [*gravibus*], just as when we are mirrored in a well with our image opposite us.[17] Also, sometimes a syllable has one or several neumes; sometimes a neume is divided among several syllables. These or any other sort of neume may be varied, if in the first place they begin with the very note, elsewhere with different notes according to various degrees of laxity and strictness. Also, at the end all *differentiae* move to the principal tone, that is, to the *finalis*, or else one may correctly choose the *confinalis* in its stead.[18] And sometimes the same tone that terminates all neumes, or closes several *differentiae*, begins the incipit, as the curious may find with Ambrose. Indeed, there are songs almost like prose, which conform to these

---

discussing the more detailed concept of time values in relation to the beat, in contrast to the more general concept of time in relation to the larger divisions of melody.

14. The horizontal *virgula*, the dash, was an accent mark in prosody (see Priscian, Section 3.3). The vertical *virgula* was a single-note neume or the stem of a note.

15. For an explanation of the proportions, see Euclid (Section 2.2). Of great importance here is the fact that Guido associates the ratios both with pitches of an interval (*numero vocum*) and with time values (*ratione tenorum*).

16. *Distinctio* is translated variously as *melodic phrase*, *grouping*, and *differentia*, the latter referring to a melodic phrase at the close of a melody (see Aurelian, Section 4.5).

17. Retrograde motion in a melody.

18. The *finales* d, e, f, g, had the corresponding *confinales* (*affinales*) a, b, c′, d′ (see Chart 5).

precepts to a lesser degree. Then, in the manner of prose, it does not matter whether some phrases and *differentiae* are devised more extensively, others less, without discrimination.

However, I say that songs are metrical, because often we sing as if we were scanning verses by feet.[19] This is also the case when we sing meters in which we must avoid including too many two-syllable neumes without an admixture of three- and four-syllable neumes. For just as the lyric poets create by adding to certain feet at one time to different feet at another, so those who create songs rationally compose distinct and diverse neumes.[20] Indeed, the distinction is rational if the variety of neumes and phrases is regulated so that neumes correspond to neumes and phrases to phrases, always answering each other in suitable imitation, that is, in a dissimilar similarity in the manner of the most dulcet Ambrose.[21] The relationship between meter and song is evident when neumes stand for feet and melodic phrases stand for verses, with one neume moving through dactyllic, another spondaic, another iambic meter; with one melodic phrase perceived in tetrameter, another in pentameter, and yet another as if in hexameter.[22] And there are many other relationships, such as an ascent or a descent either by itself, or one placed above, below, next to, or between another similarly or dissimilarly. With regard to the interval, one may be conjunct, another disjunct, another mixed. Likewise, the phrases and groupings of neumes and words must end together, so that a long time value does not occur on a so-called short syllable, or a short time value on a long one, since that would constitute a disfigurement which would only rarely be beneficial.

Likewise, the effect of the song should imitate the outcome of the circumstances so that in sad situations the neumes are grave, in tranquil situations, jocund, in those fortunate, exultant, and so on. Likewise, often we place grave and acute accents over notes, since often we effect certain situations by greater and also by lesser impulse, to such a degree that often a repetition of the same note seems to be a rising or a falling.

Likewise, in the manner of a running horse, at the end of phrases the notes always occur more sparsely toward the place of breathing, as if with a burdensome delay they arrive at the resting place exhausted. Dense but yet sparse—it is quite appropriate to furnish a sign for composing notes of this kind. Indeed, long notes dissolve in the manner of letters, in such a way that the beginning of one limpidly goes over to the other, without seeming to be finished. Furthermore, we place a point over the liquescent note as if dotting it. If, however, you desire to utter it more fully, not making the

19. The basic poetic feet used for musical as well as poetic meter are trochee, iamb, dactyl, anapest, spondee, and pyrrhic.
20. *Componere* means *to compose* in the literal sense of putting things together. The close association between composing poetry and music is reinforced by the term *lyric poets*. In an eleventh-century musical dictionary, *Vocabularium Musicum*, the entry for LYRA reads, "A type of cithara called *lyric* because of the variation of the verses. Whence the poets are called *lyrici* because they create different sounds."
21. Guido may be referring to Ambrosian modal characteristics such as a predilection for the *affinalis*, the dominant, instead of the *finalis*, the tonic.
22. A verse in iambic pentameter has five iambic feet. Tetrameter refers to four feet in the verse, and hexameter to six feet.

liquescence, it does not matter; on the contrary, often it is more pleasing. And all that we have said should be done neither too rarely nor too consistently, but with discretion.[23]

Concerning the Multiple Variety of Tones and Neumes: *Micrologus*

Do not be astonished that such an abundance of diverse songs may be formed from so few tones. There are only six tones, joined either in ascent or descent. Since their syllables are generated by only a few words, it is possible to remember the body of syllables. Yet, an infinite plurality of members may arise from the syllables. With regard to meter, the kinds of meter produced from a few feet are just as extensive. A meter of a single kind, such as the hexameter, may be found in a great many varieties. How that happens is the concern of the grammarians, and should be dealt with elsewhere. We will concern ourselves, if we may, with the ways in which we are able to construct various neumes.

The motion of voices stemming from the six tones, as has been said, occurs by rising and falling, that is, by the twin motion of arsis and thesis. In other words, each neume consists of an arsis and a thesis, whether repeated or simple. Besides, arsis and thesis are either joined to themselves, as arsis to arsis and thesis to thesis, or are connected to each other, as arsis to thesis and thesis to arsis. Thus, the connection may be of similar or dissimilar motions. However, a dissimilarity from the aforesaid motions of tones, semitones, ditones, and others, would occur if one member had more or fewer notes than another, or had conjunct or disjunct notes to a greater extent. Furthermore, a motion is constructed dissimilarly or similarly to an allied motion. Either it is placed above, that is, among the higher tones; or it is placed below; or it is adjacent, as when the end of one motion is on the same note as the beginning of another; or it is placed between, that is, when one motion is placed after another, and is lower or higher; or mixed, that is, if it consists to some extent of middle placement, to some extent of low or high or adjacent placement.[24] And again, these placements may be divided according to freedom and strictness, according to lengthening and shortening, and according to the different characteristics of the intervals. And the neumes may always be varied through these intervals in arsis and thesis; the phrases may sometimes be varied in these ways. We supply the example on page 65 to make it easier visually.

4.10 JOHANNES DE GROCHEO (fl. c. 1300)

By the turn of the fourteenth century, Johannes de Grocheo, who was possibly a lecturer in the faculty of the arts at the University of Paris, made

23. A liquescent neume consists of a stronger note followed by a note that fades away. This passage indicates Guido's attention to dynamics, as well as tempo.
24. In the hexachord system a note above the highest note of the hexachord (*la*) was sung a semitone higher (*fa* of the adjacent hexachord). The rule was: *Una nota super la semper est canendum fa* (a note above *la* is always sung as *fa*). The change from one hexachord to another was called mutation.

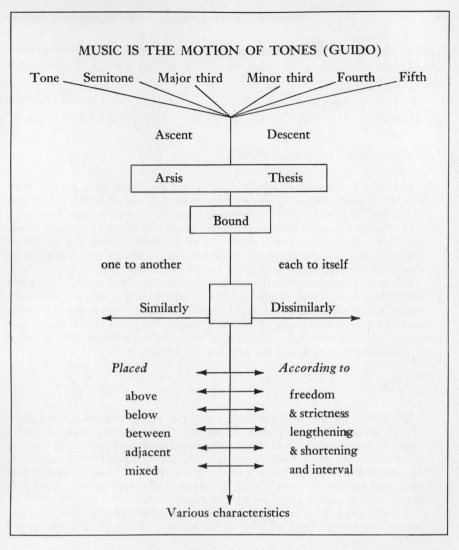

MUSIC IS THE MOTION OF TONES (GUIDO)

Tone   Semitone   Major third   Minor third   Fourth   Fifth

Ascent   Descent

Arsis   Thesis

Bound

one to another   each to itself

Similarly   Dissimilarly

Placed   According to

above   freedom
below   & strictness
between   lengthening
adjacent   & shortening
mixed   and interval

Various characteristics

a distinction between folk or popular music stemming directly from the people, and art music composed according to some system.

The basic difference between folk music and art music is that the former is anonymous and the latter is conceived by a definite composer. However, some music does not fit exactly into either of these categories. Among the exceptions were the songs of the Goliards, wandering scholars who roamed through Germany, England, and France from the tenth century on, singing in *vulgar* Latin. The songs of the troubadours in the south of France to the vernacular *langue d'oc*, and those of the trouvères in the north to the *langue d'oil* also defy categorization in this respect. The music of the Goliards that has been preserved is for the most part composerless, written in undecipherable staffless neumes. The troubadour and trouvère melodies, even where the composer is identified, have accurate pitches but lack meter signatures. The same song may now be transcribed in duple or in triple time, depending on the prognosis of the transcriber.

The elusive types make us all the more grateful to de Grocheo for the generalizations in his *De Musica*, from which portions are cited below.

Folk Music and Composed Music*

For us it is not easy to divide music correctly, since, in a correct division, the dividing factors ought to exhaust the full nature of the whole that is divided. The parts of music are many and diverse according to diverse uses, diverse idioms or diverse languages in diverse cities or regions. However, we will consider music according to its usage among the people of Paris . . . since in our day the principles of all the liberal arts, and those of almost all the mechanical arts, are diligently explored there.

Let us say, therefore, that the music which the Parisians use can be broken down into three broad categories. One category is that of civil or simple music, which they call vulgar music; another, that of composed or regular music by rule, which they call measured music. The third type is that which is built on these two and to which these two are best adapted. This is called ecclesiastic and is designed for praising the Creator.[25]

Vocal Forms

We call a song in which the deeds [*gesta*] of heroes and the achievements of our ancient fathers are told, a *cantus gestualis*.[26] This kind of cantus ought to be provided for old men, working citizens and for average people when they rest from their accustomed labor, so that, having heard the miseries and calamities of others, they might more easily bear up under their own, and so that their own tasks be more gladly approached. Thus, this kind of cantus acts as a support for the whole state. . . .

A particular type of song is called *round* or *rotundellus* by many, for the reason that it turns back on itself in the manner of a circle and begins and ends in the same way. . . .[27]

From Johannes de Grocheo, Concerning Music (De Musica), trans. Albert Seay (Colorado Springs: Colorado College Music Press, 1967), pp. 10–11, 15–16, 18–19.

25. Here de Grocheo provides the rationale for the following century when a Mass such as *L'Homme armé* [*HAM*, Vol. I, No. 66 and *MSO*, Part 1, p. 28] or *Se la face ay pale* (*MM*, No. 15) was built on a secular folk song as a cantus firmus.

26. The *cantus gestualis*, known more familiarly by its French name, *chanson de geste*, was seldom written down because the simple melody, repeated over and over again for each successive verse of the text, was easy to remember.

27. In a round each voice enters in succession, repeating the phrase of the previous voice. The phrases in a round for three voices could be diagrammed as follows:

```
a   b   c   d
d   a   b   c
c   d   a   b
```

The song called *stantipes* is that in which there is a diversity in its sections and in its refrain, not only in the rhyme of the words but also in the melody, just as the French *A l'entrant d'amors* or *Certes mie ne cuidoie*. This type causes young men and girls to concentrate because of its difficulty and turns them from improper thinking.[28]

A ductia is a light song, rapid in its ascent and descent, which is sung by young men and girls while dancing in a ring, a *chorus* like the French *Chi encor querez amoretes*. This influences the hearts of girls and young men and keeps them from vanity and is said to have force against that passion which is called love or Eros. . . .

Concerning musical forms which are performed by the human voice enough has been said. Let us now turn to those for instruments.

Instrumental Forms

Of all the instruments of the string family, we think that the vielle is the most important. Just as the human intellect envelops virtually all the other natural forms, just as a tetragon includes a triangle, and as a larger number includes a smaller, so the vielle includes virtually all the other stringed instruments. Whereas some instruments by their sound may move the souls of men more than others, for example, the drum and trumpet in war games and tournaments, the vielle provides for a more thorough understanding of all musical forms.

A good performer on the vielle normally uses every cantus and cantilena and every musical form. Those, however, which are commonly performed before the wealthy in feasts and games, are normally reduced to three types, that is, coronate cantus (*conductus*), ductia and stantipes.

A ductia is a piece without text, measured with an appropriate percussive beat. I say *untexted* because, although it can be performed by the human voice and represented in notation, it cannot be written with words, for it is lacking in word and text. But I say *with an appropriate percussive beat* because these beats measure it and the movement of the performer, and excite the soul of man to moving ornately according to that art they call dancing, and they measure its movement metrically while playing, and dancing in a ring.

A stantipes is also an untexted piece, having a complicated succession of concords, determined by puncta. I say *complicated succession*, etc., since, because of its complicated nature, it makes the soul of the performer and also the soul of the listener pay close attention and frequently turns aside the souls of the wealthy from depraved thinking. I also say *determined by puncta* since it is lacking in that percussive beat which the ductia has and is recognized only by the difference between its puncta.

The sections of ductia and stantipes are commonly called *puncta*. A punctum is a systematic joining together of concords making harmony in ascending and descending motion, having two sections alike in their begin-

28. The vocal stantipes was derived from the sequence, in which each two-line stanza was sung to a repeated melody (see Section 4.7, fn. 1). Although the lines within a single stanza were equal both in length and meter, the paired lines varied considerably from one stanza to the next.

ning, differing in their end, which are usually called the *close* and the *open*. I say *having two sections*, etc., in a comparison of two lines of which one is greater than the other. The greater includes the lesser and is at the end different from the smaller.[29] People have set the number of puncta in the ductia at three, setting it by comparison with the three perfect consonances. There are, in addition, certain pieces called *notae* of four puncta, which can be considered as a form of ductia or imperfect stantipes. There are also some ductiae having four puncta, as, for example, the ductia *Pierron*. Some, using the pitch syllables as a basis, place the number of puncta in stantipes at six. Others, again inspired perhaps by the number of the seven concords or led by natural inclination, as, for example, Tassinus, augment the number to seven. There are stantipes of this type with the seven concords, as the difficult Tassinus' pieces.[30]

4.11 DANTE ALIGHIERI (1265–1321)

The trend toward composing in the common language of the people spread to Italy where, at the beginning of the fourteenth century, "vulgar" Latin began to yield to the Italian vernacular. The cosmopolitan poet Dante, who was born in Florence and educated in Bologna, Padua, Paris, and probably at Oxford too, called those who wrote Italian lyrics *vulgares eloquentes* (eloquent commoners). Dante describes the concept behind

29. The instrumental stantipes, also called the *estampie*, was similar to the vocal sequence in that it consisted of a number of sections within each of which the melody was repeated. The instrumental composition, however, had the form aa, bb, cc, etc.; there was no single verse standing alone at the beginning as in the vocal type. The instrumental section, lacking words, had to have a name comparable to the vocal stanza. A section was therefore designated as a *punctum*. Within each punctum a repetition occurred. Often there was one ending for the first statement of the theme and a different ending for the second statement. The first ending was open (Fr. *ouvert*, It. *aperto*) and the second was closed (Fr. *clos*, It. *chiuso*). Changing the ending, or varying the goal of a motion on repetition, is one of the indispensable techniques for creating musical form.

   Following is the middle punctum of an estampie for vielle to which words were added by a troubadour, Raimbault de Vaqueiras (d. 1207).

Kalenda Maya *(HAM* I, No. 18d)

30. The estampie normally had from four to seven puncta. De Grocheo's comparison of the number of puncta in a composition to such factors as the number of perfect consonances, or the number of pitch syllables in a hexachord, is evidence of the medieval fascination for playing with numbers whether or not they are relevant to the situation of the moment.

Italy's favorite lyric, the canzona, calling poetry "nothing else but a fiction (*fictio*) expressed in rhetoric and music." [31] The union between poetry and music was so close that melody was consumed by the literary art that engendered it. Dante's treatise on the vernacular, entitled *De Vulgari Eloquentia*, was written in the Latin language, with words borrowed both from ancient Greek and the Italian then current. Some words which he used, such as *fictio*, meaning imaginative invention, or figment of the imagination, had not customarily been associated with music. By thinking of music in terms of creative fancy, he helped to establish music as an art rather than as a science (see Sections 3.4, 3.5).

Musical Implications in Italian Vernacular Poetry*

Having prepared the sticks and cords for our faggot, the time is now come to bind it up. But inasmuch as knowledge of every work should precede performance, just as there must be a mark to aim at, before we let fly an arrow or javelin, let us first and principally see what that faggot is which we intend to bind up. That faggot, then, is the song [*cantio*]. Wherefore let us see what a song is, and what we mean when we speak of a song. Now *cantio*, according to the true meaning of the name, is the action or passion itself of singing [*canendi*], just as *lectio* is the passion or action of reading. But let us examine what has been said, I mean whether a song is so called as being an action or as being a passion. In reference to this we must bear in mind that a song may be taken in two ways. In the first way, as its author's composition, and thus it is an action; and it is in this way that Virgil says in the first book of the Aeneid, "I sing of arms and the man" [*Arma virumque cano;* see Section 3.3]. In another way, when, after having been composed [*fabricata*] it is uttered [*profertur*] either by the author or by someone else, whether with or without modulation [*modulatio*] of sound; and thus it is a passion. For in the first case it is acted, but in the second it appears to act on someone else; and so in the first case it appears to be the action of someone, and in the second it also appears to be the passion of someone. And because it is acted on before it acts, it appears rather, nay, altogether, to get its name from its being acted and being the act of someone than from its acting on others. Now the proof of this is, that we never say, "This is Peter's song," meaning that he utters it, but meaning that he has composed it.

Moreover, we must discuss the question whether we call a canzone [*cantio*] [32] the composition of the words which are set to music [*verborum*

From A Translation of the Latin Works of Dante Alighieri (London: J. M. Dent & Sons Ltd., 1904), Book II, Chap. 8, pp. 94–96. Reprinted by permission of J. M. Dent & Sons Ltd.

31. *De Vulgari Eloquentia*, Book II, Chap. 4.
32. *Cantio* is translated here variously as *song*, referring to lyrical poetry in general, and as *canzone*, referring to a specific type of poem.

armonizatorum],[33] or the music itself; and, with regard to this, we say that
a modulation is never called a canzone, but a sound [*sonus*], or tone
[*tonus*], or note [*nota*], or melody [*melos*]. For no trumpeter, or organist,
or lute-player [*citharedus*] calls his melody a canzone, except in so far as it
has been wedded to some canzone; but those who write the words for music
call their words canzoni. And such words, even when written down on
paper without anyone to utter them, we call canzoni; and therefore a canzone appears to be nothing else but the completed action of one writing
words to be set to music. Wherefore we shall call canzoni not only the
canzoni of which we are now treating, but also ballate[34] and sonnets
[*sonitus*], and all words of whatever kind written for music, both in the
vulgar tongue [*vulgariter*] and in Latin [*regulariter*]. But inasmuch as we
are only discussing works in the vulgar tongue, setting aside those in Latin,
we say that of poems in the vulgar tongue there is one supreme which we
call canzone by super-excellence. Now the supremacy of the canzone has
been proved in the third chapter of this book. And since the term which
has been defined appears to be common to many things, let us take up again
the common term which has been defined, and distinguish by means of certain differences that thing which alone we are in search of. We declare
therefore that the canzone as so called by super-excellence which we are in
search of is a joining together in the tragic style of equal stanzas without a
ripresa [refrain] referring to one subject, as we have shown in our composition *Donne che aveta intellecto d'amore*.[35] Now the reason why we call

33. The word *armonizare* is used in the sense of fitting the tones or harmonies to the
    words. Dante is making a distinction between vocal music, with text, and instru-
    mental music, without text. A canzone is a song, whether for one voice or several
    singing in harmony.
34. The poetic ballata was a form frequently set to music with two or three voice
    parts by such composers as Francesco Landini (1325–1397) (*MSO*, Part 1, pp.
    24–25) and Giovanni da Florentia (*HAM*, Vol. I, No. 51). There were two sec-
    tions of music, associated with the poetry in the following way:

    Verse: 1   2   3   4   ⌈1
    Music: A   b   b   a   ⌊A
                                  Closing refrain or
                                  beginning of next stanza

(Small letters indicate change of verse during repetition of music.)
35. This is the opening line of the first canzone of the *Vita Nuova*. Dante is here
    distinguishing between the canzone, which does not have a refrain, and the ballate,
    which does have a refrain at the beginning and end of the stanza.
    One of the musico-poetic forms that did not have a refrain was the Italian
    madrigal. The fourteenth-century madrigal consisted of several stanzas each of
    which had three or five lines sung to two sections of music, as follows:

                          1   2   3
    Verse: _____   1   2   3   4   5
    Music: a   a   (a) b (b)
                                  Ritornello which may be in a different
                                  meter from the other section.

Although we do not have evidence of Dante's poems having been set to music
during his lifetime, we do have musical settings of Petrarch (1304–1374). The
latter's madrigal *Non al suo Amante* was set to music by Jacopo da Bologna
(*HAM*, Vol. I, No. 49).

it "a joining together in the tragic style" is because when such a composition is made in the comic style we call it diminutively *cantilena*. And thus it appears what a canzone is, both as it is taken generally, and as we call it in a super-excellent sense. It also appears sufficiently plain what we mean when we speak of a canzone, and consequently what that faggot is which we are endeavouring to bind up.

4.12 GUILLAUME DE MACHAUT (1300–1377)

Owing to political pressures in Rome, from 1305 to 1378 the popes lived at Avignon in the southeast of France. French and Italian musicians, poets, and painters congregated at this central location, exchanging ideas as they strove to glorify the papal establishment. By 1324, secularization was setting in with such rapidity that Pope John XXII (papal reign, 1316–1334) issued a decree directing composers toward more sacred ideals.

> Some disciples of the new school are greatly concerned with the measurement of time values. They introduce new notes, preferring to sing in their own style rather than in the old way. They dissect their melodies with hockets, lubricate them with discants, and sometimes impose on them two upper parts with secular words. In the meanwhile, they lose sight of the foundations on which they are building to the extent that they distort the Antiphonal and the Gradual.
>
> They are ignorant of the modes, which they do not keep separate. Completely confused by the multiplicity of their notes, they obscure the modest ascents and temperate descents of the plainchant, by which the modes themselves are distinguished from each other. Indeed, their notes run rather than stand still, intoxicating rather than pacifying the ear, telling tales as they are uttered. Consequently, worship, which should be sought after, is disregarded, and frivolity, which should be avoided, is propagated.

At the time of the papal bull, Guillaume de Machaut, then in his early twenties, was secretary to King John of Bohemia. The king, who traveled extensively, took Machaut with him as far as Poland and Russia. King John also brought Machaut to the attention of the pope, who bestowed on him several ecclesiastical positions which Machaut held while yet in the service of the King. In 1337, after King John's death, Machaut became canon of Rheims and was thus able to lead a more sedentary life, devoting himself to the composition of music and poetry. By the time Machaut wrote his *Mass of Notre Dame*, a setting of the texts of the Ordinary for four voices, Pope John XXII was probably no longer on the scene to berate the musical extravagances of the work that was to become the most famous sacred composition of the fourteenth century.

In the realm of secular music Machaut helped to define the forms, which were inextricably bound to the text. He demonstrated seven musico-poetic forms in the *Remède de Fortune*, a gigantic poem during the course of which Machaut interpolated music for a *lay*, a *complainte*, a *chanson roial*, a *baladelle*, a *ballade*, a *virelay*, and a *rondelet*. These compositions were written for from one to four voices. Machaut was probably the last composer in western Europe whose reputation is to some extent based on monophonic songs. After the single-voiced virelay,[36] the sixth musical composition in the *Remède de Fortune*, the poem, continuing without music, dwells on the abundance of instruments in use at the time. It is from this source that the passage below has been translated.

Musician and Poet on Instruments of the Ars Nova: *Remède de Fortune**

When fully entertained by the singing,
each man withdrew
to shed his battle garments
and put on an open vest.
Afterwards everyone repaired to a room
which was neither shabby nor dingy
where, to my mind,
everyone was honored and served well.
In such manner, were we given wine and meat
to still the demands of body and appetite.
And there I took my sustenance,
while reflecting upon the heroic conduct,
the halt, deportment, and arms-bearing
of those who were killed in battle.
After the banquet, who should appear
but the minstrels, free from danger,
well groomed and freshly attired!
Thereupon they wrought many diverse harmonies.
For I saw there, all in a circle,
viol, rebec, gittern,
Moorish lute, micanon,
citole and psaltery,
harp, tabor, trumpets, nacaires,[37]

**From Ernest Hoepffner*, Oeuvres de Guillaume de Machaut *(Paris: Librairie de Firmin Didot et Cie, 1911), II,145–147; and Friedrich Ludwig*, Guillaume de Machaut Musikalische Werke *(Leipzig: Breitkopf & Härtel, 1926), I, 102.*
The translation of this excerpt from the Remède de Fortune *is by Mary Rowen Obelkevich.*

36. The form of the virelay is: Verse: 1 2 3 4 1
                                   Music: A b b a A

37. Arabian *naqqāra*. Kettledrum of the East which became known to the thirteenth-century European crusaders. For other instruments see Sibyl Marcuse, *Musical Instruments, A Comprehensive Dictionary* (New York: Doubleday & Company, Inc., 1964).

organs, horns in more than ten pairs,
bagpipes, flageolets, chevrettes,[38]
douçaines,[39] cymbals, bells,
timbrels, the Bohemian flute,
and the big German cornet,
flutes, panpipes, pipes,
bagpipe of Aussay, little trumpet,
buzines, eles, monochord
where there is only a single string,
and shawm, all together.
And surely, it seems to me
that such melody was never before
seen nor heard.
For each of them, in accordance
with the tuning of his instrument,
played without discord, be it
viol, gittern, citole,
harp, trumpet, horn, flageolet,
pipe, bellows, bagpipe, nacaire,
tabor; and whatsoever could be rendered
with finger, quill, and bow
could be heard and seen in that chamber.
Then they danced an estampie,[40]
the ladies with their partners
sallying forth in twos and threes,
linked together by their fingers,
till they came to a very beautiful room;
and there neither men nor women were left unprovided,
for whosoever wished to rejoice,
dance, sing, or feast
with tables, wenches, or bells,
in games, singing, or playing,
could find these without cease
readied according to his pleasure.
And if these musicians
were indeed armed with better and greater science
in old and new invention
than music which produces song,
not even Orpheus, who sang so well
that all the beasts of hell were enchanted
by the sweetness of his song,
would know how to sing before them.

38. A bagpipe whose bag was made from a particular type of skin.
39. A double-reed woodwind.
40. See de Grocheo, Section 4.10, fn 5.

5

The Emergence
of Polyphony

5.1 THE *MUSICA ENCHIRIADIS* (c. 895)

Despite his admonition against composing motets by adding melodies
with secular words to the Gregorian chant, Pope John XXII said in his
decree of 1324 (Section 4.12):

> We do not intend to prohibit certain consonances which enhance the
> melody, such as perfect octaves, fifths, and fourths composed above the
> simple ecclesiastical cantus, especially on feast days or in the solemn rites
> of the Mass, and in the aforementioned divine Offices. This must be done,
> however, in such a way that the cantus itself remains unimpaired, and
> nothing in the beautiful character of the music is changed. In this way the
> consonances please the auditor to the greatest extent, arousing his devotion
> without stifling the religious feeling of the singers.

In effect, the pope was sanctioning the earliest polyphonic practice as
described in the *Musica Enchiriadis* (Musical Handbook), a work formerly ascribed to Hucbald and now possibly attributed to Hoger of
Werden (d. 915) or Otger of St. Pons (d. 940). According to this practice, over each note of the chant the composer sets a note at the distance
of a perfect interval, thus providing the chant with a counterpoint. The
given note in the main voice, the *vox principalis*, and its companion in the
composed voice, the *vox organalis*, together constitute a *symphonia*, a
concordant interval. The resulting series of *symphoniae* comprise a note-
against-note *organum*.

74

Since the *Musica Enchiriadis* is concerned with fixed pitches, the author is careful to identify them in three ways—namely, placing each syllable of the text in a horizontal track that corresponds to the height of the pitch on which it is to be sung; labeling each track with a symbol corresponding to one pitch; and indicating whether the interval from one track to the next is a tone or a semitone. Because the symbols in front of the tracks are derived from the Greek aspiration sign ⊢, the *dasia* (Section 3.3), this set of tetrachords came to be known as the Dasian system. Inherent in the notation are an augmented fourth from B♭ to e, and augmented octaves from B♭ to b♮ and f to f♯.

Graves	Finales	Superiores	Excellentes	
ꟼ ꟼ ╲ ꟼ	Ⅎ Ⅎ ╱Ⅎ	⅃ ⅃ ⊃ ⅃	♭ Ϲ ✕ ♭	ᴖ ᴖ
G A B♭ c	d e f g	a b c′ d′	e′ f♯′ g′ a′	b′ c♯″
	1 ½ 1			

Concordant Intervals *[Symphoniae]**

Not all tones blend together equally well, nor do they always render harmonious effects in song in every kind of combination. Just as letters brought together at random often do not produce either connected words or syllables, so in music only certain fixed intervals may constitute *symphoniae*. A *symphonia* is a pleasant concord of dissimilar tones joined to one another.

There are three simple or prime *symphoniae*, from which the rest are compounded. Of these one is called a fourth [*diatessaron*], another, a fifth [*diapente*], and the next, an octave [*diapason*]. *Diatessaron* is associated with four, partly because its tones are sounded at the interval of a fourth, partly because it is an arrangement of four sounds in succession, as shown in the example below. You may either refer to the fourth tone, or you may infer four tones in succession, thus:

SYMPHONIA OF A FOURTH

Thus the tones proceed in varied groups, four by four, forward and back again.

---

*Martin Gerbert, Scriptores ecclesiastici de musica sacra potissimum (St. Blasien, 1784), I, 160–162, 165–166, 169.

Diapente is associated with five either because it consists of a succession of five tones, or because tones a fifth apart sound concordant. . . .

Likewise, *diapason*, which is associated with "from all," from octave to octave, produces a consonance containing in its entity both of the above, that is, the fourth and the fifth. This *symphonia* is called "from all" because the ancients used no more than eight strings. As I was saying, one should call the tones not so much "consonant" as "equisonant," for the basic tone is renewed at the octave. While this is more evident with musical instruments, if these are not at hand, let one person hold a tone at any pitch whatsoever, while another sings fourth after fourth in succession, until he reaches the end. You will hear that the last tone to the first, that is, octave to octave, yields a perfect consonance. The following example shows how to proceed using these equisonant tones:

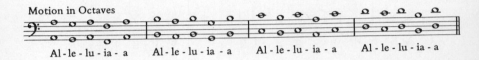

Motion in Octaves

Al - le - lu - ia - a   Al - le - lu - ia - a   Al - le - lu - ia - a   Al - le - lu - ia - a

Compound Intervals

From these simple intervals others are put together, such as octave and fourth, octave and fifth, and double octave [*disdiapason* or *disdiplasion*]. For example, when to two male voices singing in consonance at the octave, a boy's voice is added as a third, equisonant voice, then the highest and lowest voices are singing at the double octave. The voices sounding this consonance are a fifteenth apart. Between them is heard the octave, equidistant from the others.

Organum at the Fourth

We have already demonstrated how each tone in the tetrachord is different from the others according to its special position. From such agreeable diversity arises the different species of modes and tropes. Also, we have indicated by how many steps the individual tones must be separated from each other in order to produce logical intervals.

Now we will explain what perfect intervals are and why they are called *symphoniae*, that is, how the voices [*voces*] are related to each other in singing. For this is what we call *diaphonic cantilena*, or more commonly, *organum*. It is called diaphony because it does not consist of a single song, but of an agreeable union of divergent sounds. Although this name is common to all *symphoniae*, it is usually reserved for those at the fourth and the fifth. Here is an example of organal song at the fourth. In the illustration below, two tones singing together are introduced at the distance of a fourth. One voice corresponds to the other in this way:

Tu   pa - tris   sem - pi - ter - nus   es   fi - li - us.

Organum Doubled at the Octave

Not only may a single voice be brought together with a single voice, but a single voice of an organum may be matched with a voice doubled at the octave, or a voice doubled at the octave may be matched with a single voice. Or, if you double both at the octave, you will feel how delightfully the voices resound together in this relationship, as in the following example:

Vox Organalis
Vox Principalis
Vox Organalis
Vox Principalis

Tu   pa - tris   sem - pi - ter - nus   es   fi - li - us.

Concerning the Order of Consonances— Consonance and Dissonance

Concerning the octave and double octave there is no need for further explanation. Since all ages mingle naturally in singing, these need not be taught by a treatise. Concerning the perfect interval of the double octave, it is enough to say that the middle voice is in the relationship of an octave to each of the outer voices, while the outer voices correspond to each other at the distance of a fifteenth. However, we must still speak about the proper measurement of the individual perfect intervals. The interval of a perfect fourth consists of two tones and a semitone, and two disjunct perfect fourths make a perfect octave. Therefore, within the interval of a perfect octave the various tones reverberate back and forth in the greatest perfection.

Next is the interval of a fifth. Since the sounds at the interval of a fourth do not all, without exception, produce consonances throughout the whole series of tones, certain intervals of the composition should not be sung exactly. Therefore, in this kind of song the voices are marvelously accommodated to each other by a certain rule. For through the entire series of sounds the third step of one tetrachord is not consonant with the second step of the tetrachord above. A dissonance is created by them, because the interval exceeds the measurement of a perfect fourth, the upper note being three whole tones away from the basic pitch a fourth below. And because of this, the voice which is called *organalis* must be constructed with the other voice called *principalis* in such a way that in any tetrachord whatsoever, on any syllable whatsoever, it neither descends to a position below the fourth note of a tetrachord, nor rises imperfectly, causing a dissonance with the third note of the tetrachord (which is a whole tone below the fourth note of the tetrachord).

To clarify this, we are providing an example so that it may be scrutinized carefully.[1]

1. This organum is composed to a double verse of a sequence in the form a a b b, of which the first section, a a, is given here. If the *vox organalis* were to start on

Rex Coeli

Dasian notation

T								
T		maris\			squali\			
S		mine/	un\		ti di/	di\		
T	do/		di\		ni/	que\		
T	li/	maris\	\ ni	nis/	squali\	\ li		
T	coe/	mine/	un\ so/	ta/	tidi/	di\ so/		
T	Rex/ coeli do/	di/		Ty/ta nis ni/	que/			

Transcription

Rex coe-li, Do-mi-ne ma-ris un-di-so - ni,   Ty - ta -nis ni - ti - di squa-li-di-que so-li.

If you sing in two parts according to this description, you will easily realize why you cannot begin the *vox organalis* on the fourth below C. Likewise, it is not possible to proceed in this way at the end. When the *vox principalis* closes on a higher note, the voices converge at the unison to create the best position for the organum.

5.2 LEONIN AND PEROTIN
THROUGH ANONYMOUS IV (c. 1275)

Toward the second half of the twelfth century, during the period known as the Ars Antiqua, the techniques of polyphonic composition radiated from Paris, as Leonin and then Perotin headed the musical activity at the Cathedral School of Notre Dame. They composed music for the cycle of variable texts in the services of the church year in the *Magnus Liber Organi, The Great Book of Organum for the Gradual and the Antiphonal.*[2]

---

the G a fourth below the opening C of the *vox principalis*, a tritone would result from B♭ to e. Proceeding in parallel fourths, the same tritone would appear when the *vox principalis* ends on e.

Vox
Principalis

In the organum the tritone is avoided by proceeding in oblique motion from the unison to the fourth, or by leaping directly from a fourth to a unison. Both double verses of *Rex coeli* appear in *MSO*, Part 1, p. 15.

2. The music for the Mass is contained in a book called the *Gradual*. The music of the Office, performed at designated times during the liturgical day, such as Matins

Both Leonin and Perotin composed by adding one or more melodies to a given melody, the *vox principalis* or *cantus firmus*. When the given melody was a Gregorian chant that was sung responsorially, Leonin composed an additional melody, a *vox organalis*, only for the portion of the chant originally sung by the soloist, thereby creating a two-part organum for two soloists. In places where the original soloist sang a melisma—that is, where he performed many notes to one syllable of the text—Leonin found it necessary to put both the chant melody and the added contrapuntal part into rhythmic modes so that the two soloists would know how their parts fitted together. These measured sections, because they were self-contained, were called *clausulae* or *puncta*. In place of Leonin's two-part clausulae, Perotin substituted clausulae written for three and four parts.

The system of rhythmic modes used by Leonin, Perotin, and other composers of the time is described by an anonymous author. In the nineteenth century, Charles Coussemaker assigned the number IV to this author because his was the fourth anonymous treatise included in Coussemaker's collection of medieval musical sources.

The Rhythmic Modes*

Since the modulation of melodies according to the method of the eight modes used and practiced in the Catholic faith is well known, here we shall concentrate on their measurement according to length and brevity as described by the ancients. Master Leo and many others have composed more successfully by combining both rhythm [*ordines*] and pitch [*colores*], as follows.

The consideration of a mode according to time values involves the length and brevity of its melodic tones. In general there are six rhythmic modes.

The first consists of longa–breve, longa–breve, longa–breve, etc. The second consists of breve–longa, breve–longa, breve–longa, etc. The third consists of a longa and two breves, a longa and two breves, a longa and two

*Charles Edmond Henri de Coussemaker, Scriptorum de musica medii aevi (Paris: Durand, 1864–1876), i, 327–328, 342, 344.

(morning), Vespers (evening), and Compline (after nightfall), is contained in a book called the *Antiphonal*.

The texts of the Mass are divided into two categories, those of the Ordinary which are the same for every service, and those of the Proper which vary according to the day or holiday of the church year that is being celebrated. The invariable texts of the Ordinary are: Kyrie, Gloria, Credo, Sanctus, Benedictus, and Agnus Dei. The variable texts of the Proper for which music is composed include the Introit (entrance), Gradual (performed on the steps, *gradus*), Alleluia (jubilation or exultation), or Tract (penitence), Offertory (offering), and Communion (togetherness) (Section 4.5).

breves, etc. The fourth consists of two breves and a longa, etc. The fifth, of longa, longa, longa, etc. The sixth, of breve, breve, breve, etc.[3]

The ordo of a mode depends on the number of notes before a rest.[4]

Use of Shorter Time Values

Master Leonin, whom they used to call "the best composer of organum" [*optimus organista*] prepared *The Great Book of Organum for the Gradual and the Antiphonal* to augment the divine service. It was in use until the time of Perotin the Great, who wrote in shorter note values, and composed much more skillful *clausulae* or *puncta* because he was "the best composer of discant" [*optimus discantor*], and more adept than Leonin, except with regard to the subtlety of organum.

Indeed, this very Master Perotin composed the best Quadrupla, such as *Viderunt*, and *Sederunt*, with the wealth of colors in the harmonic art. In addition, he wrote the most renowned Tripla, such as *Alleluia: Posui adjutorium, Nativitas*, etc.[5]

3. The basic values were the *breve* ■ (short) and the *longa* ❙ (long), often reduced in modern time values to the ♩ and ♪, respectively. These were combined in six ways into musical feet known as the rhythmic modes. Each rhythmic mode was based on a group of three beats. The basic group, the *perfection* (♩ ♪) was notated by a two-note ligature, the ascending podatus ♫ 2nd note / 1st note   or the descending clivis ♪■ 1st note / 2nd note . Thus, all of the rhythmic modes were compatible and could be combined with each other.

THE RHYTHMIC MODES

Time Values	Poetic Feet
1. ♩ ♩ ♪ ♩	‒ ◡ trochee
2. ♩ ♩ ♩ ♪	◡ ‒ iamb
3. ♩. ♩ ♪	‒ ◡ ◡ dactyllic
4. ♩ ♩ ♩.	◡ ◡ ‒ anapest
5. ♩. ♩.	‒ ‒ spondee
6. ♩ ♩ ♩ ♩ ♩ ♩	◡ ◡ ◡ pyrrhic

4. Several successive feet plus a closing note constituted a rhythmic phrase called an *ordo*.

5. The two-part organum *Viderunt omnes* by Leonin is transcribed in *TEM*, No. 9. Perotin's Quadrupla, a four-part composition to this text, appears in facsimile in the thirteenth century Florence Manuscript of the Biblioteca Medicco-Laurenziana, Pluteo 29, 1, folio 1r-2r (facsimile ed. by Luther Dittmer, the Institute of Medieval Music Brooklyn, N.Y.). The Quadrupla *Sederunt* is in the Florence ms. f. 4r-5r.

He likewise composed triple Conductus, such as *Salvatoris hodie*, and duple Conductus, such as *Dum sigillum summi patris*, and simple Conductus, such as *Beata viscera*, and *Justitia*, among many others.[6]

The book or books of Master Perotin were in use until the time of Master Robert de Sabilone, not only in the choir of the church Beatae Virginis Majoris in Paris, but also in others from his time until the present day.[7] Furthermore, Petrus, "the best notator," and Johannes, called "the foremost" by some others, from an older period right up to the time of Master Franco the First and the other Franco of Cologne, began to notate somewhat differently in their books. For this purpose they taught other special rules suited to their books.[8]

Most of the knowledge of our ancestors was presented orally without written substantiation. Yet they were familiar with the entire series of consonances, including octave, fifth, and fourth. Accordingly, they used to

---

Perotin's three-part *Alleluya* addition to the antiphon verse *Nativitas* is transcribed in *MM*, No 9. A facsimile of this composition from the manuscript Wolfenbüttel 677 appears in Carl Parrish, *The Notation of Medieval Music* (New York: W. W. Norton, 1957, 1959), Plate XXV.

6. The monophonic conductus, a song composed to a nonliturgical text, was often used as a processional to conduct or lead characters onto the stage of a musical play (see *HAM*, Vol. I, No. 17). The two- and three-part conductus which Anonymous IV mentions were composed by adding parts to a free cantus of this kind. Perotin's triple conductus, *Salvatoris hodie* is preserved in the Florence ms. Pluteo 29, 1, folio 201r. The work alternates between syllabic sections with all three voices moving simultaneously to the meter of the text, and vocalizations or melismatae called *caudae* (tails) with all three voices in rhythmic modes. Following is the opening verse of *Salvatoris hodie*, with its cauda:

7. Beatae Mariae Virginis was the main church before the Cathedral of Notre Dame was built (cornerstone laid 1163).
8. Petrus de Cruce or Pierre de la Croix (13th cent.) introduced a system of notation

consider the upper melody in relation to the lower, and they taught others saying, "Listen and remember this as you sing." But they had an inferior way of writing it down, and they used to say, "Under these conditions the upper note [*punctus*] sounds well with the lower note." And this used to satisfy them. And thus for a long time people learned by word of mouth.[9]

But a notation with the symbols necessary for indicating shorter note values had been practiced at the time of Perotin the Great and a little before him, and the use of a note shorter than the breve was taught. And furthermore, Master Robert de Sabilone taught using the shorter note most extensively, but he made the vocal melody appear excessively luxuriant.

A Parisian by the name of Master Petrus Trothun, from Aurelianum [a commune southwest of Paris], was greatly esteemed in the realm of plainchant, but he neither knew nor taught much about the consideration of time values. On the contrary, Master Robert, mentioned above, understood these best and used to teach them accurately.

After him, following his example, came Master Petrus, *optimus notator*. The latter notated his books well and exceedingly accurately, according to the usage and custom of his master.

And at that time there was a Thomas de Sancto Juliano called "the old Parisian," who did not notate with their method, but did well in the manner of the older notators.

Indeed, there was another Englishman also teaching at that time who used the method of Anglican notation.

After them a certain Joannes already mentioned continued the methods of all these men until the time of Master Franco. There were other masters too, such as Master Theobaldus Gallicus, and Master Simon de Sacalia, besides Master de Burgundia, and also a certain fine man from Picardy whose name was Joannes le Fauconer.

There were good singers in England, and they sang most delightfully, such as Master Joannes *filius Dei*, Makeblite in Winchester, and Blakesmit in the service of His Imperial Highness, the late King Henry.

Bibliograhical Notes

For a summary of the Roman liturgy from a musical point of view see Albert Seay, *Music in the Medieval World* (New Jersey: Prentice-Hall, Inc., 1965), pp. 26–31.

---

in which the breve might be divided into as many as nine notes to accommodate the florid upper parts of his motets. Otherwise his motets were constructed like others of the time, with a textless cantus from a Gregorian melisma as the lowest voice, and two upper voices with French texts (*HAM*, Vol. I, No. 34).

Johannes (*Primarius*, the foremost) de Garlandia, born in England (c. 1195), studied at Oxford and then at the University of Paris. In his *De musica mensurabili positio* Johannes described the rules of composition in the style of Perotin.

There is a great deal of confusion about the various Francos. Master Franco the First may have flourished in the eleventh century. In the thirteenth century Franco of Cologne devised an exact system of notation with time values and rests shorter than the longa and breve. His *Ars cantus mensurabilis* is translated in *SRMH*, pp. 139–159.

9. In the organal style, where one or both of the melodies were not written in rhythmic modes, the singers had a difficult time staying together.

The entire *Magnus Liber* of Leonin is transcribed by William G. Waite in *The Rhythm of Twelfth-Century Polyphony* (New Haven and London: Yale University Press, 1954).

5.3 PHILIPPE DE VITRY AND JEAN DE MURIS (fl. 14th cent.)

During the second decade of the fourteenth century, while the center of Parisian musical activity was gradually moving from the Cathedral to the University, several treatises appeared in France indicating the arrival of a new musical era. In distinction to the Ars Antiqua (old art) of such masters as Leonin and Perotin, the Ars Nova (new art) heralded innovations in both the character and the combination of rhythmic and pitch patterns in a melody.

To replace the ternary rhythmic modes of the Ars Antiqua (Section 5.2), the exponents of the Ars Nova made provision for duple as well as triple meter. The latter also expanded the concept of rhythm by allowing for four rhythmic levels, each related to a given time value divisible by 2 or 3. The central level was the *tempus*, whose unit value was the breve ■ . Larger than the tempus was the *modus*, whose unit value was the longa ¶ . Still larger was the *maximodus*, whose unit value was the maxima ⊓ . Smaller than the tempus was the *prolation*, whose unit value was the semibreve ◆ .

With reference to the pitch pattern or *color*, musicians in the Ars Nova were accustomed to introducing chromatic alterations during the performance of a melody. This so-called *musica ficta* (fictitious music) or *musica falsa* (false music) involved tones that were not accounted for in the *musica vera* (true music) of the Guidonian gamut (see **Appendix 1,** Chart 2). Systems in the diatonic genus had made provision for b♭ as well as b♮ since the time of the ancient Greeks (Section 4.6). In the Middle Ages musicians had already recognized the fact that a note above *la* was a semitone higher than the top note of the hexachord, and the note below *ut* was a semitone below the finalis of the mode (*subsemitonium modi*). Now the musicians of the Ars Nova were acknowledging the existence of accidentals other than b♭ and b♮ within a diatonic genus. The word *chromatic*, derived from *color*, is still with us today in connection with the use of semitones, whether in a diatonic or a chromatic genus.

In France two of the treatises actually had the word *new* in their Latin titles. They were the *Ars novae musicae* (Art of New Music, 1319) of Jean de Muris, a scholar at the Sorbonne in Paris, and the *Ars nova* (New Art, c. 1320) of Philippe de Vitry, a composer in the service of Duke Jean of Normandy. De Muris, in another manuscript entitled *Libellus cantus mensurabilis,* mentioned the combined function of *talea* and *color,* the rhythmic and pitch patterns of the isorhythmic motet.

Concerning Music: *Ars Nova**

Music is the knowledge of singing correctly, or the easy way toward the perfection of singing.

There are thirteen intervals, such as unison, tone, semitone. The unison is every tone which is found on the same line, anywhere in the gamut, whatever the note or tone might be. And the word is derived from *unus* and *sonus,* having one and the same sound according to both note and pitch. According to another point of view, a unison is the pitch of one single tone [*vox*] from which no progression may be made; it always has to be one, whether on the same line or in the same space. If indeed there is a progression from any note to the adjacent neighbor, then sometimes a tone, sometimes a semitone is produced.[10] However, it is known that a unison by itself is not a consonance, but is the foundation of other consonances; without the unison no consonance is possible.

What is a unison? A unison is the tone on which we first begin to sing.[11] This tone neither ascends nor descends and, according to the quality of the singer, is placed either at an upper or low-lying pitch. It is put in any clef which might be necessary.

Concerning the Semitone

A semitone is the distance between two unisons, which, in conformity with the human voice, may not be divided by placing something in the center. It is found between any B♮ and C, E, and F, or A and B♭, in the middle and of course after the hexachord.[12] Between *fa* and *mi* there would be a seventh, but between the pitches *mi* and *fa* one hears the same interval as if a sign were added to a note, lowering it. Therefore between *mi* and *fa* there is a semitone.

The semitone, as Bernard said, is the sugar and spice of all song, and without it the song would be gnawed to pieces, transformed and mutilated.[13] Boethius, on the other hand, indicates the boundaries of the semitone in order to solve this problem [Section 3.4]. For it sometimes happens that

---

*Edmond de Coussemaker, Scriptorum de musica medii aevi *(Paris: Durand, 1864–1876), Philippi de Vitriaco,* Ars nova, *III, 17–18, 21; Johannes de Muris,* Libellus cantus mensurabilis, *III, 58.*

10. We still refer to a motion from a tone to the tone a whole step or a half-step above it and back as a *neighbor motion.*

11. We still enumerate the tones of a scale starting with the l or unison, and determine the size of an interval from the lowest tone as l.

12. The hexachord was built on the tones *ut re mi fa sol la,* with a semitone between *mi* and *fa.* The rule was, "any note above *la* is always called *fa.*" Hence the interval between *la* and the tone above it was a semitone also. (Look at the distance between *E la mi* and *F fa ut* on Chart 2.)

13. Berno, Abbot of Reichenau, wrote a tonary (11th cent.). He taught Hermannus Contractus, composer of the *Salva Regina* and *Alma Redemptoris Mater.*

through *musica falsa* we make a semitone where it ought not to be. In mensurable music we see that when the tenor or repeated melody of some motet or rondellus has ♭fa ♮mi, sung as b♮, in the second melody a fifth above it is necessary to sing *mi* on f♯ [f *acute*]. This is done through *musica falsa*, because the fifth from b♮ to f is not a perfect consonance. From b♮ to f there are two tones and two semitones, a combination which is not consonant, and it is necessary that there be a perfect fifth from one voice to another, making a good and true consonance.

And therefore, obviously, from this the following question arises. In regular music [*musica regulari*] what is the necessity for *musica falsa* or false mutation, when something regular ought never to admit the false, but rather the true [*vera*]? To this one may say that false mutation, or false music is not useless; on the contrary, it is necessary for inventing a good consonance and avoiding a bad one.

According to what has been said, there are two signs for *musica falsa*, namely the round (♭) and the square (♮). And they each have a characteristic property. In a descending motion the round ♭ changes a semitone into a tone; in an ascending motion it changes a tone into a semitone. And conversely, in a descending motion the figure ♮ changes a tone into a semitone and in an ascending motion a semitone into a tone. However, in those places where these signs are required, as was mentioned above, they were not false, but true and necessary, since it is not possible to sing any motet or rondellus without them.

Red Notes

Let us examine briefly the use of red notes in motets. Two reasons must be acknowledged. Principally, the red notes are sung in a meter [*mensura*] different from the blacks, as in *Thoma Tibi Obsequa*. That is why, in the tenor of that motet the reds are sung in perfect time in the imperfect mode, and the blacks conversely. One also sometimes uses reds because they proceed in a different mode, as in the motet *In arboris*. In the tenor of this motet the reds indicate that three beats must be heard as constituting a perfection, but the blacks indicate only two beats. Otherwise one uses the reds here and there, in ballades, rondeaux,[14] and motets, to redistribute the notes to conform to the other perfections, as in *Plures Errores*.

In a second way one uses red notes when they are really to be sung at the position an octave away, as in *Gratia Miseri* and in the motet entitled *Quant Amors*. In the tenor of these motets all of the red notes are sung at the

14. Like the Italian Ars Nova madrigal (Section 4.11, fn 4.), the French *ballade* was strophic. The music for each stanza of the French ballade was also in two sections, but with a text refrain at the end (letter C).

Text: 1 2 3 4 5 6 7 4
Music: a a b C a a b C

The French *rondeau*, another musico-poetic form, had two sections of music for one stanza of poetry, as follows:

Text: 1 2 3 4 5 6 7 8
Music: A B a A a b A B

octave. Sometimes the red notes are used to distinguish what is proper, that is, the simple and plain chant, from what is not plain and proper chant, as in *Claerburg*.

Concerning *Color: Libellus cantus mensurabilis*

A pattern of pitches, in a single melody, repeated many times in the same voice-part of a composition, is called *color* in music. This is significant because numerous singers distinguish between *color* and *talea*.

For they say *color* when the same tones [*voces*] are repeated; and *talea* when similar time values [*figure*] are repeated, and they fashion the notes of the different tones accordingly. This diversity may be observed in a considerable number of motet tenors; however, it is not used in the *motetus* [the upper voice] itself. Extensive examples occur in the motets.[15]

Bibliographical Notes

A French translation of de Vitry's *Ars nova* appears in *Musica Disciplina* XI (1957), pp. 12–30. There is an English translation by Leon Plantinga in *The Journal of Music Theory*, V, No. 2 (November, 1961), 204–223.

See Hugo Riemann, *History of Music Theory*, trans. Raymond H. Haggh (Lincoln: University of Nebraska Press, 1962), chaps. 3 and 10.

5.4 MARCHETTUS OF PADUA (fl. 14th cent.)

Many of the characteristics of the Ars Nova evolved in Italy at the same time as they did in France. One of the first musicians to deal with duple meter in terms of a new fashion was Marchettus of Padua, in his

---

Machaut (Section 4.12) was the outstanding composer of ballades, rondeaux, and motets. Few of de Vitry's compositions survive. The works he cites were not necessarily his own. See Leo Schrade, "Philippe de Vitry: Some New Discoveries," *The Musical Quarterly*, XLII, No. 3 (1956), 330–354. De Vitry's motet, *In Arboris*, is in *Polyphonic Music of the Fourteenth Century*, I, 88.

15. In contrast to the strophic ballade, rondeau, and virelai (Section 4.12), the *motet* was through-composed. Like the clausula, the motet was based on a melismatic portion of the chant, identified by the word (*mot*, Fr.) or syllable where the melisma originally occurred. (Section 5.2) However, in contrast to the textless clausula, a three-part motet had two different texts (at this time in French) in the upper voices. In an isorhythmic motet (iso- meaning same), one or more of the lower voices, usually the tenor and sometimes the contratenor besides, had a *talea* and a *color* which were repeated.

For example, an anonymous motet, with a triplum or upper voice on the French text, *En non Diu!*, and a motetus or duplum on another French text, *Quant voi*, has an isorhythmic tenor based on melismatic portions of the Alleluia verse, *Vidimus stellam ejus in Oriente* (the chant in *LU 1*, p. 460; Motet in *MSO*, Part 1,

Pomerium in arte musicae mensuratae (1318).[16] For the Italians Marchettus established a theory of notation based on the breve ◧ as a fixed measure, divided into two or three semibreves ◆ and subdivided into groupings of from four to twelve minims ↓ . His explanation of voice production encourages us to try to hear the low notes, high notes, and very high notes the way Italians of his time did.

Concerning the Clef, What It Is and How Many There Are*

The clef refers the written notes of a melody to any place desired. For just as the path toward correctness is determined by the clef placed at the beginning, so the representation of the melody, the identification of the names of the notes, and their distinction from each other, are determined

*Martin Gerbert, Scriptores ecclesiastici de musica sacra potissimum (St. Blasien, 1784), III, 120, 134–5, 172.

---

p. 18). The tenor has two *colores*, one on the syllable *e* and the other on *en*, each of which is repeated. It has only a single talea (♩ ♪♩ 𝄽). At the repetition of *color* 1 (mm. 1 and 7), the *talea* is not in phase with the *color*, whereas at the repetition of *color* 2 (mm. 14 and 20) they are together.

16. Literally, a *pomerium* was an orchard.

by the clef. The clefs universally used are two, namely, F *grave* and c *acute*. Through the distinct placement of these on lines, every melody, whatever its tones are, may be established rationally. For they are constructed at the distance of a fifth from each other, with F in the low notes [*graves*] and c in the high [*acutae*].

But someone may say, "What is a *grave*, an *acute*, and a *superacute* tone?" We say that a *grave* tone, formed in the chest voice, is the closest to silence in any human voice. It has a low resonance and is very near the windpipe, where the tone is produced. Thus, it is called *grave* because it is first produced in this low place. And in the order of the [Guidonian] hand there are seven of these, namely, A B C D E F and G [17] We call *acutae* those which produce the high sounds with respect to the aforementioned low sounds. For the *acutae* are produced in a higher place, that is, in the throat voice, and thus these high sounds emerge. And there are seven of these, which are not differentiated in name from the first. Those which produce the high sounds above the preceding are called *superacutae*. And the reason is because they are produced in a more elevated place, namely, in the head voice. And there are four of these, namely, a b♮ c and d. In fact, we add another,

a b♮ c and d

namely, e, to complete the series begun at c *acuto*. It should be noted that

e

in every human voice, no matter how many times it may ascend and descend, or whatever the length of the ascent or descent may be, these grave, acute, and superacute tones are inevitably distinguishable.

Concerning a Certain Sign
Which Is Commonly Called *Falsa Musica*

Let us consider a certain sign commonly called *falsa musica*, concerning which we may proceed in this order. First we may say that it is necessary to introduce this sign into measured music in order to recognize dissonances which occur in measured song. For we can invent these dissonances only with one or another of these two signs, namely, ♮ *quadratum* and ♭ *rotundum*, which occur or may occur in any plainsong and song with measured rhythm.[18] Secondly, we may ask what name would be logical for this occurrence. Since this kind of sign was devised in music to enhance and make the consonances more beautiful, and since, on the other hand, *false* always pertains to the bad side rather than the good (because something false is never good), we say, therefore, without derogation, that this music should more properly be called *colored* rather than *false*, for through the latter name we attribute to it the connotation of falsity.

17. Guido related the pitches to positions on the palm of the hand.
18. The *quadratum* or square ♮ was the sign for b♮, and the *rotundum* or round b was the sign for b♭. By analogy, the sign ♮ applied as an accidental to a note other than b, was an indication to raise the pitch a semitone, and the sign ♭ meant to lower the pitch a semitone. However, during the *ars nova* and into the Renaissance the accidentals were not always written in. The singers were expected to know where these *false* or *feigned* notes should occur.

Concerning the Application of Imperfect Time to Notes, That Is, the Basic Unit and Its Multiplication

Imperfect time in general, both with regard to the basic unit and its multiplication, is related to notes to the same extent that perfect time is.[19] Notes of three beats, of two, and of one, are devised in the same way, expressing imperfect time as well as perfect. They are even notated in the same way. All incidental indications in a song in imperfect time, such as rests and tails and dots, are exactly comparable to all those in a song in perfect time. And the reason for this is: there can never be substantial knowledge, nor even a sensible concept of imperfection, except through the discovery of perfection. For never, neither through intellect nor through the senses can we perceive that anything is imperfect, unless we understand what is necessary to make it perfect. Therefore, knowledge, as far as those things which refer either to the intellect or to sense perception is concerned, always deals with the perfect. Music therefore, both as far as the notes and as far as the incidental signs are concerned, always deals primarily and principally with perfect time, with the intellect subtracting a part to make imperfect time.

But you say, "In what way does one know when a song must be in perfect time and when in imperfect, if, according to you, the resemblance is completely uniform in notes and in incidentals?" We say that this is left solely to the mastery of the composer, perfectly familiar with the science of music. But, so that one may know the wish of the composer, when one should sing in imperfect time and when in perfect, we say that when a song is composed, a sign of some kind, in imperfect or perfect time, should be added at the beginning. Thus, through the meter signature one may understand the will of the composer who constructs different kinds of song. For from the configuration of the notes alone it is not possible to discover the natural diversity of song.

5.5 PROSDOCIMUS DE BELDEMANDIS
(fl. early 15th cent.)

In his *Treatise on Counterpoint* (1412) the Paduan scholar Prosdocimus de Belemandis distinguishes between polyphony that is sung and that which is written. He accounts for the existence of seventeen pitches in the octave, including a d♭ as well as a c♯, an e♭ as well as a d♯, etc. so that music may be composed with sharps and flats when necessary. Furthermore, Prosdocimus differentiates between strict counterpoint

---

19. Through to the end of the Renaissance, without changing the configuration of the notated symbols, a melody could be read in either triple or duple time, depending on whether the meter signature was a complete circle O , perfect time, or a half-circle C , imperfect time.

(note-against-note) and expansive counterpoint (several notes against one) a clarification that was to gain greater attention in the Renaissance. In order to insure the independence of the voices, he prohibits parallel fifths and octaves, a rule that still dominates the study of counterpoint today.

Note-Against-Note Counterpoint*

It is possible to invent one melody against another in two ways, namely: several notes occur against a single note and are written or sung above or below it; or, a single note alone occurs against another single note and is written or sung above or below it. We know that counterpoint may exist in two ways, namely: expansively or broadly, and individually or strictly. Counterpoint expressed in a melismatic fashion, or expansively, consists of many notes against a single note alone, any place in the melody.

Strict counterpoint is expressed in individual notes, a single note alone against another single note alone, throughout the cantus. This is real counterpoint, because in it lies true opposition [*contrapositio*].

Furthermore, we know that the characteristic of this kind of counterpoint is two-fold, namely, vocal and written. Vocal counterpoint is sung and written counterpoint is notated.

Prohibition of Parallel Fifths and Octaves

For the succession of intervals in strict counterpoint, these are the rules to be practiced.

The first rule is this: what we call discords, namely, the second, fourth, seventh, and diminished fifth, diminished and augmented octaves and their equivalents, are intervals never used in counterpoint, because they are averse to agreeability in harmony by nature of their dissonance. They are used, however, in shorter note values, because in the latter they are not considered dissonant on account of the speed of the notes.

The second rule is this, that counterpoint should begin and end only on perfect intervals, namely, at the unison, or at the perfect fifth or octave or their equivalents. And here is the reason why. If the listener has been disturbed by the harmonies in the course of the counterpoint, at the end he must be inspired with harmonies more dulcet and amicable by nature, the perfect consonances named above. Thus the main consonances are emphasized. Finally, I mean that the listener himself should be moved by harmony that is agreeable and sweeter by nature. Surely, the spirit of the listener must be affected by the introductory sweet consonance, by the strict consonance of the final, and by the harmonies between, for he is lured on by enjoyment and pleasure.

*Edmond de Coussemaker, Scriptorum de musica medii aevi *(Paris: Durand, 1864–1876), III, 194, 197–198.*

The third rule is this, that when constructing a counterpoint above or below a melody, we ought never to ascend or descend with the same perfect interval in succession, such as unison, fifth or octave, or their equivalents. However, we may proceed correctly with different perfect intervals in succession. And the reason is this: when one person sings the same thing as another, which is what happens when you sound the same interval consecutively in different voices, that is not the intent of counterpoint. Rather, the intent should be as follows: what is sung by one person should be different from what is expressed by another, and this should be done through good intervals arranged suitably.

The fourth rule is this, that we ought not to construct counterpoint with successions of imperfect intervals (thirds and sixths) continuously without interpolating a perfect consonance, because to sing in this way would be harsh, since in it no harmony is deeply perceived, and the intention of all music is harmony.

6

The Humanization of Music

6.1 ANTONIO SQUARCIALUPI (1416–1480) TO GUILLAUME DUFAY (1400–1474)

A letter written to the famous composer Guillaume Dufay in 1467 by Antonio Squarcialupi embodies the human element, the interest of one musician in the work of a fellow artist. Squarcialupi, a composer himself, whose works somehow did not survive the test of time, wrote the letter in Florence where he was the organist at the church of Santa Maria del Fiore. Squarcialupi enjoyed the patronage of the Medici family, a position that enabled him to turn his efforts toward stimulating the outstanding talent of his day, and also toward collecting the works of specific composers of the past century. A collection of fourteenth-century polyphonic music which he owned and may have compiled is still known as the *Squarcialupi Codex*. Now in the Biblioteca Medicea-Laurenziana in Florence, the codex contains groups of compositions by twelve of the most famous composers of the preceding era, including Francesco Landini, Gherardello da Firenze, Niccolò da Perugia, and Giovanni Cascia (Johannes de Florentia).

Dufay, the famous canon of Cambrai, was known to Squ intimately than through mere reputation, since the Bu had been a member of the Papal Chapel at Flore In addition to his monumental production composed settings for chansons corres vocal types of the time. In this le

his talents once again toward an Italian text, as Dufay had done in his youth when he wrote compositions dedicated to the Malatesta family, which governed the Italian city of Rimini.

Human Interest in Musical Composition*

To the Reverend Father Guglielmus, Master of the Musical Art, most honored Canon of Cambrai,
My venerable Father, above all most worthy of respect by merit,

With the greatest joy and attention I read and reread your very considerate [*humanissimus*] letter, and I cherish with all my heart the group of singers which you have sent from your church, the best, just as you wrote me, and I who have heard them, have easily come to believe it. For they are indeed excellent, both for their sweetness of tone and for their knowledge and skill in singing, and are worthy of you, their master. One cannot say what pleasure you gave to our Magnificent Piero [Petro] de Medici, who greatly esteems your paternity and always speaks of you in a most honorable manner. And he maintains, as I also willingly maintain too, that you are the most brilliant jewel of our age. Likewise, Lorenzo de Medici, son of Piero, admires you exceedingly. Just as he enjoys the other fine arts, thanks to the superiority of his divine genius, he also passionately enjoys more polished music such as yours.

And consequently he admires your art, and honors and respects you like a father. Also he desires to possess personally something significant of your very excellent talent. That is why a cantilena is attached to this letter, which he wants you to set and ornament in song. I therefore beg you to do this immediately and to send it to him. He is worthy of your favor because of his virtue and his liberality. You would also give me the greatest pleasure and I would give you many thanks. If I could only see and hear you:— something which you also seem to desire from your letter. Certainly, I would not place anything above this pleasure. I am always yours. I send regards to you.

Florence, May 1, 1467.
Antonius de Squarcialupi of Florence,
called Master Antonius, Organist of Florence

CANZONA

Amore, chai visto ciascun mio pensiero
e chonosciuto el mio fedel servire,
fammi chontento, o tu mi fa morire, etc.

[Love, who sees each of my thoughts,
And knows my faithful devotion,
Satisfy me, or you will cause me to die.]

Giovanni Gaye, Carteggio inedito D'Artisti dei secoli XIV, XV, XVI. *(Florence: Giuseppe Molini, 1839)*, I, 208–209.

6.2 THE MASTERSINGERS OF NUREMBERG
THROUGH J. C. WAGENSEIL (1633–1708)

The German mastersingers of the fifteenth and sixteenth centuries were nonprofessional composers whose musical customs were built around the very life of the towns in which they carried on their daily trades. A historical investigation into the musical activity of the folk of Nuremberg was conducted in the next century by Johann Christoph Wagenseil, a professor of law at the University of Altdorf. His published work, entitled *Book of the Mastersingers' Graceful Art: Its Beginning, Continued Practice, Usefulness, and Precepts* (1697), was one of Richard Wagner's main sources for studying the lives and customs of *Die Meistersinger* while he was planning the libretto for his opera of that name. In the second scene of the third act Hans Sachs, the shoemaker, teaches Walther von Stolzing, a young knight from Franconia, how to write a mastersong according to the rules. Wagner combines historical accuracy with artistic genius as he has Sachs and Walther go through the theoretical paces leading to the creation of a song stanza with two sets of verses and a conclusion (a a b).

Concerning the Origin and Beginning of the Art of the Mastersingers*

According to the city of Mainz, the art of the mastersingers flourished especially in the cities of Nuremberg and Strassburg, as is shown by twelve old Nuremberg masters in the profession whose names are: 1. Veit Pogner, 2. Cuntz Vogelsang, 3. Hermann Ortel, 4. Conrad Nachtigal, 5. Balthasar Zorn, 6. Sixtus Beckmesser, 7. Fritz Kohtner, 8. Niclaus Vogel, 9. Augustin Moser, 10. Hannss Schwartz, 11. Ulrich Eisslinger, 12. Hannss Foltz.

During the Reformation of the previous century, while purity in religious matters, the study of sacred and humane letters, and the study of languages were being reestablished, at the same time there arose the art of the mastersingers. Since Hans Sachs of Nuremberg made the greatest contribution, it stands to reason that he is considered to be the patriarch of the mastersingers. In his youth he learned the cobbler's trade. Yet, he also took great delight in poetry and mastersong. Thus he went to Leonhart Nunnebecken,

---

* *Joh. Christophori Wagenseilii.* De Sacri Rom. Imperii Libera Civitate Noribergensi Commentatio, Accedit, De Germaniai Phonascorum Von Der Meister-Singer Origine, Praestantia, Utilitate, et Institutis Sermone Vernaculo Liber. *Altdorfl Noricorum. Typis Impensisque Jodoci Wilhelmi Kohlesii, 1697.*
Appendix: Buch von Der Meister-Singer Holdseligen Kunst Anfang Fortübung Nutzbarkeiten und Lehr-Sätzen, *pp. 515–544.*

a mastersinger, from whom he received introductory training. Afterwards, with tireless energy, he devoted himself to the art, at which he achieved such perfection that he far surpassed all who preceded him, and made it likely that he would surpass all to come. After he returned home from his travels, for many years he carried on the cobbler's trade. But his understanding stretched far beyond footwear. Next he became a schoolmaster, and continually composed poetry. He also brought the art of the mastersingers to such prominence that in his time over two hundred and fifty mastersingers were located in Nuremberg.

Hans Sachs lived to be 81 years old. His memory will be cherished by the common people no less than that of Homer, Virgil, Ovid, and Horace is remembered by the learned—as long as the world stands.

The Complete Tablature [1] of the Meistersinger: The Mastersongs, Their Art and Characteristics

Each *Bar* of the mastersong has its own number of rhymes and syllables, prescribed and determined orally by the masters. All singers, poets, and markers must know how to measure and to count on their fingers.

A *Bar* for the most part contains a distinct *Gesätz* [stanza] or piece, or as many of them as the poet wishes to compose. A *Gesätz* usually consists of two *Stollen* [portions] which have the same melody. A *Stollen* consists of several verses, and, when a mastersong is written down, its end is often marked by a little cross. Then follows the *Abgesang* [aftersong] also consisting of several verses, but with its own special melody, different from the *Stollen*. Finally, again a *Stollen* or part of a *Gesätz* appears, with the melody of the preceding *Stollen*.

Concerning the Customs and Practices of the Meistersinger at the Song-Session and Contest

Several days before a song-session is to be held, the markers or heads of the Meistersinger cooperating societies announce it. Each society that is called to the song-session is bound to appear, and if it cannot come, it must send its apologies.

In the midst of Catherine's Church, in front of the choir, a low dais is set up. On it are placed a table with a large black lectern, and seats around the table. This dais, which is for the marker, is completely enclosed by curtains, so that from the outside one cannot see what is happening inside. The small seat on which the person who sings a mastersong sits, is called the song-stool. It stays permanently in its place, not far from the large pulpit from which the sermons are delivered.

When the day for the song-session is determined, it is advertised by four

1. The *Tabulatur* or tablature was a wooden board on which the table of mastersinger rules was recorded.

or five posters hung publicly in the city, of which three are placed on various poles in the great market, and the fourth on the outer gate through which one goes to Catherine's Church.

The markers, who are considered to be the most outstanding leaders of the society, sit at the table in front of the large lectern on the enclosed dais. They are usually four in number. One, the oldest, has lying on the lectern before him the Bible according to Luther's translation. He opens it to the place from which the singer says he took his song, and pays careful attention as to whether the song agrees both with the contents of the Scripture and with Luther's clear translation.

The second marker, sitting opposite the first, takes care to see that the context of the song fits all the laws prescribed by the tablature. If any are broken, he notes on the lectern with a piece of chalk, the mistake and its penalty, that is, how many syllables are lost. The third marker writes down the syllable for each verse or rhyme-ending and, as he sees whether everything is correctly rhymed, he notes the mistakes. And the fourth marker pays attention to the tone, so that it is followed correctly, not incorrectly. Also he sees to it that the *Stollen* and Aftersongs are suitable for each other.

6.3 CONRAD PAUMANN (c. 1410–1473)

By the fifteenth century the use of traditional German folk song as a cantus firmus was swept into the polyphonic current. In his *Foundation of Organizing* (1452) the German organist, Conrad Paumann, shows how to ornament basic melodic and contrapuntal motions by breaking their notes up into decorative tones with shorter time values. Going far beyond a mere explanation of the vertical intervallic relationships between the cantus and the organal voice, he delves into a concept of the simultaneous decoration of two independent melodies. This art of ornamentation was either called *diminution*, owing to its division of the rhythmic beat into shorter note values, or *coloration*, owing to the interlacing of the melodic motion with decorative pitches.

Blind from birth, Paumann was not inclined toward long literary explanations. He expressed himself best on his instrument, as demonstrated in his perceptive musical examples notated in organ tablature,[2] two of which are transcribed here.

2. Paumann's organ tablature was a notation using letter names for the notes of the bass part and note symbols for the upper part. Compositions are transcribed in *GMB*, Nos. 45, 47, 48; also in *HAM*, Vol. I, No. 81. A facsimile of a page from the *Fundamentum organisandi* is in Apel, *The Notation of Polyphonic Music* (Cambridge, Mass.: The Mediaeval Academy of America, 1953), p. 45.

Contrapuntal Decoration by Diminution and Coloration*

Descent through G F E D C³

Descent by 5ths⁴

* Jahrbücher für Musikalische Wissenschaft, *Vol. II (1867); (Reprint, Hildesheim: Georg Olms, 1966). A facsimile edition by Konrad Ameln was published in 1925.*

3. This example shows a descending motion through five notes, G, F, E, D, C, in the lower voice. After playing G and F without decoration, Paumann ornaments E. Basically the five notes would be of equal duration, each lasting a dotted whole note. However, the decoration of E lasts longer, depriving the following note, D, of part of its time value. The concluding note, C, has the basic time value. Above this decorated descent Paumann composes a counterpoint, with a string of parallel sixths where the diminution of E occurs in the bass. The two voices together constitute a characteristic cadence formula that Paumann uses in his compositions.

4. A bass motion in fifths is the most fundamental harmonic progression possible, because the fifth has the simplest harmonic ratio of any interval other than the unison or octave. This bass line combines two descending hexachords, a cantus

6.4 SEBASTIAN VIRDUNG (fl. early 16th cent.)

In his *Musica Getuscht* (Music Germanized, 1511), written in German rather than the learned Latin, Sebastian Virdung explains to his friend Andreas in simple terms why the keyboards of organs and harpsichords are divided into a specific arrangement of black and white keys. The question still perplexes many a performer now, and Virdung's answer still holds true. Relating the keyboard to the Guidonian gamut (Chart 2), Virdung starts with a diagram in which the keyboard has only two black keys, both b flats. His next step is to infiltrate the diatonic genus with the chromatic. By adding thirteen black keys to the two with which he started, Virdung arrives at the pattern of white and black keys that has remained standard to the present day.

Arrangement of Notes on the Keyboard*

SEBASTIAN: I believe the clavichord to be what Guido Aretinus called the monochord, consisting of a single string and its division or apportionment.[5] It was described and regulated only according to the diatonic species. I found in Guido's writings that such a monochord had a long four-cornered frame like a trunk or a chest. On it was stretched a string which could produce the entire cycle of consonances based on the proportions, those which already existed, as well as those that had been invented or imagined. I will never know the reason why a key, made for each note according to its measure, which strikes the string exactly on the

---

*Musica getutscht und aussgezogen durch Sebastianum Virdung Priesters von Amberg *(Basel, 1511)*.

---

firmus on the C hexachord, and an organal voice on the G hexachord a fifth above.

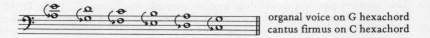

organal voice on G hexachord
cantus firmus on C hexachord

For the hexachords, see Chart 2. For the technique of organizing in fifths, see the *Musica Enchiriadis*, Section 5.1.

5. A clavichord is built with strings of uniform length. When the performer depresses a key, it causes a metal pin to hit the string, dividing it into two parts. One section of the string is thus dampened, while the other vibrates, producing the designated pitch. This mechanism is in contrast to that of the harpsichord, whose strings are themselves of varying lengths and are plucked with quills. The generic name for all keyboard instruments, including the organ, is *clavier*.

same spot or point, produces just this tone and no other; yet, the proportions are destined by nature to yield these notes. Also, I do not know who had dubbed or called the instrument *clavichord* according to these keys.

ANDREAS: Will you not also describe to me how one should measure the monochord?

SEBASTIAN: There is enough written about this elsewhere in the book, so that in my opinion it is not necessary to include it for you here. Now I only want to teach you how to learn to play from tablature on the instruments.

ANDREAS: Then what will you do to teach me the tablature?

SEBASTIAN: First I want to tell you about the keys and strings of the clavichord, also how one should name them, and then how to use these signs in the tablature.

ANDREAS: Then tell me how many keys and strings the clavichord should have.

SEBASTIAN: I cannot tell you any exact number that it should have. It might have this amount or that, and not more or less than is customary in the instrument called the monochord. I believe that one may use as many strings as one wishes.

ANDREAS: Yet, if an instrument has more than one string, you can no longer call it a monochord, but you must designate it according to the number of strings, such as, tetrachord for four strings, pentachord for five strings, etc.

SEBASTIAN: It is of little consequence how many strings there are. Whether the strings are many or few does not matter as long as they are all in tune with each other [*umsonum*], so that for equivalent pitches one is not higher or lower than the other.

ANDREAS: Why must that be?

SEBASTIAN: Because the division of the whole monochord depends only on one string. Thus, if there are more strings they should have the same pitch. Otherwise the measurements would be incorrect when the strings are divided; and the pitches would be completely false.

ANDREAS: Then is it also enough to have only one string on the clavichord?

SEBASTIAN: No. Of necessity there must be more than one.

ANDREAS: Why?

SEBASTIAN: Because on a single string one cannot produce any consonance simultaneously, or sound one tone against the other. They may only be heard successively. Therefore it is necessary that there be many strings so that one may hear the sweetness of consonances with two voices, with three, with four, and even with more voices against each other, which could never be done on one string alone.

ANDREAS: Then how many keys must there be?

SEBASTIAN: When Guido wrote about the monochord, he considered
                only the diatonic genus, and, according to that, the clavi-
                chord for a long time had no more than twenty keys, as is
                shown here:

<u>G</u> A B C D E F G a b c d e f g aa bb cc dd ee

                But others came after him who did it more subtly. They
                had also read Boethius, and divided the monochord ac-
                cording to the other species, called *chromatic*.

ANDREAS: You speak a great deal about unusual species. Tell me,
                then, what the diatonic genus is, and also about the others,
                so that I might better understand what you are talking
                about.

SEBASTIAN: The diatonic genus is as Boethius describes it in the first
                book of his *Musica*, chapter xxi. Today, in the same way,
                we construct what we call a fourth from two whole tones
                and a minor semitone, or from four keys or four pitches.

ANDREAS: How can I understand that?

SEBASTIAN: Well, do this. In the diagram drawn for you above, start
                at one of the keys, whichever you wish, and begin to
                count, from the lowest to the highest, or the other way
                around, from the highest to the lowest, and always count
                four keys to a fourth. If you always take four keys, the
                fourth will be constructed correctly, from two whole
                tones and a minor semitone. I exclude only *b fa mi*, (b♭
                and b♮). I will not discuss this here, because it has two keys
                which are counted as one.[6]

ANDREAS: Then what is the chromatic genus?

SEBASTIAN: *Croma* is just about the same as color, and *cromaticum* is
                like something colored. Besides, at times one might also
                say that it means something extended or well decorated.
                Thus, the art of instrumental music is expanded, and is
                even more subtly decorated, through the use of the semi-
                tone from the chromatic genus. Accordingly, one may
                construct the fourth from the combination of five semi-
                tones. In other words, this fourth has six notes or keys
                which produce five semitones. And thus, according to the

6. In the Greek system there was already a choice between b♮ and b♭, a combination
which on a keyboard instrument requires that there be two keys for one letter.

said chromatic genus, thirteen semitones are constructed, and distributed above the main keys. To this, one key may be added below the gamut, and some tones may also be added above *e la*. Basically, counting from the lowest key up to the highest, three octaves are included. Sometimes people add yet another key and a semitone, thus creating the double genus, now common, with thirty-eight keys, as follows:

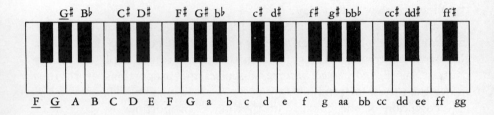

ANDREAS: Then what is the third genus?

SEBASTIAN: It is called enharmonic. But since it does not exist in the instruction and usage of the organist and organ-builder, I will not speak about it here at present, except to mention it and nothing further.

6.5 JOHANNES TINCTORIS (c. 1435–1511)

Within a year or two after the death of Dufay, about 1475, the Belgian Johannes Tinctoris put together his *Terminorum Musicae Diffinitorium*. This dictionary of musical terms was dedicated "to the most intelligent maiden and the most illustrious lady, Princess Beatrice of Aragon," daughter of King Ferdinand of Sicily. The highly condensed treatise contains many significant definitions, such as the following:

CANON: A canon is a rule showing the wish of the composer beneath a certain obscurity.

FUGA: Fugue is the identity of the parts of a composition with regard to the value, name, and arrangement of their notes and rests, sometimes even with regard to the placement of these notes and rests.

In the Renaissance the *canon* or rule gave the singers directions as to how the part should be read. For example, two singers reading from the same part might be told to read in different clefs, or to read in different meters, or to read forward and backward, thus creating polyphonic diversity from one voice. Sometimes the rule was purposefully veiled in secrecy so that only the initiated would be able to understand it.

Tinctoris' definition of *fuga* is what we think of today as imitation or canon, with the voices separated by an interval of time and possibly by an interval of pitch also.

From such entries, as well as from the music of the time, we realize that many of the terms which Tinctoris defines had not yet taken on the connotations they have today.

In all Tinctoris wrote twelve treatises on specific technical aspects of music. For example, his *Liber de Arte contrapuncti* goes into detail about the use of contrapuntal intervals from the unison to the triple octave. In contrast, his *Proportionale musices* discusses the proportions of rhythm rather than those of pitch.

Recognition of the concept of rhythmical proportions is vital to an understanding of Renaissance music. Composers were not willing to limit their rhythms to the basic meters grouped by three and two in perfect and imperfect time. In a single melody, once the basic time values were established by the meter, they wanted to be able to change the relationship between the notes, and they could do so instantaneously by inserting a sign of proportion wherever they pleased. In a combination of melodies they could show the relationship between the different parts by placing the signs of proportion immediately after the meter signatures in each part. Whether we know how to follow the intricacies of the notational system of the fifteenth and sixteenth centuries or not, we should be aware of the avenues open to the composers as we feel the rhythmic freedom expressed in their music through the rhythmic proportions.

Certain Observations Concerning Proportions*

I think that after having discussed in detail the kinds of unequal proportion and their special characteristics, I should now comment on them in general, considering *how, when,* and *where* proportions of unequal measure are indicated.

How Proportions Should Be Indicated

First of all, so that you may know *how* proportions ought to be indicated, let me say that every proportion is written correctly with the numerals appropriate to it. . . .

* *Edmond de Coussemaker,* Scriptorum de musica medii aevi *(Paris: Durand, 1864–1876), IV, 153,* Proportionale musices, *Book 3, Chaps. 1–4.*

If the larger number of the proportion refers to the smaller, then you, the composer, will put the larger numeral above and the smaller below. If, on the contrary, the smaller is related to the larger, you will place the smaller above and the larger below, as follows:[7]

Example 1

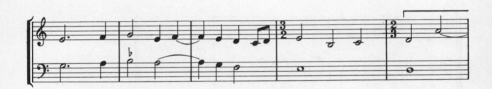

When Proportions Should Be Indicated

The second matter concerns *when* proportions should be indicated. The most commendable way is to indicate as soon as possible any proportion of inequality you wish to generate so that it may be understood immediately.

Where We Should Indicate Proportions

The third matter concerns *where*, that is, in what part and in what place we should indicate these proportions. Let us say that if there are two, three, or more parts in any composed work, whether the parts composed subsequently are in a one-to-one proportion with the first, or if the other parts are in different proportions with respect to the first, the proportions

---

7. In transcribing these examples into modern notation the values were halved.

should be indicated without ambiguity. To do this properly the sign of the chief proportion should be shown at the beginning of each part, thus:[8]

Example 2

The Order of Composing the Parts

The first part of the whole composition to be composed is the fundamental voice, the principal part with respect to the others. Most frequently, or I should say, almost always, this is the tenor, so called because it seems to hold [*tenere*] the other parts in subjugation. This happens in an infinite number of vocal compositions. If the tenor were left out, the other parts would offend our ears harshly and severely with sounds discordant to each other. Occasionally the soprano is the principal part, as happens when we first compose a melody directly in the upper part and add one or more parts to it, as shown in Example 3:[9]

8. In Example 2 the tenor, which has the basic beat, is in imperfect time (C), with a whole note equal to two half-notes in modern notation. The soprano, proportional to the tenor, is in perfect time (O), with a proportion of three half-notes to one half-note in the tenor. The contratenor, also in perfect time, has a proportion of two dotted half-notes to one half-note in the tenor.
9. In Example 3 there is a proportional diminution of two whole notes in the contratenor to one whole note in the soprano and tenor voices. The use of the term *diminution* for rhythmic proportion is more usual today than the Renaissance use of the term for melodic decoration (see Paumann, Section 6.3).

Example 3: *Pour vous la belle*

—or when we take the soprano of some composed chanson and write another new part to it, as here.[10]

Example 4

10. In Example 4 the soprano is the beginning of the upper part of a three-part chanson by John Dunstable (c. 1370–1453), *O rosa bella.* (*HAM* Vol. I, No. 61) The tenor is from the folk song *L'Homme armé*, which was used as a cantus firmus in numerous masses. The dot inside the circle is the sign for the greater prolation

The contratenor, however, is rarely or never a principal part. Despite this, if we wish to work with the contratenor as a precomposed cantus, we produce a principal part like this:[11]

Example 5

Secondary parts are all those dependent on the principal part, the fundamental basis of the relationship.

Bibliographical Note

Tinctoris' *Dictionary of Musical Terms* has been translated by Carl Parrish opposite the original Latin (London & New York: The Free Press of Glencoe, 1963).

6.6 FRANCHINUS GAFURIUS (1451–1511)

Tinctoris, Belgian by birth, spent his most fruitful years at Naples. His contemporary and close intellectual counterpart, Franchinus Gafurius, was a native Italian.

(♩ = ♪ ♪ ♪). For the Kyrie of Missa L'homme armé by Jean de Ockeghem (c. 1430–1495), see *MSO*, Part I, 29 f.

Examples 4 and 5 have conflicting or partial signatures with b♭ in one voice and not in another. In his treatise on the nature and property of the modes. Tinctoris says that in a polyphonic composition one part may be in one mode and another part may be in another mode; or one part may be authentic and the other plagal (Coussemaker, *Scriptorum* IV, 29).

11. In Example 5, where the contratenor is the principal part, Tinctoris writes a

Gafurius' approach to vocal movement or rhythm is based on the work of the ancient Latin grammarians who recognized a short syllable as one unit of time and a long syllable as two. A syllable was short or long naturally, by its position in relation to the next consonant, or by poetic license. After dealing with the rhythm of poetry, Gafurius turns to the "practice of music" (*Practica musicae*, 1496). His analogy between the beat in rhythm and the human pulse-beat, one of the earliest attempts to assign an absolute duration to the musical beat, is a valuable clue in an understanding of Renaissance tempo.

Like Tinctoris, Gafurius also paid a great deal of attention to the individual function of each interval. Gafurius' discussion of the interval of a fourth in fauxbourdon helps us to understand how this interval was perceived in the musical ear of his time.

Absolute Duration of the Musical Beat: Book 2, Chap. 1*

Musicians themselves have assigned to the quantities of sound certain characters as their own appropriate names. With these they can compose every song in a diversity of the time units expressed, much like the way that verse is made up of many feet.

Physicians agree that the correct measure of a short unit of time ought to be matched to the even beat of the pulse, establishing arsis and thesis as equal to that which they call diastole and systole in the measurement of each pulse. Nevertheless, it is clear that in the pulse of sick people, who are the physicians' responsibility, diastole and systole undergo an increase or change in unequal proportion. The Greek word *diastole* means dilation or expansion; *systole*, on the other hand, means contraction. Poets, moreover, have arsis and thesis, that is, rise and fall in their metrical feet. Arsis and thesis provide the basis for the existence of these metrical feet. They use them in recitation so that the verse can strike the ear and caress the mind with a more pleasing sound.

Even though it is possible to find arsis and thesis in the feet whenever poetry is composed, nevertheless it is the apt and smooth conjunction of words which makes them exceedingly clear and assists in graceful articulation. An interweaving of words suitable for delivery in one or another fashion, according to the various kinds of verse, is made, so that the very texture of the verses reveals the feet, which run swiftly, as races are run, and with a fixed order of the verbal connections, unveils the smooth, spontaneously flowing rhythm.

---

*From The Practica Musicae of Franchinus Gafurius, *trans. and ed. Irwin Young (Madison, Milwaukee and London: The University of Wisconsin Press, 1969), pp. 69, 140. Reprinted by permission of the University of Wisconsin Press.*

---

cadence with the tenor leap from 1 to 5, and the soprano filling in the closing harmony with the (minor) third. A complete triad at the end is unusual for this period. Example 3 has a more typical cadence.

Interval of a Fourth in Fauxbourdon: Book 3, Chap. 5

When tenor and cantus proceed by means of one or more sixths, then the middle voice, the contratenor, will always occupy the fourth below the cantus, always maintaining a third above the tenor. Musicians call this kind of counterpoint *fauxbourdon*. In it this middle contratenor quite frequently follows the notes of the cantus, proceeding at an interval of a fourth below it; it is often observed by musicians in the performance of the psalms. And so such a fourth, arranged between a contratenor and a cantus, even in semibreves, breves, and longs, is accepted as harmonious in counterpoint. This technique is aptly demonstrated in the following harmonization:[12]

6.7 PIETRO ARON (1480–1545)

Ever since the ninth century, when the *vox organalis* was first constructed on a *vox principalis*, musicians composed layer by layer, considering the set of intervals between the tones of the principal part and the corresponding tones of each of the other voices, until all of the voices became part of the composition (Sections 5.1, 6.5). Identifying himself and the musical style which he champions as hailing from Tuscany, Pietro Aron describes a new procedure, that of composing all of the parts at once, in his treatise entitled *The Tuscan in Music* (1523).

How the Composer May Begin to Compose*

Many composers have assumed that first the soprano ought to be created, then the tenor, and after the tenor the contrabass. And thus, because they constructed the contralto later, it was very difficult for them to compose. Because they had to be careful to avoid unisons, rests, and ascending and descending leaps difficult to sing, the contralto melodies were left with little sweetness and harmony.

*Pietro Aron, Il Toscanello in Musica *(Venice, 1523), Book II, Chaps. 16–20, 31.*

12. A fauxbourdon hymn by Guillaume Dufay appears in *MSO*, Part 1, p. 27 f. When notating a composition in fauxbourdon style the composer wrote only the outer parts. The singer of the middle part improvised at the fourth in the manner described by Gafurius in this passage.

Therefore the moderns have decided, as is evident, that throughout a composition, whether it be written for four, five, six, or more voices, each part should be in its suitable, proper, position. We consider all of the parts together, and do not proceed in the manner described above. Now you may decide to compose the soprano, tenor, or contrabass first; the style and the rule are up to you. At present people frequently say that the principal part may be stated either in the contrabass, or the tenor, or the contralto. To prevent them from thinking that the correct and convenient way is to begin with the principal part and then to add part by part, the practice should henceforth be categorized in some way to demonstrate the opposite rule and style.

Method of Composing for More Than Four Voices

When you want to compose for more than four voices, you must know how to add a fifth part. That fifth part should be a second soprano crossing the first back and forth, and exchanging tones with it. You should compose the second soprano in such a way that it does not exceed the upper and lower limits of the first soprano, and so that you do not disturb the other parts below. And what is customarily suitable for the first soprano, what good composers ordinarily do, is likewise applicable to the two sopranos, when matched together as one. And there is no other advice, except that great care should be used. It is not necessary for you to avoid the fourth no matter what happens in one or the other part, above or below. And in the diminutions dissonances are only allowed in the middle notes, as explained above.[13]

The same procedure is intended when one or more tenors or contraltos are added, always, however, observing the rule that you should do it in the easiest way possible. . . . When you want to compose a composition for five, six, or more voices, you must not devise a part without first considering whether all the other parts can have suitable positions, so that you don't get involved in rests, unisons, and other errors.

6.8 HENRICUS GLAREANUS (1488–1563)

In his *Dodecachordon* (literally the Greek word for *twelve strings*), published in 1547, the Swiss theorist Glareanus demonstrates the Renaissance recognition of twelve usable modes. In addition to the eight church modes, included are the Aeolian, equivalent to today's natural minor, and

13. In a previous paragraph on consonance and dissonance Aron said, "And in decorating the melodies with smaller time values you should be warned that the first and last notes in a diminished passage must always be consonant, and the notes in the middle may be varied with as much dissonance as the original passage will bear. Depending on the speed of the diminished tones some dissonances are not displeasing to the ear of the singer."

the Ionian, closest to our major, each with its authentic and plagal versions. To illustrate the Aeolian and Ionian modes Glareanus uses compositions by Jacob Obrecht (1452–1505), Adam von Fulda (c. 1440–1505), and Josquin des Prez (1450–1521), among others.

While increasing the number of modes, Glareanus also provides means for decreasing their number. When he discusses the interchange between modes, he is anticipating the trend toward a two-mode system, major and minor.

The True Determination of the Modes*

Thus far we have discussed concisely and simply all the essential principles of this subject which we considered relevant, partly theoretical, partly practical. Now the loftier and more distinctive portion of our work remains to be explained. This is to be viewed as the promised land, the harbor of this rough sailing. Indeed, we will handle the twelve modes of the ancient musicians as a topic worthy of the men of our age, and we will show the reason why at the beginning of these books we called this treatise *Dodecachordon*. Many erudite men by this time may doubtless wonder why we have made mention of twelve modes. They themselves label only eight. Some even insist that three are sufficient, as they sing *ut, re, mi*, the way performers commonly do.

Concerning the Alteration of One Mode into Another

One mode may be altered into another mode, but not all changes are equally successful. Sometimes the borrowing is scarcely detected, even by an acute ear; sometimes it is clearly heard with great pleasure. We have demonstrated over and over again that the change from the Lydian to the Ionian is very common today.[14] This is understood by those who play instruments and by those who know how to sing the verses of poets to rational music.[15] Indeed, they deserve great praise if the proportions are suitable, especially when they change Ionian into Dorian. In other cases, however, such as Dorian to Phrygian, the change is hard, and scarcely without serious offense to the ear. And therefore, those who play the organ in church encounter this difficulty whenever they improvise on songs for their congregation; unless they are experienced and prepared, they often incur the ridicule of erudite listeners. Whence I think the adage was born: From Dorian to Phrygian, from natural to less natural, or from composed

---

*Henricus Glareanus (Heinrich Loris), Dodecachordon (Basel: 1547), II, 65, 90–91, 101; III, 239–241.

14. The pure Lydian mode on F has a B♮. The Ionian mode transposed from C to F has a B♭. See the example of the Ionian mode by Josquin, in the key of F with B♭ in the signature, at the end of this chapter.

15. By "rational music" Glareanus means music with proportional pitches and rhythms, in contrast to free-flowing chant with indeterminate pitches and unmeasured rhythms.

to discordant, from pleasant to disagreeable. In short, from that which fluctuates to that which falls apart.

Despite the fact that many exceptional men of our age have written about this adage, among them the two who are especially esteemed by me are Franchinus [Gafurius] and D. Erasmus of Rotterdam, whom I never mention without a laudatory introduction.[16] The former taught me silently, the latter, orally. I am immeasurably indebted to them.

I never really saw Franchinus. Although he is said to have been in Milan twenty-two years ago when I was there, I was not yet engaged in this subject. In later years, however, (as I freely admit because it is true) this man's writings taught me much, and have given me the wonderful opportunity of reading, rereading, and absorbing Boethian music culture as much as I desire. For a long time no one approached the material; indeed no one thought it was intelligible.

I have been friendly with Erasmus for many years. Although we did not live in the same house, we were so close that we met and supped together every day, while we had continual extensive discussions about the use of language, and other difficult topics which we digested for general student consumption. And thus we took it upon ourselves to advise, to deliberate, to correct. I, as the younger, gave way to his seniority. He, as the older, put up with my conjectures. Although he sometimes found fault with them, he was an enthusiastic supporter of my studies.

Short Recapitulation of the Division of the Modes

The finals of the twelve modes have the following pitches in accordance with their characteristics: Aeolian and Hypoaeolian on A, Ionian and Hypoionian on C, Dorian and Hypodorian on D, Phrygian and Hypophrygian on E, Lydian and Hypolydian on F, Mixolydian and Hypomixolydian on G. The B key has been omitted, because songs very seldom end on it.

Examples of the Twelve Modes

Thus far we reviewed the canons or precepts of this new art as clearly and concisely as possible. It remains for us now to illustrate it with examples in all the modes which we revealed in the preceding book. This subject has

---

16. For Gafurius see Section 6.6. Desiderius Erasmus (c. 1466–1536), the Dutch humanist scholar who worked on a retranslation of the Bible from Greek to Latin, was against the theatricalization of sacred music by means of polyphony. In a commentary on *I Corinthians* XIV, 19, Erasmus wrote:

We are persuaded to leave work for the theatrical music of the churches where there is a worse clatter of sounds than ever was heard in the Greek or Roman theaters. They make noise with every sort of pipe [*tubus*], bronze trumpet [*lituus*], hollow reed [*fistula*], and stringed instrument [*sambuca*]; and with these compete the voices of the men. . . . Now who are more stupid than those who, while training for the musical art, cannot celebrate the festival of the day without using a certain kind of distorted singing which they call *fauxbourdon*. This neither uses a prescribed theme, nor does it observe the harmonies of a work of art.

been distorted by just about all the displeased and defiant singers of our age. However, nature is so plentiful in her gifts that, without understanding her, we still follow the leader. We propose to use good, simple, graceful songs that are easy to sing and are not ornate. Some are chosen from the folk, where the strength of nature lies, translated for us into a mental image. The reader is left to his own decision, for not all things please everyone. We disparage what we have heard only once, while it seems to me that we always admire a song we have learned, just as those who particularly wish to be thought of as honest musicians, judge the rehearsed song of a poet not only through the ear, but also with the mind.

Those who publish books of letters often mingle the work of others not expressed as clearly with their carefully finished epistles, obviously so that the contrast of opposite against opposite, as the philosophers say, is all the more apparent. Angelo Politian appears to have done this shortly before our time.[17] We felt that it was necessary to do likewise in these examples. Thus, to the expert songs of Josquin des Prez,[18] and other first-rate composers (*Symphonetae*),[19] we added the less polished songs of others, so that the reader would be able to judge from the antithesis the extent to which some were more beautiful. It is important for the reader to know, moreover, that we have made a tripartite division, with examples from three periods. The first examples (although we are presenting just a few of these), old and simple, belong to the infancy of this art, which is, (as far as we can tell), no more than seventy years old. Sometimes I am exceedingly pleased with the simplicity of the old song (I say candidly what touches my heart), when I contemplate the integrity of the olden days, and I ponder about the intellectuality of our tempered music. For theirs is blended with a marvelous dignity, a majesty which soothes the heart of man through his ears, more than the senseless babbling and the lascivious din.

Another group of examples belong to an adolescent art now beginning to grow up, which advanced to a higher stage of maturity in the fashion in which it was sung forty years ago. These are very pleasing examples, inasmuch as they are soothing, really comforting to the spirit. The third group belongs to an already perfected art. Since nothing may be added to it, nothing more advanced is to be expected from it, than the manner in which it has been sung for the past twenty-five years. Unfortunately, this art has now become so lascivious that the educated people have almost tired of the style. And there are many reasons for this, above all the following. Since we are ashamed to follow in the footsteps of our elders who observed the reasoning of the modes exactly, we have stumbled on a certain kind of confused singing which has no advantage, except for the fact that it is new.

17. The humanist poet Angelo Poliziano, whose real name was Angelo Ambrogini (1454–1494), was under the patronage of Lorenzo de Medici. In addition to writing his own works, Poliziano translated some of Homer and Plato into Latin.
18. Glareanus deliberately excluded some of the most familiar examples, such as Josquin's five-part *Stabat Mater Dolorosa*, which he cites as a "noble composition in the Ionian mode."
19. *Symphonetae* refers to composing in parts, in keeping with *symphonia*, consonance.

Example in the Ionian Mode by Josquin des Prez

7

The Musical Renaissance

7.1 NICOLA VICENTINO (1511–1572)

Nicola Vicentino sought to resurrect Greek musical thought in the Renaissance by insisting that the ancient diatonic, chromatic, and enharmonic genera should all be used in contemporary polyphonic composition. His persistence in this matter led him to a musical duel with Vincentio Lusitano.

Vicentino described this wager in his book, *Ancient Music Reduced to the Modern Practice* (1555). He not only related the ancient genera to vocal practice but also invented keyboard instruments with enough keys in the octave to accommodate the performance of music in any genus. Vicentino provided diagrams for an archicembalo with six keyboards and an octave divided into thirty-one pitches for this purpose.

A broadsheet distributed in Venice in 1561 contained the following description of a somewhat smaller instrument of this kind, also invented by Vicentino, the portable arciorgano.

On this instrument it is possible to play all sorts of songs and airs in accordance with the idiom natural to each nation of the world. That is, if the composer were to hear a Spaniard, a Frenchman, a Pole, an Englishman, a Turk, or even a Hebrew sing, because each nation in the world has a different pronunciation and variety of accent, he would write and compose his polyphonic compositions for four or more voices with a greater multiplicity of tones and intervals than one generally hears in music.[1]

Centuries before the production of microtones through electronic media, Vicentino envisaged keyboard instruments on which one could play the tones and microtones of any genus, in the hopes of accommodating the music of all people and dialects.

The Enharmonic Genus in the Renaissance:
A Musical Dispute*

I, Don Nicola, residing in Rome in the year 1551, was at a gathering at which there was singing and speculation about music, when there arose a sort of dispute between the Reverend Don Vincentio Lusitano and myself. Our principal discussion was as follows. The said Don Vincentio was of the opinion that the music that is sung nowadays is diatonic. And I, by way of dispute, responded that it is not diatonic alone, and that compositions, according to the current practice, are a mixture of the most ancient types: the chromatic genus, the enharmonic, and especially the diatonic genus—along with our diatonic genus. And not to take too long, and to give the substance of our dispute, I will omit most of the words which occurred in the dispute. In short, we bet two gold crowns, and together we chose two judges who would listen to our differences. And each of us agreed that there should be no appeal from the verdict.

One of the judges was the Reverend M. Bartholomeo Escobedo, priest of the Diocese of Segovia, and the other was M. Chisilino Danckers, cleric of the diocese of Liège, both singers in the chapel of His Holiness. And in the presence of the most illustrious and most reverend lord, Hyppolito II da Este, Cardinal of Ferrara, my lord and patron, with an audience of many scholars, we debated once. And then in the Chapel, in the presence of all the singers who were gathered that morning in the Chapel of His Holiness, both parties offered the reasons for their opinions to the judges, elected by us in the presence of many people, close to the above-mentioned singers. And in the presence of the most reverend and most illustrious Cardinal of Ferrara, my lord and patron, our differences were heard solely by a single judge, who was the priest, M. Bartholomeo Escobedo, because the other judge, M. Ghisilino, was detained by certain business of his own, and could not be present at that time. On the same day, therefore, I sent him a long letter, telling him how, in the presence of my most illustrious and most reverend patron, the Cardinal of Ferrara, I had proved to the said Don Vincentio that the music which is sung was not diatonic alone, as he had

---

* *Nicola Vicentino*, L'Antica Musica ridotta alla moderna prattica *(Rome, 1555)*, p. 95 f.

1. Henry W. Kaufmann, "Vicentino's Arciorgano; an Annotated Translation," *Journal of Music Theory* V, No. 2 (1961), 32–53, contains the original Italian for this quotation on pp. 36–37.

said, and that the said music was a mixture of the most ancient types: of the chromatic and enharmonic genera, and especially of the diatonic, with this very genus. I am not sure whether Don Vincentio was aware that I had written the above to the judge M. Ghisilino, but Don Vincentio also wrote to him. And after four or six days, the said judges were in agreement together, and passed the sentence against me, as everyone may see it signed here. And the judges requested that it be presented to the illustrious Cardinal of Ferrara, in my presence, by the hand of the aforesaid Don Vincentio. My most illustrious lord, after reading the sentence, told me that I was sentenced to paying him 2 gold *scudi* [2] and so, then and there, I paid him.

7.2 GIOVANNI PIERLUIGI DA PALESTRINA (c. 1525–1594) AND ORLANDO DI LASSUS (1530–1594)

Giovanni Pierluigi da Palestrina and Orlando di Lassus, two of the most skillful Renaissance composers, rarely give us the opportunity of penetrating their creative workshops.

However, in letters written to Duke Guglielmo Gonzaga in Mantua, Palestrina, who was then music director of the Seminary in Rome, does express some views verbally. In the letter of 1568 Palestrina shows concern for the clarity of the musical text, one of the musical goals set by the Council of Trent (1545–1563). In the letter of 1570 he makes significant pedagogical remarks aimed at correcting the compositional efforts of his royal pupil. Unfortunately, the Duke's madrigal and motet, which were composed in part-books, and the scores which Palestrina made from them for the purpose of constructive criticism, are both lost.

The Netherlander Lassus, a talented linguist, spent his literary efforts in chatty letters to Duke William of Bavaria. They defy translation into one language because of their intermixture of French, German, Italian, and Latin, whichever language momentarily pleases the writer. This composer of French chansons, German lieder, Italian madrigals, and Latin motets was truly an internationalist.

In 1559 Lassus composed his *Psalmi Davidis Poenitentiales* (Penitential Psalms of David). It is in the Latin preface to this work, written by Samuel à Quickelberg, that the famous reference to *musica reservata* as an expression of the affect of the text appears. Quickelberg was a physician in the court of Duke Albert of Munich, the patron who commissioned the Penitential Psalms. He wrote the Preface mainly to discuss the pictures illustrating the manuscript.

2. About 2 dollars.

Clarity of the Musical Text*

Palestrina's Letters to Duke Guglielmo Gonzaga in Mantua

February 2, 1568

Most illustrious and excellent, most respected Lord,

I am certain that my modest learning is not equal to the great desire which I have for serving your Excellency. Yet, it seemed to me more impudent and thoughtless to show you my inadequacy than to be discourteous by hiding it, since I was commissioned by so Excellent a lord, in the handwriting of such an exceptional virtuoso as M. Giacches [de Wert], to create this Mass, enclosed, which I did just as M. Aniballe Cappello instructed me.[3] If in this first attempt I have not satisfied the intellect of Your Excellency, may it please you to tell me how you want it, whether short or long, or so that the words are perceptible. I will try to serve you in accordance with my ability, all of which I will always devote to the service of Your Excellency.

March 3, 1570

Most excellent Lord and most attentive Master,

After having favored me with allowing me to hear Your Excellency's Motet and Madrigal, your virtuoso requested on your behalf that I freely offer my opinion. I say that, just as Your Excellency exalts nature in all your works, so in music you transcend those who worthily pursue the profession. And, in order to study it better, I scored [partito] the Motet.[4] And, having seen the beautiful workmanship, far from ordinary, and the lively spirit given to the words according to their meaning, I marked some passages which I think would sound better with less use of such harmonic progressions as: the sixth to the unison with the parts moving simultaneously; the sixth to the fifth ascending and descending in similar motion; some unisons which the imitations [fughe] [5] forcefully impose on the parts. Also, I think that, through the close texture of the imitations the words are obscured from the listeners, who do not enjoy them as in ordinary music. It is apparent that Your Excellency knows all these details better than I, but I have said this to obey you, and thus I shall always obey you when

* Knud Jeppesen, "Pierluigi da Palestrina, Herzog Guglielmo Gonzaga und die neugefundenen Mantovaner-Messen Palestrina's: Ein ergänzender Bericht," Acta Musicologica XXV, No. 4 (October-December, 1953), 147-148, 156-157.

3. Palestrina was commissioned to compose this Mass for the Church of Santa Barbara in Mantua. At the time Giaches de Wert (1535-1596) was the maestro di cappella both at this church and at the court of Mantua.
4. Part songs at this time were not yet printed in score form. However, this sentence furnishes early evidence that the composer or teacher might align the parts while in the act of creation or study.
5. For Tinctoris' definitions of fugue and canon, see the introduction to Section 6.5. In the Renaissance motet each successive phrase of the basic melody was treated imitatively through all the voices.

you do me the favor of commanding me, your affectionate and most obli-
gated servant.

Musica Reservata: Quickelberg's Preface to Lassus' *Penitential Psalms**

To the Viewers of the Pictures and the Readers of the Explanations:

The most illustrious Duke [Albert V] commissioned his most excellent
musician, Orlando de Lassus—our age has produced no one more outstanding
and delightful than he—to compose these Psalms for five principal voices.
Indeed, whenever he creates a work, he accommodates an expressive and
crooning tone to the subject and words, and fashions the import of the
individual affects so effectively, that it is as if he were placing the action
before our eyes. One cannot tell whether the sweetness of the affects is
decorating the expressive tones to a greater extent, or whether the expressive
tones are decorating the sweetness of the affects to a greater extent. Indeed,
in this kind of music, which is called *musica reservata*, Master Orlandus mar-
vellously reveals to posterity the durability of his genius, just as he does
in his other vocal works, which are almost innumerable. After these *Seven
Penitential Psalms* and the two other psalms on the *Laudate* text had been
composed by Orlando, they were esteemed to the greatest extent by the
most illustrious emperor, who alone among the rulers of our generation
rewards music by taking the trouble to have it inscribed on the finest
parchment and adorned with the most opulant pictures. In fact, as splendid
and opulent as the painting is, just as costly are the clasps and magnificent
gems that he ordered for the binding.

Bibliographical Note

Lassus' music, although mysteriously steeped in the contrapuntal artistry of the time, is forthright and expressive, with the intricate devices
concealed by the composer's musical genius. For example, in the 6th
Penitential Psalm, *De profundis* (*MSO*, Part 1, pp. 47–51), Lassus works
the Hypolydian cantus firmus through the various voices, which com-
positely produce the newer mode of G Ionian. In Verse 1 the cantus is
heard in Tenor II, starting on the reciting tone B. In Verse 2 there is a
Fuga in subdiapente, that is, a canon with the cantus firmus stated in the
Alto and resolved one measure later a 5th lower in Tenor II.

7.3 FRANCISCO SALINAS (1513–1590)

In their effort to account for the music of all humanity, for the people
of every country and every language, Renaissance musicians sought to
combine the Greek genera. Virdung superimposed the chromatic on the

---

Henri Florent Delmotte, Biographische Notiz über Roland de Lattre bekannt unter
den Namen Orland de Lassus *(Berlin: Gustav Crantz, 1837), pp. 28–29.*

diatonic, uniting them on one keyboard with twelve keys to the octave. Vicentino, hoping to include the enharmonic besides, split the tones even further, arriving at an unwieldy octave with thirty-one keys. Other musicians, seeking to condense rather than to proliferate the divisions within an octave, went in the direction of tempering to the point where two pitches a microtone apart might be fused into one. Gafurius, Aron, Zarlino, Praetorius, and Salinas, among others, developed systems of temperament involving equivalent pitches that could serve in more than a single capacity.[6]

In his book entitled *Concerning Music* the Spanish organist, Francisco Salinas, provides ratios not only for pitch but also for rhythm. For the rhythmic illustrations Salinas draws on Spanish folk song, thus establishing a source which would otherwise have been lost to posterity.

Concerning the Various Species of Trochaic Meter*

We speak now about the trochaic meters, of which there are as many species as the iambic, and almost the same types.[7] As among the poets, both pure and mixed types are allowed. The pure types are those which consist of trochees alone, or of tribrachs in their place, with the same number of beats, hand-claps, or strokes.[8] The mixed, however, also allow every sort of four-beat foot on even beats, just as the iambic does on odd beats. Yet, music loves only the pure, and those which are impure among the poets, should be sung as pure by the musicians. Furthermore, there is a certain great affinity between iambic and trochaic meters, for one is the offspring of the other. For the iamb is nothing but an inverted trochee and a trochee is likewise an inverted iamb, as disclosed above. Whence, if in front of a pure iamb you place a two-beat note, you produce a trochee. If, on the contrary, you take it away from the trochee, you return to the iamb, as in this iambic meter:

ᵕ – ᵕ – ᵕ – ᵕ

Celer phaselus ille.

If the syllable *Est* is placed in front, it becomes trochaic.

– ᵕ – ᵕ – ᵕ – ᵕ

Est celer phaselus ille.

And if the syllable *Est* is taken away, it becomes iambic again.

Francisco Salinas, De Musica (Salamanca: Mathias Gastius, 1577), Preface and pp. 304–306.
6. See J. Murray Barbour, *Tuning and Temperament, A Historical Survey* (East Lansing: Michigan State College Press, 1951; reprint New York, Da Capo Press, 1972), Chap. 3, Meantone Temperament.
7. The trochee is a foot with two syllables (long–short, accented–unaccented) or three beats. The iamb is a foot with two syllables (short–long, unaccented–accented) or three beats.
8. The tribrach consists of three short time values, two of which belong to the downbeat, and one to the upbeat.

This even appears in song. For the iambic is this:

Ce - ler   pha - se - lus   il - le

The trochaic is this:

Est   ce - ler   pha - se - lus   il - le.

And, on the contrary, every pure trochee that is composed likewise may receive a short syllable in front, turning it into iambic meter, as when you say,

Ad - est   ce - ler   pha - se - lus   il - le

Many songs among the Spaniards are found to be constructed in this kind of meter, such as this one:

Pen - so el mal   vil - la - no   Que   yo   que   dor - mi - a

To - mo es - pa - da en ma - no, Fuesse   an - dar   por   vi - la.

The following hymn seems to consist of this kind of meter, even though it is an outlawed meter:

Ave maris stella
Dei mater alma. [*LU 1*, p. 1254]

During the days of the octaves,[9] of the Feasts of the Blessed Virgin, in certain cathedral churches it is customary to compose songs to the following melody, or to one similar to it.

Yo   me   yua   mi   ma - dre   A   vi - la   re - a - le,

Er - ra - ra   yo el   ca - mi - no   En   fuer - te   lu - ga - re.

9. An octave is the eight-day celebration of a greater feast or holiday. It is interesting

7.4 ERYCIUS PUTEANUS (fl. c. 1595)

Abstract Renaissance musical thought culminated in the acceptance of an octave with seven syllables, and an eighth syllable identical with the first. Centuries before this system was recognized, the Spaniard Ramos de Pareja, in his *Musica practica* (Bologna, 1482), had proposed using the eight syllables of the words *psal-li-tur per vo-ces is-tas* (Let us sing through these tones).[10] Somewhat later the Belgian composer-theorist, Hubert Waelrant, who had studied with Willaert in Venice, started a school in Antwerp in 1547, where he taught the syllables as *bo, ce, di, ga, lo, ma, ni*. However, it remained for two men from the Netherlands, Simon Stevin and Erycius Puteanus, apparently working independently at the end of the sixteenth century, to identify the seventh syllable in accordance with the Guidonian names (see Section 4.9 and **Appendix I, Chart 2**).

After designating the tones as *ut, re, mi, fa, sol, la, si*, Stevin, a scientist, contended that it would be more convenient for the acoustician if all the half-steps were equal, with each semitone as the twelfth root of the octave ratio 2:1. He wanted to bypass working with the 3:2 ratio of the fifth, which leads to intervals with troublesome fractions that he assumed could not be differentiated by ear from the equally tempered intervals.

Puteanus, from Venloo, Upper Gelderland, further refined the solmization system by using the first syllable to refer to the starting tone of each successive octave. His homage to the Greeks is indicated in the title of the work, *Modulata Pallas* (Musical Athena), the word *Pallas* being an epithet of Athena, Greek goddess of artistic and intellectual genius. The subtitle, *Septem discrimina vocum ad harmonicae lectionis*, defines the substance, *Seven District Syllables for Harmonic Reading*.[11]

The decided advantage of the octave system over the hexachord system lies in doing away with the necessity for mutation or change from one interval of a sixth to another. Changing from one octave to another is

---

to note that this song has the range of an octave. *Penso el mal villano* and *Yo me yua mi madre* have Spanish texts, whereas the explanatory examples based on *Celer phaselus ille* (This fast light boat) and the *Ave maris stella* (sung on Feasts of the Blessed Virgin Mary) are in Latin, the latter being the language of Salinas' treatise as a whole.

10. The word *psallare*, to play or sing to the accompaniment of a stringed instrument, originally referred to the psaltery, an instrument with a series of strings stretched across a frame or sounding board (see Section 1.1, fn. 2).
11. The six Guidonian hexachord syllables were commonly known as the *voces musicales*. The book was published in Milan, where Puteanus settled as a professor.

infinitely preferable, because the outline of the octave constitutes the most perfect interval in nature.

Relationship and Number of Harmonic Notes*

In days gone by, under Emperor Henry II, Guido of Arezzo was among the first of his generation to introduce into the knowledge of music a method for singing with six syllabic notes. *Ut, re, mi, fa, sol, la,* are derived from the sacred hymn of St. John. . . . The six notes thus contrived are used extensively in musical progression up and down, but sluggishly and in a difficult manner. Do you notice the delay caused by the mutations, the confusion of keys, the substitution of tones? You see many people needlessly devoting a good lifetime to this art, and even accomplished ones progress poorly for years before reading in this manner. Obviously, difficulty obstructs and causes delay for many, with some completely rejecting the cycle and others encountering a lifetime of downfall. With only a slight divergence or change I will construct a course which will present the whole thing simply and without impediment. The intention is not to do something completely different, but rather to avoid the main pitfalls to smooth music. . . . To the complex of six notes in the *Pallas Modulata* I add another from the same hymn, namely, *bi. Solve polluti laBli reatum.* I use the following series: *ut, re, mi, fa, sol, la, bi.*

Close and Distant Positions; Comparison
of the Notes and Numbers

Now I will further demonstrate this *Palladem* of the voices. If you adapt my seven notes, *ut, re, mi, fa, sol, la, bi* correctly, you will accommodate every possible harmony [*concentus*] and read every possible melody, whether you want simple Aeolian, or complex Asian, or murmuring Lydian, or religious Phrygian, or bellicose Dorian. But, you say: most of the modulations are not confined to the limitations of these notes, but exceed them, and even extend higher than the human voice. They exceed, but not, however, without smooth utterance. They exceed by producing tone, not by forsaking it. For just as in the numbers from 1 to 10, when the first of the groups has reached its limit, we go on duplicating and joining them to infinity; likewise, in these groupings in our harmonic reading, after any seven initial tones, they are simply repeated, with the first after any seventh note. And thus in succession the second note (of the tones in any register) agrees with the ninth, the third with the tenth, the fourth with the eleventh, the fifth with the twelfth, the sixth with the thirteenth, the seventh with the fourteenth, etc. If words fail to shed light, try using your ears in an experiment on any musical instrument. I furnish the example on the following page, citing it as evident proof for your eyes. Also, if desired, you may go further.

*Erycius Puteanus, Modulata Pallas, sive Septem discrimina vocum ad harmonicae lectionis (Milan: Pontianos, 1599), Chap. 8, 12, 16, 17.

Numbers	Tones	Notes
16	2	re
15	1	ut
14	7	bi
13	6	la
12	5	sol
11	4	fa
10	3	mi
9	2	re
8	1	ut
7	7	bi
6	6	la
5	5	sol
4	4	fa
3	3	mi
2	2	re
1	1	ut

There are three classes, namely, numbers, tones, and notes. In the notes and tones I notice a twofold arrangement, tension and relaxation. I raise one tone and lower another, because, in order to proceed correctly, any director or master of sound makes preparation beforehand and conducts softly. Although I increased the numbers, they are the conventional ones familiar to us.

Transition to Letters: What Each Note Is Called; on What Line or Space It Appears

Concerning the number and names of the notes enough has been said. I increase the letters by which the notes are identified on the writing tablet [*tabella*] to these seven: A, B, C, D, E, F, G. Today the notes are still named by our musicians in even number and are practiced in uneven number. They are still named according to the six conventional syllables. Yet, for a long time I have clearly demonstrated how they may be named according to seven, not by lengthening the series, but rather by using a cycle similar to that of our calendar or something like it.[12] Actual acceptance of this has been proved again and again. Thus, in letters I consider two factors: how each note is designated, and on what line or space it appears. First I distinguish two harmonic types: the old, which is the only one I find identified in musical use, and the new which has been reconstructed here. They are differentiated on the basis of whether or not the letter B designates a semitone. In the F hexachord (the *mollis*, with b♭), A corresponds to *mi*, B♭ to *fa*, C to *sol*, D to *la*, E to *bi*, F to *ut*, G to *re*. In the G hexachord (the *durum*, with b♮), A stands for *la*, B for *bi*, C for *ut*, D for *re*, E for *mi*, F for *fa*, G for *sol*. The varied placement of the semitone

---

12. In the church calendar the seven letters A through G are used to designate the seven days of the week.

creates the difference in genus. Musicians construct the following patterns:
For the old genus:

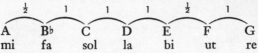

For the new genus: [13]

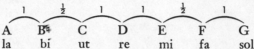

The diligent reader will consider this most attentively, and will apply it advantageously to musical intervals.

Explanation of Notes in the Table of Invention

Concerning the line or space where the clef lies, I say briefly and clearly, and I repeat thoughtfully, that harmony as a whole is defined through the tones, and the tones become recognizable through the notes. There are characteristic letters for the notes, of which four are basic, namely, B, C, F, and G.[14] These are not bound together, but are used singly or are paired at the beginning of a line. In what appearance or form? The form descended from our ancestors is barbaric and almost unknown; the current form is kept alive by the use of writing. For example, C is written any place on the staff for the low, middle, and high notes, in each of two ways, on the first, second, third, and fourth lines.

Similarly, F is used solely for the low notes, in each of two ways, on the third and fourth lines.

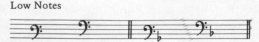

Analagously, G, whose true form is solely for the high voice, appears on the second line, in each of two ways, thus:

13. The pattern of whole and half steps in Puteanus' old genus is the Phrygian mode with its minor second, third, sixth, and seventh. The new genus is the pure minor mode with minor third, sixth, and seventh.
14. Included among Puteanus' characteristic letters are the clefs C, F, and G, and the signature b, which stood for bb.

Finally—occasionally B♭ is written as a reminder to us, without any concealment or mask. But this is done solely in the old style, for which it is a suitable sign. It appears on all lines and spaces, but always with a clef before it, as shown by the illustrations.[15]

You realize that the remaining letters are not noted in the same way as these four. From the letter shown, you know whether to ascend according to the seven letters of the alphabet already enumerated, and besides this, whether to descend, to go in crab [16] and in contrary motion. But the motion is by step, from line to space, from space to line, and thus in succession. If you leap or cross over, the whole progression becomes confused. I will now present an example for your further consideration.

In this example you see many notes known to you, but known through letters. You read them one by one in ascending order from C, just like the scale.[17] The names of the notes in the opposite order are:

C	B	A	G	F	E	D	C
ut	bi	la	sol	fa	mi	re	ut

And in this way you relate all the remaining letters one by one, through letters to notes, through notes to tones, which is the summit of harmonic reading.

7.5 GIOSEFFO ZARLINO (1517–1590)

Gioseffo Zarlino was well equipped for the role he played as investigator, innovator, and moderator of Renaissance musical thought. He was born in Chioggia, Italy, where he studied philosophy, astronomy, mathematics, chemistry, Greek, and Hebrew. During his twenties he moved to Venice, where he decided to pursue his childhood inclination toward music. There he studied with Adrian Willaert (1490–1562), the famous Flemish composer who was then maestro di cappella at St. Mark's Cathedral. Zarlino himself held this post after Willaert was succeeded by another of his students, Cipriano de Rore (1516–1565).

In his writings concerning abstract music without words, Zarlino thinks of the subject of a composition in two ways, either as a basic melodic line running through the entire work like a cantus firmus or as a composite exposition of a theme occurring in all the voices simultaneously. He pro-

15. In the old hexachord system a flat indicated the semitone, *mi-fa*. In the new system a note may be flatted without reference to its position in a hexachord.
16. Crab motion is a melody read backwards.

17. This scale is the major mode, 11½ 111½.

vides examples of both of these types of *subject*—the independent, self-contained bass line and the exposition suitable for further invention or fantasy—in the third edition of his *Harmonic Foundations* (Le Istitutioni Harmoniche, 1573). Some of these examples did not appear in the original version published in 1558. They are all the more important since there are few compositions by Zarlino extant, other than those in his theoretical works.

Zarlino carried on the Venetian musical tradition, viewing the organization of tone both as an abstract expression of the modes, and as an adjunct to the words. However, for Zarlino the music itself was the main consideration, because the musician works with materials divergent from those of the orator, and even further removed from those of the actor. When he discussed the effect of words on music, Zarlino found himself at odds with one of his own pupils, Vincenzo Galilei, who wanted the composer to follow the precepts of the tragedian.

Vincenzo Galilei (1520–1591) was the father of the famous astronomer, Galileo. Vincenzo, an advocate of Greek musical thought, played the lute and violin well. He and other prominent artists met at the home of Count Bardi to explore the possibility of imitating Greek dramatic declamation in music for a solo voice with accompaniment. Galilei and other members of the Bardi Camerata, such as Peri and Caccini (Section 8.1), listened to each other's compositions in this rather simple style, known as monody in contrast to more complicated contrapuntal composition.

A literary duel ensued, starting with Zarlino's contention in the *Istitutioni*, followed by Galileo's attack in the *Dialogo della musica antica e della moderna* (Venice, 1581), and Zarlino's counterattack in the *Supplimenti musicali* (Venice, 1588). Zarlino claimed that exaggerated imitation is caricature, while Galilei urged the musicians to take a lesson from the actors performing in tragedies and comedies. There lay the essence of the struggle which culminated in the emergence of opera in Italy at the beginning of the 17th century.

Good Counterpoint: Le Istitutioni Harmoniche*

Now I will discuss counterpoint. But before I begin this discussion, one must realize that many conditions exist in every good counterpoint, or in every other type of good composition. If one of these is missing, one would say that it is imperfect. The first factor is the subject, without which nothing can be done, for, as the agent always pays attention to the outcome in each

*Gioseffo Zarlino, Le Istitutioni Harmoniche *(Venice: Senese, 1573), Part III*, Chaps. 26, 63.

of his transactions, and bases his work on some material which we call the subject, so the musician pays attention to the outcome of his work. What inspires him to work is found in the material, or subject, on which he happens to base his composition, and then he proceeds to bring his work to perfection, according to the goal proposed. . . .

The second condition is that the counterpoint should be composed principally of consonances; and it should have many subsidiary dissonances.

The third condition is that the parts of the cantilena should proceed well, that is, the modulations should proceed through true and legitimate intervals which arise from the sonorous numbers, so that by their means the use of good harmonies is acquired.[18]

The fourth condition that exists is that the modulations and the concert be varied, because harmony arises from nothing but a diversity of modulations and from a diversity of consonances placed together with variety.

The fifth condition is that the cantilena be organized by a prescribed and determined harmony, or mode [*modo*], or tone [*tuono*], as we say, and that it not be disorganized.

And the sixth and final condition (besides others that might be added) is that the harmony contained in it should be accommodated to the text, that is, to the words, so that with cheerful material the harmony should not be plaintive, and on the contrary, with plaintive material the harmony should not be cheerful. . . .

The subject of each musical composition means the part from which the composer derives his invention [*inventione*] to create the other parts of the *cantilena*, as many as desired.[19] And the subject may exist in many ways.

First, it may be an invention proper, which the composer had discovered by himself. Then it may be what he borrowed from other compositions, accommodating it to his own cantilena, and decorating it with various parts and various modulations, as he pleases, according to the loftiness of his own ingenuity. And such a subject may be discovered in two ways. Either

18. The *senario*, or six sonorous numbers, 1 through 6, play a large role in Zarlino's teaching. Their ratios may be compared with the harmonic series (see Chart 3). To show the basis for the authentic and plagal modes, Zarlino divided the octave as follows (*Istitutioni*, Book 4, Chap. 9):

He also divided the fifth, placing a major third below for a gay harmony, and above for a sad harmony (*Istitutioni*, Book 3, Chap. 31):

19. The concept of the subject as the basis of musical invention is implicit in the title of J. S. Bach's two-part *Inventions*.

it may be a tenor, or any other part of a cantilena he chooses, from a *cantus firmus* or from a *cantus figuratus*.[20] Or it may be two or more parts with one following the other as in *fuga* [subject] and *consequenze* [answer],[21] or in some other way. The variety of such types of subject is infinite.

After a composer has the subject, he creates the other parts in a way that we shall see. Working in such a manner is called composing, or, according to our practice, creating a counterpoint. But when he does not start by inventing a subject, the part which first appears, or that with which the composer begins his cantilena, whether a low part, a high note, or in the middle, always constitutes the subject. To this he then fits the other parts as subject and answer, or in any other way that pleases him, accommodating the harmonies to the words in accordance with their content. When the composer proceeds by deriving the subject from the parts of the cantilena, that is, when he derives one part from another, creating the composition as he goes along, that section which he presents before the others, on which he will then compose the remainder of his composition, should be called the subject. And such a way of composing is referred to by those who practice it as "composing by fantasy." It may also be called "contrapuntalizing," or "making a counterpoint," as one wishes.

Counterpoint for Three Voices Composed at Sight [a mente]

Example 1. The consequent follows the guide a fifth above, after a half-note rest[22]

20. Zarlino distinguishes between two types of pre-existing melody—the simple, unadorned *cantus firmus* with notes all of equal value, and the more ornate *cantus figuratus* with notes of diverse time values. The pre-existing melody occurs in the *cantilena*, a vocal composition for several voice parts.
21. Essentially the two main types are (Example 1) a cantus firmus (*soggetto*) to which other contrapuntal parts are added, or (Example 2) a statement of the theme (*fuga*) with its imitation (*consequenza*). For the term *fuga* see Tinctoris, Section 6.5.
22. The *soggetto* for this counterpoint is the hymn, *Veni creator spiritus* (*LU 1*,

tes   tu - o - rum   vi -

si - ta,   Im - ple

su - per - na

gra - ti - a;   Quae

tu   cre - as -

p. 885). Where the imitation is strict, what we would now call canon, several voices could be read at sight from one part. In a fantasy, however, where the imitation was not strict throughout, the composer would have to write out all the parts to express his intention.

- - ti   pec - - - to - - ra.

Example 2. Double consequent at the fifth below and at the octave above, with a whole-note rest

Imitation in Composing and Reciting Music or Melody [Melopeia]

Imitation or gesture [*attione*, action] is not a matter of little importance, either in poetry, as in the teaching of Aristotle, or in music.[23] On the contrary, it is one of the principal constituents that the poet and the musician must have, since in the principle of poetry itself, they say that imitations are commonly found in the epic, the tragedy, the comedy, in dithyrambic poetry, and likewise in the greater part of the art which serves in the practice of the tibia or pipe and of the cittern [*cetera*, zither, lute]. . . .

One may laugh at the scant accuracy of the musicians and composers of our time in imitation. We strongly recommend that they learn how to imitate so that they do not receive praise for writing something like this: [24]

When for recreation the modern practicing musicians go to the tragedies and comedies which the zanies recite, sometimes let them quit their unrestrained laughter, and for a change let them observe, please, the style of utterance, the manner of voice, approximately how high or low, the quality of sound, and the quantity, the kinds of accents and gestures, the amount of speed or delay of motion with which one placid gentleman converses with another. Let them notice somewhat, the diversity occurring in various situations, as when someone speaks to one of his servants, or when the latter speak among themselves; let them observe the prince when he happens to be talking to one of his subjects and vassals, or to the suppliant pleading for himself; also, the infuriated or agitated man, the married woman, the young girl, the unpretentious child, the cunning harlot, the enamored speaking to the woman he loves, preparing her for his desires, those who lament, those who cry aloud, the timid man, and the man exulting joyfully. After observing these diverse situations intently, and considering them carefully, they will be able to conceive of names suitable for the expression of any other ideas on which they would like to try their hand.

O, fine talk truly worthy of the great man he thinks he is! From it we may well conclude that he wishes, in fact, to greatly reduce the dignity and reputation of music. He urges us to go to hear the zanies in the comedies and tragedies and to become completely transformed into actors and buffoons. But what has the musician to do with those who recite tragedy or comedy? . . .

Now, excluding the zanies, the zanninies, and the zannolies from song, let us discuss the matter of how one should speak of an imitation made by

---

* Sopplimenti Musicali (*Venice, 1588*), *II, 316–320.*

23. Here Zarlino is comparing musical imitation to Greek poetic imitation (see Aristotle on imitation, Section 2.3) The Renaissance musician had even fewer fragments of actual Greek music before him than we have today.

24. This quotation is from Vincenzo Galilei's *Dialogo della musica antica e della moderna* (Venice, 1581).

means of music. . . . It is what is called *Melopeia* [25] exclusively by the musicians; that is to say, the invention [*fattione*], fabrication [*fabrica*], or construction [*fattura*] of song. *Melopeia* does not go beyond the consideration of things dealing with such matters as the arrangement of sounds and tones. In this way the modern musician need consider only the harmony, which he admits belongs to the art, imitating with sounds and voices those words which he wishes to express in song. . . .

Perhaps the reason why he will see and should know that the recitation of their compositions cannot be clothed in the person of the poet reciting his poetry, nor in that of the orator reciting his oration, is that in reciting to the sound of the lyre, while using some sort of harmony which is required by the quality of the poem, he cannot use those actions which the orator uses in his snarling utterances. The latter, steeped in his importance, can use these imitations which are necessary for the expression of the material well and admirably in about half of the actions. Not only is the quality of the voices and words enhanced by them, but also the gestures of the body are accompanied with movements appropriate and suited to such a situation. These accompany the words in a way which is good, because they are very influential in moving the spirit of the listeners and in turning the opinions of the judges in every case. . . . But musicians do not have need of similar actions. It is sufficient for them to have only those imitations which may be produced with the voice and heard with the sense. These are necessary so that their compositions may not be deficient in properties which they can imitate. But they can do this neither in the guise of poets nor in that of orators. Although they contrive to represent these things in their compositions in the manner in which they were then expressed, some of these imitations seem strange and awkward, are unsuited to breathing properly, and have no rapport with good harmony. These should not be attributed to art, but to artifice, with little skill and little expertise in such matters, like an orator with little aptitude for speaking with dignity when he is deficient in the deportment mentioned above. Yet, our modern critics criticize the breathing which they can neither execute nor understand.

However, composers should not refrain on this account from trying to use means suitable for exploring the subject, with as much grace and serious intent as possible. And it would not be unsuitable or erroneous, something which those with little instruction do not understand. I need not mention the orator who is allowed to adjust his recitation according to the material he discusses. Sometimes he uses a high and horrible voice, shouting and screaming, to express his intention. And when he speaks of matters which he wishes to inure with fright and terror, sometimes he uses a low and deep voice. When he wants to express pity, a subject not unusual for the musician, he uses equivalent actions, reciting his compositions up high and down low, now in a shrill voice, now in a deep voice. Perhaps our learned men will say that singing is a different matter from orating or growling, and that using these means is not more becoming to the musician in singing than to the orator in his oration. These means are becoming: I too have already said this above. But I do not say that the singer ought either to shriek or to shout while singing, because these things have neither proportion nor propriety.

25. *Melopeia or Melopoeia*, a combination of the Greek *melos* (song) and *poiein* (to make), means "the art of inventing melody."

Yet, I do say that he is allowed to use the actions which are granted to the reciters of tragedy and comedy while reciting. These, if good to the breath, do not conflict with the other actions, but speak separately and by themselves express some of their thoughts. It should not be necessary for anyone to hear these actions; it is as if they are spoken in secret. On the other hand, the performer is allowed some realism [*verisimile*], so that the spectators, those who are far from the scene, as well as those who are close by, may hear what is said to the extent of understanding the thing perfectly. Since there are those who may say that only true imitation should be allowed, it should be mentioned that some do speak in the scene by themselves, without wishing to be heard by any of the others. It does seem unsuitable, as indeed it is, for the actor to speak in a high voice as if he were speaking to a deaf person, all the more so because the person who is supposed to hear him is not more than two steps away from him. Just as the reciter is allowed to do this for the convenience of the listeners, so the singer should also be allowed some actions in singing, while adhering to the strictness of imitation, the convention nobody should be able to bypass. And perhaps every art and every science is called less imperfect when the fewest things are missing. Modern musicians know, with regard to inspiration of this kind, that in imitation with harmony and with movements that are truly realistic, the action inherent in verbal subjects is missing. They wanted to add this sort of imitation to their art to show how much artificiality they can use in their compositions. But if in their singing, the singers want to use those actions that the zanies use while reciting comedy, I do not know how those who hear and see them will be able to refrain from laughing.

7.6 GIOVANNI MARIA ARTUSI (1540–1613)

A student of Zarlino, Giovanni Maria Artusi, in his treatise entitled *On the Imperfections of Modern Music* (1600), is first concerned with performance practice. He deals with the balance between voices and instruments, the effect of the instrumentation, and how to tune an orchestra. In the second part of the work, on contrapuntal technique, he demands that dissonance be prepared and resolved properly, even if the meaning of the words suggests special treatment to the composer. Unfortunately for Artusi, he directed these less penetrating comments toward attacking Monteverdi's use of dissonance, thus initiating a dispute which propelled Monteverdi into a new musical practice (see Section 8.3).

The setting for Artusi's informative discussion of performance is Ferrara, at a celebration honoring a double marriage—that of Philip III of Spain, of the Habsburg line, to Margaret of Austria, and that of Philip's sister, Isabella, to Albert of Austria. The dialogue is between two fictitious gentlemen, Signor Vario and Signor Luca, who became acquainted there.

A Well Unified Concert*

Toward the end of the year 1598, Her Royal Highness, Queen Margaret of Austria arrived at the noble city of Ferrara. . . . accompanied by princes, titled noblemen, ambassadors, duchesses, princesses, and noblewomen. Her Majesty and escort went to the Convent of the Holy Nuns, who were more than one hundred in number. Finally, after visiting many public halls and special rooms which gave Her Majesty great satisfaction, she arrived at the room usually designated and reserved for concerts. After everyone was quiet, cornetts,[26] trombones, violins, viole bastarde,[27] double harps, lutes, cornamuse,[28] flutes, harpsichords, and voices were all heard at the same time with such sweetness and delicacy of harmony, that the place seemed like Mt. Parnassus or Paradise itself, not like anything human. At the end of the concert there was an incredible silence, while the rare harmony lingered in the ears of the auditors. Signor Vario was so impressed that he said to Signor Luca, "It has been many months and years since I heard such a concert, in which everything is as well unified as in this one. Here one perceives an extraordinary proficiency and excellence on the part of women. But why do I speak of women alone? In my opinion most of the people of Italy could not have given me as much satisfaction, nor could they have done more than what was done by these nuns. My opinion will be clear if we examine point by point the factors contributing to a well unified concert, noticing improvement both in the perfection of the art and of the performing artists.

"Let us begin with the place as one of the principal factors, because without it nothing could be done. The proportions on which it is built must be such that the place is resonant in relation to the most distant parts, whether they be vocal or instrumental. . . .

"Secondly, we must consider the choice of compositions. We want them to be arranged according to the nature of the instruments and of the voices which enter into the concert, so that the melodies are distributed between the voices and instruments in correct proportion. I wish to say that there is no need for the parts to ascend or descend to the high and low notes to a greater extent than what is allowed by nature and the property of each instrument, natural and artificial. If they stay in their own ranges, the concert is more unified and more gratifying to the listeners.

"In the third place, there should be the proper distance between the performers and the listeners. Without doubt the distance of these holy nuns, whether they are further away or closer to the place where the harmony is heard by the listeners, makes a great difference. . . .

"In the fourth place, we say that not all instruments are good for such concerts. The instruments made by excellent artisans, not those which are ill-proportioned, should be chosen. Furthermore, they should be excellently constructed, so that they have sonority, not muteness, in the low

---

*Giovanni Maria Artusi of Bologna, L'Artusi overo Delle Imperfettioni della Moderna Musica (Venice: Giacomo Vincenti, 1600), pp. 1–4, 13.

26. The cornett was a wind instrument, usually made of wood, sometimes slightly curved in length and octagonal laterally, with a cup-shaped mouthpiece.

27. The viola bastarda, or lyra viol, between the bass and tenor viols in size, had six strings tuned in fifths and fourths.

28. The cornamuse was a double-reed instrument with cylindrical bore.

notes, and do not render the sounds dull or dim. Likewise, the high notes should be vivacious [*vivace*] and cheerful [*allegro*],[29] and there should be corresponding parity in the middle and low notes.

"In the fifth place, any person who has to perform either with the voice or on an instrument, should perform more with the ear than with the voice or instrument."

LUCA: Do you mean that the ear, which has neither hand nor voice, should perform? Or do you wish to infer that there is something good about the ear?

VARIO: I wish to say that it is necessary for one person to listen to another and, by listening, they can decide whether or not the companion is succeeding either in singing or in playing an instrument. In this way equality of voice and of sounds are achieved in such a sweet manner that the listeners derive infinite pleasure.

LUCA: Now I understand you. This is one of the warnings: it is not only reasonable but necessary, by all means, that the singers and players listen to each other, since it would be rather distorted if one sang with a powerful, strong and sonorous voice, and the other with a sweet, tender voice, weaker than the first. . . .

VARIO: Now I want to tell you about music that is distorted or, as we might say, disparate. I will describe an ensemble of two instruments, of which one has a rather large and robust body and the sound of the cornett; and the other is of common size and medium volume, gentle in nature. The former is predominant and does not blend. The latter, being by nature weak rather than vigorous, sounds very charming and graceful, and the listeners are extremely fond of it. Both are heard in any of the famous cities where concerts with various instruments are given, but sometimes with so much displeasure and lack of satisfaction to the listeners, that the style is more annoying than pleasant.

"In the sixth place you ought to bring into consideration the choice of compositions for the concert. I am speaking of what goes into good and excellent workmanship. I wish to say that it is not enough for the instruments to be in proper balance with the voices. The compositions themselves must be the result of practical experience, as are those of Sig. Claudio [Monteverdi], Costanzo Porta, Andrea Gabrieli, Giovanni Palestrina, Giovanni Giacomo Gastoldi, Benedetto Pallavicino, Ruggiero Giovanelli, Giovanni Maria Nanino, and others who are and have been excellent.[30]

"In the seventh place, after all the aforementioned things are prepared,

29. The words *vivace* and *allegro*, here associated with the upper register, soon were to become terms commonly used as tempo designations.

30. Costanzo Porta (c. 1529–1601), a pupil of Willaert active in Padua, wrote madrigals, motets, masses, and other contrapuntal choral works.

Andrea Gabrieli (c. 1520–1586), also a pupil of Willaert, wrote vocal compositions as well as instrumental ricercari, fantasias, canzoni, and organ intonazioni.

Giovanni Maria Nanino (1545–1607), a student of Palestrina, was the first Italian to establish a public music school in Rome. Palestrina taught there.

it is necessary that the performers have some parts which are suitable for them, as one may notice among these nuns. Those who are experienced on the trombone know how to adapt themselves to other instruments. However, they do not merely forsake this part for that, but they use the instrument on which, through long practice and natural inclination, they are excellent. They do not neglect proper instinct and natural choice, for example, by choosing the lute or double harp when they know how to play on other instruments more skilfully. Instead they pay attention to those toward which nature has given them particular inclination, and on which they have practiced long and assiduously. Likewise, they sing the parts which suit their disposition. They sing in such a beautiful fashion, decorated with so many beautiful passages, that the listener is completely captivated. The opposite effect occurs if instead of singing the part that is suitable for her by nature, she sings something unsuitable, going either too far into the low notes or too high. Whence, in all respects one may conclude that this is the most excellent, unified and well proportioned musical group in all of Italy."

LUCA: This conclusion pleases me. I concur in your thoughtful opinion.

Tuning and Temperament

VARIO: There is yet another consideration, the eighth, of great importance, perhaps greater than any other. . . . It is worthy of being noted specifically. All the instruments of this concert are reduced to the temperament of a single ear. One of the nuns is designated to make sure that every instrument, namely, the viols, violins, double harps, lutes, harpsichords, and the viole bastarde are all in tune with the other instruments entering into this concert.

LUCA: Are you telling me that two or three talented people do not know enough about tuning to reduce many instruments to a single, well unified temperament!

VARIO: They may know how to tune, but not as if they were one. The reason is that there is not just one sense of hearing, but many. Sometimes the sense of hearing in one person is quite different from that in another. It is not possible to tune with several ears to such a degree of excellence as with one alone. Thus Quintilianus [Section 2.5] states this proposition: "The sounds of the strings cannot be determined by just any ear whatsoever." And Aristoxenus [Section 2.4], the most excellent musician of his time, said that it was necessary to have a sense, not always the same in all men, which is perfectly accustomed either to remaining steadily on a certain spot, or capable of moving. However, at the same time one must know the differences between the tones, their construction, whether consonant or dissonant, and all those things which together or separately belong to this faculty. And Gaudentius [Section 2.6], in the beginning of his introduction to music, begs all those who are unrefined and coarse, who do not have an ear accustomed to harmony, to refrain and stay away from those who are excellent in this and can recognize both repetition and motion.

I therefore conclude that a single ear, accustomed to the recognition of similar treatment, would be more secure than many. That is why one single nun has the burden of tempering and uniting these instruments together. This by no means minimizes her great skill and utmost perception in the art.

LUCA: Now I understand that it is necessary to assemble the parts well in the body of the concert, so that it is well unified, with all the parts related to each other, one above the other, with the human voices appearing in the same equal relationship to the instruments, as well as other details which occur in similar concerts.

Tonguing

VARIO: Next I want to tell you how to discern intelligently the discourse of the parts from which sonatas are produced, the pleasure which it gives, the beautiful manner of performing the tirate, how to give vivacity to the passaggi,[31] how to play good instruments, such as those which sound like cornetti, cornamuse, and bent pipes, how to tongue well, and how to reinforce the nature of the instrument in any part. . . .

LUCA: Would you please tell me about a term that applies to wind instruments?

VARIO: What is it? Tell me because I would like to satisfy you.

LUCA: I would like to know how to tongue well.

VARIO: Some instrumentalists say that the tongue is more important in the practice of playing the cornett effectively and beautifully than anything else. It may rival all else as the most important means of producing the sound. Therefore it is necessary to know that there are three principal tonguings. The first principal tonguing is called *Rinversa* and is the main one of the three because it is related to the *gorgia* [throat]. Some call it "the tonguing of the *gorgia*." It goes as fast as possible and is difficult to control. You beat the tongue directly on the palate in three ways. The first, *ler, ler, ler*, is sweet and gentle. The second, *der, ler, der, ler, der, ler*, is moderate. The third, which is rougher than the others, is produced by *ter, ler, ter, ler, ter, ler*.

The second principal tonguing is a beating near the teeth. It is produced with *tere, tere, tere*. This is highly praised by instrumentalists, and is good for the small time values like eighth notes, and sixteenth notes, since it is easy to control.

The third principal tonguing is beat on the palate near the teeth and is by nature crude. It is produced by *teche, teche, teche*. It is good for those

31. For definitions of the *tirate* and *passaggi* see Praetorius, Section 7.8.

who wish to invoke astonishment, and to do more than is needed. This tonguing is not pleasing to the ear, but rather offends it. By nature it is rather fast and difficult to produce.

There are many others, one of which is produced at the teeth *te, te, te,* and serves the instrumentalist for the production of notes up to the value of the eighth note. Another is produced *de, de, de,* and is not very fast, but rather somewhat slower. Although all of these are possible, the first three are the principle tonguings and those which are practiced and adopted by good masters.

7.7 WILLIAM BYRD (1543–1623)
AND THOMAS MORLEY (1557–1602)

In the English Renaissance vocal and instrumental music both received a strong impetus from the composer William Byrd and his equally famous pupil, Thomas Morley. The popularity of singing, which pointed the way toward the English interest in works for large chorus, was encouraged by Byrd in the introduction to his *Psalms, Sonnets, and Songs of Sadness and Piety* (1588). Morley described the various types of instrumental composition current at the time in *A Plain and Easy Introduction to Practical Music* (1597), a book dedicated to Byrd.

Reasons Briefly Set Down by the Author,
to Persuade Everyone to Learn to Sing: Byrd*

First, it is a knowledge easily taught, and quickly learned, where there is a good master, and an apt scholar.

2. The exercise of singing is delightful to nature, and good to preserve the health of man.

3. It strengthens all parts of the breast, and opens the pipes.

4. It is a singularly good remedy for a stuttering and stammering in the speech.

5. It is the best means to procure a perfect pronunciation, and to make a good orator.

6. It is the only way to know where nature has bestowed the benefit of a good voice; which gift is so rare, as there is not one among a thousand that has it. And in many that excellent gift is lost, because they want art to express nature.

*William Byrd, Psalmes, Sonets, & Songs, a manuscript in the British Museum, has been transcribed and edited by Edmund H. Fellowes in The Collected Vocal Works of William Byrd (London: Stainer & Bell Ltd., 1948), Vol. XII. [The quotations here have been transcribed into modern English.]

7. For instruments there is no music whatsoever, comparable to that which is made for the voices of men, where the voices are good, and the same, well sorted and ordered.

8. The better the voice is, the more fitting it is to honor and serve God therewith. And the voice of man is chiefly to be employed to that end. *Omnis spiritus laudet Dominum.*

> Since singing is so good a thing,
> I wish all men would learn to sing.

Instrumental Music: Morley*

The most principal and chiefest kind of music which is made without a ditty is the *fantasy*, that is, when a musician takes a point at his pleasure and wrests and turns it as he likes, making either much or little of it according as shall seem best in his own conceit. In this may more art be shown than in any other music, because the composer is tied to nothing, but that he may add, diminish, and alter at his pleasure. And this kind will bear any allowances whatsoever tolerable in other music, except changing the air and leaving the key, which in *fantasy* may never be suffered. Other things you may use at your pleasure, such as bindings [suspensions] with discords, quick motions, slow motions, proportions, and what you like. This kind of music is, with those who practise instruments of parts, in greatest use, but for voices it is but seldom used.

The next in gravity and goodness unto this is called a *pavan*, a kind of staid music ordained for grave dancing, and most commonly made of three strains, whereof every strain is played or sung twice. A strain they make to contain eight, twelve, or sixteen semibreves, as they like, yet fewer than eight I have not seen in any pavan. In this you may not so much insist in following the point as in a fantasy, but it shall be enough to touch it once and so away to some close. Also in this you must cast your music by four, so that if you keep that rule it is no matter how many fours you put in your strain, for it will fall out well enough in the end, the art of dancing being come to that perfection that every reasonable dancer will make measure of no measure, so that it is no great matter of what number you make your strain.

After every *pavan* we usually set a *galliard* (that is a kind of music made out of the other), causing it to go by a measure which the learned call *trochaicam rationem*, consisting of a long and short stroke successively, for as the foot *trochaeus* consists of one syllable of two times and another of one time, so is the first of these two strokes double to the latter, the first being in time of a semibreve and the latter of a minim. This is a lighter and more stirring kind of dancing than the pavan, consisting of the same number of

---

A Plaine and Easie Introduction to Practicall Musicke. By Thomas Morley, Batcheler of musick, & one of the gentlemen of his Maiesties Royall Chappell. To the most excellent Musician Maister William Birde one of the gentlemen of her Maiesties Chappell (London: Peter Short, 1597), Part III, pp. 179–182.

strains. And look how many fours of semibreves you put in the strain of your pavan, so many times six minims must you put in the strain of your galliard.[32] The Italians make their galliards (which they term *saltarelli*) plain, and frame ditties to them, which in their masquerades they sing and dance, and many times without any instruments at all, but instead of instruments they have courtesans disguised in men's apparel, who sing and dance to their own songs.

The *alman* is a heavier dance than this (fitly representing the nature of the people whose name it carries) so that no extraordinary motions are used in dancing it. It is made of strains, sometimes two, sometimes three, and every strain is made by four. But you must mark that the four of the pavan measure is in dupla proportion to the four of the alman measure, so that as the usual pavan contains in a strain the time of sixteen semibreves, so the usual alman contains the time of eight, and most commonly in short notes.

Like unto this is the French *branle* (which they call *branle simple*) which goes somewhat rounder in time than this, otherwise the measure is all one. The *branle de Poictou* or *branle double* is quicker in time (as being in a round tripla) but the strain is longer, containing most usually twelve whole strokes.

Like unto this (but more light) are the *voltes* and *courantes* which, being both of a measure, are, notwithstanding, danced after sundry fashions, the volte rising and leaping, the courante traversing and running, in which measure also our *country dance* is made, though it be danced after another form than any of the former. All these are made in strains, either two or three, as shall seem best to the maker, but the courante has twice as many in a strain as the English country dance.

There are also many other kinds of dances, such as *hornpipes, jigs,* and infinite more. . . . And as there are different kinds of music, so will some men's humors be more inclined to one kind than to another. Some will be good descanters and excel in descant, and yet will be bad composers; others will be good composers and be bad descanters extempore upon a plainsong. Some will excel in the composition of motets, and being set or enjoined to make a madrigal will be very far from the nature of it. Likewise some will be so possessed with the madrigal humor that no man may be compared with them in that kind, and yet, being enjoined to compose a motet or some sad and heavy music, will be far from the excellency which they had in their own vein. Lastly, some will be so excellent in points of voluntary upon an instrument that one would think it impossible for him not to be a good composer; yet, being asked to make a song, he will do it so simply that a scholar of one year's practice might easily compose a better one.[33] And I dare boldly affirm that if you find someone who thinks he is the best descanter of all his neighbors, and ask him to compose a Scottish jig, he will grossly err in the true nature and quality of it.

32. A pavan in duple time followed by a galliard in triple time, by Morley, appears in *MSO*, Part 1, pp. 41–44.
33. Here *points of voluntary* refers to improvising on an instrument with a given theme. English composers such as John Blow (1648–1708) and Henry Purcell (c. 1659–1695) used the title *voluntary* for organ pieces of an improvisatory nature.

7.8 MICHAEL PRAETORIUS (1560–1629)

Michael Praetorius, a German composer born in Kreuzberg, Thuringia, confessed his indebtedness to the Italians for their method of singing, especially to Caccini, whom he called Giulio Romano (Section 8.1). In the area of rhythm Praetorius directly related the poetic foot to the dance, coordinating musical quantitative and metrical accent in the process. The excerpts quoted here are from the third volume of his systematic collection of writings on music entitled *Syntagma Musicum* (1619).

Songs Put Together from Many Pieces, Such as the Messanza and Quodlibet*

The *Messanza* or *mistichanza* is a *quodlibet* [34] or mixture of all sorts of cabbages (*Kräutern*),[35] a salty, humorous medley, which all together is called a *quodlibet*. That is, from many sundry motets, madrigals, and other German secular, comic songs, a half or whole line of text is taken with its melody and notes, and from many little pieces and chips a whole pelt is put and patched together.

There are three kinds of these *quodlibets*.

1. Some have a special and complete text in each of the voices. One of these which occurs to me has in one voice *Erhalt uns Herr*, in another, *Ach Gott vom Himmel*, in a third, *Vater unser im Himmelreich*, in the fourth *Wir glauben*, in the fifth *Durch Adams Fall*, all fitting together.[36]

2. Some have a special text in each voice, but completely mangled and broken up, as in Nicolai Zangi's *Quodlibet*.[37]

3. Some have the same text in all the voices, but it is also incomplete and

---

Michael Praetorius, Syntagma Musicum *(Wolfenbüttel: 1619), III, 17–21, 229–240, 73–75.*

34. Example 4 of Section 6.5 is a quodlibet by Tinctoris on *O rosa bella* and *L'homme armé*.

35. J. S. Bach wrote a quodlibet as the third variation of *The Goldberg Variations*. One of the two German folksongs which he used starts with the text *Kraut und Rüben haben mich vergrieben*. A translation of the complete verse is:

Cabbages and turnips drove me away.
    Had my mother cooked meat,
    Longer would have been my stay.

36. These five chorales were all set by J. S. Bach.

37. Nikolaus Zangius (c. 1570–1618) was Capellmeister for John Sigismund, elector of Brandenburg. Zangius' secular songs and quodlibets were published in Berlin in 1620. (Modern edition: *Denkmäler der Tonkunst in Österreich*, Vienna, 1894, vol. 87.)

disconnected, and soon another catches us by surprise, as in Melchior Franck's quodlibets.[38]

Songs Used in Frolicking [*Grassaten*] and Merrymaking, Such as Giustiniani, Serenata, and Balletti

1. *Giustiniani,* called rough and light music by some, are the love songs of a noble suitor from the city Bergama. They are in the language of Bergamasca, and have mostly three voices.[39]

2. A *serenata* is an evening song with three or more voices. It is sung when one goes strolling on the streets in the evening or *Gassaten gehet,* and, as it is called in the universities, pays court or addresses the young ladies.[40] Instrumental *ritornellos* are played between [the stanzas of the song].

3. *Balli* or *balletti* are of two kinds:
    First, there are special songs which are sung in succession for dancing (for *ballare* means to leap, that is, to dance). Very lovely and charming *balletti* of this kind have been published by Giovanni Gastoldi and Thomas Morley.[41]
    Second, there are other kinds of *balli* or *ballette* which have no text. And when these are played for dancing by shawms or pipes, they are called *stampita.* The French use the name *Ball* for a medley of dances of one kind, such as *branles, courants, voltes, gagliards,* etc. But a *ballet* consists of special dances for buffoonery and pageantry, which are played for masquerading. These are presented in designated forms [*inventiones*].

Usually each *ballet* has three sections: 1. The *Intrada,* when the characters in the pageant make their appearance. 2. The figures which the masked characters make while standing, walking, and changing places, or while forming a circle, cross, triangle, square, hexagon, or other shape, or when winding in and out. In other words, this part is the whole *Invention* and essence of the ballet. 3. The *Retrajecte,* that is, the conclusion or exit with which the *Invention* and the whole ballet is ended and closed. And while this section is no longer necessary, still it is part of the masquerade. The *Retrajecte* may consist of another lovely song opening and closing with in-

38. Melchior Franck (c. 1599–1639), Saxon capellmeister at Coburg from 1603, wrote German secular songs and dances for four, five, six, and eight voices (1604). In 1613 his *Ferculum Quodlibeticum, Menu of Quodlibets with various Dishes and Rhopalic Verses Scraped Together,* for four voices, appeared. A rhopalic verse is a line in which each word has one more syllable than the word immediately before it.
39. Praetorius is referring to the people of Bergamo in Italy, who were playfully ridiculed as being clownish.
40. For the relationship of the expression *Gassaten gehet* to the serenade, the cassation, and the divertimento, see R. H. Rowen, *Early Chamber Music,* (New York: Da Capo Press, 1974) pp. 140 ff.
41. Giovanni Giacomo Gastoldi, maestro di cappella in Mantua, wrote *Balleti a 5 per cantare, suonare, & ballare,* "for singing, playing, and dancing" (Venice, 1591–1595). One of these light, popular pieces with all of the voices moving simultaneously in measured rhythms, is in *HAM,* Vol. 1 No. 158.

strumental music. There are numerous examples of these as well as others among the various French dances and songs, such as *branles, courants,* and the like, in my *Terpsichore.*

Instruction in the Modern Italian Manner
for Boys with a Special Love and Desire to Sing

The domain of the orator is not only to decorate an oration with beautiful, pleasant, lively words and masterful figures, but also to articulate correctly and to move the affects. While he raises his voice or lets it fall, he speaks in a voice sometimes intense and soft, sometimes whole and full. Likewise, a musician has to do more than sing, no matter how artistic and pleasant his singing may be, if he wants to reach the heart of the listener and to move the affects. And thus he creates and directs song toward trying to attain his goal. For a singer must acquire and attain a masterful voice not only from nature, but also from a good understanding and complete knowledge of music.

Three factors pertain to singing in a lovely, correct and beautiful style, as well as to the other skills, namely: Natural Talent [*natura*], Skill or Instruction [*ars seu doctrina*] and Practice [*exercitatio*].

1. *Natural Talent.* First of all, a singer by nature must have a voice, for which three prerequisites and three characteristics may be noted.

   The prerequisites are these: A singer first of all must be able to ornament with a beautiful, lovely, tremulous and vibrating [*bebenden*] voice (yet not the kind sometimes usual in schools, but with special moderation), and a smooth round neck. Secondly, he must be able to hold a steady long breath without inhaling much. Third, he should choose a voice, such as cantus, or tenor, which he can produce with full and clear sonority, without falsetto (that is, a half and forced voice).

   And the following is to be observed about the characteristics:

   Intonatio is how to begin a song. And there are different meanings for this. Some people want to start on the keynote [*dem rechten Thon,* the correct tone]; some on a second below the keynote; some descend with the voice and then ascend in the same way, some go through a third, and some a fourth. Some want to begin with pleasant, subdued sounds which in various styles are recognized mostly under the name of *accents.*

   Exclamatio is the real means of moving the *affects.* It must coincide with a raising of the voice, and may be introduced and used on all half notes, as well as dotted quarter notes, in descending. And characteristically the following note moves forward somewhat more quickly, with more affect. The whole note, which in a rise or descent of the voice occurs more frequently without *exclamation,* also has more grace.

   The defects [*vitia*] in the voice are that some are produced with much respiration and breath; some sing through the nose and with constriction of the voice in the throat; and some sing with the teeth clenched together. All of this is not very praiseworthy. Rather it deforms the harmony and makes it unpleasant.

2. *Skill or Instruction.* On the other hand, a singer must have real knowledge to form the diminutions (often in general called *coloraturas*) lovingly and appropriately.

Diminution is when a long note resolves and is broken into many other fast and smaller notes. These are of various types and kinds. Some of them are stepwise, like *accents*, *tremulo gruppi* and *tirata*.

Accents occur when notes like the following are produced in the throat:

Initial and final note at the unison.

Ascending through a 2nd.   Descending

Ascending through a 3rd.   Descending

Ascending through a 4th.   Descending

Ascending through a 5th.   Descending

Tremolo, or *tremulo* is nothing but a shaking of the voice on a note. The organists call it *Mordanten* or *Moderanten.*

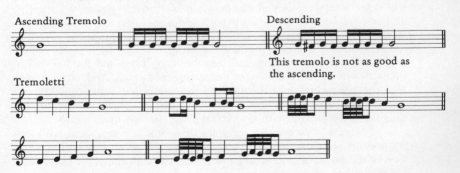

Ascending Tremolo   Descending

                                           This tremolo is not as good as
                                           the ascending.

Tremoletti

And this is directed more toward organs and quilled instruments (*instrumenta pennata*, harpsichords) than to human voices.

Gruppo or *groppi* are used in cadences and formal endings, and must be attacked more exactly than the *tremolos.*

Tiratas are long fast runs going by step up and down the keyboard.

The more swiftly and more exactly these runs are executed, yet, in a way that one may hear and almost distinguish each note very clearly, the better and more charming they will be.

The diminutions which do not proceed by step are the *trill* and the *passaggi.* The trill is of two kinds. One is performed on a single note, whether it be on a line or in a space, with many fast notes repeated one after the other.

And this kind may be found in Claudio de Monteverdia.[42]

The other kind of trill has many varieties. Indeed, it is impossible to learn how to perform a trill correctly from written instructions. It should be sung and performed live before a teacher. A person is shown how to to do it by hearing it sung beforehand by someone else, just as one bird learns by imitating the other. Therefore, to this date I have still not seen these kinds of trill described by any Italian author with the exception of Giulio Caccini. When a trill is to be performed, all they do is to put a *t, tr,* or *tri* over the notes. Nevertheless, I have deemed it necessary to include some of the types here in passing, so that the uninformed beginner may explore and may come to know approximately what a trill means.

Passaggi are fast runs which are composed and executed either by step or leap through all intervals, ascending as well as descending, on notes with some time value.

And they are of two kinds. Some are composed in longer note-values, such as, either half notes or quarter notes; or, with half notes and quarter

42. See Monteverdi's *Possente spirto* (*MSO*, Part 1, pp. 71–80).

notes at the same time. Some are broken into shorter values, such as eighth notes or sixteenth notes; or, eighth notes and sixteenth notes at the same time. (Quarter notes are called *chromata* by the Italians. Eighth notes are called *semichromata*. Sixteenth notes are called *bischromata*.) [Now these values are halved.]

But beginning students of this art should first start with the *passaggi* in longer note values, and then practice carefully and intensively those diminished with eighth notes, and finally they may get to those with sixteenth notes.

3. *Practice.* So that one may be able to remember better what has been presented here in condensed form, everything should be demonstrated with diminutions in examples of all kinds, in different styles.

Concerning Sextuple or Diminished Trochaic Meter

Sextuple meter, used as far back as the ancients, has now reached full maturity. Indeed, at this time *sextupla* refers to six semiminims to a measure, indicated by the number 3 written above or below three or six semiminims, in this manner: ♩ ♩ ♩ . But beside this I find yet three other ways in which sextuples are designated and indicated by the Italians and the British. For example:

1. In the first kind of equal notes, as in *hemiola minore*, are all black. This calls to mind the ternary division of the beat in duple time, *alla breve*, ¢, in which three black minims ♩ ♩ ♩ or one black semibreve and one minim ♦ ♩ are sung and played on the downbeat with the next three on the upbeat. The signature is $\frac{6}{1}$, meaning that six semiminims or black black minims are necessary for a whole measure.[43]

2. In the other kind (mostly used by the Italians and French in their courants, sarabandes and other similar pieces) the minims and semiminims are handled in the same way as the blackened semibreves and minims of

---

43. Ordinarily a semibreve was divided into two white minims ◊ = ♩ ♩ In *hemiola minore* a semibreve was divided into three black minims ◊ = ♦ ♦ ♦ or its equivalent, ◊ = ♦ ♩ . Since the black minim ♦ is identical in appearance with the semiminim ♩, the signature $\frac{6}{1}$ means that

6 { black minims } are equivalent to a breve.
  { semiminims }

□ = ◊ ◊
□ = ♦ ♦ ♦ ♦ ♦ ♦

The sign of proportion, $\frac{6}{1}$, indicated the number of units in the measure, without giving the time value of the unit.

the first type. The signature is $\frac{6}{4}$, indicating that six semiminims must be worth the same amount as four semiminims were worth previously.[44]

Among the French there are many different kinds of rhythm, conforming to each type of dance. More about this has been said in my *Terpsichore Musarum*.

Examples of sextuples appear in English pavanes and in various songs of the British and French. See the Fifth Part of *Musarum Sioniarum Germanicum*, Nos, 156, 157, 158, etc. In the *Hymnodia* Nos. 134, 135. In the *Megalynodia* No. 14, and in the *Terpsichore* many examples are to be found.

3. The third type I had to invent partially by my humble self. For I observed and noticed that (as in my *Polyhymnia* II, the *Omnes gentes*) this really was extremely difficult to do, and that therefore it could not be started without confusion. And so, in my *Te Deum laudamus* for twenty-two and twenty-six voices, the third part, the *Tu Rex Gloriae Christe*, was to be measured in sextuple with duple tactus (for I purposely planned it that way). And because in some schools they found it extremely difficult and almost impossible to convey this meter, I have had to think of another means by which to indicate and to notate the character of such sextuples, so that both duple and triple meters (*Tactus aequalis und Inaequalis*) may hereafter be observed and perceived at every convenient and desirable opportunity.

The sextupla may very well be called the diminished trochaic measure [*tactus*]. Just as in the simple trochaic sesquialtera only three minims or semiminims are counted in a measure, so the sextupla has six minims or semiminims in a measure, of which three provide the downbeat, and three respond on the upbeat. And in this way it is a duple measure.[45]

44. The French and Italian proportion, $\frac{6}{4}$ shows the value of the unit as well as the number of units in the measure. On the theory of proportions, see Tinctoris, Section 6.5.
45. The whole note in the chorale equals six quarter-note beats in the other voice.

And in this manner one can consider and very easily perform all triple and sesquialtera proportions in the German Choral Psalms and in all other songs in triple meter against duple meter (*Tactu Inaequali ad Tactum Aequali*).

Within a measure Praetorius combines two spondees, each of which is divided into a trochee, as follows:

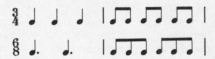

Praetorius uses "trochaic" as a generic term to describe any triplet division, whether trochee ♩ ♪, iamb ♪ ♩, or tribrach ♫♪ .

The concept of two levels of simultaneous rhythmical activity is most important for the understanding of compound meters to the present day. We still think of hemiola as a measure that may be divided in two ways, either as three beats each in duple subdivision, or as two beats each in triple subdivision.

8

Thoroughbass and Counterpoint in Theater, Church, and Chamber

8.1 GIULIO CACCINI (c. 1546–1618)

In 1601 Giulio Caccini heralded a new era with a treatise entitled *Le Nuove Musiche*. Caccini, born in Rome, moved to Florence where he was a member of the intellectual elite that met at the home of Signor Giovanni Bardi to discuss matters pertaining to the arts. Under the influence of Vincenzo Galilei (Section 7.5), among others, Caccini turned from composing madrigals in the polyphonic style to writing in the monodic style, expressing his musical intentions through solo recitative performed to his own accompaniments on the archlute. In slavish adherence to the rhythm of the text it is possible that Caccini and the composers around him were substituting the fetters imposed by the words for the fetters of counterpoint.

Preference of Monody to Counterpoint*

At the time when the admirable Camerata of the most illustrious Signor Giovanni Bardi, Count of Vernio, was flourishing in Florence, with not only many of the nobility but also the foremost musicians, intellectuals, poets, and philosophers of the city in attendance, I too was present; and I can truly say that I gained more from their learned discussions than from my more

Giulio Caccini, Le Nuove Musiche, ed. H. Wiley Hitchcock (Madison, Wisconsin: A-R Editions, Inc., 1970), pp. 44–45. Reprinted by permission of A-R Editions, Inc., Madison, Wisconsin.

than thirty years of counterpoint. For these most knowledgeable gentlemen kept encouraging me, and with the most lucid reasoning convinced me, not to esteem that sort of music which, preventing any clear understanding of the words, shatters both their form and content, now lengthening and now shortening syllables to accommodate the counterpoint (a laceration of the poetry!), but rather to conform to that manner so lauded by Plato [Section 2.1] and other philosophers (who declared that music is naught but speech, with rhythm and tone coming after; not vice versa) with the aim that it enter into the minds of men and have those wonderful effects admired by the great writers. But this has not been possible because of the counterpoint of modern music, and even more impossible in solos sung to one or another stringed instrument, wherein not a single word has been understood for the multitude of *passaggi* on both short and long syllables and in every sort of piece—although precisely because of these some have been extolled by *hoi polloi* and proclaimed mighty singers.

Having thus seen, as I say, that such music and musicians offered no pleasure beyond that which pleasant sounds could give—solely to the sense of hearing, since they could not move the mind without the words being understood— it occurred to me to introduce a kind of music in which one could almost speak in tones, employing in it (as I have said elsewhere) a certain noble negligence of song, sometimes transgressing by [allowing] several dissonances while still maintaining the bass note (save when I wished to do it the ordinary way and play the inner parts on the instrument to express some affect—for which, however, they are of little value). Thus originated those songs for a single voice (which seemed to me to have more power to delight and move than several voices together) which I composed at that time: the madrigals *Perfidissimo volto, Vedrò'l mio sol, Dovrò dunque morire*,[1] and others like them, and particularly the air on the eclogue of Sannazaro, *Itene à l'ombra de gli ameni faggi*, in that very style I later employed for the fables performed in song at Florence.[2]

8.2 LODOVICO DA VIADANA (1564–1645)

The predominance of monody, a style based on accompanied melody with attention directed to the outer parts, coincided with the appearance of the *basso continuo* or thoroughbass. The earliest explanation of this important new term lies in the preface to *100 Ecclesiastical Concertos for One, Two, Three, and Four Voices, with Basso Continuo to be Played on the Organ. New Invention suitable for all sorts of Singers, and for Organists*, by Lodovico Viadana (1602). Lodovico Grossi, named

---

1. The music for these three vocal solos with figured bass is transcribed and realized by Hitchcock, pp. 77, 81, 95.
    Caccini's madrigal, *Amarilli mia bella*, for solo voice and basso continuo appears in *MSO*, Part 1, pp. 68–69 without the inner notes and in Hitchcock, p. 85, with them. (For an explanation of the basso continuo, see Section 8.2.)
2. Jacopo Sannazaro (1458–1530) established the model for the pastoral drama.

Viadana after his birthplace near Mantua, called his compositions *concertos* in the original Italian edition. In a German translation published by Nicolaus Stein of Frankfurt (1613) they were called *motets* which "should be sung by singers and musicians who are endowed not less with understanding than with a good voice." The ecclesiastical concerto of the late sixteenth and early seventeenth centuries actually was a motet with instrumental accompaniment, as distinguished from earlier motets in unaccompanied, a cappella style. In the new category were Adriano Banchieri's *Concerti ecclesiastici* (1595), double choir motets with continuous organ bass.

When Viadana speaks of "new invention" in his title, he is referring to the idea of writing pieces for variable numbers of vocal and instrumental parts, with whichever part is momentarily the lowest participating in the continuous bass. The other aspects of the basso continuo—such as the use of figures to denote the intervals above the bass, and the doubling of the keyboard bass by a string bass—which were incorporated as the concept took shape, were not part of his claim.

The Basso Continuo or Thoroughbass*

To the Kind Readers

Many were the reasons, dear readers, which induced me to compose this sort of concerto. Among them one of the principal ones is the following: I saw that certain singers, wishing to sing to the organ either with three voices or with two, or with one voice alone, sometimes were compelled, because of the lack of compositions suited to their purpose, to resort to using one, two, or three parts of a motet with five, six, seven, or even eight voices. Owing to the fact that these parts ought to be heard in conjunction with the others because of the imitations [*fughe*], cadences, counterpoints, and other characteristics throughout the song, there are long and frequent rests, missing cadences, lack of melody, and lastly, very little continuity or taste. This is aside from the interruption of the words, sometimes omitted in part, and sometimes separated at unsuitable places,[3] which rendered the style of singing either imperfect, or annoying, or noxious. It was of little pleasure to those who stayed to listen, not to mention the very great trouble it was to the singers who performed it. Having frequently given great consideration

---

The original Italian text, as well as Latin and German versions, are in Opere di Lodovice Viadana, *ed.* Claudio Gallico *(Kassel: Barenreiter, 1964). The Italian text with a modern translation into English appears in F. T. Arnold,* The Art of Accompaniment from a Thorough-Bass *(London: The Oxford University Press, 1931), pp. 2-33.*

3. In establishing his "Rules to be Observed in Dittying," Morley warned,

We must also take heed of separating any part of a
word from another by the rest, as some dunces have
not slacked to do, yea one whose name is John Dunstable.

to such difficulties, I struggled to find a partial substitute for such a notable deficiency, and I believe, thank God, that I have at last discovered it. Toward this end I composed some concertos for a single voice, for soprano, alto, tenor, or bass. I composed some others for the same voices in different combinations, in an effort to give satisfaction to all kinds of singing. I coupled the voices together in every sort of pair, so that if anyone wants a soprano with a tenor, a tenor with an alto, an alto with a cantus, a cantus with a bass, and a bass with an alto, or two sopranos, two altos, two tenors, two basses, he will be accommodated here to the fullest extent. And whoever wants these voices in larger groupings will find them in the concertos for three or for four voices. Here, every singer, according to his taste, should be able to conveniently locate plenty of songs with which he may further his reputation.

Then you will find some others that I have composed with various instruments, thereby indicating my intentions more completely and making the concertos more useful and diversified.

Besides, I have taken particular care not to insert rests unless they enhance the character and disposition of the song. . . .

I have taken pains for the words to be placed exactly beneath the notes, so as to insure their proper articulation with continuity of meaning throughout, and to make it possible for the listeners to understand them clearly, provided that the singers pronounce them distinctly.

Instructions

1. This kind of concerto should be sung gracefully, with discretion and charm, using accented dissonances [*accenti*] with reason and ornamental runs [*passaggi*] with moderation, and in their right place. Above all, nothing should be added to what is in print, even though there are now certain singers who, because they are favored by nature with a flair for gurgling, never sing the songs the way they are written. It does not occur to them that today the likes of them are not welcome. On the contrary, they are held in very low esteem, particularly in Rome where the true profession of singing well flourishes.

2. The organist should adapt his part from the full score [*partitura*] simply, usually playing with the left hand. If he wishes to perform some motion with the right hand, such as decorating a cadence or some appropriate passage, he should play in such a way as not to cover or confuse the singer or singers with too much motion.

3. It would be a good thing for the organist to have previously looked through the concerto which is to be sung, since, by understanding the nature of the music, he will always perform the accompaniments better.

4. The organist should always take care to perform the cadences in their correct position. That is to say, if a concerto for a single bass voice is being sung, the organist should perform a bass cadence, for a tenor voice a tenor cadence, for an alto or discant, each should be played in its own position, since it would create a bad effect if while the soprano was singing its cadence, the organ were to play a cadence in the tenor,

or while the tenor was singing its cadence, the organ were to play in the soprano.[4]

5. When a concerto is found which begins in the manner of a fugue, the organist starts playing alone [*tasto solo*] [5] and when the other parts enter it is up to him to accompany them as he pleases.

6. No keyboard score [*intavolatura*] [6] has been made for these concertos, not to avoid the trouble, but to make it easier for the organists to play them, since not everyone can improvise from a reduced score, and most people would have less trouble playing from the open score [*partitura*]. However, the organists can make the said *intavolatura* if they so desire, which, to tell the truth, is much better.

7. When one plays all the voices on the organ, hands and feet are both used, but without additional stops, because the nature of these thin and delicate concertos is not commensurate with the great din of the full organ. Besides, there is something pedantic about the use of the organ in small concertos.

8. Every care has been taken in assigning all of the accidentals, ♯ ♮ ♭, where they belong, and therefore the wise organist should pay attention to playing them.

9. The *partitura* is never obliged to avoid two fifths or two octaves, but the parts sung by the voices are.

10. If anyone wishes to sing this sort of music without an organ or another keyboard instrument he will not create a good effect. On the contrary, for the most part dissonances will be heard.

8.3 CLAUDIO MONTEVERDI (1567–1643) AND GIULIO MONTEVERDI (b.1573)

In 1601 Giulio Caccini and Jacopo Peri, another singer who frequented Count Bardi's home, each set *Euridice* in the monodic style. These earliest operas were composed to a libretto on the legend of Orpheus and Euridice written by Ottavio Rinuccini, a poet also active in the Camerata at Florence. At that time, Claudio Monteverdi, who was soon to compose an *Orfeo* of his own to a libretto by the poet Alessandro Striggio, was

---

4. For the cadences suitable for each voice, see Tinctoris (Section 6.5).
5. As the technique of thoroughbass accompaniment became codified, the term *tasto solo* continued to indicate that the keyboard instrument was to play only a single melody.
6. Unlike the German keyboard tablature which used letters for the bass, the Italian *intavolatura* or condensed score was a reduction for keyboard with notes on two staves. The staff for the right hand had five or six lines, while the staff for the left hand had six to eight. Each staff accommodated an outer voice, with the inner voices distributed between both. For an example of an Italian keyboard score, see Willi Apel, *The Notation of Polyphonic Music*, Fifth edition (Cambridge, Mass.: The Mediaeval Academy of America, 1953), p. 5; for a *partitura* or open score, see p. 17.

composing madrigals and sacred polyphony while in the service of Vincenzo Gonzaga, Duke of Mantua.

In 1600 Monteverdi had circulated some madrigals which came to the attention of Giovanni Artusi (Section 7.6). The latter picked on isolated passages in his treatise entitled *On the Imperfections of Modern Music*, criticizing Monteverdi's use of unresolved dissonance without considering the relationship between the music and the text. Artusi tried to subject Monteverdi's style of composition to rules such as those formulated in Artusi's *Art of Counterpoint* (Venice, 1586, 1589, 1598).

In an open letter printed as a preface to his fifth book of madrigals (1605), Monteverdi defended himself, saying that his words were in the Second Practice (*Seconda Pratica*) of music, rather than the First Practice (*Prima Pratica*). As symbols of the practice which preceded him, Monteverdi cited Willaert in composition and Zarlino in theory. Although Monteverdi promised to write a further explanation, he never did. Instead, he went on composing and developing the new style.

Monteverdi's opera, *The Fable of Orpheus*, was first performed at Mantua in February of 1607.[7] In July of that year, the *Scherzi Musicali for Three Voices* were published. These compositions, which had instrumental ritornelli to be played at the end of each stanza, were edited by Claudio Monteverdi's brother, Giulio, who added three pieces of his own at the end. Giulio also took the opportunity to explain Claudio's letter of 1605, quoting it line by line and interspersing pertinent commentary as he went along. If after reading what the two brothers had to say about the Second Practice we still wonder what the term really meant, we should turn to the music which Claudio subsequently wrote, including *The Combat of Tancred and Clorinda* (Venice, 1624)—in which he introduced pizzicato in the strings to portray the clashing swords—and the *Madrigals of War and Love* (Eighth Book, Venice, 1638) for six voices, two violins, and *basso continuo*—in which he introduced tremolo as an aid toward expressing agitated emotions.

The Second Practice of Music: Explanation of the Letter Printed in the *Fifth Book of Madrigals**

There was published (a few months ago) a letter by my brother Claudio Monteverdi. Someone, under the assumed name of Antonio Braccini da Todi, has been striving to make the subject with which it dealt appear

*The facsimile of the preface to the Scherzi Musicali *is contained in* Tutte Le Opere di Claudio Monteverdi, *ed. G. F. Malipiero (Asolo: Universal, 1926–1942), Vol. X. It is translated completely in* SRMH, *pp. 405–415.*

7. Monteverdi's *Orfeo* called for a large orchestra including instruments that could play chords and those that could play a melody. Among the chordal instruments were two harpsichords, a double-strung harp, two theorbes, 2 small wooden or-

to the world as a chimera and vanity. Therefore I, spurred on by my love for my brother, but much more by the truth in this letter, seeing that he prefers to pay attention to facts rather than to appraise the words of others, not being able to bear the thought that his works are blamed so very wrongly, want at this time to answer the attacks made on them. Throughout I will explain more fully what my brother has compressed into short terms in the said letter, in order that he [Artusi] and his followers may know that the truth contained in it is very different from what he shows in his discourse. Thus says the letter:

Do not be astonished that I give these madrigals to the press without first answering the attacks which Artusi made

By "Artusi" he of course means, *L'Artusi ovvero delle imperfetioni de la moderna musica*, the book by that title which disregards the civil precept of Horace: "Neither should you praise your own studies nor find fault with someone else's" [*Epistularum*, Bk. 1, Chap. 18, line 39].

And without any specified motive, and therefore unjustifiedly, he says the worst things possible about some musical compositions of my brother Claudio.

against some minute fragments of them,

Those fragments, called "passaggi" by Artusi, and which have been so badly lacerated by the said Artusi in the second discourse, are part of the harmony of the madrigal *Cruda Amarilli* by my brother, and the harmony of it grows from the melody on which the madrigal is composed.[8] For

---

gans, one portable reed-pipe organ, and three leg viols. Among the melody instruments were ten arm viols in different ranges, high violins, four trombones, two cornetti, one high flute, one clarino (a natural trumpet on which harmonics were played) and three other trumpets. For the opening toccata and the sinfonias Monteverdi expected any instruments of suitable range and character to play the appropriate parts. However, he designated particular instruments and wrote out the embellishments for the aria *Possente Spirto* (Act 3) so that Orfeo could demonstrate the full strength of his musical powers, (*MSO*, Part 1, 72–80), *SSMS*, pp. 145–151.

8. *Cruda Amarilli* is the first madrigal of the Fifth Book (*MSO*, Part 1, 69–72). The text is from the second scene of *Pastor Fido* by Battista Guarini (1537–1612).

In Artusi's *On the Imperfections of Modern Music* (Section 7.6) Luca shows Vario some excerpts one or two measures long, without the words. Seven of the examples are from *Cruda Amarilli MSO*, Part 1, pp. 69–72, (meas. 13–14, 19–20, 21–22, 35–36, 37–38, 41–42, 53–54) and two are from madrigals in Book 4, *Anima mia perdona* and *Che se tu s'il cor mio*.

Concerning these works Vario says,

Signor Luca, you bring me new things which astonish me greatly. At my age I am happy to see a new type of composition, but it would give me much more pleasure if I found that these Passaggi were based on some reason which might satisfy the intellect. But such castles in the air, chimeras built on sand, do not please me. They should be blamed, not praised. (p. 40)

that reason, my brother, considering all the factors of which melody consists, calls these *particelle* [particles, fragments] and not *passaggi* [passages].

because I, being in the service of His Venerable Highness, have not yet had enough time at my disposal.

My brother said this, not only because of his responsibility for the music in the church as well as the chamber, but also because of other extraordinary services. In the service of the Grand Prince, the greater part of the time he is busy either with the tournaments, or with the ballet, or with the comedy and with various concerts, and finally with playing the two viole bastarde. . . .

I have nevertheless written the answer to let it be known that I do not compose my works at random.

My brother says that he does not compose his works at random. I attest that, in the type of music in question, his intention has been that the words should be the mistress of the harmony, not its servant. And his composition should be judged from the point of view of the construction of melody, speaking of which Plato says: "Melody consists of three things, the words, the harmony, and the rhythm" [Section 2.1].

And as soon as it is recopied it will come out under the title of *Seconda Pratica* or *The Perfection of Modern Music*.

Since his adversary intends to attack modern music, and to defend the old, which two types of music are really very different from each other (in the way of using consonance and dissonance, as my brother will explain), and since the difference is not known to his adversary, for greater clarity and also for truth, let the characteristics of each be understood by all. Both are honored, revered, and praised by my brother. To the old he has given the name *Prima Pratica*, it being the first practical method, and the modern he has called the Seconda Pratica, it being the second practical method. *Prima Pratica* means that which deals with the subject of the perfection of harmony; that is to say that it considers the harmony not commanded, but commanding, and not servant but mistress of the words. And this was begun when songs were first composed for more than one voice with our kind of notes. This was followed and amplified by Ockeghem, Josquin Desprez, Pierre de la Rue, Jean Mouton, Créquillon, Clemens non papa, Gombert, and others of those times, ultimately perfected by Sir Adriano with practical action, and by the most excellent Zarlino with most judicious rules.[9]

9. Jean de Ockeghem (c. 1430–1495), born in Flanders, was *maître de chapelle* for three successive kings of France. He wrote canons in which the second voice, entering after a specified lapse of time, repeats the melody at the unison or at some other interval. The repetition might be in augmentation (proportionately slower), diminution (proportionately faster), inversion (opposite direction), or cancrizans (backwards). He also wrote mensuration canons in which the voices

The Second Practice, of which the divine Cipriano Rore has been the first innovator using our kind of notes, as my brother will show, followed and amplified not only by the masters mentioned, but by Ingegneri, Marenzio, Giaches Wert, Luzzasco, and likewise by Giacoppo Peri, by Giulio Caccini, and finally by the most elevated spirits and connoisseurs of the true art, means that which is founded on the perfection of melody.[10] That is to say that it considers harmony the commanded and not the commanding, and puts the words as mistress of the harmony. For such reasons he calls it the Second Practice and not the New Practice. He has said *practice*

---

start together and proceed in different meters, and double canons involving two or more canons at the same time. Ockeghem even wrote a canon for thirty-six voices which Glareanus mentioned in the *Dodecachordon* as a "chattering song" which he had not seen. These contrapuntal complexities occurring in compositions of the *Prima Pratica* were obviously not conducive toward promoting clarity of the words. In such compositions as *Missa L'homme armé* Ockeghem also indulged in the practice of using a folk melody as cantus firmus, without the original French text (*MSO*, Part 1, 28–29).

The Netherlander Josquin Desprez (c. 1445–1521), who might have studied with Ockeghem, worked in a number of cities, including Modena, Florence, where he became friendly with Pietro Aron (Section 6.7), and Ferrara, the locale of Artusi's treatise. Desprez was a master of imitative counterpoint in which each voice announced the subject in succession while producing a harmonically unified texture. (See *Gloria* of *Missa Pange lingua*, *MSO*, Part 1, 30–33.)

Pierre de La Rue (d. 1518), composer of forty masses and numerous motets and madrigals, was at the court of Burgundy and later at the court of Margaret of Austria.

Jean Mouton (c. 1470–1522), active in the courts of the French kings Louis XII and Francis I, taught Willaert.

The French musician Thomas Créquillon (d. 1557) was at the court of Charles V of Spain from 1544 to 1547.

Clemens non Papa (c. 1510–1556) used tunes popular in the Netherlands for his three-voiced psalm settings entitled *Souterliedekens* (published in four books by Tielman Susato in Antwerp 1556–1567).

The Fleming Nicholas Gombert (c. 1490–1556), possibly a pupil of Josquin, was known for his works for multiple choruses. He wrote some 250 chansons and motets which were published in arrangements for lute and guitar during his own day.

Sir Adriano refers to the Fleming Willaert (c. 1490–1562), who after serving as a musician in courts at Ferrara and Milan became maestro di cappella at St. Mark's in Venice (see Zarlino, Section 7.5). Willaert composed French chansons, some with strict canons, others with a cantus firmus in the tenor. He also wrote Italian villotte, villanesca, and madrigals in a chordal style with the melody in the soprano. His instrumental compositions included ricercare with motetlike imitations, and canzone that were more sectional.

10. Cipriano de Rore (1516–1565), born in Antwerp, was successor to Willaert at St. Mark's. De Rore paid special attention to the declamation of the words in his madrigals, whether composing syllabic or melismatic passages. See Alfred Einstein, *The Italian Madrigal*, trans. Alexander Krappe, Roger Sessions, and Oliver Strunk (Princeton, N.J.: Princeton University Press, 1971), I, pp. 384–423.

Marco Antonio Ingegneri (1545–1592), maestro di cappella at the cathedral in Cremona, taught Monteverdi.

For information on Giaches de Wert, see Section 7.2 fn. 1.

Luzzasco Luzzaschi (1545–1607), born in Ferrara, was a pupil of de Rore, and in turn became the teacher of Frescobaldi (see Section 8.6). Luzzaschi wrote madrigals for one to three sopranos, accompanied by a keyboard instrument.

and not *theory* since he intends to put his discussion on the subject of the way to use consonance and dissonance into practical action. He has not said *Institutioni Melodiche,* since he confesses that it is not a subject of such a great undertaking, but he leaves to Cavalier Ercole Bottrigari [11] and the Reverend Zarlino the composition of such noble writings. Zarlino called his work *Harmonic Institutions* because he wanted to teach the laws and rules of harmony. But my brother called his *Seconda Pratica,* that is the second practical method, because he wants to deal with considerations of that method, that is, with melodic considerations. And in his discussions he will use only those considerations by which he can defend himself against his adversary. . . .

But they may be certain that on the subject of consonance and dissonance there is still another practice different from the standard one, which by application of reason and good sense defends the modern way of composing. And this is what I wanted to express because this term *Seconda Pratica* has not yet been used by others.

The adversary was most confused in his discourse, saying, "Perhaps you are so sensitive about this term because you fear that it may be stolen from you." This would almost be equivalent to saying, "You need not fear such fury, since you are not a subject worthy of being imitated, nor of being stolen." Thus I make known that if the matter were to be considered in the following light, he would not have the slightest arguments in his favor. Was not my brother, particularly with regard to the *canto alla francese* in this modern manner, which appeared in the publications of three or four years ago either under the title of motets, or madrigals, or canzonetts and arias— was he not the first to carry it back to Italy on his return from the baths of the Spa in the year 1599? And was it not he who began to adapt them to Latin texts and to the vernacular in our language? Did he not compose these Scherzi at that time? [12] Then these facts should speak in his favor . . .

And also because some ingenious people might consider other secondary questions on the subject of harmony just as well.

"On the subject of harmony," that is, on the subject, not of the isolated fragments or *passaggi* of the song, but on all of it. If his adversary would have thought about the harmony of my brother's madrigal *O Mirtillo* as a

11. Ercole Bottrigari (1531–1612) was at the court of Este in Ferrara, and later went to Bologna as music professor at the university. In 1593 he wrote *Il Patrizio ovvero de' Tetracordi armonici di Aristosseno,* published in Bologna. This was followed in 1594 by *Il Desiderio* or "Concerning the Playing Together of Various Musical Instruments," trans. Carol MacClintock (American Institute of Musicology, 1962).
   Artusi's *Seconda Parte delle Imperfettioni* (1603) was directed against both Bottrigari and Monteverdi. Nonetheless, Artusi had the audacity to dedicate the entire work to Bottrigari. Bottrigari answered Artusi in the *Aletelogia di Leonardo Gullucio a benigni e sinceri lettori,* in which he defended Monteverdi.
12. The *Scherzi,* although published in 1607, were written in 1599 when Monteverdi returned from a voyage made with Duke Vincenzo Gonzaga to the baths of the Spa in Belgium.

whole, he would not have said these exorbitances on the subject of its mode in his discourse.[13] Artusi has likewise discussed and demonstrated the confusion which is produced in the songs which begin with one mode, follow with another, and, at the end, close with that which is altogether distant from the first and second thought. He says that it is like hearing the talk of a fool who beats at random, so to speak, either on the hoop of a cask or on the cask itself. The unfortunate one does not perceive that while he wants to appear to the world as a teacher in this matter, he falls in error by denying the mixed modes.

8.4 HEINRICH SCHÜTZ (1585–1672)

In the preface to his *Sacred Choral Music* (1648) Heinrich Schütz seeks a balance between the new thoroughbass or *basso continuo* style and the old contrapuntal style. At the age of 63 Schütz could look back to his training in Venice where he studied with Giovanni Gabrieli, through a long career as capellmeister to the Elector of Saxony, forward to his present location at Dresden. Although Schütz loved the Italian madrigal and the Latin motet, stimulated by his Lutheran persuasion, he felt that the German language too should be expressed in music with the utmost artistry. He had already composed works to German text, from the *Psalmen Davids* (1619) for multiple choirs and instruments, to the *Becker Psalter* (1628) in simple four-part metrical text setting, to the *Kleine geistliche Konzerte* (1636–39) for solo voice or ensemble and continuo.

While the *Geistliche Chor-Musik*, for five, six, and seven voices, to be performed both vocally and instrumentally, allows for the possible use of a continuo, Schütz does not actually provide a part for the keyboard player. The voices are either doubled by instruments or set in contrast to them. In either case Schütz makes it clear that his ideal is a good contrapuntal foundation, whether or not the basso continuo is present. Tucked away between the works admitting instruments is a transcription of Andrea Gabrieli's Latin motet *Angelus ad pastores*, in Schütz's version

---

13. *O Mirtillo* is the second madrigal of the fifth book, on a text from the second scene of *Pastor Fido*. Luca comments on it in *On the Imperfections of Modern Music* (Section 7.6) as follows:

> I heard a madrigal not many days ago which began on one note of the twelfth mode, b♭. Then there was a change to the first mode by means of a b♮. The words of the madrigal, *O Mirtillo*, were taken from *Pastor Fido* by Guarini. It gave me much to think about, since it did not sound as if it were composed with the skill of a talented composer. Rather, it was brimful of imperfections similar to those known as far back as the time when the muses first put their lips to the fountains at Helicon. (p. 48 b)

called *Der Engel sprach zu den Hirten.* In more ways than one, Schütz reverts to the past. His final sentence in the preface sounds like an echo of Viadana's sixth point (Section 8.2). Schütz too gives the organist the prerogative to make a tablature so that he will be able to play the keyboard part with intelligence if it is to be included in the performance.

Balance Between the Contrapuntal and Thoroughbass Styles*

Preface to *Geistliche Chor-Musik*

As everyone knows, since the concertizing style of composition over a *basso continuo* came from Italy to the attention of us Germans, it has been most successful and popular here.[14] In fact, it has gained more followers than any other style we ever had. The varied musical works now scattered hither and yon in the book shops of Germany offer sufficient evidence for this. By no means do I find fault with such publications. Rather do I see among them and also among those in our own German nation, all sorts of geniuses, well suited and inclined toward the profession of music, whose fame I readily grant and willingly concede.

On the other hand, no musician, not even those trained in a good school, can approach the most difficult study of counterpoint or any other well-regulated style of composition and handle or deal with it properly, unless he has previously gained sufficient skill in the style without the basso continuo, and has mastered the necessary requisites for regular composition. These are (among others): orderly arrangement of the modes; simple, mixed, and inverted fugues; double counterpoint; differentiation of diverse styles in the art of music; modulation of the voices; succession of themes, etc., and similar subjects on which the learned theorists write voluminously. Also important are the instructive counterpoints studied with live voices at school practice sessions [*in Scholâ Practicâ*]. Without these no composition can survive, even if it is written by an experienced composer and even if it seems like heavenly harmony to those whose ears are not properly trained in music. For then it would not be worth much more than an empty shell [*eine taube Nuss,* a deaf nut].

Thus I came to write this little work without basso continuo, so that the type may take root again and perhaps inspire some, especially some of the young German composers. Before they proceed to the concertizing style, as

---

*Musicala ad Chorum Sacrum, Das ist: Geistliche Chor-Music, *with 5, 6, and 7 Voices, to be performed both vocally and instrumentally. Composed by Heinrich Schütz, Capellmeister at the Electoral Court of Saxony. Although the General Bass is provided here for use at one's discretion, it is not necessary. First Part, 1648, Op. 11, Dresden.*

14. For a sacred composition by Schütz with basso continuo see *Symphoniae Sacrae,* No. 10 (*MSO,* Part 1, pp. 95–97). Schütz's *Christmas History* (1664) gave evidence of the Italian monodic style with instrumental accompaniment. Toward the end of his life, seeking to come closer to the German Protestant spirit, Schütz not only abandoned the basso continuo but also wrote unaccompanied recitative to German text. Thus, in his three Passions he had the characters express themselves through a German sacred chant, rather than in a manner that in any way resembled a theatrical style.

a first test they should crack open this hard nut, in which the real kernal and the actual basis of good counterpoint is to be found. For in Italy, where the real university of music lies (where in my youth I first began to learn the fundamentals of this profession), it was the custom for beginners first to compose [*ausarbeiten*, work out] each short spiritual or secular work properly and diligently without the basso continuo. Probably this fine procedure is still followed there. I wish to point out that my remarks about the advancement of music and the increase in the fame of our nation are made with the best of intentions and not to anyone's detriment.

I would also like to say that this style of church music without the basso continuo (which I have therefore called *Spiritual Choral Music*), is not always the same. Some of the compositions are really intended for the pulpit, for solo voices; others are for full choir with both vocal and instrumental voice-parts. Some of the latter are set so that, for a better effect the parts are not doubled, tripled, etc., but are split into vocal and instrumental divisions, and in this way may be played with good effect on the organ or sung in several choruses (if a composition has eight, twelve, or more voices). Both of these types may be found in my present work, written for only a few voices. I have not supplied the text for the compositions at the end because the intelligent musician will be able to examine the pieces at the beginning and then know how to proceed with a suitable arrangement.

Herewith I wish to publicly affirm and pray that no one will think that what I mentioned above would seem as if I wished to present and recommend this or any other of my published musical works to anyone as the essence of knowledge or as a definitive model. I myself well understand their trifling nature. Rather do I wish to direct each and every one to the most important composers of all, the glorious Italians, and other old and new classical authors. Their most admirable and incomparable works should be studied diligently by those who wish to compose in a similar manner. In one style or the other they shine as a brilliant light, indicating the right path toward the study of counterpoint. Besides, I still live in the hope of receiving news that a musician celebrated both in theory and in practice will soon publish a treatise on this subject which will be very informative and useful, especially to us Germans. I shall diligently endeavor to support this undertaking toward promoting the study of music in general.

Finally, if any organist so wishes, he has my permission to take this little work originally composed without basso continuo and write it in tablature or score [*Partitur*]. He may do this without compunction, for this kind of music would then achieve its desired effect so much the better.

8.5 ANGELO BERARDI (c. 1635–c. 1700)

The Italian theorist Angelo Berardi undertook to clarify Monteverdi's differentiation between contrapuntal compositions of the First and Second Practice. Berardi, a student of Marco Scacchi (c. 1602–c. 1685), was maestro di cappella at Spoleto (1681) and at Viterbo (1687). There is some question as to which portions of the *Documenti armonici* (1687) were developed by the master and which by the student. Scacchi had started to write while he was principal conductor of the royal chapel in Warsaw. When he returned to Italy in 1648, to the town of Gallese near Rome, he continued with his theoretical work, some of which had been published in Venice while he was in Warsaw. The *Harmonic Documents* on which he was working during his last years were completed under Berardi's name.

In this work Berardi penetrated to the depths of *real* and *artificial* motions and rhythms. Baroque investigation into ancient musical theory had revealed that some intervals were proportioned by nature and others were tempered artificially by man. In 1650, with Aristoxenus' equal division of the whole tone in mind, Athanasius Kircher tried to close the circle of fifths to facilitate the tuning of instruments.[15] Whereas in the

15. In the *Musurgia Universalis* or the *Great Art of Consonance and Dissonance* (p. 462) Athanasius Kircher (1602–1680) illustrated the following harmonic motion by alternately going up a fifth and down a fourth (see Section 1.2).

Kircher's Cycle of 5ths

In this diagram the shift from sharps to flats comes where he use G♭ instead of F♯. The x's show the temperament implicit in the chromatic diesis (Chart 4). Earlier in the book Kircher had a section entitled "The System of Eleven Mean Proportionals by Which the Octave Was Divided into Twelve Equal Semitones by Aristoxenus." Kircher also refers to the division by Marin Mersenne, which Mersenne summarized in his *Harmonie Universelle* (Paris, 1636) as follows:

Mersenne's System, or Octave Divided into 12 Equal Semitones

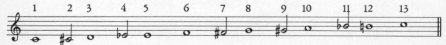

Thus Kircher indicates that he considered both natural and artificial intervals while constructing the cycle of fifths.

What the cycle of fifths meant in terms of composition becomes clearer when

Renaissance the mysterious regions were regarded as *musica reservata*, music reserved for the initiated, in the Baroque period artifices were exposed so that they might be utilized openly in composition.

Composers had been grappling with the problem of how to use the circle of fifths on a simple keyboard that did not have split keys for the microtones, or even how to sing polyphonically in remote keys without getting into chromatic and enharmonic commas between the voices. Following in Kircher's path, Berardi concluded that a note with a flat sign may be the enharmonic equivalent of the sharp on the letter name below. It is difficult for us to follow the notation of the compositions which Berardi gives as musical examples, since we are not used to supplying accidentals in the manner of *musica ficta*, nor are we trained to compensate for aberrations in pitch that accrue as a chain of fifths is in progress. However, without becoming technically involved in Berardi's reasoning, we can still sense the aura of living counterpoint in the less technical portions of his treatises.

---

it is compared with the harmonic cycle of the hexachord system. John Bull (c. 1562–1628) wrote a set of variations entitled *Ut, re, mi, fa, sol, la,* which appears in the *Fitzwilliam Virginal Book* (edition by J. A. Fuller Maitland and W. Barclay Squire, I, 183–187). Bull's theme is the hexachord pattern (tone, tone, semitone, tone, tone) presented in a cycle of keys in the order indicated below:

¹ G	² A	³ B	⁴ C♯	⁵ D♯	⁶ F	
	⁷ A♭	⁸ B♭	⁹ C	¹⁰ D	¹¹ E	¹² F♯

     G

Kircher's cycle of fifths, similarly charted according to keys, would look like this:

¹ F	² G	³ A	⁴ B	⁵ C♯	⁶ D♯	⁷ E♯
	⁸ G♭	⁹ A♭	¹⁰ B♭	¹¹ C	¹² D	¹³ E

In both cases there are two whole-tone rows with the second row starting a semitone above the first. Whereas Bull does not reach the octave until he goes through all of the intervening semitones, Kircher arrives at E♯, the enharmonic octave of F, before dealing with the second row. As a result, Bull does not include all the successive letter names in his first row and Kircher does. The latter, more modern concept, with its use of G♭ instead of F♯, enabled Berardi to "solve" the performance of Willaert's duo *Quid non ebrietas,* which otherwise would end in an enharmonic comma between the voices rather than a unison. This and other compositions cited by Berardi are discussed in the following studies: Joseph S. Levitan, "Adrian Willaert's Famous Duo *Quidnam Ebrietas*," *Tijdschrift der Vereeniging voor Nederlandsche Musiekgeschiedenis*, XV (1938), 166–233; Edward E. Lowinsky, "Adrian Willaert's Chromatic 'Duo' Re-examined," *Tjschrift voor Musiekwetenschap*, XVIII (1958), 1–36; Lowinsky, "Echoes of Willaert's Chromatic 'Duo' in Sixteenth- and Seventeenth-Century Composition," in *Studies in Music History, Essays for Oliver Strunk* (Princeton, N.J.: Princeton University Press, 1968), pp. 183–238.

Enharmonic Equivalents: *Documenti armonici**

Clearly one can observe the deception of the ear, because these notes, which are indicated at the interval of a second, for the sake of the harmony are considered to be unisons, a practice which can be used with all consonances and dissonances.

Unisons
A semitone lower

A semitone higher

Syncopated Counterpoint

There are a great many counterpoints which are invented at the caprice or fancy of the contrapuntists. Most of these are of the variety called *artificial counterpoint*. Since it is impossible to demonstrate all of them, I will try to give you examples of the more common counterpoints, namely: syncopated [*alla zoppa*],[16] stepwise [*alla diritta*], by leap [*saltando*], by suspension [*perfidia d'un sol passo*],[17] and fugal [*fugato*]. Some are stripped of certain consonances, others are called *answering* counterpoints because they must divert the given notes of the cantus firmus, and so on, including double counterpoint.

Contrapunto alla zoppa is counterpoint in which the half note is syncopated, that is, before the half note there is a quarter note, and after the half note are two quarter notes.

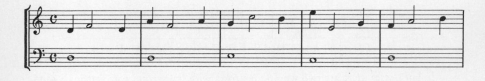

---

* *Angelo Berardi*, Documenti armonici (*Bologna, 1687*), *pp. 12–15, 36–40, 62*. Miscellanea musicale (*Bologna, 1689*), *pp. 38–41, 58–70, 78–80.*

16. *Zoppa* is the Italian for limping or hobbling along.
17. Corruption of a single beat.

Contrapunto alla diritta is counterpoint in which the melodic motion is by step, either ascending or descending.

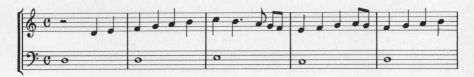

Contrapunto saltando is counterpoint in which the melodic motion is always by leap, not by step.

The artificial counterpoints indicated above may be used in capricci and ricercari, as may be seen in the capricci of Frescobaldi (Section 8.6). An obligato part may be improvised at the octave, but only in stepwise motion with the other four parts.[18]

Concerning Fugue

The fugue is a statement [*replica*] or answer [*reditta*]. It may be an exact imitation of a theme; or sometimes it may be a complete modification of the original melody. Similarly, fugue means that one part presents the

18. Berardi is concerned here with adding a fifth part to a four-part composition. Among Frescobaldi's works there is a *capriccio* "to which a fifth obligato part may be sung without being played, with the obligato part always on the given theme." This capriccio has a section in which chromatic motion appears in one part or another. Berardi is cautioning the improviser not to get into difficulty with the other parts when they are not moving diatonically.

subject and another follows it on the same course or path. The statement, an exact presentation note for note, is a name perfectly clear in itself. The answer, in responding, relates to and refers to what the other part sang originally. *Imitation,* a copy of the original, searches with all its powers for ways to imitate, whether by interval or by beat, in every kind of motion, trying to get at the core of everything that was said originally. . . .

We will divide the fugue into different species, showing the more artificial types. Let us begin with the real fugue, the type in which the parts really answer the leader, or subject, not only with the same intervals, but also in the same mode, the same pattern of tones and semitones.

This fugue does not adhere to the formation of the mode, because a mode is not constructed on two fifths; nor does it consist of two fourths. To avoid the soprano's reaching a ninth,[19] the alto and bass would have to answer as in the example on the following page. This would give shape to the mode.[20]

19. In the *real fugue* the opening leaps of the subject and answer combine to form a ninth. Since the combined leaps do not constitute an octave, which is the range of a mode, they do not lie within a single mode. (For the eight church modes see Chart 5.) We may think of this subject as being in transposed Aeolian. (For the Aeolian mode see Glareanus, Section 6.8.)

20. In a *tonal fugue* the answer is contrived to stay within the mode or *tone.* Therefore a subject that leaps a fifth is answered by the interval of a fourth to complete the octave.

Tonal Answers

Alto   Bass

Vocal Styles for Church, Chamber, and Theater: *Miscellanea musicale*

In their musical progressions our ancestors did not use certain dissonant intervals, like the diminished fifth, the tritone, and others now used today in the Second Practice, which create new harmony, and are necessary for expressing the words. The said intervals will be used in due time to produce a third type of musical progression, totally different from the usual. This is proved by the authority of various excellent composers. Monteverdi in the beginning of *Lasciatemi morire* uses the diminished fifth in a way that moves one to pity.[21] Nenna uses the same interval in the first of his madrigals for four voices, at the word *Humiltà*.[22]

Cipriano uses the tritone in his madrigal *Poiche m'invitta amore*, at the words *Dolce mia vita*. Giaches does it in the madrigal *Misera non credea* in the eighth book at the word *essangue*. Besides, Luca Marenzio, and many other famous masters use the tritone, as may be seen in their publications.[23]

The moderns use the bare seventh as a deception [*inganno*] and accent, or as a dissonance if it is softened by the accompaniment of the other parts. This new progression renders a new effect on the ear, as may be observed in the ninth book of madrigals of Luca Marenzio at the beginning of *E io come in un punto* at the words *maggio durrezza*, and in the second part at *da i colpi*. Brevity prevents me from naming many others who have used the seventh in a different manner from the First Practice.

Modern musicians are seeking to separate themselves from the ancient style in a definite way, for no other reason than to discover an individual expression of the words in order to move the affects and passions of the soul to a great degree. This was not done by our ancestors, who perceived only a moderate style and a common school of thought in making use of the consonances and dissonances. And this is proved in the works that have come to light.

If we consider Palestrina, the chief and father of music, a composer who did not live so long ago, we find that among his madrigals and motets there is little difference in terms of variation of style.

21. Berardi is referring to the Second Practice mentioned by Monteverdi (see Section 8.3). The *Lament of Arianna* for solo voice and bass accompaniment is the only remainder we have of Monteverdi's opera *Arianna*, commissioned by the Duke of Mantua in 1608. Monteverdi also made a madrigal arrangement of the *Lament of Arianna* for five voices without accompaniment, published in his sixth book of Madrigals in 1614. Apparently Monteverdi had no qualms about reversing a process that many of his contemporaries were trying to steer in the other direction.
22. Pomponio Nenna (1550–1618), the teacher of Gesualdo, wrote eight books of five-voiced madrigals and one book for four voices.
23. Luca Marenzio (1553–1599), famous Italian madrigalist, was active at Rome and Ferrara in Italy and also at the Polish court of Sigismund III.

We might look at the popular works in the French and Dutch languages, like the *Twenty-Six Musical Chansons;* and also the Third Book containing *Twenty-Two New Chansons for six and eight Parts,* published in the years 1545, 1546, and 1549; [24] and in the years 1550 and 1552 the works of different composers like Créquilon,[25] Ianluys,[26] Petit,[27] Landelatere, Iaques, Vaet, Vulnerant,[28] Baston,[29] Clemenz Morel, Clemens non Papa, Iusquino, Jan Gerard, Simon Cardon, Ricourt, Adriano, Noel Balwin, Jan Ockenheim,[30] Verdelot and many others, who have been omitted, from various nations. If we consider their compositions, we do not find any difference between ecclesiastical and secular melody, except for some who use a slightly more joyous melodic progression, such as *La belle Margarite, La Girometta,* and *La Bataille* of Clément Janequin, and some compositions by Verdelot.[31] For his motets, masses and madrigals the latter provides music from which the funny and joyous is little or no different from the serious except for the text. And he uses consonances and dissonances in a way that clearly shows that our ancestors had one style, and a single practice. The moderns have three styles, for the church, for the chamber, and for the theater. There are two practices. The first, which is older, provides that *the harmony is mistress of the words;* the second, that *the words are mistress of the harmony.*

24. Pierre Attaignant published thirty-five books of chansons from 1539 to 1549, with over 900 part songs by French and Flemish composers. Tielman Susato published thirteen books of chansons at Antwerp from 1543 on.
25. Thomas Créquillon (d. 1557), a French contrapuntist, was also mentioned by Monteverdi (Section 8.3).
26. By Ianluys Berardi probably means Jean Louys of Belgium who set the Psalms of David in the French text of Marot and de Bèze, "composed musically following the song of the folk [*le chant vulgaire*]" (Antwerp, 1555).
27. Adrien Petit Coclicus (c. 1500–1563), a Flemish musician, studied with Josquin. He wrote *Compendium musices* (1552), in which the term *musica reservata* is mentioned.
28. For Waelrant's use of syllables, see the introduction to Puteanus, Section 7.4. Some of Waelrant's compositions were published by the firm he founded with Jean Laet; others came out with Tylman Susato at Antwerp, Pierre Phalèse at Louvain, and other publishers at Venice.
29. Josquin Baston wrote chansons published by Susato. For Baston and many of the other chanson composers mentioned by Berardi, see Charles van den Borren, "The French Chanson" in *The Age of Humanism 1540–1630,* Vol. IV of *The New Oxford History of Music,* ed. Gerald Abraham (London: Oxford University Press, 1968).
30. For Clemens non Papa, Josquin, Adrian Willaert, and Ockeghem, see Section 8.3.
31. Clément Janequin (1485–c. 1560), a pupil of Josquin, wrote French program chansons, such as *La Bataille* (The Battle). This work imitates the sounds of fanfares and drums using only four unaccompanied voices, with the harmonies repeated in declamatory fashion and redistributed through the parts to create varying effects.

    Philippe Verdelot (d. c. 1550), a Flemish composer, was one of the early writers of Italian madrigals. Twenty-two of his works were arranged by Willaert for solo voice with lute accompaniment (printed in tablature, Venice, 1536). In 1545 Verdelot added a fifth voice, which could be performed optionally, to Janequin's *Bataille,* published in Antwerp by Tylman Susato.

The CHURCH STYLE is considered in four ways:

1. Masses, Psalms, Motets, Hymns for several voices, in the old practice.
2. Vocal compositions with the organ, for a great many voices, in a more advanced style.
3. Psalms, Motets, and Masses for several concertizing voices with instruments.
4. *Concertinos* in the modern style, such as Dialogues, Motets, and musical portions of the Oratorio.[32]

The CHAMBER STYLE is divided and conceived as three styles:

1. Madrigals for the table [*madrigali da tavolino*].[33]
2. Concerted madrigals [*madrigali concertati*] with basso continuo.
3. Concerted vocal compositions [*Cantilene concertate*] with various sorts of instruments.[34]

The THEATER STYLE, in this respect, consists only of words with melody and of singing with words. . . .

I am omitting the music for Serenades, Canzonette, Cantatas interspersed with the deteriorating Recitative style, Ariette of different types, such as sonnets, ottava (rima), laments, etc., since these are practiced daily with worthy invention and uplifted spirits by modern composers, who continually struggle to reduce music to its ultimate end, that is, to delight and to uplift the human passions, as all the philosophers say.

8.6 GIROLAMO FRESCOBALDI (1583–1643)

In contrast to vocal music, which engendered the expressive style in the interpretation of the words, keyboard music, lacking text, sought expression in the skillful treatment of ornamentation and the flexible coordination of tempos within a composition. In the preface to his *Toccatas and Partitas* (1614) Girolamo Frescobaldi, organist at St. Peter's in Rome, elucidated these means toward enhancing the emotional impact of organ and harpsichord music.

32. The term *concertino* might refer here to compositions like Viadana's concertos for vocal soloists with organ (see Section 8.2). The Dialogue sometimes had only two singers who alternated with questions and answers.
    In seventeenth-century instrumental music the word *concertino* referred to the small group of soloists in contrast to the full orchestra, the *ripieno*.
33. *Table music,* to be performed at mealtime (*Tafelmusik* in German), was popular in Mozart's day.
34. In seventeenth-century vocal music the term *coro concertato* referred to the small group of soloists and *coro ripieno* referred to the full chorus.

Although Frescobaldi does not specify which compositions were to be played on the harpsichord and which on the organ, the toccata and partite were obviously intended for the keyboard.[35] The verb *toccare* literally means "to touch" in Italian, while the verb *partire* means "to divide." Over the individual compositions Frescobaldi used the noun *toccata* in the singular, designating *Toccata prima*, *Toccata seconda*, and so forth. However, he used the noun *Partite* in the plural, to mean variations or divisions, as in *Partite 14 sopra l'Aria della Romanesca*, fourteen divisions on the traditional harmonic bass called the *Romanesca*, and *Partite six sopra l'Aria di Follia*, six divisions on the traditional *Follia* melody. *Cento Partite sopra Passacagli* were 100 divisions on a simple bass, two and sometimes four measures long. In the latter work Frescobaldi stopped enumerating with division number 11. He said that the performer need not play all the sections of the work, and that the divisions that are played should be coordinated by adjustment of the tempo from one variation to another. By describing the means of ornamentation within a division as *passaggi* (fast runs, Section 7.8) and *affetti*, (affect, passion, sentiment) he fuses the very concept of embellishment with emotion.

The Expressive Style on the Keyboard*

Preface to the Toccatas and Partite

Realizing the great popularity of playing with songlike affects and a variety of passages [*passi*], I decided to show my interest by publishing my slight contribution, presenting it in print with the following observation: I aver that I appreciate the discernment of others, and I shall be grateful to all who may approve of the affect with which I approach the studious and polite readers.

1. First, this manner of playing need not be subject to the beat [*battuta*]. As in the case with modern madrigals, no matter how difficult they may be, they are made easy by means of the conductor's beat, sometimes slow, sometimes fast, or evenly sustained, according to the affect or sense of the words.

2. In the toccatas, not only have I provided for an abundance of different passages and affects, but I have also made it possible for each section to be played separately from the other, so that the player may stop where he pleases without being obliged to play them all to the end.

---

*Toccate d'intavolatura di cimbalo et organo, Partite di diversi arie et Corrente, Balletti, Ciaccone, Passachagli, *by Girolamo Frescobaldi, Organist at St. Peters in Rome. Book 1. Printed in the year 1637 by Nicolo Borbone.*

35. These compositions appeared in prints and reprints with varying titles from 1614 to 1637. They were written in the Italian condensed keyboard score with a staff of six lines for the right hand and eight lines for the left (see Viadana, Section 8.2, fn. 4).

3. The beginnings of the toccatas should be played *adagio* and *arpeggiando*. Tied notes [*ligature*] and real discords [*durelli*], such as those in the middle of the work, should be played on the beat, so that the instrument should not sound empty.[36] This playing on the beat and arpeggiation may be done at the discretion of the performer.

4. Hold the last note of a trill, as well as that of passages by step or leap, whether the said note be an eighth note, a sixteenth note, and so forth, for such a pause prevents the confusion of one passage with another.

5. Cadences, even when they are written in rapid note values, should be suitably sustained. When coming to the end, play the passage or cadence more slowly. The conclusion of a passage, and its separation from the next occurs when a consonance in half notes is written for both hands at the same time.

6. When there is a trill in either the right hand or the left, while the other hand has to play a passage at the same time, do not play note against note, but simply try to play the trill rapidly, and perform the passage less rapidly and expressively. Otherwise confusion will arise.

7. When passages occur in eighth notes in one hand, and in sixteenth notes in the other at the same time, you should not play too quickly. The hand which has the sixteenth notes should perform them in a dotted manner, that is, not the first note but the second should have the dot. Continue thus, alternating with one not dotted and the next dotted.

8. Notice that where there are double passages with both hands in sixteenth notes, you must stop on the preceding note, even if it is black. Then play the passage with determination, thus making the dexterity of your hands seem so much the greater.

9. In the Partite where ornaments and affects are found, it would be well to use a *largo* tempo. This observation also applies to the Toccatas. The unornamented sections may be played with a somewhat faster beat. It is left to the good taste and excellent judgment of the player to establish the tempo, on which the spirit and perfection of this manner and style of playing depend.

The Passacaglia sections may be played separately, as one pleases, adjusting the tempo at will from one section to another—the same for the Chaconne sections.[37]

8.7 SEBASTIEN DE BROSSARD (1655–1730)

In 1703 Sebastien de Brossard, Grand Chaplain and Master of Music at the Cathedral of Meaux in France, summarized the musical knowledge at his command in the alphabetical organization characteristic of a dictionary. The title of his work, *Dictionary of Music, Containing an Ex-*

---

36. The eighth toccata is entitled *Toccata ottava, di durezze e ligature*.
37. This paragraph applies to the *Cento Partite sopre Passacagli*.

planation of the Greek, Latin, Italian, and French Terms Most Used in Music, indicates the proximity of French and Italian thought at the time. Brossard's articles on style and on the forms then current are highly informative because he had a consummate knowledge of the music about which he wrote. In fact, he was such an avid collector of the music of other composers that in 1724, starting with the manuscripts from Brossard's private library, Louis XV initiated the music collection of the Bibliothèque Nationale in Paris.

Definitions*

Cantata (in the plural, *Cantate*)

People are beginning to use *Cantate* as the French term. It is a long piece, whose words are in Italian, varied by Recitatives, by Ariettes, and by different movements, ordinarily for a solo voice and basso continuo, often with two violins or several instruments, etc. When the words concern piety or morality, one calls them *Cantate morali ò spirituali;* when they speak of love, they are *Cantate amorosè.*

Suonata (in the plural, *Suonate*)

It is thus that the Italians commonly write this word. However, one also often finds it without the *u,* as *Sonata.* It is what the French are beginning to translate with the word SONATE. This word comes from *Suono* or *Suonare,* because it is uniquely with the sound of instruments that one plays this kind of piece. They are with respect to all sorts of instrument what the Cantata is with respect to the voice. That is to say that Sonatas are properly long pieces, Fantasies, or Preludes, etc., varied by all sorts of movements and of expressions, by refined or extraordinary harmonies, by simple or double fugues, etc., and all that purely according to the fantasy of the composer, who without being subjected to the general rules of counterpoint, nor to any fixed number or particular kind of meter [*mesure*], gives his effort to the fire of his genius, changing the meter and mode when he thinks it suitable, etc. One finds them for one, two, three, four, five, six, seven, and eight parts, but ordinarily they are for a solo violin or for two different violins with a basso continuo for the harpsichord, and often a more ornamented bass for the viola da gamba, the bassoon, etc. There are, so to speak, an infinite number of styles, but the Italians ordinarily reduce them to two types.

The first comprises the *Sonates da Chiesa,* that is to say, suitable for the Church, which ordinarily begin with a slow and majestic movement suited to the dignity and holiness of the place, followed by a gay and animated Fugue, etc. This is what one properly calls Sonatas.

* *Sebastien de Brossard,* Dictionnaire de Musique *(Paris: Christophe Ballard, 1703).*

The second type consists of *Sonates* which are called *da Camera*, that is so say, suitable for the Chamber. These are properly suites of several short pieces suitable for dancing, and composed in the same mode or tone. This kind of sonata ordinarily begins with a Prelude, or short Sonata which serves as a preparation for all the others. Afterwards come the Allemand, the Pavane, the Courante, and other dances or serious airs. Finally come the Gigues, the Passacaglias, the Gavottes, the Minuets, the Chaconnes, and other gay Airs. Everything is composed in the same tone or mode, and, played in succession, composes a Sonata da Camera.

Stilo (meaning, Style)

That is in general the manner or particular fashion of expressing one's thoughts in writing or doing something else. In music one speaks of the manner which each one in particular has of *composing*, or of *playing*, or of *teaching*. And all of this is very different according to the nature [*genie*] of the author, of the region, and of the nation, as also according to the materials, the place, the time, the subject, the expression, etc. Thus one says the style of Carissimi, of Lully, of Lambert, etc.[38] The style of the Italians, the French, the Spaniards, etc. The style of gay and joyful music is very different from the style of grave or serious music. The style of the music of the church is very different from the style of music for the theater or the chamber. The style of Italian compositions is piquant, florid, expressive; that of the French compositions is natural, flowing, tender, etc. From this come various epithets for distinguishing all these different characteristics, such as ancient and modern style; Italian, French, German style, etc; ecclesiastical, dramatic, chamber style; gay, joyful, florid style; piquant,[39] pathetic, expressive style; grave, serious, majestic style; natural, flowing, tender, affectionate style; grand, sublime, gallant style; familiar, popular, low, crying style, etc.

8.8 ARCHANGELO CORELLI (1653–1713)

The Italian trio sonata is exemplified in the works of Archangelo Corelli, who wrote four sets of trio sonatas for two violins and basso continuo. Opus 1 (1683) and Opus 3 (1689) were *Sonate da Chiesa* for three

38. Giacomo Carissimi (1605–1674), active in Rome, veered from the strict a cappella style of Palestrina. Carissimi wrote oratorios which, beside polyphonic choruses, has recitative in a polished monodic style, with instrumental accompaniment. Carissimi also composed motets and masses.

    Michael Lambert (c. 1610–1696), singer and lutenist, was master of chamber music for Louis XIV. He was Lully's father-in-law. Lambert wrote *Airs et brunettes*, light songs on popular subjects, and *Airs et dialogues*.

39. Brossard clarifies *Stile Picquant* under his entry for STACCATO, as follows:

    That is to say, on all bowed instruments the bow strokes [*coup d'archet*] must be sharp, without dragging, and well detached or separated from one another. It is almost what we call *Picqué* or *Pointé* in French.

parts, played by two violins in the treble and a violone (double-bass viola da gamba) or archlute below, reinforced with a bass for the organ. Opus 2 (1685) and Opus 4 (1694) were *Sonate da Camera* for three parts, played by two violins and a violone or harpsichord.

The following passage from Corelli's chamber sonata Opus 2, No. 3, visually abounding in parallel fifths, became the center of a controversy which indicated that the seventeenth-century Italian instrumental style was by no means uniform throughout Italy. The complete sonata consists of the following movements: *Preludio* (Largo), *Allemanda* (Allegro), *Adagio*, and *Allemanda* (Presto).

Allemanda

Padre Matteo Zani was the spokesman for the leading virtuosi of Bologna who met at the home of the president of the Accademia Filarmonica, Giovanni Paolo Colonna, to play and discuss the music of the day. Even though Corelli had left Bologna for Rome some fourteen years earlier, this piece was on their minds in 1685 because Corelli's Opus 2 had just been published in Bologna, only months after it first appeared in Rome.

According to Zani, the Bolognese musicians actually scored the work to examine the fifths more closely. Parallel fifths had already been observed in the more popular styles of the villanelle by Morley and Praetorius.[40] Here the allemand came in for its share of freedom from

40. In the *Synatagma Musicum* (1619) Michael Praetorius wrote:

> The name *villanella* comes from *villa* [country estate, farm], that is, a village, and *villano*, a farmer. Thus *villanello*, the diminutive, means something like "slightly rustic." Hence, villanella, a farmer's song which the peasants and common artisans sing. Therefore composers often purposely take pains to use four or five fifths, even though they rarely occur in succession according to the rules of music, since peasants do not sing according to art, but rather according to what occurs to them. It is peasant music for peasant taste. Sometimes such songs are also called *villotta, vilatella*. That was the way a small village was formerly designated. Formerly in France the farmers' dances which were composed [inventirt] by the farmers themselves, and were performed with shawms and fiddles, often with two, three, and more people to a part, were called *villages*. And until the present the songs had text; now some occur without text.

the strict rules. Corelli wrote the rests as deliberately as he did the notes, and he took into account the harmonies which lingered in the ear through these rests.

Hearing Through Parallel Fifths*

Matteo Zani's Letter to Archangelo Corelli

Bologna, September 26, 1685

Because your compositions for the church as well as the chamber are so beautiful, our virtuosi have had the occasion to put them into score [*partitura*] to study how they are constructed. And since in scoring the last chamber sonata published, they happened to come across some parallel fifths, and not being able to understand the reason for them, the more because Your Lordship marks the fifth with the visible sign of the number, which you do intentionally, they indicated that they wanted to consult you to find out the reason for it. But I who am so smitten with your corrections, and who know that you would not have published anything which was not completely perfect, beseech you to tell me something about this, so that I may be able to tell them what Your Lordship intends, so that they may learn what they do not know.

Corelli's Reply to Matteo Zani

Rome, October 17, 1685

I received in your most accomplished letter the page with the passage from the third sonata, where your virtuosi are having difficulty. This does not at all surprise me, but rather helps me to understand very well the extent of their knowledge, which barely stretches beyond the first principles of composition and harmonic modulation. If they had made further progress in the art and would have understood its finesse and profundity, and what the substance of harmony might be, and in what way it may charm and comfort the human mind, they would not have had such scruples, which ordinarily arise from ignorance. I, with careful attention for many years, following the practice of the most esteemed professors of music in Rome, have attempted to perceive their proofs and their examples, knowing very well that everything one does must be regulated by reason, or by the example set by the most excellent professors.

Nevertheless, I will make myself clear in some respects to satisfy the curiosity of your virtuosi, and to show them that I understand and know the basis for this passage which is obscure to them, as well as for all others that I have published, why I have composed and wish to compose in this way. Indeed, in this passage one sees for oneself that I have marked the fifths over the bass to make it obvious that I expressed my intention, knowing what I wanted a fifth to do, not by error, but by my choice. For if, instead of the

---

* *This correspondence is preserved in the library of the Liceo Musicale at Bologna. It is listed in the* Catalogo della biblioteca del Liceo musicale di Bologna, *compiled by Gaetano Gaspari (Bologna: Libreria Romagnoli dall'Acqua, 1890–1943), I, 74.*

eighth-note rest [*mezzo sospiro*],[41] I would have added a dot of the same value to the preceding note, the musical beginners who compose only with the primary rules would not notice any difficulty. But I wanted the note to be detached [*stacchi*] and to fade away [*smorzi*] [42] because I thought that if I composed it that way, it would be felt to better advantage. Besides, to shed some additional light on my intention for those who are in the dark, if they will give thought to the start of that short modulating passage, they will find that a rhythm [*tempo*] begins and continues. Anyone who understands the art must be able to follow this, if he wants the beauty of the harmony to last. In the teaching of Euclid the saying goes: Time is motion measured according to the past and the future. Whence, consider the beginning, the middle, and the end of my modulation, and you will understand my intention. Furthermore, to satisfy your virtuosi, and not to rely entirely on my opinion, I have shown the troublesome passage to the Signori Francesco Foggia, Antimo Liberati, Matteo Simonelli, and all, of the same opinion, have agreed with me that it stands up very well, and that someone who has difficulty with it does not understand the tie [*la legatura*], and that if anyone else were to compose a similar passage in a similar motion [*andamenti*], they would always feel obliged to defend it.[43]

I am not pursuing this any further, because it seems to me that this short explanation should be sufficient to satisfy the curiosity of your virtuosi, and likewise to teach them a little bit about their apprenticeship in the art.

Bibliographical Notes

Discussions of this passage in Corelli's Opus 2, No. 3 are contained in F. T. Arnold, *The Art of Accompaniment from a Thorough-Bass as practised in the 17th and 18th centuries* (Oxford University Press, 1931; London: The Holland Press, 1961), pp. 901–903; also, Marc Pincherle, *Corelli, His Life, His Music*, trans. Hubert E. M. Russel (New York: W. W. Norton & Company, Inc., 1956), pp. 47–50.

8.9 HENRY PURCELL (1659–1695)

The Italian violin style quickly made its way into English chamber music, despite writers of the old school like Thomas Mace in *Musicks Monument* (1670). Mace preferred a chest of viols consisting of two

41. *Mezzo sospiro* literally means half a sigh or breath. The unit value for the rest would thus be a quarter note, since half of it was an eighth note.
42. The intangibles of performance, the minute time value deducted from a note when it is played *staccato*, and the liquescence when a note fades away as in *smorzando*, occur for Corelli during the rest.
43. Francesco Foggia (c. 1604–1688) had spent many years in the service of the German courts. At the time of this letter he was maestro di cappella of Santa Maria Maggiore in Rome.

    Antimo Liberati, a student of Gregorio Allegri and Orazio Benevoli, wrote several letters in defense of Corelli's passage.

    Corelli had studied counterpoint with Matteo Simonelli.

trebles, two tenors, and two basses, to a disproportionate ensemble in which "the scolding violins will out-top them all." In contrast, Henry Purcell in the preface to his *Sonatas of Three Parts: Two Violins and Bass, to the Organ or Harpsichord* confesses his desire to imitate the Italian trio sonata.

This work, published in part books in 1683, did not appear in printed score until two centuries later. As had been the custom since the time of Viadana, provision for a score was up to the keyboard player rather than the publisher. The part books were for first and second violins, viola da gamba, and basso, four in all. The gamba and bass parts, although separate, were identical except for the use of figures in the latter to show the chords to be played on the harpsichord or organ.

Imitation of Italian Chamber Music Style:
Purcell's Preface *

To the Reader

Ingenuous Reader,

Instead of an elaborate harangue on the beauty and the charms of Musick (which, after all the learned Encomions that words can contrive, commends itself best by the performances of a skilful hand, and an angelical voice) I shall say but a very few things by way of Preface, concerning the following Book, and its Author. For its Author, he has faithfully endeavoured a just imitation of the most famed Italian Masters; principally, to bring the serious-ness and gravity of that sort of Musick into vogue, and reputation among our Country-men, whose humor, 'tis time now, should begin to loath the levity, and balladry of our neighbors. The attempt he confesses to be bold, and daring, there being Pens and Artists of more eminent abilities, much better qualified for the employment than his, or himself, which he well hopes these his weak endeavours, will in due time provoke, and enflame to a more acurate undertaking. He is not ashamed to own his unskilfulness in the Italian Language; but that's the unhappiness of his Education, which cannot justly be accounted his fault, however he thinks he may warrantably affirm, that he is not mistaken in the power of the Italian Notes, or elegancy of their Compositions, which he would recommend to the English Artists. There has been neither care, nor industry wanting, as well in contriving, as revising the whole Work; which had been abroad in the world much sooner, but that he has now thought fit to cause the whole Thorough Bass to be Engraved, which was a thing quite besides his first Resolutions. It remains only that the English Practitioner be informed, that he will find a few terms of Art perhaps unusual to him, the chief of which are these following: Adagio and Grave, which import nothing but a very slow movement: Presto Largo, Poco Largo, or Largo by itself, a middle movement: Allegro, and Vivace, a very brisk, swift, or fast movement: Piano, soft. The Author has no more to add, but his hearty wishes, that his Book may fall into no

---

* *Henry Purcell*, Twelve Sonatas of Three Parts, *ed. J. A. Fuller Maitland (London and New York: Novello, Ewer and Co., 1893). Preface in facsimile.*

other hands but theirs who carry Musical Souls about them; for he is willing to flatter himself into a belief, that with such his labours will seem neither unpleasant, nor unprofitable.

8.10 JOSEPH ADDISON (1672–1719)

The Italian impact reached England not only in the medium of the trio sonata, but in opera as well. Still used today are the Italian tempo designations mentioned by Purcell, and operatic terms such as *aria* and *recitative*. The Italian hold on opera was satirized by Joseph Addison in one of his penetrating essays in *The Spectator* (1710–1711).

English Satire on Italian Opera*

Wednesday, March, 21.

It is my design in this paper to deliver down to posterity a faithful account of the Italian opera, and of the gradual progress which it has made upon the English stage; for there is no question but our great grandchildren will be very curious to know the reason why their forefathers used to sit together like an audience of foreigners in their own country, and to hear whole plays acted before them in a tongue which they did not understand.

Arsinoe was the first opera that gave us a taste of Italian music.[44] The great success this opera met with produced some attempts of forming pieces upon Italian plans, which should give a more natural and reasonable entertainment than what can be met with in the elaborate trifles of that nation. This alarmed the poetasters and fiddlers of the town, who were used to deal in a more ordinary kind of ware; and therefore laid down an established rule, which is received as such to this day, "That nothing is capable of being well set to music, that is not nonsense."

This maxim was no sooner received, but we immediately fell to translating the Italian operas; and as there was no great danger of hurting the sense of these extraordinary pieces, our authors would often make words of their own, which were entirely foreign to the meaning of the passages they pretended to translate; their chief care being to make the numbers of the English verse answer to those of the Italian, that both of them might go to the same tune. Thus the famous song in Camilla:

Barbara si t'intendo, &c.
(Barbarous woman, yes, I know your meaning)

which expresses the resentments of an angry lover, was translated into that English lamentation:

Frail are a lover's hopes, &c.

*The Works of Joseph Addison (*New York: Harper and Brothers, 1850*), I, 42, 43.
44. *Arsinoe, queen of Cyprus,* an opera after the Italian manner by Thomas Clayton. It was first performed at the Theatre Royal, Drury Lane, in 1707.

And it was pleasant enough to see the most refined persons of the British nation dying away and languishing to notes that were filled with a spirit of rage and indignation. It happened also very frequently where the sense was rightly translated, the necessary transposition of words, which were drawn out of the phrase of one tongue into that of another, made the music appear very absurd in one tongue that was very natural in the other. I remember an Italian verse that ran thus, word for word:

And turn'd my rage into pity

which the English for rhyme sake translated,

And into pity turn'd my rage

By this means the soft notes that were adapted to pity in the Italian, fell upon the word rage in the English; and the angry sounds that were turned to rage in the original, were made to express pity in the translation. It oftentimes happened, likewise, that the finest notes in the air fell upon the most insignificant words in the sentence. I have known the word *And* pursued through the whole gamut, have been entertained with many a melodious *The,* and have heard the most beautiful graces, quavers, and divisions, bestowed upon *Then, For,* and *From;* to the eternal honour of our English particles.

The next step to our refinement was the introducing of Italian actors into our opera; who sung their parts in their own language, at the same time that our countrymen performed theirs in our native tongue. The king or hero of the play generally spoke in Italian, and his slaves answered him in English. The lover frequently made his court, and gained the heart of his princess, in a language which she did not understand. One would have thought it very difficult to have carried on dialogues after this manner without an interpreter between the persons that conversed together; but this was the state of the English stage for about three years.

At length the audience grew tired of understanding half the opera; and therefore to ease themselves entirely of the fatigue of thinking, have so ordered it at present, that the whole opera is performed in an unknown tongue.

8.11 JEAN-BAPTISTE LULLY (1632–1687)
THROUGH LECERF DE LA VIÉVILLE

Italian opera prospered in a number of different cities, notably in Florence, Mantua, Rome, and Venice; French opera flourished in Paris and Versailles, near the king. Louis XIV reveled in the activities of Jean-Baptiste Lully, composer to His Majesty and music master of the royal family. In 1672 Lully gained a royal privilege which meant control of the Royal Academy of Music and with it a monopoly on the national opera, an institution which still exists as the *Grand Opéra.*

Lully, who managed music as well as he composed it, under certain circumstances wrote only the outer voices of the score himself, enlisting the aid of one or another of his secretaries, Jean-Baptiste-François Lalouette and Pascal Colasse, to fill in the less essential inner voices. This type of cooperation was possible mainly in the sections dependent on basso continuo style, with its emphasis on the upper voice and the reinforced bass. The chief ensembles and choruses received the master's attention throughout. Lully's work habits are described in an early eighteenth century essay by Leçerf de la Viéville, Sieur de Fresneuse (1647–1710), entitled *Comparison of Italian and French Music* (1704–1706).

Quinault as Lully's Librettist*

Lully was attached to Quinault; he was his poet. Quinault used to find and lay out several operatic subjects. He then brought them to the king, who chose one. When Quinault wrote a plan of the design and of the continuity of his piece, he gave a copy of this plan to Lully, and Lully, examining the intent of each act, prepared divertissements, dances, and chansonettes of the shepherds, sailors, etc. Quinault composed the scenes; as soon as he finished some, he showed them to the French Academy. After having received and profited by the opinion of the Academy, he brought these scenes to Lully.

Lully at Work on an Opera

M. de Lîle Corneille is the author of the words of *Bellérophon*.[45] Lully drove him to despair at every turn. For the five or six hundred verses contained in that piece, M. de Lîle was compelled to write two thousand. Finally Quinault felt so badly about it that Lully accepted a scene. Lully read it until he almost knew it by heart. He sat down at his harpsichord, singing and resinging the words, striking the harpsichord and playing a basso continuo. When he had finished his song, it was so well impressed on his mind that he could not mistake a note of it. Lalouette or Colasse came, to whom he dictated it. The next day he would hardly remember it. He did the same with the symphonies connected with the words, and on the days when Quinault gave him nothing, he worked on the airs for the violin.

When he sat down to work and did not feel in the humor for it, he would very often quit. He would get up during the night to go to his harpsichord; and wherever he was, he would leave whenever an inspiration came to him.

*Jean-Laurent Leçerf de la Viéville Sieur de Fresneuse, Comparaison de la Musique Italienne et de la Musique Françoise in Pierre Bourdelot-Pierre Bonnet, Histoire de la Musique et de ses Effets (Amsterdam, 1725), III, 195, 198–199.

45. Although Philippe Quinault (1635–1688) was Lully's favorite librettist, Quinault was not necessarily the originator of the literary material that he presented to Lully for musical treatment. Initially *Bellérophon* was a play by Thomas Corneille 1625–1709); it was transformed into an opera libretto by Quinault, and then into an opera by Lully (1679).

He never lost a good moment. This was a very clever and sensible method, for it is an established fact that a good moment well taken and well used is worth more and leads much further than a day of reluctant application. He wrote an opera a year; for three months he devoted himself to it completely with extreme application and diligence. The rest of the year he did little—an hour or two from time to time on nights when he could not sleep, or on mornings not otherwise pleasurably occupied. However, he directed his thoughts for the whole year to the opera on which he was working, or which he had just written. As proof of this, whenever he was heard singing, it usually was something from his opera.

8.12 KING LOUIS XIV (1638–1715)

Lully had such powerful control over the production of opera in France that after his death in 1687 King Louis XIV had difficulty finding a comparable musical personality to uphold the French style in the face of Italian infiltration. The most likely successors to the operatic mantle were André Campra (1660–1744) and his student, André-Cardinal Destouches (1672–1749).

In his youth Destouches went to a Jesuit school in Paris, whence he was sent to Siam with a missionary in 1686. Later, after his return to France, Destouches wrote three songs for Campra's opera-ballet of 1687 entitled *L'Europe Galante*. In the same year Destouches' reputation was made when his own opera *Issé*, a "heroic pastorale" performed at the Trianon, caught the fancy of the king.

It was while Destouches was serving as Superintendent of the Music of the King and Inspector-General of the Académie Royale de Musique that the two decrees quoted below were issued by order of King Louis XIV.

Statute Concerning Opera Decreed at Versailles,
January 11, 1713*

His Majesty being informed that, since the decease of the late Monsieur Lully, there has been a surreptitious slackening of law and order within the Royal Academy of Music, despite the care that the directors have taken to avoid it, and that, by the confusion which has occurred there, the said Academy has been considerably overcharged with numerous debts, and the public exposed to the deprivation of a show which for a long time has always been uniformly acceptable; and consequently, his Majesty, wishing to avoid similar inconveniences, has resolved the present Statute, which he wishes to be followed and executed according to its form and terms.

*Jean Marie Bernard Clement, Anecdotes Dramatiques *(Paris, 1775), III, 533–534, 539–551.*

Article I

Monsieur de Francine, Honorary Patron of the said Academy, and Director, should take care to choose the best persons that he can find for singing as well as for dancing and for playing instruments. None of the said persons may be accepted without the approbation of Monsieur Destouches, Inspector-General.

Article II

To succeed in helping suitable persons to achieve what they are lacking, there will be established a School of Music, one of Dance, and one of Instruments; and those who will be admitted there will be taught there free of charge.

Article III

All the people employed in the service of the show will be ready for the performances as well as the rehearsals at the places and hours indicated by the Director, under penalty of a fine of 3 pounds; [46] and the said fine, just as all the others ordained by the present Statute, will be applicable to the General Hospital.

Article IV

All the Actors and Actresses of Music and Dance will be required to accept and to perform the roles or parts which are assigned to them, either to perform the said roles or parts as principals or as understudies, under penalty of being deprived of a month's wages for the first time, and of being dismissed in case of a second offense.

Article V

If it happens that any of the Actors or Actresses of Music and Dance or any of the Symphonists of the Orchestra is reported as disturbing the good order necessary for the progress of the show, a fine of 6 pounds will be imposed the first time, and in case of a second offense will be dismissed immediately.

Statute on the Subject of Opera Decreed at Marly, November 19, 1714

The King, by judgment issued to his council this day, having terminated the disputes which had arisen between the Owners of the license of the Royal Academy of Music and the Assignees of the said license, and deeming

46. The livre or pound was worth about 20 cents.

it necessary on this occasion to make some changes and additions to the rules prescribed for the regulation and administration of the said Academy by the Statute of 1713, His Majesty has revoked the said Statute, and has ordained the one which follows.

Article I

The Trustees of the Creditors, the Assignees of the license for the Opera should meet immediately to deliberate, choosing and naming two from among themselves. Of these one should be in sole charge of supervising and managing the rehearsals and performances in such a manner that the Actors and Actresses, Clerks and Workmen of the Opera House, need report only to him; the other should have charge of the warehouse, of damage and everything pertaining to it.

Article V

The order of the pieces which should be presented at the theater should be determined six months before the first performance of the one chosen for the opening, so that the plan for winter is always made during Easter Week, and the plan for summer during the month of November. This should be done at a meeting of the Trustees in charge of the management of the Theater, supervised by the Inspector.

Article VI

The winter productions should always begin with a new tragedy, which will be ready, together with costumes and decorations, for the 10th or 15th of October, so that it may be presented to the Public the 24th of the same month at the latest.

Article VII

As soon as the new piece has been played a sufficient number of times, performances should cease. Two weeks later an old Opera of Monsieur Lully should be substituted. The latter should always be ready, if possible, almost at the same time as the first piece which precedes it.

But if it happens that performance of the first piece is extended until Lent, then instead of the Opera of Monsieur Lully, which will not be played, the third piece mentioned in Article IX should be given, not to waste it.

Article VIII

With regard to the summer performances, if the last piece of the winter plan could not be presented by Easter, the performances on the first Sunday after Easter will always begin with a new Tragedy, or one by Monsieur Lully, which will be followed by a Ballet.

Article IX

Beside the four Operas, two for the winter and two for the summer, there should also be a third piece for each season, in case the others cannot be supplied.

Article XIII

The words intended for musical setting should be examined by the knowledgeable People on the Committee, before the Musician may begin to work on it.

Article XIV

After the piece of poetry has once been approved, it should be accepted by a resolution of the Trustees charged by the administration and supervised by the Inspector. The Author will always be responsible for naming the Composer of whose services he intends to avail himself, unless he has already been provided with one.

Article XV

When the music has been completed, the Composer will be responsible for having it heard and for exposing it entirely finished to the judgment of the People on the Committee, as prescribed in ARTICLE XIII. This should be performed six months before the piece may be presented in the Theater.

Article XVI

The Authors of Tragedies in four acts, for the Verses as well as for the Music, are paid on the production of the performances of their pieces, the Poet at the rate of 100 pounds, and the Musician likewise at a rate of 100 pounds for each of the first ten performances; and at the rate of 50 pounds for each of the next twenty performances, provided, however, that the said pieces were played without interruption. In the event that the pieces cannot be given the said number of performances because of the disfavor of the Public, the said Authors cannot claim anything after they are discontinued. Any performances of the said pieces in excess of the above amounts, no matter how many there are, belong to the Academy, and they may be presented again without the said Authors being entitled to anything.

Article XVII

The same rules apply to the Ballets and pieces in three acts, with the difference that the Authors, of the Verses as well as the Music, will be paid only at the rate of 60 pounds each for each of the first ten performances, and at the rate of 30 pounds for each of the next twenty performances.

Article XVIII

Actors and Actresses, male and female, Dancers, and Members of the Orchestra cannot be accepted at the Opera until after they have given proof of their competency in several performances, and have merited the approbation of the public. And they cannot be hired, nor can they be positively discharged without a meeting of the Trustees called by the Administration of the Theater, supervised by the Inspector.

Article XIX

Neither Actors nor Actresses may be admitted without knowing enough music to be able to study the roles and parts which may be assigned to them by themselves, unless they are not playing Characters of great importance. And in that case they will be obliged, just like those who actually participate, to acquire this degree of proficiency within one year. Otherwise they will be dismissed.

Article XXI

All the Actors and Actresses, with the exception of those who have the eight leading roles, are obliged to serve in the Choruses and to sing there, even if they may be assigned to some small roles. After they finish performing them, they resume their usual places.

Article XXII

The distribution of the roles and the entrances of the Dance are set by a meeting of the Trustees, supervised by the Inspector, on the advice of the Composer. If it is a new Opera, the Actors and Actresses, male and female Dancers, are required to accept the place which has been assigned to them, and to perform their functions there without making any excuses, on penalty of a fine of 6 pounds the first time, deprivation of a month's wages for the second, and being dismissed for the third.

Article XXIII

They are also required to play, dance and sing with the costumes given them for the purpose, without substituting others.

Article XXIV

If any male or female Singer and Dancer, or any Instrumentalist in the Orchestra causes trouble, disturbing the order necessary for the presentation of the spectacle, he will be fined 6 pounds the first time, will be deprived of a month's wages for the second, and will be dismissed for the third.

Article XXVI

The posts of Beater of Time [*Batteur de Mesure*] and that of Master of Music [*Maître de Musique*] for the Actors and Actresses, which have been confused for some time, will be distinguished and separated in the future, in view of the impossibility of having the functions of these two different occupations filled by the same person.

Article XXVII

That of Beater of Time is not only responsible for beating the time in the performances as well as in the rehearsals, but also for overseeing all the Members of the Orchestra; for keeping track of what should happen at precise hours so that they may perform their duties, and to prevent their leaving their places and their instruments during the Opera. And he should inform both the Inspector as well as the Trustees of any irregularities that he notices so that they may be corrected.

Article XXVIII

The function of the Master of Music is to go, at least three times a week, for the whole morning, at 9 o'clock precisely, to the Warehouse, where he will be assigned to a Hall or Room in which he will be able to study and rehearse the roles with the Actors who are to meet him there for that purpose. He is also in charge of demonstrating the Music to those who do not know it.

8.13 FRANÇOIS COUPERIN (1668–1733)

The polarization of treble and bass parts in the thoroughbass style encouraged composers to focus their attention on melody and harmony. Some musicians thought in horizontal terms, trying to articulate melody by emphasizing the accents and cadences with suitable ornamentation; others were more concerned with the vertical relationships that permeated the musical texture. Brossard (Section 8.7), in his dictionary article entitled *Motion*, found that the horizontal and vertical factors, intertwined with rhythm, produced musical motion. With respect to melody Brossard said the motion pertains to "the passage from one tone to another by interval, whether the melody goes through all the intermediate degrees within the interval or whether it only uses the two outer tones of the interval." With respect to harmony, Brossard observed, "One compares the way in which an upper part moves from one tone to another with the way in which the bass part moves from one tone to another at the same time."

François Couperin, a keyboard virtuoso in the highly embellished rococo style, sought to refine and identify the characteristics of motion that escape exact notation but are vital to performance. At the end of his treatise entitled *The Art of Playing the Harpsichord* (1717) he demonstrates how to perform the ornaments that cannot be spelled out in definite note values. Among them is one that Couperin actually calls *Aspiration* (inhaling), which he illustrates as follows:

The harpsichordist as well as the singer breathes while performing, reducing the time value of the decorated note by a rest approximating a sixteenth note.

In other embellishments Couperin included time values as short as a sixty-fourth note, and pitches above, below, or in between the given notes, always seeking to pinpoint the elusive, the immeasurable, the indefinable details of melodic motion.

Ornamentation: The French Harpsichord Piece Compared to the Italian Violin Sonata*

It is advantageous for those who instruct young people to import to them gradually a knowledge of the intervals, of the modes, of their cadences, perfect as well as imperfect, of the harmonies, of the suppositions.[47] This constitutes for them a kind of memory storage which makes them more secure, and which helps them to remember intelligently when they have forgotten.

Concerning batteries or arpeggios, whose origin is in the sonatas, my advice is that the number played on the harpsichord should be limited somewhat. This instrument has its own characteristics, as does the violin. If the

---

*François Couperin, L'art de toucher le Clavecin (1717).

47. The supposition is the contrapuntal structure of the work. According to Brossard,

> *Supposition* is when one part holds a note firmly, and the other part moves against that note through conjunct steps in two or more notes of less value. This is one of the ways of fashioning counterpoint that the Italians call *contrapunto sciolto* (free counterpoint). Others call it *celer progressus* (fast development), still others *ornement du chant* (embellishment of song), etc. But one of the greatest uses that one makes of *supposition*, is that by this means one makes the most dissonant sounds appear as if they were good, or at least as if they could improve one's impression or perception of the consonances.

In the article on *supposition* Brossard continues with a discussion of counterpoint with two and four notes against one in duple meter, and then with three notes against one in $\frac{6}{4}$, $\frac{6}{8}$ or $\frac{12}{8}$ meters.

harpsichord cannot swell its sounds, if the ornaments repeated on the same note are not completely suited to it, it has other advantages which are, precision, clarity, brilliance, and extent. Therefore one should sometimes take a middle path, which would be to adopt the fast movements of the sonatas, and to avoid the slow ones, whose basses are not at all suited to amalgamating the lute-like and syncopated passages of the harpsichord. But the French willingly absorb novelties to the detriment of truth, which they believe they comprehend better than the other nations. After all, we must be in agreement that pieces made expressly for the harpsichord always suit it better than the others. However, in the fast movements of the sonatas, there are some which thrive well enough on this instrument. These are the ones where the upper part and the bass are always busy.[48]

What usually makes moderately skillful players cling to the sonatas, is that few ornaments are used there, except for arpeggios. But what happens! These same players forever render themselves incapable of being able to play real harpsichord pieces. On the other hand, those who have first played the pieces well, perform the sonatas perfectly.

It might be worthwhile here to say a word about French motions and how they differ from the Italian. I believe that in our fashion of writing music there are faults which are related to the method of writing our language. That is, we write differently from the way we perform it. This is why foreigners play our music less well than we do theirs. On the other hand, the Italians write their music in the true values with which they conceived it. For example, we play several successive conjunct eighth notes in a dotted manner, even though we notate them equally. Our practice has enslaved us, and we still continue. THEREFORE, LET US FIND OUT WHERE THIS CONTRADICTION COMES FROM!

I find that we confuse *measure* with what is called *cadence* or *motion*. Measure defines the number and uniformity of the beats; and cadence is really the spirit and soul which must be combined with it. The sonatas of the Italians are not very receptive to cadence. But all of our airs for the violin, our pieces for the harpsichord, for the viols, etc., denote and seem to want to express some feeling. Thus, not having invented signs and characters for communicating our particular ideas, we try to remedy this by placing at the beginning of our pieces some words, like *tenderly*, *quickly*, etc., to show approximately how we would like them to be heard. I hope that someone will take the trouble of interpreting us for the benefit of foreigners. And may they thus gain the means of judging the excellence of our instrumental music.

With regard to delicate pieces which are played on the harpsichord, it is good not to play them quite as slowly as one would play them on other instruments, because of the shortness of duration of its tones. There cadence and taste by themselves may take care of the increase or decrease of speed.

48. Couperin gives an example here of an Allemande with perpetual sixteenth-note motion, appearing in one hand or the other, or both together.

9

Compositional Practices from the Baroque to the Classic Era

9.1 JEAN-PHILIPPE RAMEAU (1683–1764)

An overwhelming change in the concept of harmonic motion was introduced by Jean-Philippe Rameau, organist at the Cathedral at Clermont-Ferrand in France, when he wrote his *Treatise on Harmony* in 1722.[1] We can understand Rameau's innovation all the more fully if we pursue further Brossard's Dictionary article on *Motion* with respect to harmony (Section 8.13). Brossard enumerated three types of relationship between the voices, namely: (a) *direct motion*, when both the treble and bass ascend or descend together at the same time; (b) *contrary motion*, when the treble descends as the bass ascends, or vice versa; and (c) *oblique motion*, when one of the parts remains on the same tone while the other moves in either direction.

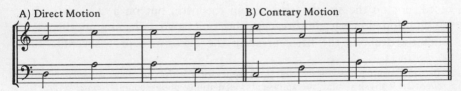

A) Direct Motion   B) Contrary Motion

1. The year after the *Traité de l'Harmonie* was published Rameau settled in Paris, where he wrote the *Nouveau Système* in 1726 to clarify his theories proposed four years earlier. The passages quoted here are from the latter work, the *New System of Music Theory, in Which One Discovers the Principle of All the Rules Necessary for the Practice; To Serve as an Introduction for the Treatise on Harmony.*

C) Oblique Motion

In each of Brossard's examples the bass includes the harmonic leap of a fourth or a fifth. The motions of the treble and bass are united in time contrapuntally, note against note by interval. In contrast, Rameau chose to consider harmony first and melody as springing from harmony, rather than the other way around. Each tone in a harmonic motion generated a chord above it and generated the next tone of the motion besides.

The union of three notes as two conjunct thirds, one major, the other minor, within the interval of a perfect fifth, had already been calculated by Zarlino in 1558 (Section 7.5). A chord on each letter name of the musical alphabet, and what was eventually called the first inversion, had been identified by Joachim Burmeister in *Musica Poetica* (Rostock, 1606).[2] The term *trias harmonica*, harmonic triad, had been used by Johannes Lippius in 1609. In 1611 Johann Alsted had said, "The consonant *trias* is that in which a third and a fifth concur, as if arising from two thirds. . . . The harmonic *trias* is the root of all the harmony that can be invented." [3] In 1650 Kircher had demonstrated the cycle of fifths (Section 8.5, first fn.). Brossard had described the cadential motive as the bass moving alternately by intervals of a descending fifth and an ascending fourth.[4] But it was Rameau who derived the *basse fondamentale*, the fundamental bass in which each tone is the root of a chord, in which each tone is itself a fundamental note harmonically related to the next fundamental note.

In contrast to the *basso continuo*, which was a real bass line actually played on an instrument, the *basse fondamentale* was a hypothetical bass, imagined but not played, resulting from placing the roots of the chords in succession. Rameau conceived of each chord of a composition as being based, not on the simple triad within the fifth, but on a seventh chord. He envisioned every chord except the tonic triad as having another conjunct third above the fifth, creating the dissonance of a seventh. This

2. In the Baroque era there were three types of treatise on music—namely, *musica theorica* (physical and metaphysical speculations about sound), *musica practica* (instruction on performance for voice and instrument), and *musica poetica* (how to compose).
3. Johann Heinrich Alsted (1588–1638), *Templum Musicum* (1611), trans. as *A Compendium of the Rudiments Both of the Mathematical and Practical Part of Musick* by John Birchensha (1644).
4. Brossard describes *motive* as that which "induces us to create something."

association of dissonance with the chord placed the emphasis on each vertical harmony, thus minimizing the attention to horizontal voice-leading. Eventually he changed his mind about using only seventh chords and let notes of the scale other than the tonic support a simple triad. He always considered the triad to be the "perfect chord," as Burmeister had done before him, because it was outlined by a perfect interval. In his desire to account for the harmonic drive toward the tonic, Rameau implied the circle of fifths wherever he could, reinforcing the progression by a bass that leaped down a fifth or up a fourth. Posterity has continued to recognize the progression of the dominant seventh chord to the tonic chord, both in root position, as the most conclusive harmonic cadence.

Preliminaries of Music*

Music is the science of sounds. It is separated into theory and practice. The theory of music considers the various ratios [*rapports*] between the sounds, investigates the principal, and provides the reason for the rules necessary in the practice. The practice of music teaches composition and performance.

The theory and practice of music are separated into harmony and melody. Harmony consists of the union of two or more sounds, by which the ear is affected agreeably. Melody is formed by many sounds heard successively, as when we sing.

We will see in the course of this treatise that melody grows from harmony.

Concerning Natural Melody

Melody is, as we have already said, the song of a single voice. Song may be formed only by the progression of fundamental sounds, and by one which is composed of chords. These progressions are natural to us, as is easily proved by the three different sounds which one distinguishes in a single sound of the voice, in a single string, etc.

A sound, then, directs our voice to intone after it those which have the most rapport with it. At the same time it becomes the arbiter of the modulation which we ought to follow, and everything which we sing later is governed by the first impression which we receive from it.

Finding the Basse Fondamentale Naturally

Here we are concerned with a fact of experience which all people slightly sensitive to harmony, from children of 8 to 9 years old up, may prove, despite the manner of instruction with which they started.

Jean-Philippe Rameau, Nouveau Système de Musique Théorique *(Paris: Ballard, 1726), pp. 1, 48–49, 54–55.*

Open a book of music. Keeping time, sing everything that is there from the beginning of an air until the first place where you believe you may rest. As that place is always the first note of a measure, apply to that first note the penultimate syllable of a word of which the last syllable is silent, like *tendre, aimable,* &c. Then allow your voice to fall at least a third below that first note, to pronounce the last silent syllable, and pronounce it immediately without stopping. Besides, do not impose on your voice any inflection other than that to which you feel inclined naturally. Do not be preoccupied except with the song which you have examined to that point, and you will find that, without thinking, you will begin to sing the real *basse fondamentale* of the note which you have chosen for this purpose.[5]

"How can I tell," you say to me, "whether I really intone the *basse fondamentale* of the chosen note?" This is the way.

You sometimes sing the major third below that note, sometimes the minor third below, sometimes the fifth below, and sometimes the fourth below. At times you notice that finding the fourth gives you more trouble than the other consonances, because it is not direct, and, because of its deficiency you can only sing the unison or octave of that note. These different consonances are thus found beneath a note. Without your knowing exactly which they are,

5. The beginning of the monologue from Lully's *Armide,* quoted by Rameau in both his *Nouveau Système* (p. 80) and his *Observations sur notre instinct pour la musique* (Paris, 1754) (p. 70) is a good vehicle for the experiment Rameau suggests. If you sing to the D of measure 3 and allow your voice to fall, you will find G is the root, as he does.

Lully: Monologue from *Armide*

key of E minor:

key of G major

you must without doubt be persuaded that there is at least something extraordinary which you cannot understand. But if you were only interested in finding the key [*ton*], that is, the principal tone [*son*] of the song which you had examined, you would see that you had always sounded either the principal tone, or at least the dominant of that principal tone.

It is always necessary to sing everything which precedes the note where one wishes to stop. Only through our concern for the modulation of the complete portion of the song examined thus far, do we receive the impression of the *basse fondamentale*, where our voice moves naturally.

Sometimes we make a mistake between the relative keys [*modulations*], such as G major and E minor. But they are easily recognized by certain signs, and this is not the place to discuss the matter. Besides, such a mistake cannot damage the proposed experiment, since it only serves to show the effect of the great rapport that the modulations which give birth to it have for each other.

If one can explore the modulation through a *basse fondamentale* discovered in this way, and if one knows besides that the progression of the *basse fondamentale*, in other words, of the fundamental tones, goes from fifth to fifth through each modulation, what can one think of the great difficulties that have been sown up to the present time in the rules of composition and accompaniment? Have we recognized those rules which have no principal other than a *basse fondamentale* whose seed, whose bud is in us? But we are not satisfied with this. We still have to offer another experience, for which it is good to know about dissonance, the different combination of chords, and the coordination inherent in each modulation.

Example of Errors Found in the Figures in Opus 5 of Corelli [6]

One sees, from the *basse fondamentale* placed below the *basso continuo* of Corelli, the real chords which are found there according to the liaison which the fundamental progression of fifths should maintain most naturally in each modulation. This progression should only be interrupted after a principal note, except for broken or interrupted cadences.

Corelli is guided much less by understanding than by the intervals between the treble and bass which his ear made him practice when he figured the chords which this bass must support.

Since there is the same basis of harmony in both of these progressions, the notes at the beginning of each progression should be figured in the same way. But apparently Corelli only considered the violin part, which formed the sixth and the fifth with the note in measure 5, while it only forms the sixth with the note at measure 8. Examples such as these appear in many other places in the same Allegro and elsewhere.

6. The example is from Corelli's Opus 5, No. 1, a sonata da chiesa. Rameau only quotes half of measure 8 and two beats from measures 8–9, supplying the basse fondamentale only for these passages. In the first note of the first passage to which Rameau refers the solo violin has a double stop. The connecting passage has been supplied here so that the reader will see the minute length of the places being singled out.

Corelli: Sonata Op. 5, No. 1

Bibliographical Notes

Rameau's theories are explained in Matthew Shirlaw, *The Theory of Harmony* (Illinois: 1955), chaps. 3–9.

Rameau's *Traité* has been translated in its entirety by Philip Gossett as *Treatise on Harmony* (New York: Dover, 1971).

9.2 JEAN-JACQUES ROUSSEAU (1712–1788)

From 1751 to 1772, two outstanding French scholars edited a twenty-eight-volume encyclopedia entitled *Encyclopédie ou Dictionnaire Raisonné des Sciences, des Arts et des Métiers.* Denis Diderot (1713–1784) and Jean Le Rond d'Alembert (1717–1783) enlisted the help of other specialists during the course of their work. Music was high on the priority list, since d'Alembert himself had written an explanation of Rameau's theories entitled *Eléments de musique, théorique et pratique, suivant les principes de M. Rameau,* first published in 1752.

Diderot and d'Alembert approached Rameau, at the zenith of his fame, to write the articles on music for the *Encyclopédie*. When Rameau declined their offer, they called on Jean-Jacques Rousseau, outstanding philosopher and self-trained musician, who had read a paper on modern music before the Académie in Paris in 1742 and was currently trying his hand at opera. Rameau never quite forgave Rousseau for daring to undertake the task. Subsequently Rousseau's articles were published separately in an enlarged revision entitled *Dictionnaire de musique* (1767).

Melody*

Melody is a succession of sounds ordered according to the laws of rhythm and modulation, so that it seems agreeable to the ear. Vocal melody is called song [*chant*], and instrumental, symphony [*symphonie*].

The idea of rhythm necessarily enters into that of melody. A song is only a song when it is measured. The same succession of sounds may have as many guises, and as many different melodies as there are different scansions. The change of note values alone may disfigure the succession to the point of rendering it unrecognizable. . . .

Melody has two different principles, according to the manner in which one considers it. Taken as the relationship of sounds and as the rules of the mode, its principle lies in the harmony, since it is harmonic analysis which provides the degrees of the scale, the chords of the mode, and the laws of modulation, unique elements of song. According to this principle, the entire strength of melody is limited to soothing the ear with its agreeable sounds, just as one may soothe the eye with agreeable mixtures [*accords*] of color. But taken as an art of imitation by means of which one may affect the spirit of different images, to move the heart with divers sentiments, to excite and calm the passions, to produce, in a word, some moral effects which go beyond the immediate domain of the senses, one must find another principle. For we do not see anyone captivated by harmony alone, and all that proceeds from it affects us in the same way.

What is the second principle? It is by nature like the first. But in order to discover it, a finer but simpler observation is necessary, with great sensitivity in the observer. This is the same principle as that which causes the tone of a voice to be varied when one speaks according to the things which one says, and the movements which one goes through while saying them. It is the accent of the languages which determines the melody of each nation. It is the accent which makes one speak in a sing-song manner. One speaks with more or less energy according to whether the language has more or less accent. That which has a more marked accent must produce a livelier and more passionate melody; that which has no accent or only a slight one can only produce a languid and cold melody, without character and without expression.

Jean-Jacques Rousseau, Dictionnaire de musique (Geneva, 1767).

Unity of Melody

All of the liberal arts have a certain unity of purpose, a source of pleasure which they give to the soul. Divided attention is never restful, and when we busy ourselves with two subjects, it is proof that neither of the two satisfies us. There is in music an inherent unity which abides in the subject, and by which all the divisions, smoothly coordinated, compose a single one, perceived as an entity with everything fitting together. . . .

The art of the composer takes the unity of melody into account (1) To determine the mode by the harmony when it is not sufficiently determined by the melody. (2) To choose and turn the chords so that the most prominent tone may always be the one that sings, and so that the one which provides the best close may be in the bass. (3) To add to the energy of each passage with harsh chords if the expression is harsh, and sweet ones if the expression is sweet. (4) To consider the dynamics [*forte-piano*] of the melody in relation to the accompaniment. (5) Finally, to manage so that the singing of the other parts, far from contradicting that of the principal part, sustains it, seconds it, and gives to it a more vibrant accent. . . .

Unity of melody requires that one should never listen to two melodies at the same time, but not that the melody should never pass from one part to the other. On the contrary, often some elegance and taste are necessary to arrange the passage neatly, even to relate the song to the accompaniment, so that the text may always be heard. Likewise, there are learned and well arranged harmonies, where the melody, without being in any part, results solely from the effect of the whole. Here is an example of this, a *Song Drawn from the Harmony*, which although unpolished, suffices for someone to understand what I am trying to say.

Song Drawn from the Harmony

It would take a treatise to show in detail the application of this principle to duos, trios, quartets, to choirs, to symphonic pieces. Men of genius will make it sufficiently known by extending and using it, and their works will instruct others in it. I conclude, therefore, and I say with regard to the principle which I am going to establish, it follows first, that all music which never sings is boring, no matter what harmony it has; secondly, that all music in which one distinguishes several songs simultaneously is bad, and that it results in the same effect as that of two or more words pronounced at once on the same tone. By this judgment, which allows no exception, one sees what one must think of this extraordinary dual music, where one air serves as an accompaniment to another air.

It is this principle of unity of melody that the Italians have felt and followed without knowing it, but that the French neither knew nor followed— it is, I say, in this great principle that the essential difference of the two musics consists. And it is, I believe, what every impartial judge will say about it who wishes to give the same attention to both, if that is at all possible.

When I had discovered that principle, I wished, before proposing it, to try the application myself. That attempt produced *Le Devin du village*.[7] After the success, I wrote about it in my *Letter on French Music*. It is for the masters of the art to judge whether the principle is good, and whether I have followed well the rules which spring from it.

Recitative

Recitative is speech recited on a musical and harmonious tone. It is a style of singing which comes close to the word, a declamation in music in which the musician must imitate, as well as possible, the inflections of voice of the speaker. This song is called recitative, because it lends itself to narration, to telling a story, and is used in dramatic dialogue. In the *Dictionnaire de l'Académie* it says that recitative must be declaimed. There are some recitatives which must be declaimed, others which must be sustained. . . .

One does not measure the recitative while singing. Meter, which characterizes the airs, spoils recitative declamation. It is the accent alone, be it grammatical, be it oratorical, which directs the slowness or rapidity of the sounds, as well as their rise or fall. The composer, in noting the recitative with some fixed meter, is only trying to establish a correspondence between the basso continuo and the song, to indicate approximately how one must determine the length of the syllables and cadences, and must scan the verse. The Italians only use the meter with four beats for their recitative; but the French interperse theirs with all sorts of meters. . . .[8]

In recitative, where the expressions, the sentiments, and the ideas vary every moment, one must use varied modulations which can represent in their textures the progressions expressed in the discourse of the reciter. The inflections of the speaking voice are not restricted to musical intervals. They are infinite and impossible to determine. Therefore, not being able to fix them with accurate precision, the musician, in order to follow the words,

---

7. The highly successful *Devin du village* had been performed first at Fontainbleau in 1752 and at the Paris Opéra in 1753.
8. For examples of French recitative with a variety of meters, see Lully, *Le Ciel protège les héros* from *Alceste* (*HAM* Vol. II, No. 225) and *Enfin il est en ma puissance* from *Armide* (*GMB*, No. 234); also, Rameau, *Ma Voix puissant* from *Castor et Pollux* (*GMB* No. 297). For an example of Italian recitative with four beats to a measure, see Alessandro Scarlatti (1659–1725), *Mitilde, mio tesor*, a chamber cantata (*HAM* Vol. II, No. 258).

must at least imitate them as well as possible. And in order to carry to the soul of the listeners the idea of the intervals and of the accents which he cannot express in notes, he has recourse to the transitions as a substitute for them. If, for example, he needs the interval of a major or a minor semitone, he does not notate it because he does not know how. But he gives you the idea by means of an enharmonic passage. A progression in the bass often suffices to change all the ideas, and to give the recitative the accent and inflection that the performer cannot execute.

Accompanied recitative is that to which, besides the basso continuo, one adds an accompaniment of violins. This accompaniment, which can hardly be syllabic, because of the rapidity of the delivery, ordinarily consists of long sustained notes lasting the entire measure. For this reason one writes the word *Sostenuto* on all the instrumental parts, principally on the bass, which, without this would play only dry and detached strokes on each change of note, as in ordinary recitative. Instead, it must spin out and sustain the sounds according to the value of the notes.[9]

Bibliographical Notes

For a detailed discussion of the relation of the Encyclopedists to Rameau's theories, see Alfred Richard Oliver, *The Encyclopedists as Critics of Music* (New York: Columbia University Press, 1947).

9.3 JOHANN MATTHESON (1681–1764)

Rameau's *Traité*, published in 1722, had an immediate impact on the musical world (Section 9.1). His theory of harmony was dependent neither on a pre-existent melody, whether sacred or secular, nor on a melody created by the composer. Rameau thought of harmony as springing directly from tone, without melody as an intermediary. To composers used to looking toward song for their inspiration, this concentration on the chord as the generator of both vertical and horizontal relationships came as a total shock.

Johann Mattheson, German composer, biographer, theorist, and critic, agreed with Rameau on one essential point, the fact that an interval sounded vertically in a harmony must be equal to an interval whose notes are heard successively in a melody. Without this compatibility composition was not feasible. Past this point Mattheson was intuitively a champion of melody. For inspiration he advocated widespread use of the German chorale. In theory he showed how a chordal succession of tones was a combination of several melodies.

9. Here Rousseau spells out the difference between what the Italians called *recitativo secco* (dry recitative accompanied only by the basso continuo) and *recitativo accompagnato* (recitative accompanied by the orchestra).

The passages quoted here are from *Der Vollkommene Capellmeister* [*The Complete Chapelmaster*]. Mattheson's technique of *breaking*, combining several melodies into one voice part or, conversely, arpeggiating a chord into a single line, became important in the shaping of the classical style. Mattheson starts with a harmonic interval on two lines, which he compresses into a single melody before inserting passing tones. His approach is contrapuntal, even as he ventures into chordal textures. His three- and four-part harmony is dependent on horizontal voice-leading to a greater extent than it is on vertical pillars of sound. We might say that while Rameau found harmony in a single melody, Mattheson found harmony in a simultaneous combination of melodies.

Melodic Invention*

Some people might think this is an excellent title, for here beautiful flashes of fancy must pour forth audibly. But I fear that he who does not bring with him natural talent, will derive little comfort from this study. Notwithstanding, we shall willingly try to propose every imaginable means of help. . . .

Most invention comes from an innate turn of mind and a successful arrangement of the cells in the brain. Inventing something of genuine value also depends to no small extent on the time when the person does it, as well as on his good humor.

It does not always happen that our inclination is perfect. One often thinks that a thing should turn out excellently, and decides to put something special down on paper, only to find that it often falls apart completely.

I knew a Capellmeister who derived his inspiration for the start of an invention from the bell-playing of the tower of St. Peter's which at certain hours only sounded a tetrachord, or the interval of a fourth, by means of a clock mechanism.

Some use the most well known morning and evening songs, as well as other Lieder. I am thinking of melodies of spiritual songs, from which they borrow one phrase or another, and often elaborate it pleasingly, for example:

---

* *Johann Mattheson,* Der Vollkommene Capellmeister, *That is, Basic Proof of everything one needs to know, to be aware of, and to understand thoroughly in order to direct a chapel [a private orchestra and choir] creditably and profitably (Hamburg: Christian Herold, 1739), pp. 121–122, 203–204, 352–356.*

Inexhaustible sources of invention are found everywhere, in every place, even in the smallest thing. Although it is by no means possible to count them, they are readily noticed, if you look for them. Seek and ye shall find, even though something forced might run beneath that did not flow from the soul, but was pulled by the hair or was drawn from a strange well.

The Difference Between Melodies for Singing and Playing

All music is produced either by singing or playing, the latter on certain organs suited to it, which preferably are called instruments. However, the human voice also has its own natural organ. Organs are differentiated on the basis of artificiality. One type is fabricated; the other is innate. It follows that there are essentially two different classes of melody, called vocal and instrumental, because things which are produced by art must be approached differently from those which are natural and innate. . . .

The first difference between a vocal and an instrumental melody, of which there are seventeen, lies in the relationship, so to speak, of the former as the mother and the latter as the daughter. Such a comparison shows not only the degree of the difference, but also the kind of relationship. For, just as a mother must necessarily be older than her own daughter, so vocal melody, without doubt, must antedate instrumental melody in this nether-world. The former, then, not only has precedence and superiority, but also has the authority to direct the daughter to follow her mother's instructions in order to make everything melodious and flowing, so that one may hear whose child she is.

The second difference between melodies for singing and playing, is that the former precedes and the latter follows. This rule is as reasonable as it is natural, although the opposite usually happens. For who can make a good start in composition if he needs further study in vocal melody? Not every-one who knows how to play compositions, such as sonatas and overtures, etc., before he has sung and written down a single chorale correctly, can compose, let alone artistically.

I myself was brought up that way. Without heed, they taught me how to play and sing at the same time. But in composing, on the contrary, the op-posite order is observed. Everything played is a mere imitation of singing, if one remembers that people probably had use of their throats before they made instruments. For, can someone make a good copy who has never had a true original before him?

Concerning Broken Chords

A *broken chord* is the name given to the notes of a chord when they are played, not simultaneously, but successively. From this arises not only a greater opportunity for ornamenting instrumental parts, but also an endless method of variation, yes, so to speak, an inexhaustible source of invention. . . . It is suitable for solos on instruments, for accompaniments to vocal parts, and also for vocal parts themselves, if used with proper discretion.

Examples should help most toward the understanding and execution of our proposal. Therefore there is nothing better than our going to the music without further ado, and showing how the two-voiced setting may be heard in several ways as a single voice with broken chords. This is it:

Now if I wish to condense both of these voices into one through the breaking of the chords upward, the setting might appear something like this:

But if the breaking were done downwards, the following shape might result:

These eighth notes derived from quarter notes, if they are divided into sixteenths, offer almost a sheave of alterations, or so-called variations. We only have enough room to indicate the beginning of each alteration.

This kind of double-division can be continued throughout the whole setting in just as many ways. If we try it with the first, we may understand the others all the more readily.

If one wants to increase the liveliness, one may present the preceding double-division, or even the quadruple division, as follows:

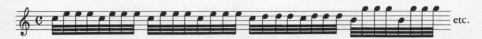

Arpeggios

We now wish to speak about arpeggios which every performing artist may use as he pleases, whether on keyboard instruments, on the violin, lute, etc., if they are presented by the composer in a manner suitable for the instrument on which they are to be played. For example, in four-voiced divisions for the violin, for which the bass makes the fifth part, there is nothing more to do than to locate the strings which are to be played and struck together, and to put the notes one under the other. We had to indicate this with dots, so that the player may know where to improvise broken chords.[10]

9.4 JOHANN SEBASTIAN BACH (1685–1750) THROUGH J. N. FORKEL (1749–1818)

In his *Well-Tempered Clavier*, completed at Cöthen in 1722, Johann Sebastian Bach affirmed the major–minor cycle of keys as we know it today.[11] The subtitle reads, "Preludes and Fugues in all the keys, com-

10. Compare the arpeggiated chords below, as Bach indicated them for improvisation in his *Chromatic Fantasy and Fugue,* with the same chords written out in a modern edition.

J. S. Bach: Chromatic Fantasy and Fugue

11. In the *Well-Tempered Clavier* Bach systematically went through every chromatic step within an octave, writing two sets of preludes and fugues in each of the

posed for the use of inquisitive musical youth, as well as for the amusement of those who are already versed in this art." By composing in all the keys Bach both acknowledged the current use of equal temperament in keyboard instruments and guaranteed its musical acceptance for the future in the most appropriate manner possible, through actual composition.

Bach's first biographer, the organist and musical scholar Johann Nicolaus Forkel, elicited the material for the biography, *Concerning Johann Sebastian Bach's Life, Artistry, and Compositions*, directly from Bach's sons. Forkel indicates how Bach learned by transcribing some of the concertos by Antonio Vivaldi (c. 1670–1740) from strings to keyboard instruments. Bach probably made his transcriptions of Vivaldi concertos when he was in Weimar between 1708 and 1717.[12] Bach had already composed his own programmatic *Capriccio on the Departure of His Beloved Brother* in honor of his brother's 1706 departure from the family to join the Swedish army. In the second movement of this keyboard composition Bach describes "the various casualties which may happen to him in a foreign country." The movement, all of nineteen measures long, consists of a fugal exposition presented in three keys in rapid succession. Bach modulates by whole tone through G minor, F minor, and E♭ major on the following theme, which itself fluctuates between parallel minor and major when the B♭ is replaced by B♮.

Adopting the title of Vivaldi's Opus 8, we may say that the "trial of harmony and invention" was well under way.

---

twelve keys, one set in the major mode interspersed with another set in the parallel minor, yielding twenty-four prelude–fugue compositions. Then he went through this entire procedure again, writing another twenty-four prelude–fugue combinations. In the autograph title Bach differentiates the major mode from the minor simply by identifying the interval of a third with which each starts. He calls his original twenty-four "The Well-Tempered Clavier or Preludes and Fugues through every tone and semitone with regard to both the major third or *Ut Re Mi* and the minor third or *Re Mi Fa*."

12. Vivaldi went far toward reconciling the art of invention with the harmonic cycle. Among the works covering a wide range of keys were several sets of compositions each containing twelve concertos. Opus 3 was Vivaldi's "Harmonic Inspiration" (*L'Estro Armonico*). Opus 4 showed the "Extravagance" (*La Stravaganza*) with which the Venetians tempered the tunings of their instruments. Opus 8, "The Trial of Harmony and Invention" (*Il Cimento dell' Armonia e dell' Inventione*), includes program concertos entitled *The Tempest, The Hunt*, and *The Pleasure*, as well as a group of program concertos each describing one of the four seasons.

Johann Sebastian Bach's Composition*

Johann Sebastian Bach's first attempts at composition were, like all first attempts, tentative. Without formal instruction to direct his progress, he had to help himself gradually, step by step, like all those who set out on a course by themselves without guidance. All beginners tend to engage in feats such as running and leaping up and down on the instrument with both hands playing as much as their five fingers will allow, and continuing in this wild state until they accidentally land on some kind of a resting place. These people are nothing more than mere finger-composers (or clavier-cavalry, as Bach called them in his later years). In other words, their fingers tell them what to write, instead of their telling their fingers what to play. But Bach did not stay on this course for long. He soon began to realize that eternal runs and leaps were no accomplishment, that order, coherence and continuity of thought were necessary, and that to achieve such a goal one needed some kind of guide. The newly published violin concertos by Vivaldi which had just come out served him as such a guide. He had heard them praised so often as important musical pieces, that he thought it would be a good idea to arrange the collection for clavier.[13] He studied the voice-leading, the relation of the parts to each other, the exchange of modulations, and many other things. While arranging the thoughts and passages intended for the violin, but not suited to the clavier, he learned how to think musically, so that after his work was completed, he no longer needed to rely on his fingers for his ideas, but could conjure them in his own fancy.

Prepared thus, he now needed only diligence and uninterrupted practice to progress and finally to reach the point where not only could he create an artistic idea for himself, but he could also hope, in time, to achieve it. He never lacked perseverance. He worked so long and so hard, that he often kept going into the night. What he wrote during the day, he learned how to play at night. Yet, despite all the attention that he gave to his own compositions at that time, he never neglected to apply himself most diligently toward studying the works of Frescobaldi (Section 8.6), Froberger,[14]

*J. N. Forkel, Über Johann Sebastian Bachs Leben, Kunst und Kunstwerke (Leipzig: Hoffmeister und Kühnel, 1802), pp. 23–26.

13. Bach transcribed the following Vivaldi concertos to solo harpsichord. Opus 3: No. 3 from G major to F major, No. 7 from F major to D major, and No. 12 from E major to C major. Opus 4: No. 1 from B flat major to G major and No. 6 from G minor to the same key. Bach also transcribed one of Vivaldi's concertos from Opus 7, a set of twelve concertos without a collective descriptive title. Bach transcribed Vivaldi's Opus 3, No. 10, originally for four violins and string orchestra in B minor, into a concerto for four harpsichords and string orchestra in A minor.

Two books that may serve the reader are Marc Pincherle, Vivaldi, Genius of the Baroque, trans. Christopher Hatch (New York: W. W. Norton & Co., Inc., 1957, 1962); and Karl Geiringer, in collaboration with Irene Geiringer, Johann Sebastian Bach, The Culmination of an Era (New York: Oxford University Press, 1966).

14. Johann Jakob Froberger (1616–1667), born in Stuttgart, studied with Frescobaldi in Rome, was organist in Vienna, Paris, and London. He is noted for composing keyboard suites with movements in the order of allemande, courante, saraband, and gigue.

Kerl,[15] Pachelbel,[16] Fischer,[17] Strunck,[18] Buxtehude,[19] Reinken,[20] Bruhns,[21] Boehm,[22] and some old French organists, who were all masters of harmony and fugue in the style then prevalent.

It was not only the excellence of these models, mostly intended for the church, but even more so the nature of his own serious temperament, that eventually led him to the development of the learned and serious style in music. In this kind of music little can be accomplished with only a moderate number of artistic expressions or tonal relationships. He soon realized that the treasure-chest of musical discourse would have to be enlarged before the artistic ideal looming before him could be attained. He conceived of music as a language, and the composer as a poet, who, regardless of the language in which he chose to write, always had to have enough expressions at his disposal to adequately represent his feeling. Since in his youth artistic expressions were not sufficiently numerous, at least not for his poetic musical intellect, and since, moreover, they were not supple enough, he sought to remedy both deficiencies chiefly by a treatment of the harmony, which, while adapted to its own nature and intent, is still unique to him.

As long as the language of music is merely melodic expression or successive tonal relationship, it may still be called poor. By the addition of bass tones, through which its relationship to the key and to the chords contained therein becomes less ambiguous, it gains not so much in richness as in precision. A melody accompanied in this way, not merely by bass

15. Johann Caspar Kerl (1627–1693), German organist, studied with Carissimi and Frescobaldi in Rome at about the same time as Froberger. He wrote organ preludes, clavier suites, and toccatas.
16. Johann Pachelbel (1653–1706) held organ posts in Vienna, Eisenach, Erfurt, Stuttgart, Gotha, and Nuremberg. He wrote chaconnes, toccatas, and chorale settings.
17. Johann Kaspar Ferdinand Fischer (c. 1660–c. 1738) was in the service of the Margrave of Baden. He wrote *Ariadne musica neo-organoedum* (Opus 4, Augsburg, 1715), twenty sets of organ preludes and fugues, each in a different key. The work was named for Ariadne, mythological daughter of the king of Crete, who provided her lover with a thread as a guide to lead him out of a labyrinth. The theme of Fischer's fugue in E major (*HAM* Vol. II, No. 247) may be compared with J. S. Bach's fugue of the same key in Volume II of the *Well-Tempered Clavier*.
18. Nikolaus Adam Strunck (1640–1700) at the age of 12 was organ assistant to his father at Celle. Eight years later he became principal violinist of the orchestra at Brunswick. A ricercar and six capriccios in the *Denkmäler der Tonkunst in Österreich* (XIII, 2), attributed to Georg Reutter, are really by Strunck.
19. Dietrich Buxtehude (c. 1637–1707) succeeded Franz Tunder as organist of St. Mary's Church in Lübeck. There Buxtehude founded the *Abend Musiken*, musical services held the five Sundays before Christmas. In 1705 Bach walked 200 miles from Arnstadt to Lübeck to hear Buxtehude. (Also see Mattheson, Section 9.3.)
20. Jan Adam Reinken (1623–1722), pupil of Sweelinck in Amsterdam, became organist in Hamburg. For his influence on Bach see Philipp Spitta, *Johann Sebastian Bach*, trans. Clara Bell and J. A. Fuller-Maitland (London: Novello & Co., Ltd; New York: Dover Publications, Inc., 1951). A sonata by Reinken for strings and continuo is quoted in its entirety in the Spitta appendix.
21. Nikolaus Bruhns (1665–1697), also one of the most famous organists of his time, studied with Buxtehude at Lübeck before obtaining a post in Copenhagen. Three of his organ pieces are in Commer's *Musica sacra*, I.
22. Georg Böhm (also spelled Boehm) (1661–1734), organist at Lüneburg, composed keyboard suites.

tones, but by middle voices which complete the chords, was always called *homophony* by our forefathers, and rightly so. The relationship is very different when two melodies are so interwoven with each other, that they converse together just like two different people of the same standing and education. There the accompaniment was subordinate; it only had to serve the first voice as the principal one. Here there is no such difference; this kind of union of two melodies gives rise to new tonal relationships and consequently to an increase of the wealth of artistic expression. Proportionate to the addition of voices and to their interweaving with each other in a free, independent manner, is the increase in the wealth of artistic expression. Finally, when the various meters and the endless variety of rhythms are added, it becomes inexhaustible. Harmony is to be considered, therefore, not merely as the accompaniment of a single melody, but as the real means of increasing our artistic expression or the richness of our musical language. But if harmony is to be an agent of this kind, it must consist not merely of accompaniment, but of the interweaving of several real melodies, each of which, whether it be an upper, middle, or lower part, carries and is capable of carrying the conversation.

Out of such an interweaving of separate melodies, which are all so melodious that each may have its turn as the upper part, and really does, emerge the harmonies of Johann Sebastian Bach in all the works which he composed from about the year 1720 on, or since he was 35 years old until the end of his life. In this he surpasses all the composers in the world.[23] At least I have not found anything similar in all the works known to me. In his four-part compositions, at times you may even omit the upper and lower parts, and still be able to hear perfectly clear and melodious music in the two middle parts alone.

9.5 JOHANN ERNST ALTENBURG (1734–1801)

Great skill was demanded of the eighteenth-century trumpeter when the composer called for the performance of consecutive notes in stepwise motion. Before the invention of valves the natural trumpet was limited to the tones of the harmonic series, which only accommodate a scale from the eighth harmonic upward (**Appendix 1,** Chart 3). The inclusion of the upper register, mainly the octave outlined by harmonics 8 and 16, is described as clarino-playing by Johann Ernst Altenburg in his *Essay on an Introduction to the Heroic-Musical Art of the Trumpet and Drum, with Historical, Theoretical and Practical Commentary, and Illustrated by Examples* (1795).

Altenburg is actually describing a practice that had been in use for some time, a notable example being the solo trumpet part in J. S. Bach's *Brandenburg Concerto* No. 2.[24] Yet, Altenburg's contribution is far from

23. Here Forkel has a note: "See Kirnberger, *Kunst des reinen Satzes*, p. 157." (*For* Kirnberger see Section 9.7.)
24. With the insertion of crooks, additional lengths of tubing to change the funda-

trivial. He helps us to understand the role of the trumpet not only as a bearer of the melody but also as a participant in the harmony. Among the variety of compositions for trumpet which he illustrates are the solo, bicinium, tricinium, quatricinium, sonata, and concerto.

Concerning Clarino Playing and Its Requisite Execution*

In former times the trumpet under discussion here, on account of its high, clear sound, in Latin was called *Clario, Claro,* or *Clarasius,* which the French translated as *Clairon* and the Italians translated as *Clarino.*[25] It is really a shorter, more tightly wound trumpet than the usual one, and was called *Clarion* by the English.[26] Mattheson says that the designation *Clarin* applies to the trumpet mainly when it is muffled by means of a mute. We understand by Clarin or by a Clarin-part approximately what is a discant in vocal music, namely a certain melody which is blown mostly in the two-line octave and is consequently high and clear. The proper embouchure for forming this sound is extremely difficult to acquire, and is not possible to determine by specific rules. Practice is the best guide here, although much also depends on the position of the lips. A stronger breath and narrow pursing of the lips and teeth are possibly the most favorable advantage here.

A person who has succeeded in tastefully blowing at the mentioned height with special skill, is usually called a clarinist. One scarcely need be reminded that there are many factors in good clarino playing, and that the effect is very different according to whether a composition is performed well or poorly.

Theoretical and practical knowledge, especially a fine, innate feeling for music, are also indispensable for the clarinist. With respect to finding the tone accurately, it would be very useful if he could have some instruction in singing beforehand.

---

*Johann Ernst Altenburg, Versuch einer Anleitung zur heroisch-musikalischen Trompeter-und Pauker-Kunst *(Halle, 1795), pp. 94–95, 103–105.*

mental tone, and later with the incorporation of valves into the construction of the instrument, players were able to produce the tones of a scale which on the natural trumpet could only be produced in the high register. Handel and Bach used crooks in C and D. In addition, Mozart called for the E♭ crook.

It became the custom always to write the trumpet part as if the instrument were in C, with the result that the performer read in relation to the harmonic series rather than reading the actual pitches.

25. The word *clarino* may refer to a type of trumpet with a mouthpiece in a particular shape and an upper register where good tones may be produced readily; or it may refer in general to the upper harmonic range of a trumpet.

J. S. Bach designated parts for the *clarino* in several of his cantatas (No. 15, Arnstadt, and Nos. 24, 48, and 167, Leipzig). However, he usually used the Italian word *tromba* for trumpet, as he did for the high trumpet part in his second Brandenburg Concerto.

Joseph Haydn designates the trumpets as *Clarini* in masses including the *Pauken-messe* (1796).

26. Altenburg has a footnote here referring to Domino du Cange's dictionary of writings on the Middle Ages (Paris, 1842). Under the caption *Clarasius, Clario, Claro,* du Cange cites the line "with the melody of the clarions resounding" from the fourth book of William of Malmesbury's *History of England* (1101).

Solo

This is never played alone on the clarin, but together with several instruments. It is called Solo, because the person who plays the main melody must be heard distinctly while the others only accompany.

Bicinium

By this I mean a small duet for two trumpets, which usually consists of two short sections. Since the performers must sometimes blow long, high notes, trumpets in the chamber pitch D are the most suitable, especially when they are made lower with a tuning device. Because these pieces always procede [*moduliren*] in a single key, one bestows on them every possible variation and melodic passage which does not fatigue the mouth too much. The more difficult pieces of this kind may be blown on shorter trumpets for practice.

Indeed, some people have written various two-part canons and fugues for trumpets, although these do not especially delight the ear. For example: [27]

27. This fuga is an adaptation of the eleventh duet for two trumpets by Heinrich
    Biber (1644–1704). In measures 7–8 Altenburg uses the E♭ of the pure minor mode,

Bibliographical Notes

Altenburg's treatise has been translated in its entirety by Edward H. Tarr as *Trumpeters' and Kettledrummers' Art* (Nashville, Tennessee: The Brass Press, 1974).

For the trumpets in use from Monteverdi to Bach and Handel see Don L. Smithers, *The Music & History of the Baroque Trumpet before 1721* (Syracuse University Press, 1973).

9.6 CARL PHILIPP EMANUEL BACH (1714–1788)

While the composer sought to solidify the harmonic progressions, the performer sought expressive means of improvisation on the structure provided for him by the composer. The art of improvisation placed

---

whereas Biber had the E♮ of the Dorian. Also, Altenburg's cadences, even within the confines of two voice parts, are harmonic, defining the dominant and tonic chords in root position, whereas Biber's cadences were determined by melodic considerations prevalent in the Renaissance.

Biber: Duet for 2 Trumpets

such heavy demands on the performer's talent that the dilettante was quickly separated from the professional. Carl Philipp Emanuel Bach, Johann's second oldest son, came to the rescue of the amateur by composing six sonatas with the "improvisations" all written out. He called them *Sonatas for the Clavier with Varied Reprise*, dedicating them to Princess Amalia of Prussia. These compositions, stripped of their variations, are like other published Baroque keyboard sonatas. Bach in effect has preserved for us a sampling of the performance practice of the time by indicating how a performer might repeat an entire movement or part of a movement at a time, varying it at will.

Preface to Sonatas with Varied Reprise*

Berlin, July 1759

Variation at the reprise is indispensable today. Every performer is expected to do it. One of my friends takes every possible pain to interpret a piece just as it is composed, pure and according to the rules of good execution; should we deny him his applause? Another often finds it necessary to compensate, through his daring in variation, for what seems to him to be missing in the expression of the prescribed notes. And for this the audience elevates him above the other. One may know how to change almost every thought at the repetition, and still have no conception of either the plan of the piece or the talent of the performer. Mere variation, especially when it is combined with a long cadenza at times decorated rather peculiarly, often stimulates most of the listeners to *Bravo!* What doesn't pass, then, for a misuse of these two real flourishes of performance! A person no longer has the patience to play the prescribed notes the first time. To wait for the *Bravo* too long would be unbearable. Often these untimely variations are contrary to the setting, contrary to the affect, and contrary to the underlying thoughts—an unpleasant matter for many a composer. But granted that the performer has all the attributes necessary for varying a piece as it should be—is he always obliged to do it? Don't new difficulties arise in unfamiliar works? Isn't the main purpose of variation this: that the performer should do credit to both himself and the piece? Must he not, therefore, produce ideas at least as good the second time? However, despite these difficulties and misuses, good variations always retain their value. I refer to what I have stated concerning this at the end of the first part of my *Essay on the True Art of Playing Keyboard Instruments.*

In the composition of these sonatas I had in mind principally beginners and such amateurs who, on account of their age or other obligations, no longer have enough patience and time to practice very vigorously. I wanted to provide pleasure for them in an easy and appropriate manner, that they

*Carl Philipp Emanuel Bach; Sechs Sonaten fürs Clavier mit veränderten Reprisen (Berlin, 1760).

may be heard playing variations without the necessity of either creating them themselves or having them written in advance by others and learning them by heart with much trouble. Finally, I have expressly indicated everything that appertains to good performance, so that one may play these pieces under all circumstances, even when not in too good a mood.

I am pleased to be the first, as far as I know, to work on this art for the profit and pleasure of his patrons and friends. How happy I would be if they would understand the special joy I derived from this attempt at service.

Bibliographical Notes

Carl Philipp Emanuel Bach's *Versuch über die wahre Art das Clavier zu spielen* has been translated as the *Essay on the True Art of Playing Keyboard Instruments* by William J. Mitchell (New York: W. W. Norton & Co., Inc., 1949). See section on Performance, pp. 165–166.

Sonata No. 1 with varied reprise is reprinted in *Anthology of Music*, Karl Gustav Fellerer, General Editor, Vol. XI, *The Variation*, ed. K. von Fischer.

9.7 JOHANN PHILIPP KIRNBERGER (1721–1783)

Since J. S. Bach taught orally without writing very much about his theories, we are doubly indebted to the valuable theoretical writings of one of his outstanding students, Johann Philipp Kirnberger.

Kirnberger, a fine musician in his own right, studied the organ with Johann Peter Kellner of Gräfenroda in Thuringia and Heinrich Nikolaus Gerber at Sondershausen. From 1739 to 1741 Kirnberger went to Leipzig, where he studied with Bach. Thence Kirnberger traveled to Poland, where for nine years he taught music in the homes of the nobility and at a convent. In 1751, on his return to Germany, he studied the violin at Dresden and became a violinist to Frederick the Great in Berlin. In 1754 Kirnberger became chapel master and composition teacher to Frederick's sister, Princess Anna Amalia (1723–1787) (Section 9.6).

Although Kirnberger was himself a prolific writer, sometimes it is difficult to distinguish his contribution from that of his student, Johann Abraham Peter Schulz (1747–1800). Both of them wrote the articles on music for an outstanding encyclopedia edited by Johann George Sulzer (1720–1779). The work, entitled *General Theory of the Fine Arts*, included, in addition to music, categories on architecture, theater, painting, drawing, dance, poetry, speech, rhetoric, and the fine arts in general.

Equal Temperament*

The introduction of the twenty-four different scales now current was brought about by establishing each of the twelve tones of the octave as a keynote so that the major and minor modes could be played in these keys. It might have happened in this way.

In the old diatonic scales there were some modes, like C and F, which had perfect fifths and major thirds. Others, like A and E, had minor thirds for their perfect fifths. In contrast, D had neither a perfect fifth nor a pure minor third, and the major third was lacking altogether.

Since B did not have a fifth, one could not play any pure scales in the major or minor mode starting on this tone.

The observation that through the introduction of the tone F♯, B could acquire a fifth and D a major third, made the composer realize that it would perhaps be possible to have a major and minor third and a fifth on every string. Already the four new tones, C♯, D♯, F♯, and G♯, which were necessary as half steps below the principal tone above, gave hope to the possibility of such a new system of music. The mere thought of it was so appealing that innumerable attempts were made to bring this to fruition.

Therefore they tried to use the four semitones C♯, D♯, F♯, and G♯ in such a way that each tone of the chromatic scale, C, C♯, D, D♯, E, F, F♯, G, G♯, A, B♭, [and] B had its fifth outlining its own major and minor third.

But they soon saw that this would be possible only if one could make the intervals either somewhat larger or somewhat smaller. For example, if one wanted to use D♯ as the pure minor third of C, it could not be the perfect fifth of G♯ at the same time. In the meanwhile they discovered that they could find ratios for these new tones which, although not yielding perfectly pure intervals, were yet bearable. This was called the tempered system.

Each organ-builder and instrument-maker, to the best of his ability, sought for a temperament which was the least inconvenient. And so matters stand until today.

After countless temperaments were conceived, some musicians finally conceived of the simplest means to solve the problem. It is this, that the tones C, C♯, D, D♯, etc., are all separated from each other by equal steps. Thus, the octave is divided into twelve equal parts, of which each is approximately a half tone. This is called *equal temperament.* Many considered this to be very advantageous, because, with it, every string of the chromatic scale is so close to the pure fourth, fifth, and sixth, that the ear scarcely notices the difference from the perfect interval.

Consequently, in this temperament one can play all tones lying throughout the chromatic system almost perfectly in major as well as minor.

But a closer examination soon discloses important disadvantages to this temperament.

*Johann Philipp Kirnberger, Die Kunst des reinen Satzes in der Musik (Berlin and Königsberg, 1776–79), I, 9–16, 156 f., 223 f.

First, it is impossible to tune it without a monochord, or something similar. With the bare ear consonant intervals may be tuned perfectly, but dissonant ones cannot be determined exactly.

Secondly, the diversity of the tones is reduced by equal temperament. Unfortunately only two types remain, for, on the one hand, all major modes, and, on the other, all minor modes are completely alike.

Therefore, through the twenty-four scales one has not really gained anything, but has lost a great deal. For the plain diatonic scale, as used by the ancients, yielded diverse modes differentiated from each other in character, from which one might choose the one which lent itself best to the expression. Equal temperament narrows the field, and merely offers the composer the choice between the major and minor mode.

Authentic and Plagal as Used Today

Following are the names of the old principal modes: C Ionian, D Dorian, E Phrygian, F Lydian, G Mixolydian, A Aeolian.

In earlier times each of these six modes was treated in two ways called authentic and plagal. In the authentic the range was from the keynote to the octave above; in the plagal, from the fourth below the keynote to the fifth above. For example, in C or the Ionian mode:

Authentic   Plagal

Thus there came to be twelve modes in all. If one were to treat today's scales in a similar manner, and build on every tone a major and minor mode in both authentic and plagal, one would arrive at forty-eight different modes.

Four-Part Composition and Orchestration

The highest degree of purity in composition is not enough to make four-part writing perfect. Each voice must have an independent and flowing melody of its own, and, at the same time, all voices must blend together agreeably.

First of all, each voice must have its own independent and flowing melody. You must not imagine that you have written a 4-part setting if there are several voices proceeding in octaves with one another.[28]

There is perhaps nothing more difficult in the whole principle of composition than this. Not only must you give each of the four voices its own independent flowing melody, but you must also give them all a uniform character, so that from their combination arises a single unified whole. In

28. Kirnberger's note: "Sometimes we see pieces which seem to consist of a great many parts, but which as a basis have only three or four. The alto goes with the bass, and the tenor doubles the discant in octaves. In this way one can easily give

this the late Capellmeister Bach in Leipzig perhaps surpassed all the composers in the world. Therefore his chorales as well as his larger works are recommended most highly as the best models for diligent study. Experienced composers too will be more easily convinced of this fact if they try to set an alto and tenor to the bass and discant of one of his chorales, and to make these voices just as expressive and singable as both of the others.

Relationship Between the Declamation of an Aria and a Chorale

At the basis of every aria lies nothing more than a chorale set according to the most correct declamation, since every syllable of the text has only one note, which is decorated to a greater or lesser degree as the expression requires. The true basis of beauty in an aria always lies in the simple melody that remains after it has been stripped of all its decorating tones. If this is incorrect with regard to the declamation, chord progression or harmony, the mistakes cannot be completely covered up by any decoration.

Anyone who takes the trouble of stripping the most beautiful arias of all its decorations, will see that the remaining tones have the shape [*Gestalt*] of a well-set and correctly declaimed chorale. A few examples will be adequate to show this: [29]

---

a setting containing only three voices the appearance of having ten, twelve or more voices. Take for example the following:

With the soprano are:
1st oboe and 1st violin in unison
1st flute an octave higher
1st tenor and 1st horn an octave lower

With the second soprano or alto:
2nd oboe and 2nd violin in unison
2nd flute an octave higher
2nd tenor and 2nd horn an octave lower

The singing bass goes mostly in unison with the second tenor, with:
the viola an octave higher
the double bass an octave lower.

This gives us the impression of sixteen voices, when only three voices form the basis."

Kirnberger has here given us a lesson in Classical orchestration. *Tenor* was the generic term for a woodwind or string instrument in a range between the alto and bass. Therefore, in the violin family the 1st tenor could have been a large-sized viola, and the second tenor a cello. In the woodwind family the first tenor could have been an English horn, and the second tenor a bassoon. The horn (*Waldhorn*) was a natural brass instrument to which a crook, an extra length of tubing, might be added to put the instrument into a lower key. Valves were not invented for the French horn until c. 1815.

29. Kirnberger removes neighbor tones, passing tones, chordal leaps, suspensions, syncopations, and other decorations, leaving note-against-note counterpoint in the final sketch. The Handel Aria has one sketch, while the Graun Aria is stripped of its ornaments in two successive stages.

Handel composed *Tamerlano* in 1724 for the Royal Academy of Music in Lon-

Aria from the Opera *Tamerlano* by Handel (1724)
"Benche mi sprezzi l'Idol ch'adoro"

Aria by Graun from the Opera *Sylla* (1753)
"Per più sublime oggetto"

---

don (see Paul Henry Lang, *George Frideric Handel* [New York: W. W. Norton, 1966], p. 182).

In 1740 Carl Heinrich Graun (1704–1759) became Kapellmeister to the newly crowned King Frederick II of Prussia. The King asked Graun to go to Italy to hire a group of singers for the Royal Opera he wished to establish in Berlin. Over a span of fifteen years Graun wrote most of the court operas, among which was *Sylla* (1753). Frederick's other favorite operatic composer was Hasse.

The Main Idea and Its Development*

In a musical composition the *period* contains the expression and the whole essence of the melody. It not only appears at the beginning, but is frequently repeated throughout the whole composition, in different keys and with various changes. This main idea [*Hauptsatz*] is generally called the theme; and Mattheson compares it, not totally without justification, to the text of a preacher, who must present in a few words what will be developed [*entwikelt*] in more detail in the discussion.

Music is really the language of feeling [*Empfindung*], whose expression is always succinct because feeling itself is uncomplicated, evidencing few discrepancies. For this reason, a very short melodic phrase of two, three or four measures can express a feeling so definitely and correctly that the listener recognizes the singer's frame of mind exactly. Thus, if a composition had no intention other than to present a feeling definitely, such a short phrase, if it were well thought out, would be sufficient. But this is not the intention of music; it must serve to keep the listener in the same frame of mind for a length of time. This cannot happen through mere repetition of the same phrase, no matter how perfect it is, because repetition of the same thing is boring and drives one's attention right into the ground. Thus one must discover a kind of melody in which one and even the same feeling may be repeated with suitable changes and various modifications as often as is necessary to produce the desired impression.

From this arose the form of most of the compositions present in music today: the concerto, the symphony, aria, duet, trio, fugue, etc. All of these agree in that, in the main section nothing but a short period suitable for the expression of the feeling is established as the main idea; that this main idea is supported or even interrupted by smaller interim thoughts which are associated with it; that the main idea is repeated with these interim thoughts in different harmonies and keys, and also with small melodic changes which are suitable for the main expression, as often as is necessary, until the mind of the listener is sufficiently saturated with the feeling and has been reached, as it were, from all sides.

Johann George Sulzer, ed., Allgemeine Theorie der Schönen Kunste (Leipzig, 1771–1774, 1792), II, 488–491.

In all of these pieces the main idea is always the most important one of the whole composition. Its creation is the work of genius; but its development [*Ausführung*] is a work of taste and of art. Even if the composer has not been successful with the main idea, he can still construct a perfectly correct, artistic piece, one that also sounds extremely well, providing he has a thorough understanding of the art; but he will lack the true power of arousing lasting feeling.

The most outstanding characteristic of the main idea is sufficient clarity or understanding of the expression, so that anyone who has heard the main idea can immediately understand this language of the heart without hesitation, or can feel like a person who is singing. If the feeling is not completely determined and understandable, the piece can never be a totally perfect musical composition, even if it had been executed by the foremost composer in the world. This intelligibility depends on the melody or the melodic progression, as well as on the motion and the rhythm, and is, as has been said, totally the work of genius, for whose feeling no rule can be made.

However, genius alone is not enough for the perfection of the main idea; art must also do its share. For all the characteristics that do not go directly toward the understanding of the expression, really depend on art. The main idea must have a certain length. If it is too short it does not provide enough room for the necessary variations [*Veränderungen*] or for the prerequisite repetitions. If it is too long, it does not generally remain in the memory clearly enough. Therefore in a fast tempo it should not be under two measures. If the composer has created an idea with a very distinct expression, he must know how to expand or contract it properly in relation to its length. For longer themes [*Hauptsätzen*] which consist of several small segments, he must be very careful to observe the continuity meticulously, so that the theme has true unity and doesn't seem to be put together from two different fragments. One should not think the theme has ended until it has been performed in its entirety. This takes both skill and judgment.

Furthermore, in the main theme there must already be present opportunities for introducing small insertions [*Zwischensätze*] through which the most beautiful modulation [*Abwechslung*] in the song is achieved. These insertions usually come at small points of rest, or at somewhat sustained tones of the theme, and must express the feeling closely and exactly. Therefore the main theme need describe the feeling only as a whole and in general, and should provide an opportunity for the fine distinctions to be inserted. This must be done with the proper modulations, without in the least disturbing the unity of the rhythm.

Sometimes these insertions first occur at the end of the main theme. This may also be artistic if everything is brought together in a natural and simple relationship in a repetition which follows immediately thereafter.

Someone who composes for instruments alone has fewer difficulties than someone who composes to a text. For in the latter case everything, the motion and the length of the movements, the small insertions or points of rest, must agree exactly with the construction of the verse, which is often no small feat.

One sees from this that, besides natural genius, much taste, art, and experience in creating and handling the main theme are demanded. There is a great deficiency in the theory of music in that one finds so little on this important subject. Here, as in various other things, we must give thanks to the good Mattheson for at least making an attempt, although he might not have been the man to handle this material most creditably. It would be of great use if a fine connoisseur were to gather together the most beautiful themes in the compositions of the great masters and would point out and explain the skill and taste in them. For, in matters where one cannot assign definite rules, consummate examples serve instead of rules.

9.8 CHARLES BURNEY (1726–1814)

In 1776 two important histories of music first appeared, both written by Englishmen, each with an independent point of view. John Hawkins (1719–1789), knighted by His Majesty George III in 1772 for his service to England as magistrate of the County of Middlesex, wrote *A General History of the Science and Practice of Music*. Charles Burney, organist and harpsichordist who received his Music Doctorate from Oxford University in 1769, wrote *A General History of Music*. Hawkins was inclined toward documenting a history of the theory of music, while Burney was attracted toward comparing national styles. Burney's desire to hear live performances before drawing historical conclusions led him to travel in France, Italy, Germany, and the Netherlands, as well as through the United Provinces.

It is from the diaries kept by Burney during his travels, not from his history, that the excerpts below are taken. These diaries in themselves become sources for what was going on, musically speaking, in the streets as well as in the concert halls and meeting rooms of the cities through which he journeyed. The discussion of a machine for recording music indicates the search that was on for a mechanical means swifter and more accurate than manual notation, to reproduce any sound exactly, whether it was intentionally composed or casually improvised.

Venice*

I had many inquiries to make, and had very sanguine expectations from this city, with regard to the music of past times as well as at present. The church of St. Mark has had a constant supply of able masters, from Adriano, Zarlino's predecessor, to Galuppi, its present worthy composer.[30] Venice has

Charles Burney, The Present State of Music in France and Italy: or, The Journal of a Tour Through Those Countries, Undertaken to Collect Materials for a General History of Music *(London, 1771)*, pp. 137–8, 297. The Present State of Music in Germany, the Netherlands, and United Provinces, *2nd ed. (London, 1775)*, 1, 94–97, II, 213–219.

30. Baldassare Galuppi (1706–1785) was a talented harpsichordist and outstanding composer of opera buffa. He was active in Venice and St. Petersburg, where he instructed many Russian composers and singers.

likewise been one of the first cities in Europe that has cultivated the musical drama or opera: and, in the graver style, it has been honored with a Lotti [31] and a Marcello.[32] Add to these advantages the *conservatorios* established here, and the songs of the *Gondoleri,* or Water-men, which are so celebrated that every musical collector of taste in Europe is well furnished with them, and it will appear that my expectations were not ill grounded.

The first music which I heard here was in the street, immediately on my arrival, performed by an itinerant band of two fiddles, a violoncello, and a voice, who, though unnoticed here as small-coalmen or oyster-women in England, performed so well, that in any other country of Europe they would not only have excited attention, but have acquired applause, which they justly merited. These two violins played difficult passages very neatly, the bass stopped well in tune, and the voice, which was a woman's, was well toned, and had several essentials belonging to that of a good singer, such as compass, shake, and volubility.

Naples

The national music here is so singular, as to be totally different, both in melody and modulation, from all that I have heard elsewhere. This evening in the streets there were two people singing alternately; one of these Neapolitan *Canzoni* was accompanied by a violin and *calascione*.[33] The singing is noisy and vulgar, but the accompaniments are admirable, and well performed. The violin and calascione parts were incessantly at work during the song, as well as the ritornels. The modulation surprised me very much: from the key of A natural, to that of C and F, was not difficult or new; but from that of A, with a sharp third, to E♭, was astonishing; and the more so, as the return to the original key was always so sensibly managed, as neither to shock the ear, nor to be easily discovered by what road or relations it was brought about.

The Mannheim Orchestra [34]

I found the orchestra of his electoral highness, so deservedly celebrated throughout Europe, to be indeed all that its fame had made me expect. Power will naturally arise from a great number of hands; but the judicious use of this power, on all occasions, must be the consequence of good discipline. Indeed, there are more solo players, and good composers in this, than perhaps in any other orchestra in Europe. It is an army of generals, equally fit to plan a battle, as to fight it.

31. Antonio Lotti (1667–1740) became maestro of St. Mark's in 1736. He wrote masses, motets, oratorios, and operas. Lotti taught Galuppi and Marcello, among others.
32. Benedetto Marcello (1686–1739) wrote *Estro poetico-armonico,* fifty settings of paraphrases on the Psalms by Giustiniani. Marcello's satire on opera, *Il Teatro alla moda,* has been translated into English by Reinhard Pauly in *The Musical Quarterly* (July 1948 and January 1949).
33. The *Calascione,* of Eastern origin, was a long-necked lute with two or three strings tuned in fourths.
34. For the Mannheim composers at the court of Duke Carl Theodor (1724–1799), Elector Palatine, see Paul Henry Lang, *Music in Western Civilization* (New York: W. W. Norton & Co., Inc., 1941), pp. 608 ff.

But it has not been merely at the Elector's great opera that instrumental music has been so much cultivated and refined, but at his *concerts*, where this extraordinary band has "ample room and verge enough," to display all its powers, and to produce great effects without the impropriety of destroying the greater and more delicate beauties peculiar to vocal music. It was here that Stamitz,[35] stimulated by the productions of Jomelli,[36] first surpassed the bounds of common opera overtures, which had hitherto only served in the theater as a kind of court cryer, with an "O Yes!" in order to awaken attention, and bespeak silence, at the entrance of the singers. Since the discovery which the genius of Stamitz first made, every effect has been tried which such an aggregate of sound can produce. It was here that the *Crescendo* and *Diminuendo* had birth; and the *Piano*, which was before chiefly used as an echo, with which it was generally synonymous, as well as the *Forte*, were found to be musical colors which had their shades, as much as red or blue in painting. I found, however, an imperfection in this band, common to all others that I have ever yet heard, but which I was in hopes would be removed by men so attentive and so able; the defect I mean is the want of truth in the wind instruments. I know it is natural to those instruments to be out of tune, but some of that art and diligence which these great performers have manifested in vanquishing difficulties of other kinds, would surely be well employed in correcting this leaven, which so much sours and corrupts all harmony. This was too plainly the case tonight, with the bassoons and oboes, which were rather too sharp at the beginning and continued growing sharper to the end of the opera.

My ears were unable to discover any other imperfection in the orchestra, through the whole performance. And this imperfection is so common to orchestras in general, that the censure will not be very severe upon this, or afford much matter for triumph to the performers of any other orchestra in Europe.

A Machine for Recording Music

This afternoon I went to M. Marpurg for the last time,[37] who was so obliging, on this occasion, as to throw out all the temptations which he could suggest in order to keep me longer in Berlin; but my want of time rendered me inflexible. However, he kindly undertook to procure and transmit to me several interesting particulars relative to the history of German music and

35. Johann Stamitz (1717–1757), concertmaster and director of the Mannheim orchestra at the height of its fame, was responsible for important innovations in orchestral playing. In 1754 at the Concert Spirituel in Paris he used clarinets in the performance of a symphony.
36. Niccolò Jommelli (1714–1774) was a prolific composer of Italian operas. He produced his works not only in his native Naples but also in Rome, Bologna (where he met Padre Martini), Venice, Turin, Padua, Ferrara, and Parma.
37. Friedrich Wilhelm Marpurg (1718–1795), famous music theorist, met Rameau in Paris in 1746. In 1763 Marpurg was director of the Royal Lotteries at Berlin. Among his voluminous writings are methods for playing the clavier, treatises on fugue and thoroughbass, an explanation of Rameau's theories, and an introduction to the art of singing.

musicians, and furnished me with the description of a machine for writing down extempore pieces of music, commonly called voluntaries, of which I had long been in search.

To fix such fleeting sounds as are generated in the wild moments of enthusiasm, while "bright-eyed fancy—

> Scatters from her pictured urn,
> Thoughts that breathe and notes that burn."

would be giving permanence to ideas which reflection can never find, nor memory retain.[38] . . .

The Berlin machine was to consist of two cylinders, which were to be moved by clock-work, at the rate of an inch in a second of time; one of these was to furnish paper, and the other was to receive it when marked by pins, or pencils, fixed at the ends of the several keys of the instrument, to which the machine was applied. The paper was to be previously prepared with red lines, which were to fall under their respective pencils.

The chief difficulties in the execution, which have occurred to English mechanics with whom I have conversed on the subject, were the preparation of the paper for receiving the marks made by the keys; and the kind of instrument which was to serve as a pencil, and which, if hard and pointed, would, in the *forte* parts, tear the paper; and if soft, would not only be liable to break when used with violence, but would be worn unequally, and want frequent cutting.

In the Berlin machine the pencils were made to terminate in a very narrow compass, so that paper of an uncommon size was not requisite; but it was *not* found necessary to prepare the paper, for the degree of gravity or acuteness of each sound was ascertained by a ruler applied to the marked paper when taken off the cylinder.

38. Among the experiments antedating the machine under discussion Burney mentions an English "demonstration of the possibility of making a machine that shall write extempore Voluntaries or other pieces of music as fast as any master shall be able to play them, upon an organ, harpsichord, etc., and that in a character more natural and intelligible, and more expressive of all the varieties those instruments are capable of exhibiting, than the character now in use" (1747); also, a German machine "so perfect that I was assured by a great performer who tried it upon a clavichord that there was nothing in music which it could not express, except *tempo rubato*."

10

Classical Sense
of Balance and Form

10.1 JOSEPH HAYDN (1732–1809)

The string quartets and symphonies of Joseph Haydn, the son of the organist of the village church in Rohrau-on-the-Leitha, Austria, epitomize the expression of Classical instrumental style. Joseph's musical talent was evident at an early age. When he was 5 years old, provision was made for him to learn to sing and play the violin. A few years later, as a boy chorister at St. Stephen's church in Vienna, Haydn, in addition to his music, studied Latin, reading, writing, and arithmetic.

When Haydn was in his seniority, one of his biographers, Albert Christoph Dies, asked him to judge the textbooks he considered to be most valuable. Haydn thought C. P. E. Bach's *Essay* was indispensable. As for Mattheson's *Complete Chapelmaster* (Section 9.3), Haydn did not find the examples attractive, so he wrote new melodies over Mattheson's basic sketches. Kirnberger, too, came in for some criticism because of his restrictive rules. Haydn liked Johann Joseph Fux's *Gradus ad Parnassum* (Vienna, 1725), a treatise on counterpoint originally written in Latin, for its organization of the species.

Haydn had not been inclined toward putting his own ideas in writing. One of the rare instances in which he formulated detailed instructions concerning tempi, accompaniment, dynamics, instrumentation, and the like came about in connection with the *Applausus Cantata*. Haydn composed this congratulatory work to honor Rainer Kollmann, Abbot of the

Benedictine monastery of Zwettl, northwest of Vienna, on the occasion of the abbot's 70th birthday. Haydn, who was in the employ of Prince Nicholas Esterházy of Hungary at the time, could not leave his duties to attend. Therefore Haydn sent a letter to the monastery with advice as to how to perform the cantata. These specifications constitute an important document in the annals of performance practice.

Accompaniment, Dynamics, and Instrumentation*

Letter Concerning the Performance of the Applausus Cantata

Since I cannot be present in person at this performance of the *Applausus*, I believe a few explanations are necessary, namely:

1. First, I beg you to take heed of the tempo in all arias and recitatives exactly and, since the entire text applauds, I should prefer to have one or another of the Allegros taken somewhat more briskly than usual, especially in the very first Ritornello and in one or another Recitative, no less than in the two bass Arias.

2. For the Sinfonia all you need to do is to play an Allegro and an Andante, because the first Ritornello takes the place of the closing Allegro.[1] If I knew the day of the performance, perhaps I would be able to send a new Sinfonia before that time.

3. In the accompanied Recitatives notice that the accompaniment should not enter until after the singer has finished singing the text completely, even though the score often shows the contrary.[2] For example, in the beginning, each time the word *metamorphosis* appears, the voice has an appoggiatura [*Anschlag*] on *-phosis*.[3] There one must be careful to allow the last syllable of the Recitative to be heard completely and then the accompaniment must come in promptly on the downbeat. For it would be ludicrous if one were to fiddle the word away from the mouth of the singer so that nothing but *quae metamo* was intelligible. But I leave this up to the cembalist because everyone else must follow him. NB: Our learned men in Eisenstadt, of whom indeed there are very few,

---

The autograph of this letter, which has been reproduced many times, is in the Archiv der Gesellschaft der Musikfreunde in Vienna.

1. Haydn is giving instructions for assembling an overture from music at hand in case he does not have time to write one. The form of the Sinfonia or Italian Overture was Allegro-Andante-Allegro. Haydn's cantata starts with an Allegro di molto, which becomes the third section of the overture.

2. This practice of completing the recitative before the cadential chords are played in the accompaniment, was common in the performances of the Baroque as well as of the Classic era.

3. The Latin text of this cantata deals with the four cardinal virtues.
   In 1753 C. P. E. Bach said that an appoggiatura to a note of duple value lasts half the length of that note. On *-phosis* Haydn uses an appoggiatura on A which takes up half the duration of G. (See Bach's *Essay*, trans. W. J. Mitchell [New York: W. W. Norton, 1949], p. 90.)

argued a great deal over the word *metamorphosis*.[4] One wanted the penultimate syllable short while the other wanted it long, not taking into account the fact that in Italian they say *metamŏrphŏsi* while in Latin I have always heard it as *metamorphōsis*. If I am mistaken, this mistake would be easy to correct.

4. The *fortes* and *pianos* are written accurately throughout, and they should be reckoned exactly, for there is a very great difference between *piano* and *pianissimo*, *forte* and *fortissimo*, between *crescendo* and *forzando* and the like. Also notice that when a *forte* or *piano* is not written down for each part in the score, the copyist should make up for this deficiency when copying the parts.[5]

5. At various academies I have often lost my temper with many a violinist who wretchedly marred the so-called ties, one of the most beautiful figures in music, by lifting the bow up in a short staccato manner on a tied note which should have been joined to the preceding one. Therefore I suggest the following to the first violinist: Since the first two notes require one bow, it would be utterly foolish if, instead of playing this [as it appears in Measure 47],

one were to play in such an unsuitable and incorrect manner as this, all staccato, as if there were no tie.

6. Please have two players on the viola part throughout, because the middle part in many cases should be heard more than the upper part. Besides, in all my compositions it is apparent that the middle part rarely doubles the bass.

7. If he has to make duplicate violin parts, the copyist should avoid everybody having to turn the page at the same time, for this takes much power away from music arranged for a few players. Also, he should see to it that the *da capo* sign SS is written in one of the first violin parts as it appears in the score, but the other can have the *da capo* about two measures after the sign appeared originally, with the sign in a suitable place.

8. Above all I recommend that the two boy soloists have good enuncia-

4. Haydn lived in Eisenstadt (then in Hungary) on the estate of Prince Nicholas, and came to Vienna only for a few months in the wintertime. Twice Haydn's house burned down and some of his operas and other compositions were destroyed.

5. As is still customary when writing a score, Haydn abbreviated in places where one part was an exact repetition of another. See the facsimile of the first page of the *Applausus* in the frontispiece to *Joseph Haydn Werke*, ed. at the Joseph-Haydn-Institut, Cologne, Vol. 27².

tion, slow in the Recitatives, so that every syllable may be understood. Likewise, the style of singing a recitative, for example,

Quae me - ta - mor - pho - sis

must be as follows,

Quae me - ta - mor - pho - sis

and not:

Quae me - ta - mor - pho - sis

Otherwise the note before the last, the penultimate G, would be completely suppressed. And this style is applicable to all the other similar cases. In this regard I have confidence in the expertise of the principal tenor who will give all the directions about it to the boys.

9. I hope that you have at least three or four rehearsals of the entire work.

10. In the soprano aria the bassoon may be left out completely. However, I would prefer that it were present at the times when the bass is entirely obbligato. I think that music with three basses, such as violoncello, bassoon, and violone, sounds better than that for six violones and three violoncelli, wherever it is difficult to perceive certain passages clearly.

Finally, I beg everyone, especially the principal musicians, for my sake as well as your own, to use the utmost care possible. If I perhaps have not divined your fancy with my work, please do not be angry at me, because neither the persons nor the place are known to me, and this mystery really made my work difficult. Yet, I hope that this *Applausus* pleases the poet, and the fine musicians, as well as the most esteemed audience [*auditorio*], all of whom I respect most highly.

Your most obedient servant Giuseppe Haydn
Chapelmaster of His Most Serene Highness Prince Esterhazy

Biographical Notes

G. A. Griesinger, *Biographische Notizen über Joseph Haydn* (Leipzig, 1810) and A. C. Dies, *Biographische Nachrichten von Joseph Haydn* (Vienna, 1810) are translated by Vernon Gotwals in *Joseph Haydn, Eighteenth-Century Gentleman and Genius* (Madison: The University of Wisconsin Press, 1963).

The technical portion of Johann Joseph Fux's *Gradus ad Parnassum* was translated by Alfred Mann as *Steps to Parnassus* (New York, 1943).

10.2 WOLFGANG AMADEUS MOZART (1756–1791)

Wolfgang Amadeus Mozart, born in Salzburg when Haydn was 24 years old, matured quickly, to the point where, in the decade of the 1770s, the two composers were influencing one another's style. Mozart had the pedagogical advantage of having a father who, although a professional violinist, conductor, and court composer in his own right, was totally dedicated to the musical advancement of his children, Wolfgang and "Nannerl." [6]

From the time Wolfgang was 6 years old, Leopold Mozart took the children on tour. The boy wonder performed on the harpsichord and on the violin, playing his own compositions, improvising, conducting from the keyboard, and generally delighting both royal and public audiences. On travels during which Mozart was separated from his father, he wrote home to describe his experiences. In one of the letters quoted here Wolfgang shows enthusiasm for the pianoforte, the new keyboard instrument then gaining favor. In the other letter, while chatting about informal music making at mealtime, Wolfgang incidentally passes on to posterity his concept of tempo rubato.

Characteristics of a Fine Pianoforte*

Augsburg, October 17, 1777

My very dear father:

I must tell you right now about Stein's pianofortes.[7] Before I had yet seen any of Stein's make, I liked Späth's Claviers the best.[8] But now I must give priority to Stein's, because they damp so much better than those made in Regensburg. When I strike the key forcefully, whether I let my finger stay there or lift it up, the tone disappears at the instant I have produced it. No matter how I decide to touch the keys, the tone is always even, never scratchy, louder or softer, or non-existent. In a word, it is consistently even. To be sure, he does not sell such a pianoforte for under 300 florins,[9] but he cannot be reimbursed for the trouble and care that he lavishes on it. His instruments have a special feature over the others in that they are made with an escapement. Although only one maker in a hundred provides for this, without an escapement it is impossible to prevent a pianoforte from

*The autographs of these letters, which have been reproduced many times, are in the Mozarteum, Salzburg.

6. Leopold Mozart wrote the most important violin method of the day, *Versuch einer gründlichen Violinschule* (Augsburg, 1756), facsimile reproduction (Breitkopf & Härtel, 1956) translated into English by Editha Knocker (London: Oxford University Press, 1948).

7. Johann Andreas Stein (1728–1792) learned the art of constructing keyboard instruments in the workshop of J. A. Silbermann in Strasbourg, and then set up his own business in Augsburg. The business was eventually continued by Stein's apprentice, Johann Andreas Streicher, who in 1802 moved it to Vienna.

8. Franz Jacob Späth (1714–1798) was a clavier-builder in Regensburg, a city in lower Bavaria, slightly north of Augsburg.

9. The Austrian florin, a silver coin, was worth about half a dollar.

scratching or reverberating. When you play on his keys, the hammers rebound at the instant that they strike the strings, whether or not you continue to depress the keys. As he told me himself, only after he has finished the construction of one of his claviers, does he sit down at the keyboard to try all kinds of passages, runs, and leaps. He prepares and works on the clavier until it functions perfectly. If he did not work solely for the good of music and not for his personal profit, he would finish the task much sooner. He often says, "If I myself were not such a passionate lover of music, and could not play a little bit on the clavier, I would certainly have lost my patience for this work a long time ago. But I am a firm believer in instruments which are worthy of the player and which are lasting."

His claviers really do last. He guarantees that the sounding board will not break or crack. After he has finished the sound board for a clavier, he places it in the air, the rain, the snow, and the blazing sun, subjecting it to all the demons so that it may crack. Then he inserts shavings and glues them in so that it becomes strong and solid throughout. He is overjoyed when it cracks; then one may be certain that nothing else can happen to it. Often he even cuts into it himself and glues it together again, really strengthening it. He has constructed three pianofortes of this kind. Just today I played on one again.

Informal Music Making at Mealtime

October 23–24, 1777

Last Sunday I attended mass at the Heiligkreuz Monastery and then went to visit Herr Stein at about 10 o'clock. That was on the 19th. We rehearsed several symphonies for the concert. Afterwards I had dinner with my cousin at the Heiligkreuz. Music [*Musique*] was played at the table [*Tafel*].[10] As poor as their fiddling is, I prefer the *Musique* in the monastery to the orchestra at Augsburg. I put together a *sinfonie* and played the Concerto in Bb by Vanhall [11] on the violin, to sweeping applause [*applauso*]. The Dean, a cousin of Eberlin,[12] is a clever, jovial man by the name of Zeschinger. He knows Papa quite well.

In the evening, at supper, I played the Strasbourg Concerto.[13] It went like oil. Everyone praised the beautiful, pure tone. After that they brought in a small clavichord. I improvised [*Präludirte*],[14] and played a sonata and the

10. Mozart has mixed his languages here in a way which seems particularly appropriate. *Musique de Table* or *Tafelmusik* was music to be performed at mealtime. Georg Philipp Telemann (1681-1767), a German composer, had written a series of instrumental suites which he entitled *Musique de Table* [*Denkmäler deutscher Tonkunst* (Leipzig: Breitkopf & Härtel, 1892–1931), Vol. 61–62].

11. Johann Baptist Vanhall (1739–1813) was a Bohemian composer who studied with Karl von Dittersdorf in Vienna.

12. Johann Ernst Eberlin (1702–1762) was court Kapellmeister to the Archbishop-Prince of Salzburg at the time when Mozart's father, Leopold, was Vice-Kapellmeister.

13. The *Strasbourg Concerto* was probably Mozart's Violin Concerto in D major, K. V. 218, written in Salzburg in 1775. The third movement, a rondo, has a musette theme similar to the Ballo Strasburghese called Musette in Dittersdorf's *Karnevals-Sinfonie*.

14. Following his conquests on the violin, Mozart turned to the keyboard on which he *preludized*, probably improvising with chordal passage work to warm up for the pieces he was about to play. The concept of *prelude* here goes back to its original meaning in connection with music indigenous to the clavier.

Variations [on a Minuet] by Fischer.[15] Then the others whispered in the Dean's ear that he should hear me play something in the organ style. I told him to give me a theme. He did not want to, but one of the monks gave me one. I took it for a stroll, and in the middle (the fugue was in G minor) I went into major with something quite jocular, but in the same tempo, reverting to the theme again, but backwards. Finally I wondered, could I not also use the jocular subject as the theme of a fugue?—I did not ask for long, but did it at once, and it fitted as neatly as if Daser had measured it.[16] The Dean was completely beside himself. "This is super, nothing less," he said. "I would never have believed what I have heard here. You are an accomplished fellow. Independently my abbot told me that in his whole life he had never heard anyone play the organ so convincingly and fervently." (For he had heard me several days before, but the Dean was not there.)

Finally someone brought out a sonata in fugal style for me to play. But I said, "Gentlemen, this is too much. I don't think that I will be able to play this sonata at sight."

"Yes, I agree," assented the Dean, because he was completely on my side. "This is too much; no one could do it."

"However," I said, "I will try it anyway."

But I continually heard the Dean behind me saying, "O, you bold rascal, o you show-off, o you, you—!"

Bombarded and, as it were, beset by fugue themes, I played until 11 o'clock. The other day, when I was at Stein's house, he brought me a sonata by Beecke [17]—I think I told you about it already.

The fact that I always maintain the beat accurately, amazes everyone. They simply cannot understand the idea that the left hand goes on as usual during tempo rubato in an Adagio. They imagine that the left hand always follows along. Count Wolfeck and others who are thoroughly enthusiastic about Beecke said openly at a concert the other day that I can shove Beecke in my pocket. Count Wolfeck kept running around the hall saying that he had never heard anything like it in his life. He said to me, "I must tell you that I never heard you play like you did today. I will tell your father about it as soon as I get to Salzburg."

Bibliographical Notes

Ludwig von Köchel, an Austrian botanist and minerologist, compiled a catalog of Mozart's works under the title, *Chronologisch-thematisches Verzeichnis sämmtlicher Tonwerke W. A. Mozarts* (Leipzig, 1862). Although the meticulous enumeration and listing of themes of over 600 works, together with the bibliographical data concerning autographs, editions, and literature, was originally done as a labor of love, Köchel's catalog has become a standard, and Mozart's works are now identified with a number preceded by a K. for Köchel. Expansion and revision of

15. K. 189a = **179** are *Twelve Variations for Klavier* on a minuet by Johann Christian Fischer, composed by Mozart at Salzburg in 1774. Apparently here Mozart played them on a clavichord.
16. Daser was a tailor in Salzburg.
17. Ignaz von Beecke (1733–1803) was a composer and clavierist friendly with Gluck and Jommelli, as well as Mozart. He wrote six harpsichord sonatas.

the catalog since Köchel's day sometimes produces a double number, as in fn 15 above.

10.3 HEINRICH CHRISTOPH KOCH (1749–1816)

The mysteries of melodic and harmonic textures were explored by the theorist Heinrich Christoph Koch in his *Treatise on Composition* (1787, 1793). Koch penetrated the distinction between melodic "modulation" and harmonic modulation, calling the former *tone progression* and considering the latter as *modulation* in the modern sense of the term. He also recognized that a mixture of learned and free styles was indigenous to a balanced quartet style. Koch's observation antedates Goethe's contention that the performance of a string quartet is "more intelligible than other instrumental music. You hear four rational persons conversing together, and fancy you get something from their discourse, and learn to know the peculiarities of their different instruments." [18]

Little is known about Koch's life. His first teacher was his father, a member of the prince's orchestra at Rudolstadt. In 1768 Koch himself became a violinist in the orchestra and rose to the rank of chamber musician in 1777.

In addition to the book on composition and a highly perceptive musical lexicon (1802), Koch wrote articles for periodicals including the *Allgemeine Musikalischer Zeitung*.

Concerning Modulation*

The melodic succession of tones considered from the standpoint of the formation and use of both of the semitones belonging to a mode, was formerly called "modulation." It is not my intention now to show that this expression and the meaning associated with it arose at the same time period of music as that in which the old Greek modes were still practiced, and that therefore this meaning no longer applies to the use of both of our modern modes. I am limiting myself in this inquiry merely to the use of the modern modes, since, outside of the old church songs, the old modes are no longer practiced. Nevertheless, today we still use the term "modulation," and usually associate it with two meanings related to each other. First, one speaks of modulation when one means the colorful changing ascent and descent of the tones of a basic tonality, mainly with regard to a tone progression. Secondly, one also calls the procedure a modulation when the composer gives more melodic and harmonic color to the entire composition, leading the succession of tones through various other keys and bringing it back to the main tonality. In the first case one speaks mainly about the modulation

---

*From *Heinrich Christoph Koch*, Versuch einer Anleitung zur Composition (*Leipzig, 1787, 1793*), II, 137–50; III, 325–27.

18. From a letter written by Johann Wolfgang von Goethe (1749–1832) in Weimar, dated November 9, 1829, to Karl Friedrich Zelter (1758–1832). Zelter's musical settings of Goethe's poems led to a lasting friendship. (Letter trans. A. D. Coleridge, 1887.)

or about the tone progression, and in the second case especially about the modulation, or about the tonal expansion or tonal extension.[19]

Concerning Tone Progression

Melodic tone succession, or tone progression, consists of a skillful and colorful changing succession of tones in the basic tonality. A tonality must be at the basis of a melodic-harmonic union of tones. But the skillful or un-skillful management of this colorful changing succession of tones must be determined partly by what the human voice, as the most beautiful instru-ment for the performance of melody, can produce with ease, partly by the nature of the basic tonality, and also, partly by the feeling of what is beau-tiful and appropriate.

All compositions which are not easy for the human voice to produce, that is, all difficult intonation, must be avoided, especially in vocal music.

This applies to the following ascending as well as descending intervals:

1. The augmented second, as in Example 1. The unsingable characteristic of this interval is improved by reordering the tones. Instead of having both tones which contain the augmented second in succession, place them so that they produce the leap of a diminished seventh, as in Example 2.

Example 1

Example 2

2. The augmented fourth, as in Example 3. Instead of this interval, the in-version of the tones into a diminished fifth is preferred, as in Example 4.

Example 3

Example 4

7. All intervals that are larger than the octave.[20] Remarks: Now and then there are many exceptions to this rule. The most important exception occurs in instrumental music, with the use of intervals that are larger than an octave. Since on most instruments there is no difficulty of in-tonation for these intervallic leaps, and, usually, as long as they do not contain any augmented interval larger than an octave, there is no melodic

19. The first type of modulation, *Tonführung*, refers to a single voice part; this type is discussed in the section on tone progression. The second type of modulation, *Tonausweichung*, concerns the transition from one key to another throughout the texture of the setting as a whole.
20. Koch also gives examples for #3, the augmented fifth; #4, the augmented sixth; #5, the augmented third and diminished sixth; and #6, the major seventh.

disadvantage. Thus, it is not necessary to renounce their use completely, if the main expression of the setting does not in itself renounce their use. This kind of leap has its best effect when it is used in a slow tempo, in stately movements, or for the expression of the sublime, for example:

But intervals which are larger than an octave are not completely banned from vocal music either. They are sometimes used in an aria if one is composing for a singer who has a large vocal range. Or they are also used for the expression of various emotions. Thus, for example, the first aria in Schweitzer's *Alceste* contains the following passage: [21]

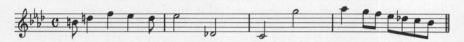

On the other hand, in choruses such wide intervallic leaps cannot be used. In a choral setting a leap larger than an octave may be used only after a cadence, or after a break where a rest occurs in the middle of the leap, or, mainly after a rest. But one must be careful to avoid having large leaps in all the voices at the same time, for example:

Among the forbidden augmented intervallic progressions there is also an exception in vocal music concerning the ascending augmented second, and the ascending as well as descending leap of an augmented fourth. The expressions of various unpleasant emotions, such as the expression of sadness, of anger and of fear, are portrayed very well with these intervals. And since they do not present any particular difficulty of intonation to talented singers, they can often be used to great advantage in the expression of such emotions. We find examples in the Aria from the opera *Alceste* from which we already quoted, such as:

21. Anton Schweitzer (1737–1787) was chapelmaster for the duke of Gotha. He wrote operas and incidental music for German plays.

In instrumental music both of these augmented intervals are used much more often than in vocal music, indeed sometimes without any justification and for emotions to which they are totally unsuited. Therefore the beginning composer should always follow the worthwhile rule that he should never use these tone progressions appropriate for expressing various unpleasant emotions, at inappropriate places. And above all he should not use them often without justification, lest through unnecessarily frequent use they become all too familiar to the ear, thereby weakening their intrinsic value for the expression of unpleasant emotions. . . .

Skill in tone progression, insofar as it is determined by the basic tonality, demands that one should never use tones in *direct* melodic succession that presume any other than the basic tonality. Otherwise the nature of the basic tonality is destroyed. And this will always happen if, for example, one wants to use in succession several intervals of a single particular size, an interval of the kind contained in the natural tonality. The nature of both of our scales is such that nowhere in the melody can two major thirds appear in succession, as is the case in Example 1 when in the minor mode the third step ascends to the fifth, and the fifth to the major seventh. If one were to use two major thirds in succession in the major mode, or if one were to use them on different steps in the minor mode, one would destroy the nature of the tonality, as the succession of Example 2, either in C major or A minor.[22]

Example 1   Example 2

But if the same tones which are not contained in the basic tonality are placed in direct succession, that is, if they are used scalewise, intermingled with the tones in the basic tonality, the result is the chromatic scale which, used properly, does not belie the nature of tonality.

Concerning the Quartet

The quartet, at the present time the most delightful type of composition for a smaller musical ensemble, is being produced most assiduously by recent composers.

22. The distribution of the intervals in Example 2 is prohibitive when a succession of natural major thirds is nvolved. However, in a system with equal temperament, where the B♯ is equivalent to C, it becomes quite possible. Following is an enharmonic progression outlining the whole-tone scale within an octave.

In pinpointing the progressions leading away from tonality, Koch is actually paving the way for their future acceptance.

If it is really to consist of four obbligato parts, of which none dominates over the other, it must be handled in the manner of a fugue.

But since modern quartets are composed in the galant style, one must be satisfied with four main voice-parts of the kind which are alternately predominant and galant, either one or the other, when the bass usual in compositions in the galant treatment occurs. While one of the voices is concerned with presenting the main melody, both of the remaining voices must proceed with related melodies which enhance the expression without obscuring the main melody. Thus it is obvious that the quartet is one of the most difficult types of composition, which should be attempted only by the most highly trained composers, experienced in writing many compositions.

Among the recent composers, Haydn, Pleyel, and Hofmeister have enriched the public with this kind of sonata to the greatest extent.[23] Also the late Mozart had six quartets for two violins, viola, and cello published in Vienna with a dedication to Haydn. Of all the modern four-voiced sonatas, these best exemplify the meaning of the true quartet. On account of their real mixture of the learned and free styles, and on account of the treatment of the harmony, they are one of a kind in the art.[24]

10.4 LUDWIG VAN BEETHOVEN (1770–1829) THROUGH E. T. A. HOFFMANN (1776–1822)

At the height of the Classical era the composer-critic E. T. A. Hoffmann called music "the most Romantic of all the arts." With instrumental music in mind, specifically writing about Beethoven's Fifth Symphony and his Trio, Opus 70, No. 1, Hoffmann considered music as independent in thought and feeling, as infinite, without boundaries, existing in a world of its own. Hoffmann illustrated this Romantic contention with works which from the standpoint of form represent the essence of musical Classicism.

Born Ernst Theodor Wilhelm Hoffmann, E. T. A. changed the Wilhelm to Amadeus in deference to his admiration for the music of Wolf-

23. In the original sense of the word, a *sonata* was a composition to be played, in contrast to a *cantata*, which was to be sung. Thus Koch calls the string quartet "a kind of sonata."

24. Haydn's first string quartets, written somewhat before Mozart was born in 1756, were mostly in a galant or homophonic style. Likewise, there was little independence of melodic line in Mozart's first string quartets (K. 155–160), written from 1772 to early 1773. Haydn introduced a new texture when in 1772 he wrote fugues for the last movements of his string quartets. Opus, 20, Nos. 2, 5, and 6. A year later, in 1773, Mozart wrote a series of string quartets (K. 168–173) with many contrapuntal features, including a fugal finale on a chromatic subject (K. 173). When Haydn produced his next set of string quartets, Opus 33, in 1781, he amalgamated the homophonic and contrapuntal textures to the extent that each instrument could carry its own distinguishable melody while the four instruments blended together. It was at this point that Mozart started to write his six string quartets, K. 387 in G major, K. 421 in D minor, K. 428 in Eb major, K. 458 in Bb major, K. 464 in A major, and K. 465 in C major, dedicating them to Haydn in 1785, after the two composers had themselves played string quartets together in Vienna.

gang Amadeus Mozart. As a composer Hoffmann is remembered for his Romantic opera *Undine*, produced in Berlin in 1816. However, it is generally recognized that Hoffmann's widespread influence on composers of the Romantic era stems from his literary rather than his musical writing.

Romanticism in Beethoven's Music*

Fifth Symphony, Opus 67

When music is discussed as an independent art, only instrumental music should be taken into account. For instrumental music, rejecting all aid from, and association with another art [poetry], clearly expresses the characteristic artistic property only to be found in music. It is the most romantic of all the arts—one might almost say, it is the only purely romantic art. Orpheus's lyre opened the gates of Orcus.[25] Music unlocks for man an unknown realm, a world which has nothing in common with the external world of the senses that surround him, a world where he may completely abandon the exact expression of thought and devote himself to the inarticulate.[26] How little the instrumental composers know about the real essence of music, who try to portray every definable emotion, or even every specific event, thus treating an art diametrically opposed to the plastic arts as if it were among them: [27] Dittersdorf's symphonies of this kind, as well as all the newer *Batailles des trois Empereurs* [28] are like comical aberrations soon to be forgotten completely.

*The two selections are from Allgemeine Musikalische Zeitung, July 4, 1810, Vol. XII, pp. 630–31, 634–36; and March 3, 1813, Vol. XV, p. 146.

25. Orcus is the Roman name for the Greek Hades, the lower world.
26. For a discussion of articulate and inarticulate sounds see Priscian (Section 3.3). The separation, combination, and contrast of the articulate sounds of words and the inarticulate sounds of absolute music has been a challenge to poet and musician throughout the ages. In 1610 the Englishman Giles Fletcher, on considering the role of musicians, wrote, "Who ever doubted, but that Poets infused the verie soule into inarticulate sounds of musique; that without *Pindar* and *Horace* the Lyriques had beene silenced for ever" (Preface to *Christ's Victorie*). In 1669 another English poet, John Dryden, endeavored to strengthen poetry in the minds of the "Enemies of the Stage" with the following analogy: "By the Harmony of words, we elevate the mind to a sense of Devotion, as our solemn Musick, which is inarticulate Poesie, does in Churches" (Preface to *Tyrannick Love*).
27. The plastic arts involve modeling, as in the sculpture of a figure or in the pose of a dancer. Wagner included the plastic arts in his universal artwork (see Section 11.10).
28. Karl Ditters von Dittersdorf (1739–1799) wrote six symphonies on subjects from Ovid's *Metamorphoses*, three of which were published by Artaria in Vienna in 1785.
    Battle scenes had been prevalent in the vocal compositions of the Renaissance—namely, *La Bataille* of Janequin (Section 8.5, fn. 31). In the eighteenth century gunfire, cannons and fanfares received full symphonic treatment. Franz Kotzwara's *Battle of Prague* (1788), Philipp Rutti's *Battle of Leipzig*, Louis Jadin's *Battle of Austerlitz*, and Beethoven's *Wellington's Siege* (first performed in 1913) all are in this category.

In song, where the participating poem indicates definite emotions through words, the magic power of the music works like the wonder-elixir of the wise, a few drops of which make any drink costly and regal. Music clothes every passion—love, hate, anger, despair, etc., as they are presented in opera—in the purple shimmer of Romanticism, and even what we have experienced in life leads us away from life into the realm of the infinite. . . .

Aesthetic surveyors have often complained about the complete lack of true unity and inner coherence in Shakespeare; only with deeper penetration does a more beautiful tree bearing buds and leaves, blossoms and fruit, spring from a single seed. So too only a very deep search into the inner structure of Beethoven's music reveals the great self-possession of the master, which is inseparable from true genius and is nourished by a continuous study of the art. Deep in his soul does Beethoven bear the Romantic art of music, which he expresses with great genius and perception in his works. Your reviewer had never felt this more keenly than in the Fifth Symphony, which in a climax mounting steadily to the end reveals Beethoven as a Romantic more than any of his other works, and leads the listener irresistibly into the wonderful spirit-world of the infinite.

The first Allegro, in $\frac{2}{4}$ meter, in C minor, begins with a main idea [*Hauptgedanke*] consisting of only two measures,[29] which subsequently is fashioned in a variety of ways, more and more penetrating.

In the second measure there is a fermata; then there is a repetition of the previous idea a tone lower, with another fermata—both times only with stringed instruments and clarinets.

The key has not yet been resolved; the listener expects E♭ major. When the second violin introduces the main idea [measure 6], the fundamental note C, played by the cellos and bassoons in the next measure, establishes the key of C minor, while the violas and first violins enter in imitation with the two-measure motive in sequence. After the motive is repeated three times (the last time with the participation of the whole orchestra), the composition proceeds to a fermata on the dominant, leaving the listener with a feeling of the unknown, of the mysterious. The beginning of the Allegro to this point of rest determines the character of the whole piece, and therefore it is quoted here for the reader.[30]

29. For the *main idea* and its development see Kirnberger, Section 9.7.
30. A comparison of the distribution of instruments in the score of Beethoven's Fifth Symphony printed in Hoffmann's article with that of a modern score printed here, reveals the importance of the stringed instruments in the polarity of the outer parts during Beethoven's day. The 2 violin parts and the viola were on top; the cellos and string basses supported the harmony from below. The woodwinds, brass (with the trumpets identified as clarini), and percussion were in the middle. Shades of the thoroughbass concept still persisted.

Beethoven: Symphony No. 5 in C minor

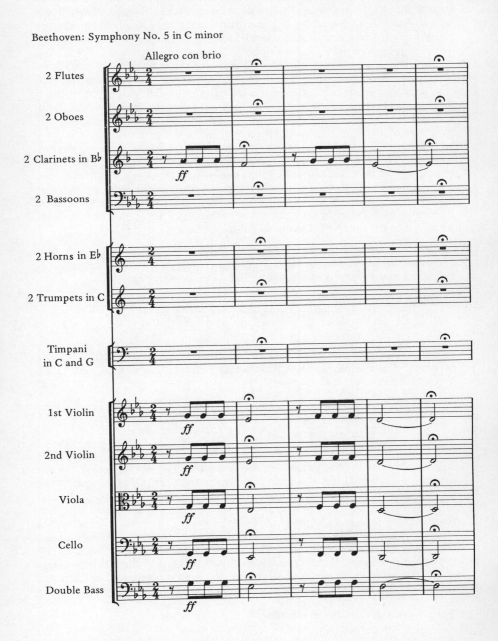

Trio for Piano, Violin and Cello, Opus 70, No. 1

The second movement, a *Largo assai ed espressivo*, bears the character of a soft pensive melancholy, comforting to the soul. The theme, in the true Beethoven manner, is composed of two very simple figures only one measure long, divided between the piano and the other instruments.

These few harmonically rich measures contain the material from which the whole movement is woven. It is remarkable how the figure of the cello in the ninth measure, so beautifully combined with the countertheme in the piano, keeps reappearing in imitation. Also, the main theme in the second measure of the piano has a striking effect when it is taken up by the cello and pursued further.

10.5 CARL CZERNY (1791–1857)

Within the span of the Classical era Kirnberger had defined the main idea (*Hauptsatz*) of a characteristic sonata movement (Section 9.7) and Koch had recognized the fact that the concept of the sonata as a whole applied to various instrumental media, including the string quartet (Section 10.3). Yet it was half a century later that Carl Czerny concisely described the overall form of a Classical sonata and the construction of the first movement of the form that had been brought to its zenith by Haydn, Mozart, and Beethoven. The chamber ensembles, orchestral symphonies, and sonatas for solo instruments had to be written before someone like Czerny could summarize their constituents.

Czerny, a pupil of Beethoven at the age of 9, also had musical contact during his childhood with Clementi and Hummel. In turn, Czerny's pedagogical aptitude was recognized at the age of 15, when Beethoven asked him to instruct his nephew, Carl.[31]

In the original German of Czerny's *School of Practical Composition*, the term *principal subject* was expressed by the word *Hauptsatz*, meaning an idea that may permeate the entire texture or setting rather than the melody alone, as the English word *subject* might seem to suggest. Remembering Kirnberger's discussion of the *main idea* helps to clarify this term. The same may be said for the secondary or middle subject (*Seitensatz*).

While presenting the attributes of the Classical sonata, Czerny carries the discussion into the realm of the Romantic. While eulogizing Classicism, he cannot avoid reference to the individuality of expression and the return to nature associated with Romanticism.

The Sonata as a Whole*

Among all the forms of composition, that of the sonata is the most important, and this *first*, because most of the other principal forms may be included in it; *secondly*, because it presents the composer with opportunity and space for displaying, in the worthiest manner, both his invention and fancy, and also his musical acquirements; and *thirdly*, because its form and construction precisely correspond with those of the symphony, the quartet, the quintet, and indeed of every significant and complete instrumental piece.

*From Carl Czerny, School of Practical Composition, *trans. into English by John Bishop (London, 1848), pp. 33–52.*

31. Czerny's autobiography was translated as "Recollections from My Life" by Ernest Sanders in the *Musical Quarterly*, XLII/3 (1956), 302–17.

    For details about Czerny's compositions, see William S. Newman, *The Sonata Since Beethoven* (Chapel Hill: The University of North Carolina Press, 1969), pp. 178–186.

The sonata usually consists of four separate and distinct movements, namely: first movement, *Allegro;* second movement, *Adagio* or *Andante;* third movement, *Scherzo* or *Minuet;* fourth movement, *Finale* or *Rondo.*

The First Movement of the Sonata

The first movement consists of two parts, the first of which is usually repeated. This first part must comprise: (1) The principal subject; (2) Its continuation or amplification, together with a modulation into the nearest related key; (3) The middle subject in this new key; (4) A new continuation of this middle subject; (5) A final melody, after which the first part thus closes in the new key, in order that the repetition of the same may follow unconstrainedly.

The second part of the first movement commences with a development of the principal subject, or of the middle subject, or even of a new idea, passing through several keys, and returning again to the original key.[32] Then follows the principal subject and its amplification, but usually in an abridged shape, and so modulating, that the middle subject may likewise reappear in its entirety, though in the original key; after which, all that follows the middle subject in the first part is here repeated in the original key, and thus the close is made.[33]

We perceive that this first movement has a well established form, and makes an organic whole; that its various component parts follow each other in a settled order, and must be entwined together; and that the whole structure presents a musical picture, in which a precise idea can be expressed, and a consequent character developed.

Like as in a romance, a novel, or a dramatic poem, if the entire work shall be successful and preserve its unity, the necessary component parts are: first, an exposition of the principal idea and of the different characters, then the protracted complication of events, and lastly the surprising catastrophe and the satisfactory conclusion—even so, the first part of the sonata-movement forms the exposition, the second part the complication, the return of the first part into the original key produces, lastly, that perfect satisfaction which is justly expected from every work of art. This property it is, which so highly distinguishes this form of composition above all others at present existing, and in which all genuine masterpieces of modern instrumental music (such as symphonies, concertos, quartets, trios, &c.) are composed.

The Modulations of the Sonata in a Major Key

The most natural modulation which the ear anticipates and desires, and with which it is most perfectly satisfied, is that from a major key to the key of its dominant; for example, from C to G, from A to E, from E♭ to B♭, &c.

---

32. The term "original key" must always be understood as the key in which the composition is set.
33. In modern terminology, the first part of the first movement is the *exposition,* which is repeated. The second part of the movement consists of the *development* section and the *recapitulation.*

This modulation must in general be employed in each piece which, according to its construction, forms a great and perfect whole, and which consequently possesses a middle subject.

It is worthy of remark that the modulation into the subdominant (as from C to F, or from E♭ to A♭), in itself so natural, appears, in this case, as well as in the simple two-part theme, very feeble, unsatisfactory, and even disagreeable; although, in other instances (as, for the Trio of a Minuet or of a March), it has a very pleasing effect.

Many composers, it is true, have essayed to conduct the middle subject and the conclusion of the first part into a more remote key—as, for example, Beethoven from C to A major, and from C to E major, and Hummel from E to A♭—but notwithstanding the good effect of this, in the particular cases mentioned, we must be careful to avoid using it frequently, or leaving the general rule; for it would generally destroy the natural course of the piece, and deprive the succeeding modulations in the second part of their best effect.[34]

The commencement of a sonata may be either mild or energetic, and may consist either of a melody, or of a short figure suitable for development; or even of chords, or moving passages. . . .

A good middle subject is much more difficult to invent than the commencement for, *first*, it must possess a new and more beautiful and pleasing melody than all which precedes; and *secondly*, it must be very different from the foregoing, but yet, according to its character, so well suited thereto, that it may appear like the object or result of all the preceding ideas, modulations or passages. . . .

The invention of the second part is always one of the most important tasks for a composer.[35] For, here, the ideas of the first part must be displayed, developed, worked up, and necessarily augmented with new ones. The whole field of modulation, art, and fancy here lies open to the composer. But this development must consist of no arbitrary rambling into many keys, no heaping together of designless modulations, and as little a Potpourri-way of connecting the subjects, or a labored display of dry learning. The most difficult thing here for the beginner is the observance of that nice boundary which lies between the Sonata and the Fantasia or Capriccio. For this first portion of the second part (until the re-entry of the principal subject) the composer must form a plan, which he must note down in figured chords, and then, in respect to the rhythmical and aesthetic connection, invent a form corresponding to the character of the first part and to the peculiarity of the subject. All harmonic complication must be calculated for the purpose of returning to the principal subject *at the proper time*. A single period too much or too little may enfeeble all that pleasing expression which the re-entry of the theme in the original key should produce, which is the true and expected end of all this development.

There are no rules for preserving a due moderation; the only means, next

34. Johann Nepomuk Hummel (1778–1837) studied for two years with Mozart in Vienna. He also had instruction from Clementi, Albrechtsberger, Haydn, and Salieri. He rivaled Beethoven as a piano virtuoso, and in his day was considered by some to be the equal of Beethoven in composition.

35. Czerny has just described the two themes of the exposition. With this paragraph he starts to discuss the development section.

to the talent and judgment of the composer being—*the study of good models*. In the construction of the second part, Haydn, Mozart and Beethoven are pre-eminent. By this remark we refer not only to their pianoforte sonatas, but also to their trios, quartets, quintets, symphonies and, generally, to all their great instrumental works. Clementi, Dussek,[36] Hummel and some others, are also to be viewed as good patterns in this respect.

As to the modulations in the development of the second part, the composer has a free choice of all keys. But he must, to a certain extent, avoid the original key of the piece, and that of its dominant, so as not to dwell in them for any length of time, or to employ them for any considerable idea, because they have been sufficiently used in the first part. After we have returned to the original key and principal subject in an unconstrained, but, as much as possible, surprising manner, the completion of the piece presents no further difficulties.[37] We then repeat the whole of the principal subject, with as much of the continuation as is required in order to make a cadence on the dominant seventh of the original key; after which the entire middle subject and the continuation following it are likewise repeated in the original key. Here some suitable changes, such as new passages &c, may be introduced; and the second part then either concludes exactly like the first, or a short coda is also added, in which perhaps, if we please, the principal subjects may be once more reproduced.

Now arises the question, in which way can the beginner soonest and most conformably arrive at the practical application of all these rules?

The best method is, undoubtedly, that which Joseph Haydn recommended to his pupils: Let the beginner, in the first place, exercise himself in little sonatas, which he must so compose *according to the models chosen*, so that the same key, time, form of the periods, number of bars, and even each modulation, shall be strictly followed. But, *he must take pains to invent ideas, melodies, and passages as different as possible from each of the models chosen*. The short sonatas of Haydn, Mozart, Clementi, Dussek and others, will be of the greatest service in this respect. . . .

From little sonatas we gradually proceed in this manner to the greater, progressively continuing to select more important and finished patterns, until at last we find ourselves sufficiently exercised to be able to write, *without a model*, with facility and regularity of form. . . .

The arbitrary, grotesque, and exaggerated in art, has, alas! at the present day, but too greatly gained the ascendancy, because it is very easily invented, and we require to learn the least for it. For neither is great talent, nor well-grounded knowledge demanded in order to produce a wild and irregular fantasia. But there is nothing more important than for the young and talented composer to return to the rules of the beautiful, to which the

36. Muzio Clementi (1752–1832) as a pianist toured some of the same circuits as Mozart. Clementi numbered among his successful pupils, John Field (see Section 11.6).

Johann Ladislaus Dussek (1760–1812), born in Bohemia, studied with C. P. E. Bach in Hamburg. Both Clementi and Dussek were acclaimed for their singing touch on the piano.

37. Here Czerny goes into the recapitulation of sonata form.

manifest arbitrariness of many modern kinds of composition is as greatly opposed, as the law of arms to that of justice and good manners. An endeavor is made to defend the present disregard of form by calling it new and original, and an extension of the bounds of art. But all the truly great masters (and particularly Beethoven) have proved how original it is possible to be within the bounds of regular forms and established order; and that what is new must be sought for in the ideas, melodies and developments, and by no means in the contempt of euphony, symmetry, and the intelligible connection of the subjects.

By way of example, we here give the 1st movement of a little sonata by Mozart, which although belonging rather to the class of the sonatina by reason of its brevity, nevertheless contains all the essential parts of a complete sonata, and the succeeding remarks will explain to the pupil all the rules previously given on the organization and construction of this species of composition.[38] . . .

The principal subject is a simple, energetic figure in unison, which extends through five bars. . . .

Sonata

In order to give the pupil a practical idea of the manner in which he should follow such a sonata as a model, we here insert a substitute patterned on the foregoing theme, which the beginner must attentively compare with the original, and then direct his own studies accordingly.

38. Czerny uses as an example the entire first movement of Mozart's Piano Sonata in D major for four hands (K. 123a = 381, Salzburg, 1772), here transcribed for two hands.

Kirnberger had described how to build a new composition on the bass of a sonata already written, in a pamphlet entitled *Method for Tossing off Sonatas* (see William S. Newman, *The Sonata in the Classic Era* (Chapel Hill: The University of North Carolina Press, 1963), pp. 441 ff.

Sonata

The Sonata in a Minor Key

The construction of the sonata in a minor key is the same as in a major; but the principal modulations are subject to the following changes.

1. In the first part, after the continuation of the principal subject, we modulate into the relative major key (for example, from A minor to C major, from F minor to A♭ major &c.), and give the middle subject, together with its continuation, and the conclusion of the first part, in this major key.

2. Or, after the principal melody, we modulate into the dominant minor key (as, from A minor to E minor, from F minor to C minor &c.) and remain in the same during the middle subject and all which follows, to the end of the first part.

The modulations in the development of the second part are left to the composer. But when the middle subject is reproduced after the return of the principal theme, if it was given in the major in the first part, it may also be in the tonic major of the original key in the second part, provided it does not naturally admit of being given in the minor. If it was minor in the first part, it must also be minor in the second. The conclusion of a minor sonata however, may pass into the tonic major of the original key, if the character of the whole composition requires it.[39]

39. As an example Czerny uses Haydn's Sonata in E minor (1778), which begins as follows:

Particular Remarks on the Minor Keys

The minor keys possess a tender, melancholy, plaintive, and tragic character, which, as is well known, pleases and attracts youth. Hence, most of the early attempts of young composers are made in them, and assume this cast.

We think of being able to infuse into such pieces more of the so-called profound, more of the romantic, and a higher degree of interest; and to bribe the mind of the hearer to a greater extent, by presenting to him pensive melodies. Moreover, the dissonant chords and harmonies to which we are involuntarily led in minor keys, impart to the compositions an appearance of particular learning and thoughtful labor. But, to say the truth, the precise reason for the preference shown to the minor keys by beginners, is this—that such compositions are *much more easily invented*. For ten sad, mournful, or tragic subjects are far more readily conceived than a single pleasing, serene, and yet noble and graceful idea. Even in poetry we much less frequently meet with grace, wit, gaiety and humor, than the opposite. And, as is well known, we possess a far greater number of excellent tragedies, than similar comedies.

The songs of barbarous and uncultivated nations, and those of rude ages, are nearly all of a sorrowful cast, and in minor keys. The noble, serene, and pleasing, on the contrary, are mostly the fruit of higher refinement, purer taste, and a more sound understanding.

The greatest composers have always avoided the too frequent use of the minor keys in their instrumental works, and have availed themselves of the effects of this expedient with judicious restraint. Of the six grand Symphonies by Mozart, only one is in the minor; and a like proportion exists in the symphonies, quartets, and other compositions of Haydn. Even the earnest Beethoven has only written *two* of his nine symphonies in minor keys; and so it is with the sonatas and other works of this and all other great composers. These masters felt convinced that we should not always call up the ghost, and that it is much more honorable to imitate the ancient Greeks, who by their works of art sought to *cheer* and *embellish* life, than to exercise our talent for the sole purpose of representing sad objects, and rendering everything dark and mysterious.

11

Romantic Feeling
for the Natural
and the Supernatural

11.1 CARL MARIA VON WEBER (1786–1826)

The first truly Romantic German composer of renown was Carl Maria von Weber. Carl Maria savored his first taste of the stage when his father, a former army officer and amateur musician, took the family along on tour with the theatrical troupe for which he was musical director. More formal musical training came from Joseph Haydn's brother, Michael (1737–1806), who taught Weber counterpoint, and from others who taught him singing and piano. Later, in Vienna, Weber continued his studies with Abbé Vogler.

In 1809 Weber predicted the future in the fantasy quoted here. The first important opportunity for this highly imaginative musician came in 1813, when he became conductor of the German Opera in Prague. Four years later the King of Saxony asked Weber to head the German Opera Theater at Dresden. While there, Weber met Friedrich Kind, a lawyer who thought of writing an opera libretto on a German subject. With Weber he chose a ghost story whose eeriness was intensified in the completed opera, *Der Freischütz*, by the inclusion of spoken and recited dialogue (Berlin, 1821). The immersion in the supernatural combined with the spirit of German folk song heralded the Romantic era.

A Musical Dream*

Very pleased about a symphony which I had completed this morning, after a first-rate lunch, I relaxed and took a nap. In my dream I suddenly seemed to be in a concert hall where all the instruments were alive. They were attending a large meeting at which the oboe presided with naively expressive nasal wisdom. At the right was a group consisting of a viola d'amore, a basset horn,[1] a viola da gamba, and a recorder [*flûte douce*], wailing together in plaintive tones about the good old days. On the left Dame Oboe was holding forth in the company of young and old clarinets and flutes, with and without the countless number of keys now in vogue. And in the middle was the gallant clavier, surrounded by several sweet violins, who were well-bred in the refined style of Pleyel [2] and Gyrowetz.[3] The trumpets and horns carried on in a corner, while the piccolo flutes and flageolets [4] filled the hall with their naive, childish cries. Madame Oboe insisted that their tones constituted a true Jean Paul arrangement,[5] raised by Pestalozzi to the height of naturalness.[6]

Everyone was happy, when all of a sudden the irritable contrabass, accompanied by his relatives, a pair of cellos, stormed through the door. He threw himself on the director's stool in such a state of ill-humor that the clavier and all the stringed instruments present involuntarily vibrated sympathetically with fear. "No!" he shouted. "The devil take anyone who persists in producing compositions like those! I just came from the rehearsal of a symphony by one of our newest composers. And although, as you know, I have a rather strong and powerful constitution, I could hardly bear it any longer. In another 5 minutes my sound post would have collapsed

*From Carl Maria von Weber, Fragment aus einer musikalischen Reise, die vielleicht erschienen wird (Fragment of a Musical Trip Which Might Possibly Happen, *1809*).

1. A basset horn was a clarinet in the key of F, G, or sometimes E♭. The wooden instrument was invented in Bavaria about 1770. Mozart used basset horns in *The Magic Flute* (1791) for the March of the Priests and the following Aria and Chorus (Nos. 9, 10).
2. Ignaz Joseph Pleyel (1757–1831) studied piano with Wanhal. In 1772 he went to live with Haydn, under whose tutelage he remained for five years. Pleyel wrote many chamber works, symphonies, and concertos for violin, for cello, and for piano. Eventually he went to Paris, where in 1807 he started to manufacture pianos in a firm that still bears his name.
3. Adalbert Gyrowetz (1736–1850) was Kapellmeister at the Vienna Opera from 1804 to 1831.
4. The piccolo flute, an octave higher than the concert flute, was first constructed at the end of the eighteenth century. It was preceded by the flageolet, a whistle flute blown at the end like a recorder. The flageolet had originated in Asia in the eleventh century. In Handel's *Rinaldo, flauto piccolo* meant the flageolet.
5. Jean Paul Friedrich Richter (1763–1825) wrote novels and romances. His essay *Reflections on Art* was published in 1804. An excerpt from this work, "The Nature of Romantic Poetry," is quoted in *SRMH*, pp. 744 ff.
6. Johann Heinrich Pestalozzi (1746–1827), Swiss educator, established an orphanage for abandoned children in 1774 and a widely acclaimed boarding school in 1801. The emphasis of his pedagogical method was on group activity with relation to concrete observation of the world around us.

and my strings, my very life-line, would have been broken. I don't want to be forced to jump around and act like a wild goat, nor to be turned into a violin for the purpose of playing the nonexistent ideas of a master composer. I would rather become a dance-fiddle and earn my bread with Müller and Kauer dance pieces.[7]

FIRST CELLO (wiping away the perspiration): Dear papa is right. I'm exhausted. I don't remember being so overheated since the Cherubini operas.[8]

ALL THE INSTRUMENTS: Tell us about it! Tell us!

SECOND CELLO: Something like this should neither be told nor listened to. According to what I learned from my wonderful master, Romberg,[9] a symphony such as the one we just played is a musical atrocity, neither suited to the nature of any instrument whatsoever, nor to the performance of a thought, nor to any purpose other than the desire to be new and original. We were made to climb up high like violins—

FIRST CELLO (interrupting him): As if we couldn't do it just as well as they can!

A SECOND VIOLIN: Each one should stay in his own yard.

VIOLA: Yes, because if I'm supposed to be between them, what will become of me?

FIRST CELLO: Oh, this has nothing to do with you. You only flow along with us in unison or shudder and shiver like agitated water, but when it comes to beautiful song—

FIRST OBOE: —then there's no comparison with me!

FIRST CLARINET: Pardon me Madame, if we also take notice of our own talents.

FIRST FLUTE: Yes—for marches and at weddings.

FIRST BASSOON: Who comes closer to the heavenly tenor than me?

FIRST HORN: Do you dare to presume that you are able to combine as much delicacy and power as I can?

CLAVIER: And what is all of this against the fullness of harmony which I encompass? Whereas all of you are only a part of the whole, I am independent, and—

7. Wenzel Müller (1767–1835), a pupil of Dittersdorf, conducted theater orchestras and wrote many popular *Singspiele*. He was director of the Prague Opera from 1808 to 1813, at which time Weber succeeded him there. Ferdinand Kauer (1751–1831) wrote about 100 operettas.

8. Luigi Cherubini (1760–1842) composed fifteen Italian and fourteen French operas. His book on counterpoint, edited for publication by his student Halévy, is indicative of his technical mastery in the art of composition. Weber eventually met Cherubini in Paris in 1826.

9. Bernhard Romberg (1767–1841), German cellist, played in France, Spain, and Russia. The cello was prominent in his concertos, concertinos, caprices, and fantasias on Swedish, Spanish, Rumanian, and Russian airs. He wrote a cello method (Paris, 1840).

ALL THE INSTRUMENTS (shouting together): Oh, keep still! You can't even sustain a single tone!

FIRST OBOE: No portamento.

TWO SMALL FLAGEOLETS: Mama is right.

SECOND CELLO: In this noise there can be no orderly placement of tone against tones.

TRUMPETS AND DRUMS (coming in fortissimo): Be still! We want to talk too. What would the whole composition be without our effect? If we don't burst out, nobody would applaud.

FLUTE: Lowly folk render noise; the highborn dwell among whispered sounds.

FIRST VIOLIN: And if I didn't lead you, what would happen to you all?

CONTRABASS (jumping up): Mind you, I hold everything together, and without me there is nothing.

ALL THE INSTRUMENTS (shouting at once): I alone am the soul; without me there is nothing!

All of a sudden the property man came into the hall and the instruments got frightened. They separated from each other, because they were afraid of the mighty hand that packed them up and took them to rehearsals. "Wait," he cried out. "Are you rebelling again? Wait! Soon the *Eroica Symphony* of Beethoven will be put on the stands, and then which of you will be able to move a limb or a key!"

"Oh, not that!" begged all of them. "We'd rather have an Italian opera because then at least we can doze from time to time," mused the viola.

"Fiddle-faddle!" exclaimed the property man. "You'll soon learn. Do you think that in our enlightened times when all traditions are cast aside, that a composer is going to deny his heaven-sent, colossal inspiration on your account? Heaven forbid! It is no longer a question of clarity and precision, of the delivery of passionate emotions, as with the artists of old like Gluck, Handel, and Mozart. No. Listen to the recipe of the newest symphony that I just received from Vienna, and judge for yourself. First there is a slow introduction comprised of short, disconnected ideas, in which one need not have anything to do with the other, with three or four notes every quarter of an hour! Such tension! Then there is a muffled roll of the drums and a mysterious passage for the viola, all bedecked with the requisite number of general pauses [10] and rests. Finally, after the listener has despaired of ever surviving the tension and arriving at the Allegro, a wild tempo ensues in which the principal concern is that no main theme should emerge, and it is up to the listener to find one for himself. Modulations from one key to another are in abundance, but this causes no embarrassment. Just do what Paër [11] does in *Leonore:* Compose a run through the semitones and stop on

10. A general pause or a grand pause is a rest for the entire orchestra. This sudden omission of all sound at a climax was one of the innovations of the Mannheim Orchestra (see Section 9.8).
11. Ferdinando Paër (1771–1839) started his operatic career in Italy. He was court Kapellmeister at Dresden at the time he composed *Leonora, ossia l'amore con-*

any note you want to; then the modulation is complete. Be sure to disregard all rules, because rules only hinder genius."

Suddenly a string broke on the guitar hanging above me. I awoke terrified, for in my dream I was on my way toward becoming a great composer in the newest style—or a great fool.

11.2 LOUIS SPOHR (1784–1839)

The Romantic musician was interested not only in furthering the demands on each individual instrument of the orchestra but also in increasing the responsibilities of the conductor. For some time the conductor, hidden among the violinists or seated at the clavier, had been trying to attract attention. In 1779 a German gentleman took issue with

> the principal violinist at the opera, seated on a stool somewhat elevated above the orchestra, so that each member of the orchestra can see him while he directs the whole work. Indeed, this seems strange enough, particularly when the high-seated Mr. Director gestures so convulsively that any moment one might think it necessary to call a doctor, to say nothing about the bad impression produced when one violin is seated up high and the rest of the violins are seated below, along with the other instruments. The violin seated above screams out over the orchestra, as if the opera consisted of a single violin, or at least as if everything depended on it.[12]

The image of the thoroughbass keyboardist conducting as he improvised, or of the principal violinist indicating the beat with his bow, was still vivid to Louis Spohr in the next century. Spohr the violinist had advanced lessons with Franz Eck, who took him to Russia where they met Clementi and John Field. Spohr also had success as a composer; Weber conducted his opera *Faust* at Prague (1816). In 1820 Spohr went to England, where with his wife, Dorette Scheidler, the harpist, he performed in concerts for the London Philharmonic Society. It was concerning his experiences there that he wrote this passage in which he considered his conducting with a baton as a startling innovation.

The Virtuoso Conductor*

After I had been welcomed in a friendly manner by the directors of the Philharmonic Society, some of whom spoke German and others French, a meeting was held concerning the program of the first concert. At this I

*Louis Spohr's Autobiography, *trans. from the German* (London, 1865), II, 76–77, 81–82.

---

jugalo (1804), on the subject which Beethoven used for *Fidelio* (1805). Weber was to include Beethoven's *Fidelio* in the repertory of operas which he conducted at Prague (1813).

12. *Wahrheiten die Musik betreffend gerade herausgesagt von einem teutschen Biedermann* (*Truths Concerning Music Honestly Presented by a German Gentleman.*) (Frankfurt, 1779), p. 42. Quoted in Georg Schünemann, *Geschichte des Dirigierens* (Leipzig: Breitkopf & Härtel, 1913), pp. 173 f.

was required to play solo twice and to lead as first violin. To this I replied that I was quite ready to perform the first, but must beg that I might be permitted to lead in one of the subsequent concerts, as my solo playing would appear to less advantage if both were required of me on one and the same evening. Although this was acknowledged to be self-evident by some of the gentlemen who were themselves solo-players, it gave rise at first to a long and earnest discussion, as it was contrary to the custom of the society. But at length it was complied with. A still greater subject of offense, however, was my request to be permitted on this, my first appearance, to play my own compositions only. The Philharmonic Society, in order to exclude from their programs all shallow and worthless virtuosi-concerti, had laid down the law, that with the exception of the pianoforte concerti of Mozart and Beethoven no similar musical pieces should be played, and that a solo player could perform only that which they should select. Nevertheless, after Ries [13] had continued the discussion in English, and therefore unintelligibly to me, and represented to the gentlemen that my violin-concerts in Germany would therefore become excluded by their ban, they at length yielded in this also. I therefore at the first Philharmonic concert came forward with my cantabile scena, and in the second part with a solo quartet in E major, and met with great and general applause. As a composer it afforded me an especial gratification that the whole of the directors now shared the opinion of Mr. Ries; and as a violinist, the greatest pleasure that old Viotti [14] who had always been my pattern and was to have been my instructor in my youth, was among the auditors and spoke to me in great praise of my playing. . . .

Meanwhile my turn had come to direct one of the Philharmonic concerts, and I had created no less a sensation than with my solo playing. It was at that time still the custom there that when symphonies and overtures were performed, the pianist had the score before him, not exactly to conduct from it, but only to read after and to play in with the orchestra at pleasure, which, when it was heard, had a very bad effect. The real conductor was the first violin, who gave the tempi, and now and then when the orchestra began to falter, gave the beat with the bow of his violin. So large an orchestra, with the performers seated so far apart from each other as in the Philharmonic, could not possibly play exactly together. And in spite of the excellence of the individual members, the *ensemble* was much worse than what we are accustomed to in Germany. I had therefore resolved when my turn came to direct, to make an attempt to remedy this defective system. Fortunately at the morning rehearsal on the day when I was to conduct the concert, Mr. Ries took his place at the piano, and he readily assented to give up the score to me and to remain wholly excluded from all participation in the performance. I then took my stand with the score at a separate music desk in front of the orchestra, drew my directing baton from my coat pocket and gave the signal to begin. Quite alarmed at such a novel procedure, some of the directors would have protested against it; but when

13. Ferdinand Ries (1784–1838), a piano student of Beethoven, lived in London from 1813 to 1824. He was a famous piano virtuoso who toured Germany, Scandinavia, and Russia.
14. Giovanni Battista Viotti (1755–1824) toured Germany, Poland, and Russia as a violinist (1780). In 1792 he went to London, where he conducted Italian operas and was soloist in his own concertos at the Salomon concerts (1794–95).

I besought them to grant me at least one trial, they became pacified. The symphonies and overtures that were to be rehearsed were well known to me; and in Germany I had already directed at their performance. I therefore could not only give the tempi in a very decisive manner, but indicated also to the wind instruments and horns all their entries, which insured to them a confidence such as hitherto they had not known there. I also took the liberty, when the execution did not satisfy me, to stop, and in a polite but earnest manner to remark upon the manner of execution, which remarks Mr. Ries at my request interpreted to the orchestra. Incited thereby to more than usual attention, and conducted with certainty by the *visible* manner of giving the time, they played with a spirit and a correctness such as till then they had never been heard to play with. Surprised and inspired by this result, the orchestra immediately after the first part of the symphony expressed aloud its collective assent to the new mode of conducting, and thereby overruled all further opposition on the part of the directors. In the vocal pieces also, the conducting of which I assumed at the request of Mr. Ries, particularly in the recitative, the leading with the baton, after I had explained the meaning of my movements, was completely successful. And the singers repeatedly expressed to me their satisfaction for the precision with which the orchestra now followed them.

The result in the evening was still more brilliant than I could have hoped for. It is true, the audience was at first startled by the novelty, and the people were seen whispering together. But when the music began and the orchestra executed the well-known symphony with unusual power and precision, the general approbation was shown immediately on the conclusion of the first part by a long-sustained clapping of hands. The triumph of the baton as a time-giver was decisive, and no one was seen any more seated at the piano during the performance of symphonies and overtures.

11.3 GIOACCHINO ROSSINI (1792–1868)
THROUGH STENDHAL (1783–1842)

The catchwords of the Romantic movement, such as "sensibility," "melancholy," "spirit," and "enchantment," the delightful intrigues, the fascination with mysticism, dissipation, the real and the imagined, were all incorporated into Stendhal's literary essays on "that mountebank called Rossini."

Stendhal was the pseudonym of Marie Henri Beyle. Born at Grenoble, a city in the southeast of France, he took as his literary name the birthplace of Johann Joachim Winckelmann (1717–1768), born at Stendal, a city in the Saxony province of Prussia, Germany. Winckelmann, the archaeologist-historian of ancient art, through his descriptions about the treasures excavated at Pompey and Herculaneum, inspired Goethe to write a monograph on him in 1805.

Stendhal at various points in his life lived in Paris, Brunswick, and Milan. He moved in artistic circles, where he mingled with Byron,

Manzoni, and Madame de Staël. In 1821 Stendhal visited England. He originally wrote the material quoted here for the *Paris Monthly Review* (January 1822). In 1823 Stendhal gathered his anecdotes, reliable or imagined, original or copied, together for a full-length biography of Gioacchino Rossini (1792–1868).

Memoir of Rossini the Composer*

Of all living composers, Rossini is the most celebrated. He has been invited to every grand theater of Europe in succession. Last year he was to have presided at the King's Theater in London; but love, or indolence, or the Italian passion for Italy, held him within the Alps. This year he has crossed them, and presides at Vienna. Paris next solicits him; and if he be not exhausted by the admiration of the French, or overladen with their opulence, he will come to London, the last, loftiest, proudest, and most lavish of capitals fed upon by men of song. . . .

Rossini went on the stage *en amateur*. In Italy the stage is not always adopted for a life profession, as in France or England. There an amateur may sing in public for a season or two, and then return to the nondescript station of a dilettante, without its affecting his future pursuits. It appears that Rossini, who is known to sing with infinite taste and spirit the introductory song in *Il Barbiere di Seviglia*, had no success as a public singer. There were at that time several detached airs of his composition circulating in society which, though modelled on the style then in fashion, displayed original vivacity. Two or three wealthy amateurs of Venice engaged him to compose an opera. The manager of the theater entertained but a slight opinion of the composer from his youth and excessive gaiety, which differed little from the reckless waggery of a school-boy. The patrons of Rossini, however, threatened the manager to withdraw their support from him, till he at length consented to bring forward his first operatic attempt. This opera was *L'inganno Felice*, in which there are two or three flashes of genius (the duo, for instance), but the rest was merely in the reigning taste. *L'inganno Felice* was played with success. Soon after, Rossini composed *Il Tancredi*, *L'Italiana in Algeri*, and *La Pietra del Paragone*, which are ranked among his masterpieces. To be entirely of this opinion, one should have seen them as they were produced at Milan; particularly *L'Italiana*, in which a prima donna and a buffo—such as Marcolini and Paccini, supported by Galli—completely developed the spirit of that beautiful composition.

The opera of *Tancredi* circulated through Italy with great rapidity. The air, *Ti n'vedrò, mi n'vedrai*, was taken from a Greek Litany that Rossini had heard chanted in one of the islets of the Lagune near Venice. This air, to be understood, should be sung, if possible, as Pasta sings it. Rossini, either through indolence, or other motives, has a strong aversion for overtures, so much so, that he did not compose one for *Tancredi*. And at present, in Italy, this opera is preceded by the overture of the *Pietra del Paragone*, or that of the *Italiana*. . . .

* From "*Memoir of Rossini the Composer,*" *Blackwood's* Edinburgh Magazine, *XII*, No. 69 (*October 1822*), *440–47.*

Rossini received offers from every town in Italy. He generally demanded about a thousand francs for an opera. He has been known to write three or four in a year. The management of a theater in Italy is curious. The director is often the most wealthy and considerable person of the little town which he inhabits. He gets together a troupe, consisting of a *prima donna, basso cantante, basso buffo,* a second female singer, and a third *basso.* He engages a *maestro* (a composer) to write a new opera, in which he is obliged to adapt his airs to the compass and volume of the company. The director purchases the words of the opera for about 60 or 80 francs, from some unlucky son of the muses. The troupe, thus organized, gives from forty to fifty representations in the town for which they were engaged, and then breaks up. This is what is generally called a season [*stagione*], the last is that of the carnival. The singers who are not engaged in any of these companies, are usually to be found at Milan or Bologna.

From this sketch of theatrical management in Italy, one may easily form some idea of the kind of life which Rossini led from 1810 to 1816. During that interval he visited all the principal towns of Italy, remaining from three to four months in each. On his arrival he was welcomed and feted by the dilettanti of the place. The first thirteen or twenty days were passed with his friends, dining out, and shrugging his shoulders at the nonsense which he was obliged to set to music. . . . When he had been about three weeks in a town, he began to refuse invitations, and to occupy himself seriously in studying the voices of the performers. He made them sing at the piano, and I have seen him more than once obliged to mutilate and "curtail of their fair proportions," some of his most brilliant and happy ideas, because the tenor could not attain the note which was necessary to express the composer's feeling, or alter the character of a melody because the prima donna sang false. . . .

Rossini has a quick mind, susceptible of impressions, and which can often turn to advantage the most trifling or passing circumstance. When composing his *Mosé,*[15] someone said to him, "What, you are going to make the Hebrews sing? Do you mean they should chant as they do in the Synagogue?" The idea struck him, and on returning home, he composed a magnificent chorus, which commences with a kind of nasal twang, peculiar to the Synagogue.

Rossini was at length called to Rome. The director of the theater there, having had the words of several operas put aside by the objections which the police made to them as containing certain allusions, in a moment of disappointment and ill-humor, proposed *Il Barbiere di Seviglia,* which had already been set to music by Paesiello.[16] The government consented. Rossini, who is intellectual enough to be modest when put in competition with true and acknowledged merit, was extremely embarrassed by the choice. He

15. Rossini composed *Moses in Egypt,* performed in Naples in 1818.
16. Giovanni Paisiello (1740–1816) wrote fifty operas, the first of which was the comic opera, *La Pupilla* (Bologna, 1764). In 1776 Empress Catherine II invited him to St. Petersburg, where he composed an opera entitled *The Barber of Seville* in 1782. The work, an immediate success, also became popular in Italy. Rossini's *Barber of Seville,* originally performed in Rome in 1816 under the title *Almaviva o sia l'inutile precauzione,* received the designation of *The Barber* six months later, when performed at Bologna.

instantly wrote to Paesiello [Paisiello], acquainting him with the circumstance. The old maestro who, though a man of undoubted genius, was somewhat of a boaster, replied that he was perfectly content with the choice which the Roman police had made, and that he had no doubt as to the result. Rossini prefaced the libretto modestly, showed Paesiello's letter to all the dilettanti of Rome, and immediately set about the composition, which was finished in thirteen days. He has said that at the first performance of *Il Barbiere* his heart throbbed violently as he seated himself at the piano. The Romans seemed to consider the commencement of this opera tiresome, and very inferior to that of Paesiello. One of the airs sung by Rosina (*Io sono docile*) appeared entirely out of character. They charged Rossini with having substituted the sauciness of a shrew for the complainings of a lovesick and gentle girl. The duet between Rosina and Figaro drew forth the first applause. The air *La Calumnia* was pronounced to be magnificent, though in fact it resembles a little too closely the air *La Vendetta* in the *Marriage of Figaro* of Mozart.[17]

The fate of this opera was singular. On the first night it experienced almost a complete failure; and on the second, it obtained the most enthusiastic applause. However, the Roman critics thought they discovered that Rossini had not only been inferior to himself in the expression of impassioned tenderness, but to all the celebrated composers. Rosina, finding in Almaviva a faithful lover instead of a faithless seducer, which she has been led to suppose he was, in place of giving herself up to a gush of ecstatic feeling, bewilders her voice, her lover, and her audience amidst the unmeaning intricacies of roulades and cadences. And yet these very insignificant and ill-placed embellishments are always applauded to the echo in other capitals. Music, and dramatic music in particular, has made considerable progress since the time of Paesiello. The long and tiresome recitative has been discarded; pieces for the ensemble are more frequently introduced, which, by their vivacity and musical uproar keep boredom at a distance. It was the opinion at Rome that if Cimarosa [18] had set *The Barber* it might have been less animated, but would have been much more comic, and infinitely more tender. They also seem to think that Rossini has not approached Paesiello in the quintet *Bona Sera*, where Basilio is entreated to go home. . . .

17. Following are the themes of this tune detection:

Mozart, Act I, No. 4
(Doctor Bartolo)
La ven - det - ta, oh, La ven - det - ta!

Rossini
La ca - lum-nia è un ven - ti - cel - lo,

18. Paisiello left St. Petersburg in 1785. Domenico Cimarosa (1794–1801) succeeded Paisiello in the service of Catherine the Great two years later. Cimarosa had gained fame as the composer of *L'Italiana in Londra* (Rome, 1778).

Rossini intends to visit London. The manager of the King's Theater, in order to rouse and stimulate his genius, should give the illustrious maestro the two excellent poems of *Don Giovanni* and the *Matrimonio Segreto* to set. It would be highly interesting to see the competition between Mozart, Cimarosa, and Rossini.[19]

11.4 ROBERT SCHUMANN (1810–1856)

Robert Schumann had the dual Romantic genius for musical composition and criticism. His inclination toward evaluating the merit and talent of other composers led him to discover the Symphony in C Major by Franz Schubert (1797–1828).

Schumann had attended Leipzig University, whence he went to Heidelberg, mainly to study with Anton Thibaut (1774–1840), a professor of jurisprudence who had a keen interest in music.[20] When Schumann returned to Leipzig, he resumed his studies on the piano, the instrument to which he had been devoted since childhood. Anxious to develop additional strength in the fourth finger of his right hand, he mechanically tried to separate it from the rest of the fingers on his hand, an experiment which proved disastrous to his piano playing. Thenceforth Schumann applied himself to composing and writing about music.[21]

19. An original footnote added by one of the magazine editors, says, "As to COMPETITION between Rossini and Mozart, was there ever a competition between a fozy turnip and a pineapple? The milk-woman poetess and Milton! Gadzooks!— C. N."

    C. N. were the initials for Christopher North, the pseudonym for John Wilson (1785–1854), a Scottish writer who was the main contributor to *Blackwood's Magazine*.
20. Thibaut directed a singing club. He wrote a book in 1825 which was later translated under the title, *On Purity in Musical Art*.
21. Schumann's penchant for associating music and letters extended to utilizing the nomenclature of the notes themselves. His *Carneval*, subtitled "Delicate Scenes on Four Notes," is a series of short pieces, each of which captures some mood or emotion. The four notes correspond to letters in the name *Schumann*, as well as to the name *Asch*, a town that held amorous memories for him. In accordance with German musical terminology, B♮ is called H (hearkening back to the B quadratum). A♭ and E♭, respectively known as *As* and *Es* in German, were therefore considered as tones corresponding to the letter *s*. Hence Schumann establishes three Sphinxes or patterns of tones as follows:

	Sphinx 1	Sphinx 2	Sphinx 3
Letters	(E)S C H A	AS C H	A (E)S C H
Notes	E♭ C B A	A♭ C B	A E♭ C B (C♭)

    In the *Carneval* these tones may appear as a motto or short subject in one part and then another (Sphinx 3 in *Pierrot*), as a decorative part (Sphinx 3 in *Papillons*), as a combination of ornamental and basic tones in a melody (Sphinx 2 in

In 1838 Schumann went to Vienna, where he satisfied his curiosity about the unpublished music of the late composer, Schubert. It was over a decade since Schubert had made the rounds with his C Major Symphony, trying to get it published and performed. Schumann visited the home of Schubert's brother Ferdinand, where he found the symphony in a treasure-pile of neglected manuscripts. As a result of Schumann's efforts, the symphony was performed and eventually published in 1849.[22]

Schubert's C Major Symphony*

Anyone who does not know this symphony, knows still less about Schubert. Indeed, this praise may seem almost unbelievable, considering what Schubert has already bestowed on the art. To the detriment of the composer, it has often been said, "After Beethoven, steer clear of the symphonic form." And this is partly true, aside from several significant orchestral works that are of more interest in judging the progress of their composers than as a determining influence on the public, or as an advance in the species. Most of the others are only a dim reflection of the Beethovenian style, not to mention the feeble, tedious, symphonic manufacturers who have the power to imitate passably the powder and periwigs of Haydn and Mozart, but without the heads that belong to them. Berlioz [23] belongs to France, and is

Schumann was the guiding force in establishing a periodical, the Neue Zeitschrift für Musik, which he edited from 1835 to 1844. The article quoted here derives from that publication (1839).

Lettres Dansantes), as structural tones in a melodic cadence (Sphinx 3 in *Chopin*), etc. In choosing as the basis for composition elements that lack internal musical cohesion. Schumann rivals the composers of the Middle Ages and Renaissance. In the duality of his emotions Schumann is a true Romantic. Whereas the Baroque composer sought to express a single emotion in an aria, Schumann constantly intermingles rival temperaments, often changing tempo and mood within a movement. For example, the gentle, tender emotion personified in the movement entitled *Eusebius* is tinged with the passionate expression which dominates the following movement entitled *Florestan*.

The *Carneval* closes with the *March of the Davidsbündler against the Philistines*, another personification of the dual nature that permeated Schumann's artistic creativity. In David's camp were composers such as Mendelssohn, Moscheles, Chopin, and Liszt, whose lofty ideals opposed the music of the "Philistines," written merely for the display of technique. Toward the middle of the movement Schumann enlists the aid of a musico-poetic-dance association when, in the manner of a cantus firmus, he weaves the seventeenth-century German dance tune, the *Grandfather's Dance* into the bass. To round out the form of the *Carneval* as a whole, Schumann repeats portions of the *Préambule* in the concluding *March*.

22. See Alfred Einstein, *Schubert, A Musical Portrait* (New York: Oxford University Press, 1951), pp. 292, ff.

23. Hector Berlioz (1803–1869) broke all Classical bounds with his penchant for large orchestras and huge choruses. His *Symphonie fantastique*, composed when he was 26 years old, brought the literary program to the symphony. Beethoven had introduced a chorus singing Schiller's *Ode to Joy* into the last movement of his Ninth Symphony (1824). Berlioz, in contrast, provided a text with the story for the

only mentioned occasionally as an interesting foreigner and hothead. As I had surmised and hoped, and perhaps many others hoped so too, it turns out that Schubert, who had already shown in so many other media that he was strong in form, rich in imagination, and versatile, had also applied these talents to the symphony, and that he had found a means therein by which he could impress the public in the grandest manner.

Certainly he never intended to follow in the tracks of Beethoven's Ninth Symphony; rather, as a most diligent artist, on his own he continually created one symphony after another. The fact that the world has just now gained the opportunity of seeing his Seventh, without having witnessed its development, and without knowing its predecessors, is perhaps the only thing that could harm its publication, that might even allow for a misunderstanding of the work. Perhaps soon his other symphonies will also be brought out; the most insignificant one among them would still bear the Franz Schubert stamp. Indeed, the Viennese symphonists did not need to look so far for the laurel which they sought, because it lay sevenfold one upon another in Ferdinand Schubert's study chamber in a suburb of Vienna. Here all at once a valuable garland was to appear. . . .

Vienna, with its St. Stephen's steeple, its beautiful women, its public pomp, interlaced by the Danube in countless ties, stretches out into the blooming plain, ever reaching out, little by little, toward higher and higher mountains. This Vienna, with all its memories of the great German masters, must provide fertile territory for a musician's fancy. Often when I watch it from the mountain tops, I am reminded of how Beethoven's eye may have at times wandered across those distant Alpine ranges, how Mozart dreamily may have frequently followed the course of the Danube which everywhere seems to fade away into bush and thicket, and how often Father Haydn may have looked up at St. Stephen's steeple, shaking his head at its dizzy height. Take the pictures of the Danube, of St. Stephen's steeple, and of the distant Alpine ranges, mixing them together in a delicate fragrance of catholic incense, and you have a picture of Vienna. And when this alluring, attractive landscape stands complete before us, strings that we had never heard before will vibrate within us. In the brilliant, blooming, romantic vivacity of Schubert's Symphony, the city appears to me more distinctly than ever, and it becomes clear to me how such a work could spring directly from environment. I will not try to give the Symphony a setting; different ages choose their literary and pictorial foundations in different ways. The 18-year-old youth often hears a world-shaking historical event in a musical work, where the man only perceives a national occurrence. In the meanwhile, the musician, without imagining either, was only producing the best music that he had in his heart.

But one must also realize that the outside world, radiant today and cloudy tomorrow, often penetrates the inner soul of the poet and musician, and that concealed in this Symphony is something more than mere beautiful melody, more than mere sorrow and joy such as that which music has already expressed a hundredfold. Indeed, it leads us into a region that we

---

program, but did not include words in the symphony itself. To keep the listeners somewhat informed about where they were in the story, Berlioz used a recurring musical theme (*idée fixe*), which he transformed according to the vicissitudes of the story.

cannot remember ever having explored before. To corroborate this, one need only hear the Symphony. Aside from the masterful musical technique of composing, herein dwells life in every fiber, color down to the finest shading, meaning throughout, the sharpest expression of detail, and finally, over the whole a romantic outpouring such as we already know elsewhere in Franz Schubert. And the heavenly length of this Symphony is like a thick novel in four volumes, perhaps by Jean Paul [24] which can never come to a close—and for a very good reason—to allow the reader to reach his own conclusion later.

11.5 FELIX MENDELSSOHN (1809–1847)

A conception of how words or pictorial thoughts are absorbed into another medium, musical composition, is expressed in a letter by Felix Mendelssohn to his friend Marc-André Souchay. The letter was written in response to Souchay's inquiry about the meanings of some of Mendelssohn's *Songs Without Words*. At the time, Mendelssohn was in Berlin, directing concerts for grand orchestra and chorus for King Friedrich Wilhelm IV. For his excellence in handling the musical groups, the king designated Mendelssohn as Royal General Musical Director. The singers whom Mendelssohn organized there became known as the *Domchor* (cathedral choir).

The first book of *Songs Without Words* (*Lieder ohne Worte*), completed at Venice in 1830, was published in London in 1832. There were eight sets of short pieces for piano solo designated by this title, six of which were published during Mendelssohn's lifetime.

The Expression of Literary Thoughts in Music*

To Marc-André Souchay, Lübeck

Berlin, October 15, 1842.

... There is so much talk about music, and yet so little really said. For my part I believe that words do not suffice for such a purpose, and if I found they did suffice, then I certainly would have nothing more to do with music. People often complain that music is ambiguous, that their ideas on the subject always seem so vague, whereas everyone understands words. With me it is exactly the reverse—not merely with regard to entire sentences, but also as to individual words. These, too, seem to me so ambiguous, so vague, so unintelligible when compared with genuine music, which fills the soul with a thousand things better than words.

* Letters of Felix Mendelssohn Bartholdy from 1833 to 1847, *trans. Lady Wallace, 1864.*

24. For Jean Paul see Section 11.1, fn. 5.

What the music I love expresses to me, is not thought too *indefinite* to be put into words, but, on the contrary, too *definite*. I therefore consider every effort to express such thoughts commendable; but still there is something unsatisfactory too in them all, and so it is with yours also. This, however, is not your fault, but that of the poetry, which does not enable you to do better. If you ask me what *my* idea is, I say—just the song as it stands. And if I have in my mind a definite term or terms with regard to one or more of these songs, I will disclose them to no one, because the words of one person assume a totally different meaning in the mind of another person, because the music of the song alone can awaken the same ideas and the same feelings in one mind as in another—a feeling which is not, however, expressed by the same words. Resignation, melancholy, the praise of God, a hunting-song—one person does not form the same conception from these that another does. Resignation is to the one what melancholy is to the other; the third can form no lively idea of either. To any man who is by nature a very keen sportsman, a hunting-song and the praise of God would come pretty much to the same thing, and to such a one the sound of the hunting-horn would really and truly be the praise of God, while we hear nothing in it but a mere hunting-song; and if we were to discuss it ever so often with him, we should get no further. Words have many meanings, and yet music we could both understand correctly. Will you allow this to serve as an answer to your question? At all events, it is the only one I can give—although these too are nothing, after all, but ambiguous words!

Bibliographical Note

For a description of the Souchay family, and their influence on Mendelssohn, see Eric Werner's *Mendelssohn*, trans. Dika Newlin (London: The Free Press of Glencoe, The Macmillan Co., 1963), pp. 297 ff.

11.6 FRANZ LISZT (1811–1886)

The article Franz Liszt wrote for his revision of the first collection of the *Nocturnes* of John Field (1782–1837) reads like a manifesto of Romanticism. Field, who was born in Dublin and died in Moscow, and who is considered to be the originator of the keyboard nocturne, was a fitting subject for Liszt's accolades.

John Field's Nocturnes*

Field's Nocturnes have retained their youth alongside so many compositions obsolete in no time! After an interval of more than thirty-six years, they still have a soothing freshness and seem to be bathed in perfume.

---

*Franz Liszt, Über John Field's Nocturne *(Hamburg, Leipzig, and New York: J. Schuberth & Co., 1859).*

Where else would we encounter such a perfection of incomparable simplicity?

In writing as well as in playing, he was absorbed with expressing his feelings to himself alone, and one could not imagine a more sincere disregard for public opinion than his. When he came to Paris, at his concerts he did not refuse to perform on square pianos, which certainly did not match the effect produced by an instrument more appropriate to the halls where he attracted an attentive public, whom he enchanted without realizing it. His almost motionless posture and his barely expressive countenance did not attract attention. His glance did not try to catch another eye. His playing streamed forth clear and limpid. His fingers glided over the keys, and the sounds they evoked seemed to follow them from a frothy wake. It was easy to see that for him his principal auditor was himself. His tranquility was almost sleepy, and public impressions were his least worry. No shock, no jerk, either in gesture or in rhythm ever intervened to interrupt his melodious revery, which lovingly diffused through the air, *mezza voce*, a delightful billow of murmuring songs, the sweetest impressions of the most charming surprises of the heart! . . .

It is to this total absence of anything that aims merely at effect that we owe the first (O so perfect!) attempt toward freeing the piano setting from the restraint which the conformists assigned to it, according to which all pieces must be performed with a regular, duty-bound beat, and made it at home with an expression of feeling and a world of dreamy imagery. Formerly compositions necessarily had to be either sonatas, rondos, or the like. Field was the first to introduce a genre which did not arise from any established category, in which sentiment and melody reign supreme, free from the fetters and impediments of obligatory form. He opened the path to all future productions which appeared under the title of *Songs Without Words*, impromptus, ballades, etc., etc., and one may ascribe to him the origin of those pieces that are destined to paint individual excitement and intimate emotions in tone. He discovered this propitious domain, so new and fertile for the imagination, more subtle than grandiose, more tender than lyrical.

The name *Nocturne* well suits the pieces which Field fancies to designate in this manner, for it immediately turns our thoughts from the present to those hours when the soul, released from the present to those hours when the soul, released from all the cares of the day, retires within itself, as it soars toward the mysterious regions of a starry sky. We see it here, aerial and winged, hovering like the ancient Philomela over the flowers and perfumes of a nature of which it is enamored.[25]

The first and fifth nocturnes of this collection are filled with a radiant joy that one might call an expression of bliss, achieved without effort, enjoyed with delight. In the second the tints are deeper, like those of the light on a shady walk. One is tempted to believe that the feeling of absence reigns in this song, as in the saying, "Absence is a world without sun."

The third and sixth nocturnes have a pastoral character; the melodies are infused with the most fragrant breezes, the mildest breaths. They seem to reflect the changing nuances coloring the vapors of dawn, when the rosy

25. According to Ovid, Philomela, daughter of King Pandion of Athens, was transformed into a nightingale.

tints become bluish, and then lilac. But in the latter stage shapes are delineated more distinctly, the contours are more precise, as if a heat, already oppressive, had dissipated the morning mist. There one encounters undulations similar to a wave with many small brilliant sparkles like diamond chips, unwinding its serpentine coils across a landscape beaming with light and bloom. This radiant clarity does not offer any dissonant opposition to the titles of these pieces, and it was not merely for the sake of being unusual that Field called one of his nocturnes, *Noontide*. Is this not the dream of someone half awake, in a summer night without darkness, like those he often saw dawning at St. Petersburg—nights draped in white veils which conceal nothing from the eye, and only cover the objects with a haze, as if clouded by a silvery curtain. A secret harmony suppresses the apparent disparity between the shadowy nocturnes and the brilliant transparencies, and one is not at all surprised as long as the vagueness of the images make us feel that they are delineated only in the dreamy imagination of the poet, not in vivid reality.

One could say that Field's entire life, free from the overexcited activity which instills in most of mankind the desire to be in the spotlight, in broad daylight, also, free from the burning rays which vivid passions project, drifting in idle fancy totally saturated in half-tints and chiaroscuro, may itself be likened to a long nocturne with no lightening from any storm, nor any gust of wind from a squall ever disturbing the calm of nature at rest.

He left England while still a youth, because of his attachment for his teacher, Clementi, whom he accompanied, first to Germany, where they spent only one or two years, then to Russia, where he remained. At St. Petersburg and Moscow his lessons were in great demand and valued very highly. For many years his time was sought so avidly that he reached the point where he had to listen to his pupils play in an adjoining room in the morning, before he got out of bed. . . .

A favorite pupil of Clementi, he learned from this great master the secrets of the most beautiful performance known at that period, and made use of it for a genre of poetry in which he will remain an incomparable model of natural grace, of melancholic simplicity, of ingenuity, and of freedom from restraint, all at the same time. He is one of the special types of an early school which one encounters only at certain periods of an art. Although the art is already aware of its resources, it has not yet reached the point of venturing to spread itself out, to show off more freely. More than once will its wings yet be bruised while it tries to break loose from its fetters.

11.7 DANIEL GOTTLOB TÜRK (1756–1813)

Frederic Chopin's nocturnes, ballades, mazurkas, scherzos, polonaises, fantasies, impromptus, valses, and études for piano allowed great rhythmic freedom to the performer, who in the first instance was usually the composer himself. As a youngster of seven, Chopin (1810–1849) was already playing original improvisations during his public concert appearances in his native Warsaw. Eventually the nuances and fluctuations of tempo inherent in Chopin's pianistic style were absorbed into his mature technique of composition. For example, in his *Ballade in G minor*, Opus 23, the following phrases, all with some common motion of pitches, appear with slight rhythmic variations over a meter with six quarter notes to a measure.

Chopin: *Ballade* in G minor

Rhythmic liberties of this kind, which in the hands of Chopin became characteristic of Romantic pianistic virtuosity, had already been known to the classicists, including Mozart (Section 10.2). Daniel Gottlob Türk, a theorist born the same year as Mozart, distinguished between the factor of varying the tempo and tempo rubato. Türk, who had studied with Johann Adam Hiller at Leipzig University, played both organ and violin professionally before he wrote his *Clavier Method*. The book was written sometime between 1779 and 1787 while Türk was music director at the University of Halle, and was published two years later. In line with the thought expressed in Mozart's letter of 1777, Türk gives specific examples for displacing the tones in one voice while maintaining a steady beat in another.

Concerning Appropriate Speeding Up and Slowing Down*

If a composer does not want a composition to be played strictly according to the time throughout, he may indicate this through the added words *con discrezione*. In such a case it is left to the desire of the performer to slow down in certain places, to hurry in others.

Daniel Gottlob Türk, Klavierschule oder Anweisung zum Klavierspielen für Lehrer und Lernende, mit kritichen Anmerkungen (*Clavier method or course on playing the clavier for teachers and students, with critical commentaries*). (Halle, 1789), pp. 374–376.

Besides, the expression "to play with discretion" also has several other meanings. Not infrequently one understands it to mean a good performance or fine taste. If, for example, a performer executes each thought with suitable insight, finesse, and judgment in accordance with the intention of the composer, one says, "He plays with discretion." Often playing with discretion also means to give in, or to accommodate oneself to someone else. Thus, when someone obliged to play with a poor performer rushes, holds back, if necessary leaves out whole measures, makes additions, etc., he plays (or accompanies) with discretion. And unfortunately one must all too often be discreet in this way.

Tempo Rubato

The so-called *Tempo rubato* or *robato* (really "stolen time") I consider the ultimate means available to the performer for expressing his taste and insight. This term has more than one meaning. Usually one understands by it a sort of shortening or lengthening of the notes, or a displacement of them. For example, part of the time value may be taken (or stolen) from one note and given to another, as in the following Examples (b) and (c).

At (a) the simple notes are given. At (b) the tempo rubato is produced by anticipation, and at (c) by retardation. One sees that the time or rather the meter is not completely displaced in this performance. Consequently, the usual but rather ambiguous German expression *verrücktes Zeitmass* (displaced time) is not appropriate. For the fundamental voice continues its progression in time (undisplaced); only the notes of the melody are pushed, as it were, from their rightful places. Therefore perhaps the more correct expression would be: the displacement or protraction of the notes or members of the measure. Even when several notes are inserted in the melody as in the following Examples (e) and (f), in each case both voices must sound together correctly at the beginning of the measure. At this place there is no real displacement of the time.

This delay of the tones, as it may also be called, must be very carefully done, because mistakes in the harmony may easily arise from it. The anticipation in Example (f) is only possible in a fairly slow tempo.

Beside the above meaning of tempo rubato, at times this expression only means a special kind of execution, namely, when the accent which appears on the good notes is applied to the bad ones, or, in other words, when one performs the tones on the weak part of the measure more strongly than those which fall on the good part of the measure (or of a beat), as in these examples.

Still another type of tempo rubato is prescribed by the composer, for example, in Pergolesi's *Stabat mater:*

11.8 WILLIAM MASON (1829–1908)

William Mason was descended from a Massachusetts family of long standing, whose tree dates back to Robert's landing at Salem in 1630. William's father Lowell Mason, who "originated the idea of assembling music-teachers in classes," [26] thought not only of music education in the broad sense but also of training the individual artist. William was shipped off to Europe where he studied and associated with the masters. One of the highlights of his career came on his return to America where he arranged for the first American performance of the Brahms Trio in B Major, Opus 8.

Student Life Abroad*

It having been decided that I should continue my musical studies in Europe, I sailed from New York for Bremen on the side-wheel steamer *Hermann* in May, 1849, accompanied by Mr. Frank Hill of Boston, who

---

*William Mason, Memories of a Musical Life (*New York: The Century Company*, 1901), pp. 27, 36–37, 90, 110,112, 127–129, 183,193–195.

26. Lowell Mason (1792–1872) published his foreign experiences in *Musical Letters from Abroad* (New York, 1854; Reprint Da Capo Press, 1966). As an American music educator he advocated teaching music to children by having them sing. Lowell Mason was also largely responsible for encouraging teachers to meet at conventions to exchange ideas on teaching methods.

had already attained some distinction as a pianist. My intention was to go directly to Leipzig to study with Moscheles.[27]

Moscheles, Beethoven, and Chopin

Moscheles, with whom I studied in Leipzig, had been a pupil of Dionysius Weber in Prague. At that time Beethoven was still a newcomer, and was regarded with skepticism by the older men, whose ideas were formed and who could not get over their first unfavorable impressions of him. Beethoven was a profound man and had strong individuality. He was eagerly accepted by the younger men, Moscheles among them; but Dionysius Weber regarded him as a monstrosity, and would never allow Moscheles to learn any of his music. Consequently, Moscheles practiced Beethoven in secret, and when he grew up he prided himself on being a Beethoven-player, and wrote a life of Beethoven which, however, is largely based on Schindler's.

At about the time I went to Leipzig the attitude of Moscheles toward Chopin was very like what Dionysius Weber's had been toward Beethoven. One of the daughters of Moscheles was very fond of playing Chopin, but her father forbade it. Afterward she married and went to London, where she played Chopin to her heart's content. It is curious how men who in their younger days are pioneers become so conservative as they grow older that they are like stone walls in the paths of progress. They forget that in their youth they laughed at or criticized their elders for the same pedantry of which they themselves afterward become guilty.

Accepted by Liszt

I had no idea then, neither have I now, what Liszt's means were, but I learned soon after my arrival at Weimar that he never took pay from his pupils, neither would he bind himself to give regular lessons at stated periods. He wished to avoid obligations as far as possible, and to feel free to leave Weimar for short periods when so inclined—in other words, to go and come as he liked. His idea was that the pupils whom he accepted should all be far enough advanced to practice and prepare themselves without routine instruction, and he expected them to be ready whenever he gave them an opportunity to play.

27. Ignaz Moscheles (1794–1870) was also Mendelssohn's piano teacher. Moscheles idolized Beethoven, as is evident in this anecdote from the editor's preface to the Beethoven biography mentioned by Mason.

It was in the year 1814, when Artaria undertook to publish a piano arrangement of Beethoven's *Fidelio* that he asked the composer whether I might be permitted to make it. Beethoven assented, upon condition that he should see my arrangement of each of the pieces, before it was given into the engraver's hands. Nothing could be more welcome to me, since I looked upon this as the long wished-for opportunity to approach nearer to the great man, and to profit by his remarks and corrections. During my frequent visits, the number of which I tried to multiply by all possible excuses, he treated me with the kindest indulgence.

Liszt's Playing

Time and again at Weimar I heard Liszt play. There is absolutely no doubt in my mind that he was the greatest pianist of the nineteenth century. Liszt was what the Germans call an *Erscheinung*—an epoch-making genius. . . .

The difference between Liszt's playing and that of others was the difference between creative genius and interpretation. His genius flashed through every pianistic phrase, it illuminated a composition to its innermost recesses, and yet his wonderful effects, strange as it must seem, were produced without the advantage of a genuinely musical touch.

Brahms in 1853

On one evening early in June, 1853, Liszt sent us word to come up to the Altenburg [28] the next morning, as he expected a visit from a young man who was said to have great talent as a pianist and composer, and whose name was Johannes Brahms. He was to come accompanied by Eduard Remenyi.[29]

The next morning, on going to the Altenburg, we found Brahms and Remenyi already in the reception-room. After greeting the newcomers, of whom Remenyi was known to us by reputation, I strolled over to a table on which were lying some manuscripts of music. They were several of Brahms' yet unpublished compositions, and I began turning over the leaves of the uppermost in the pile. It was the piano solo Opus 4, *Scherzo*, E♭ Minor, and, as I remember, the writing was so illegible that I thought to myself that if I had occasion to study it I should be obliged first to make a copy of it. Finally Liszt came down, and after some general conversation he turned to Brahms and said: "We are interested to hear some of your compositions whenever you are ready and feel inclined to play them."

Brahms, who was evidently very nervous, protested that it was quite impossible for him to play while in such a disconcerted state, and, notwithstanding the earnest solicitations of both Liszt and Remenyi, could not be persuaded to approach the piano. Liszt, seeing that no progress was being made, went over to the table, and taking up the first piece at hand, the illegible scherzo, and saying, "Well, I shall have to play," placed the manuscript on the piano-desk.

We had often witnessed his wonderful feats in sight-reading, and regarded him as infallible in that particular, but, notwithstanding our confidence in his ability, both Raff [30] and I had a lurking dread of the possibility

28. Elsewhere in his *Memories* Mason says, "At that time Liszt occupied a house on the Altenburg belonging to the grand duke. The old grand duke, under whose patronage Goethe had made Weimar famous, was still living. I think his idea was to make Weimar as famous musically through Liszt as it had been in literature in Goethe's time."
29. Eduard Remenyi (1930–1898), distinguished violinist, was born in Hungary and concertized widely through France, Germany, Belgium, Holland, England, the United States, Canada, Mexico, Japan, China, and South Africa.
30. Joseph Joachim Raff (1822–1882), a composer-satellite in Liszt's orbit at Weimar, helped in the instrumentation of some of Liszt's symphonic poems.

that something might happen which would be disastrous to our unquestion-
ing faith. So, when he put the scherzo on the piano-stand, I trembled for
the result. But he read it off in such a marvelous way—at the same time
carrying on a running accompaniment of audible criticism of the music—
that Brahms was amazed and delighted. Raff thought, and so expressed
himself, that certain parts of this scherzo suggested the Chopin *Scherzo in
B♭ Minor*, but it seemed to me that the likeness was too slight to deserve
serious consideration. Brahms said that he had never seen or heard any of
Chopin's compositions. Liszt also played a part of Brahm's *C Major Sonata*,
Opus 1.

At Work in America

When I returned from Europe in 1854 my parents had moved from
Boston, and were living at Orange, New Jersey. . . .
The idea of starting a series of matinées of chamber-music occurred to
me. I wished especially to introduce to the public the *Grand Trio in B
Major*, Opus 8 by Johannes Brahms, and to play other concerted works,
both classical and modern, for this kind of work interested me more than
mere piano-playing. So I asked Carl Bergmann, who was the most noted
orchestral conductor of those days, and thus well acquainted with musicians,
to get together a good string quartet. This he accomplished in a day or
two, and made me acquainted with Theodore Thomas, first violin; Joseph
Mosenthal, second violin; and George Matzha, viola, Bergmann himself
being the violoncellist. We very soon began rehearsing, and our first concert, or rather matinée, took place in Dodworth's Hall, opposite 11th
street, and one door above Grace Church on Broadway [New York City].
The program was as follows:

Tuesday, November 27, 1855

1. Quartet in D Minor, Strings   Schubert
2. Romance from Tannhäuser, *Abendstern*   Wagner
3. Pianoforte Solo, Fantasie Impromptu, Op. 66
   (first time)   Chopin
   Deux Préludes, D♭ and G, Op. 24   Heller
4. Variations Concertante for Violoncello and
   Piano, Op. 17   Mendelssohn
5. *Feldwärts flog ein Vöglein*   Nicolai
6. Grand Trio in B Major, Op. 8, Piano, Violin,
   and Cello (first time)   Brahms

It will be observed that we started out with a novelty, Brahms' Trio,
which was played then for the first time in America. I repeated it in Boston
a few weeks later with the assistance of some members of the Mendelssohn
Quintet Club. It received appreciation on both occasions and was listened
to attentively, but without enthusiasm. The newspapers spoke well of it in
general, but there were some who regarded it as constrained and unnatural.
The vocal pieces were inserted in deference to the prevailing idea of the
period that no musical entertainment could be enjoyed by the public with-

out some singing. We quickly got over that notion, and thenceforth, with rare exceptions, our programs were confined to instrumental music.

11.9 GIUSEPPE VERDI (1813–1901)

Italian operatic composers traveled a long, successful journey from Claudio Monteverdi (1567–1643), active in opera at the start of the seventeenth century, to Giuseppe Verdi, whose span of operatic creativity encompassed *Oberto* in 1839 to *Falstaff* in 1893.

Probably the greatest mistake ever made by the admissions committee of the Milan Conservatory was their rejection of Verdi on the grounds that his piano-playing and technical knowledge of music were not proficient enough to satisfy their entrance requirements. Verdi then studied privately with Vincenzo Lavigna (1776–1836), chief keyboardist at the La Scala opera house and a professor of solfeggio at the conservatory.

Many of Verdi's letters touch on vital issues related to his personal artistic inspiration, and to Italian opera in general. Several pertinent passages from his letters are quoted below, including an interchange of correspondence between Verdi and Hans von Bülow (1830–1894), a German pianist and conductor who presented the first Munich performances of *Tristan and Isolde* and the *Mastersingers* (1868).[31] Von Bülow also championed the music of Brahms, whom he designated as the "third B" with reference to Bach and Beethoven.

Interplay Between Composer and Librettist on *Aïda**

Verdi to Antonio Ghislanzoni [32]

St. Agata, September 8, 1870

Since your departure I have worked very little, having composed only the march which is extremely long and complex.[33] The entrance of the King with his court, Amneris, and the Priests; the Chorus of People, of

---

*The first four letters are quoted from Gaetano Cesari and Alessandro Luzio, I Copialettere de Giuseppi Verdi (*Milan, 1913*); Franco Abbiati, Giuseppe Verdi (*Milan, 1959*). The last two letters, Hans de Bülow e Giuseppe Verdi, are from "Due lettere," in Gazzetta Musicale di Milano (*1892*).

31. Large selections of Verdi's letters have been translated into English in *Verdi: The Man in His Letters*, edited and selected by Franz Werfel and Paul Stefan, trans. Edward Downes (New York: L. B. Fischer, 1942); and *Letters of Giuseppi Verdi*, selected, trans., and ed. Charles Osborne (New York, Chicago, San Francisco: Holt, Rinehart and Winston, 1971).

32. Antonio Ghislanzoni was the librettist of *Aïda*.

33. *Aïda*, Act II, Scene II, Finale and Chorus, *Gloria all'Egitto*.

Women; yet another Chorus of Priests (to be added); the entrance of the troops with all their battle equipment, and the dancing girls carrying sacred vases and other precious things; finally, Radames with the whole entourage—all of this constitutes but a single piece, the March.

But I need your help to work it out so that the chorus sings a little bit about the glory of Egypt and of the King, and a little bit about Radamès. Therefore it will be necessary to revise the first eight verses; the next eight, those of the women, are good; and eight more must be added for the priests.

October 8, 1870

Once and for all let me say that I have no intention of speaking about your verses, which are always good, but rather of giving my opinion about the stage effect. The duet between Radamès and Aïda,[34] according to my way of thinking, has turned out to be greatly inferior to that between the father and daughter. Perhaps this is because of the form, which is more usual than that of the preceding duet.[35] Of course, that string of *cantabile* passages of eight verses, declaimed by one and repeated by the other, is not contrived to create a lively dialogue! And besides, the intermediary passages between these vocalizations are also rather cold.

Then, the verses,

Amneris's anger would be inevitable;
With my father I should also have to die—

are not theatrical, that is to say, they give the performer no space for action. They do not hold the audience's attention, and the situation is ruined.

More expansion is necessary, and the expression of the words should be something like this: [36]

AÏDA: And are you not afraid of Amneris's anger? Do you not know that her vengeance would strike me, my father, and all of us like a thunderbolt?

RADAMÈS: I will defend you.

AÏDA: In vain—You could not! But, if you love me, one path of escape still remains open to us.

RADAMÈS: Which one?

AÏDA: To flee.

You may say, "But that's nonsense! My verses say the same thing." Very true—nonsense if you like, but it is certain that phrases such as, "Would strike me, my father, and all of us" and "In vain—You could not!" etc., etc., when they are declaimed properly, always hold the attention of the audience and sometimes produce a great effect.

34. Act III, Duet, Radamès and Aïda, *Pur ti riveggo.*
35. Act, III, Duet, Aïda and Amonasro, *Ciel! mio padre!*
36. In the final version the text was altered still further. Verdi is referring to the place where Aïda sings, "Nè d'Amneris paventi il vindice furor?"

Naples Conservatory: Standard of Pitch

Verdi to Cesarino De Sanctis [37]

Genoa, January 1, 1871

You wish to talk to me about your conservatory? But how could I take this position? Would I be able to succeed, with my ideas, which certainly are not the same as yours? Your ideas, once so great and progressive, are now stationary. . . . Please understand that when I use the word "stationary" I do not mean to say anything bad. Who knows! Perhaps you are right, and I am wrong. But it is certain that I cannot admit what is now taken for granted, and perhaps I would overturn the whole structure, which originally was so well built by Scarlatti, Durante, Leo, etc., etc., and has now been allowed to go toward almost total ruin.

Do you think I could do what you want, with the reactionary spirit that reigns? Don't you remember the strong opposition presented by the whole orchestra and by the two chief conductors two years ago, when I proposed adopting the normal diapason of Paris? [38] And, oddly enough, to come to an agreement with me they proposed splitting the difference, which was the most absurd thing in the world. There was no mutual understanding then, and there would not be now. If there was so much controversy in such an open and closed case, what would happen concerning more serious problems! At every moment I would hear someone say, "But Mercadante, but Zingarelli would have wanted so-and-so! [39]

Would you like me to answer, "Zingarelli and Mercadante are two great names, or, if you prefer, two great masters. But they have done nothing to satisfy the needs of the time, and besides, they have allowed those pro-

---

37. Cesare De Sanctis was a Neapolitan businessman who took a lively interest in the arts. When Saverio Mercadante, opera composer and director of the Naples Conservatory, died in December of 1870, De Sanctis and others, on behalf of the faculty of the conservatory, invited Verdi to be the director. Quoted are parts of Verdi's responses to this invitation.
38. In 1859 the Paris Academy had established the *Normal diapason*, or absolute pitch of the tone a' at 435 vibrations per second. Up to that time standard pitches had varied according to the medium of performance. For example, Praetorius, concerned with various media in his *De Organographia* (1619), designated choir, chamber, and cornett pitches. A further complicating factor in the seventeenth and eighteenth centuries was the possibility of differing pitches of the organ on which a composition was performed and on the organ for which it was originally composed.

   Verdi recognized the necessity for a universal standard of pitch. In the case of operatic composition, if a composer writes a particularly high or a particularly low note in an aria, or if he requires the chorus to sing toward the top or bottom of its range, the whole work may be distorted if the orchestra is tuned to a different a'.

   The present standard of a' at 440 vibrations per second was established in London in 1939 by the International Standards Association.
39. Nicola Zingarelli (1752–1837) was the predecessor of Mercadante as director of the Naples Conservatory. Zingarelli was also maestro at the Naples Cathedral, succeeding Paisiello in that post.

found and strict studies which have been the glorious basis of the school of Durante, Leo, etc., etc., to fall."

This is not possible; therefore I am staying in my fields at St. Agata.

Verdi to Francesco Florimo [40]

Genoa, January 4, 1871

You all tell me that your conservatory is in need of reform. . . . You may imagine how proud I might have been to occupy this post held by the founders of the school, A. Scarlatti, and then Durante and Leo. I would have been honored to instruct the students in these weighty and learned subjects, and to try to clarify for them the teachings of the founding fathers. I should have liked to have been able to stand, so to speak, with one foot in the past and the other in the present and the future (for I am not afraid of the *music of the future*). And I would have said to the young students: "Practice the fugue constantly and with perseverance, until you have had your fill of it, and until your hand has become so agile and strong that you can shape the notes as you please. Thus you will learn how to compose with assurance, how to resolve the parts properly, and how to modulate without affectation. Study Palestrina and a few others among his contemporaries. Then skip up to Marcello and pay attention specifically to his recitatives. Only go to a *few performances* of modern opera, and even then don't let yourself be carried away by the lavish harmonic and instrumental beauty, nor by the chord of the *diminished seventh*, the rock and refuge of all of us who do not know how to compose four measures without a half-dozen of these sevenths."

After they have pursued these studies, together with a fine education in literature, I would finally say to these students: "Now, place your hand on your heart, write, and (taking for granted that you have an artistic disposition) you will be composers. In any event, you will not enlarge the multitude of the imitators and quacks who try, try, and (although they sometimes show promise) never really create. In the teaching of singing I would somehow like to have the old studies unite with modern declamation."

To put into practice these few principles which seem simple on the surface, it would be necessary to supervise the instruction so carefully that, one might say, even the twelve months of the year would not be enough. I have a house, interests, property, and everything else here. I ask you—how can I do it?

Therefore, my dear Florimo, please convey my deepest regret to your colleagues and to the other musicians in your beautiful Naples, because I cannot accept this most gracious invitation. I hope you will find a learned man, above all, one who is strict in his studies. Liberties and errors in counterpoint may be allowed, and are sometimes even beautiful in the theater: in the conservatory, they are not. Let us go back to the old studies: there we will find progress.

40. Verdi's friend, Francesco Florimo, librarian at the Naples Conservatory, wrote a history of Naples and its conservatories, originally published in two volumes, from 1869 to 1871.

Comparison of Italian and German Musical Traits

Von Bülow to Verdi

Hamburg, April 7, 1892

Already eighteen years have passed since the undersigned was guilty of a great-great journalistic folly concerning the purpose and condition of modern Italian music. If I have not repented, I have felt bitterly ashamed oh so many times! . . . I had a mind blinded by fanaticism, by ultrawagnerian "silk." Then seven years later—bit by bit light trickled in. . . . At last I sew together this "stitch of knowledge." . . . I began by studying your latest operas, *Aïda, Otello,* and the *Requiem,* whose recent performance, although somewhat weak—moved me to tears at the end. I have studied it not only according to the letter, which kills, but according to the spirit, which revives! Well then, illustrious Maestro, now I admire you, I love you! Faithful to the Prussian motto, "Each to his own," I exclaim bravely, "Long live Verdi, the Wagner of our dear allies!"

Verdi to Von Bülow

Genoa, April 14, 1892

If your opinions in the past were different from those of today, you certainly did well to reveal them. I should never have ventured to object in the least. Besides, who knows—perhaps you were right then!

However that may be, your unexpected letter, written by a musician of your distinction and your importance in the artistic world, gave me great pleasure! This is not because of my personal vanity, but because I see that truly superior artists judge without prejudice of school, of nationality, or of period.

If the artists of the north and of the south have diverse tendencies, it is well that they are diverse. All of them should uphold the actual characteristics of their own countries, as Wagner very aptly stated.

How lucky you are to still be the son of Bach! What about us? We likewise are the sons of Palestrina, who in days past used to have a great school —our own! Now it has become a hybrid, and ruin threatens. If only we could start again from the beginning!

I am sorry that I cannot be present at the Musical Exposition in Vienna, where, besides enjoying the opportunity of mingling with so many illustrious musicians, I would have particularly liked shaking hands with you. I hope that the gentlemen who so graciously invited me will seriously think of my age and will excuse my absence.

11.10 RICHARD WAGNER (1813–1883)

In musical terms the Romantic spirit was expressed in freer forms, more colorful instrumentation, and heightened chromaticism. Richard Wagner, the dominant composer of German opera, despite his vision of opera as a "universal art-work," concentrated on the music, and especially on what went on in the orchestra. For Wagner, opera was to encompass tone, poetry, and dance, coordinating every aspect of production, including the acting, the positions on the stage, the scenery, and the stage effects. Of these elements he reserved for himself exclusively the creation of two; he wrote his own libretto and music.

In the *Prelude* to his opera *Tristan and Isolde* (composed in Venice and Lucerne in 1859) Wagner opened up the whole realm of musical chromaticism.[41] Wagner himself joined the *Prelude*, which has no text, to the *Liebestod* (love-death) sung by Isolde at the end of the opera. He was able to omit the vocal part of the *Liebestod* without spoiling the texture, because in the aria the melodic line of the voice was always reinforced by one or more instruments. Thus the *Prelude and Love-Death*, first performed at Karlsruhe in 1863, emerged as an orchestral composition that could be played independently from the opera.

Wagner was an avid writer, intent on presenting his views to the world through his essays. Quoted below are passages that articulate his philosophy a decade before the completion of *Tristan*. The letter excerpts characterize Wagner's attributes as an operatic politician and businessman.

Opera as the Universal Art-Work: *The Art-Work of the Future**

There is no other artistic faculty of man that answers to the character of *harmony*. It cannot find its mirror in the physical precision of the movements of the body, nor in the logical induction of the thinking brain—it cannot set up for itself its standard in the recognized necessity of the material world of show, like *thought*, nor like corporeal *motion* in the periodic calculation of its instinctive, physically governed properties: it is like a nature-force which men perceive but cannot comprehend. Summoned by outer—not by inner—necessity to resolve on surer and more finite manifestment, harmony must mold from its own immensurate depths the laws for its own following. These laws of harmonic sequence, based on the nature of *affinity*—just as those harmonic columns, the chords, were formed by the affinity of tone-stuffs—unite themselves into one standard, which sets up salutary bounds around the giant playground of capricious possibilities. They allow the most varied choice from amid the kingdom of harmonic families, and extend the possibility of union by elective affinity with the members of neighboring families, almost to free liking. They demand, how-

* *The excerpts are from Richard Wagner,* The Art-Work of the Future *(Leipzig, 1859), trans. William A. Ellis (London, 1892).*

The Letter from Wagner to the editor of the Vienna Botschafter *is translated in* Dwight's Journal of Music *(Boston, 1865).*

41. See William J. Mitchell, "The Tristan Prelude: Techniques and Structure," in *The Music Forum,* ed. William J. Mitchell and Felix Salzer (New York and London: Columbia University Press, 1967), I, 162–203.

ever, above all, a strict observance of the house-laws of affinity of the family once chosen, and a faithful tarrying with it, for the sake of a happy ending. But this end itself, and thus the measure of the composition's extension *in time*, the countless laws of harmonic decorum can neither give nor govern. As the scientifically teachable or learnable department of the art of *tone*, they can cleave the fluid tonal masses of *harmony* asunder, and part them into fenced-off bodies; but they cannot assign the periodic measure of these fenced-off masses.

When the limit-setting might of *speech* was swallowed up, and yet the art of tone, now turned to harmony, could never find her time-assigning law within herself: then was she forced to face towards the remnant of the rhythmic beat that *dance* had left for her to garner. Rhythmic figures must now enliven harmony. Their change, their recurrence, their parting and uniting, must condense the fluid breadths of harmony—as *word* had earlier done with tone—and bring their periods to more sure conclusion. . . . This rhythmic interchange and shaping did not move of its own inner necessity, but was bound by the laws and canons of *counterpoint*. Counterpoint, with its multiple births and offshoots, is *art's* artificial playing-with-itself, the mathematics of *feeling*, the mechanical rhythm of egoistic harmony. . . .

The living breath of fair, immortal, nobly-feeling *human voice*, streaming ever fresh and young from the bosom of the *folk*, blew this contrapuntal house of cards into a heap. The *folk-tune* that had rested faithful to its own untarnished grace; the simple, surely outlined *song*, close-woven with the poem, soared up on its elastic pinions to the regions of the beauty-lacking scientifically-musical artworld, with news of joyous ransom. This world was longing to paint men again, to set men to sing—not pipes. So it seized the folk-tune for its purpose, and constructed out of it the *opera-air*. But just as dance had seized the folk-dance, to freshen herself therewith when needed, and to convert it to an artificial compost according to the dictates of her modish taste—so did this genteel operatic tone-art behave to the folk-tune. She had not grasped the *entire man*, to show him in his whole artistic stature and nature-bidden necessity, but only the *singing man*. And in his song she had not seized the *ballad of the folk*, with all its innate generative force, but merely the *melodic tune*, abstracted from the poem, to which she set conventional and purposely insipid sentences, according to her pleasure. It was not the beating heart of the nightingale, but only its warbling throat that men could fathom, and practiced themselves to imitate.

Just as the art-dancer had set his legs, with their manifold but still monotonous bendings, flingings, and gyrations, to vary the natural folk-dance which he could not of himself develop further—so did the art-singer set his throat to paraphrase with countless ornaments, to alter by a host of flourishes, those tunes which he had stolen from the people's mouth, but whose nature he could never fertilize afresh, and thus another species of mechanical dexterity filled up the place which contrapuntal ingenuity had left forlorn. We need not further characterize the repugnant, ineffably repulsive disfigurement and rending of the folk-tune, such as cries out from the modern operatic *aria*—for truly it is nothing but a mutilated folk-tune, and in no wise a specific fresh invention—such as, in entire contempt of *nature* and all human feeling, and severed from all basis of poetic speech, now tickles the imbecile ears of our opera-frequenters with its lifeless, soul-less toy of fashion. . . .

Not one rich faculty of the separate arts will remain unused in the United Art-Work of the Future. In *it* will each attain its first complete appraisement. Thus, especially, will the manifold developments of *tone*, so peculiar to our instrumental music, unfold their utmost wealth within this art-work. Nay, tone will incite the mimetic art of *dance* to entirely new discoveries, and no less swell the breath of *poetry* to unimagined fill. For *music*, in her solitude, has fashioned for herself an organ which is capable of the highest reaches of expression. This organ is the *orchestra*. The tone-speech of Beethoven, introduced into *drama* by the orchestra, marks an entirely fresh departure for the dramatic artwork. While *architecture* and, more especially, scenic *landscape-painting* have power to set the executant dramatic *artist* in the surroundings of physical *nature*, and to dower him from the exhaustless stores of natural phenomena with an ample and significant background—so in the orchestra, that pulsing body of many-colored harmony, the personating individual man is given, for his support, a stanchless elemental spring, at once artistic, natural, and human.

On Producing *Tristan and Isolde*: Public Letter

Letter to the Editor of the Vienna *Botschafter*

Munich, April 18, 1865

My Esteemed Friend—You are still the only editor of a political newspaper of any importance on whose support I can reckon, whenever it is necessary for me to be put, in any way, in communication with the public. It is a real piece of good fortune for me that we should be connected by friendship of long standing. Were this not the case, on this occasion as on previous ones, I do not know to what means I should be obliged to have recourse, in order, as I naturally very much desire, to inform the more serious lovers of my art, who are scattered far and wide, that they will, in a very short time, really have an opportunity of witnessing a performance of my *Tristan and Isolde*. While, therefore, I earnestly beg you to do all you can for the propagation of this intelligence, I must beg you to allow me to accord myself the small satisfaction of directing your attention to the peculiar significance which I may fairly attach to the performance, that is actually coming off, of my work. Perhaps in giving a short history of the obstacles which have hitherto prevented this performance, I shall be furnishing you with a contribution, not unworthy of notice, to the history of modern art generally.

In the summer of 1857 I determined to interrupt the execution of my work on the *Nibelungen* [42] and commence something shorter, which should renew my connection with the stage. *Tristan and Isolde* was really com-

---

42. Wagner wrote the librettos for the cycle of music dramas, *The Ring of the Nibelung*, in reverse order. He then proceeded to compose the music in sequence, starting with *Das Rheingold* (1853–54) and going on to *Die Walküre* (1854–56). To offset "heaping one silent score upon the other," Wagner interrupted his work on the *Ring* to write *Tristan*. The interruption was not complete, however, as he simultaneously kept up with the third Ring opera, *Siegfried* (1856–71). During the negotiations for *Tristan* he was composing another non-*Ring* opera, *The Mastersingers of Nuremberg* (1862–67). At length he returned to the *Ring* and completed it with *Götterdämmerung* (1869–74).

menced in the above year, but the completion of it, from all kinds of disturbing influences, was deferred till the summer of 1859. . . . In order to render possible a first performance in which I myself should take an active part, I migrated in the autumn of 1859 to Paris. My scheme was to collect a model German operatic company there during the months of May and June, 1860. The Italian Operahouse, unoccupied every year at that period, was to have been engaged for the performances. As I found most of the artists, with whom I was acquainted and on friendly terms, inclined to take my offer into consideration, the first thing I had to do was to think of how to insure the material possibility of the enterprise. It was not difficult to find a business-director in the person of one of the proprietors of the Italian Operahouse. It was more difficult to procure the financial guarantee of a capitalist. To get a person to give it, I had to provide courage for a well-disposed wealthy man, a friend of one of my Parisian friends. At my own risk, I arranged three grand concerts in the Italian Operahouse, when I had fragments of my music executed by a grand orchestra, and—for it is not possible to do anything of the kind otherwise in Paris—at a very heavy expense. . .[43]

Thus then my *Tristan und Isolde* had become a mere fable. I was treated in a friendly manner here and there. *Tannhäuser* and *Lohengrin* were praised. Otherwise, however, it seemed to be all over with me. But fate had ordained otherwise. When all else forsook me, a noble heart beat the more strongly and warmly for the ideal of my art. It cried to the artist abandoned by the world, "What thou createst I will accept!" And this time the will was itself creative, for it was the will of a—*King!* . . . And what the nature of the power here at work is, you must conclude from the mode of its manifestation, when I inform you in what fashion *Tristan* will be presented to my friends.

The performances of *Tristan and Isolde*, of which three at least are fully guaranteed, will be of a completely exceptional and model kind. For this purpose, in the first place, the representatives of the two extraordinarily difficult leading parts were especially summoned to Munich in the persons of my dear friends, Ludwig and Malvina Schnorr von Carolsfeld. They are accompanied by my trusty old comrade on the battlefields of art, Anton Mitterwurzer, true and genuine as can be as Kurvenal. As far as circumstances will allow, too, the most judicious measures have been most magnanimously taken for the cast of the other parts. Every person concerned is friendly and devoted to me. In order that we might not be annoyed by the disturbing influences existing in a theater open every day, the cozy

43. Wagner describes the difficulties he encountered while trying to arrange for a complete performance of *Tristan*. At Paris and then Vienna he had trouble finding singers who were equal to the parts musically and physically. The delayed and canceled rehearsals caused him to run into debt with the orchestra and stagehands. One cheerful interlude occurred on the banks of the Rhine where, in his words,

> I managed to get complete performances of my opera with Bülow's inimitable pianoforte accompaniment. This happened in my room, at a time when no one offered me the opportunity of doing so much on any stage.

Wagner felt himself in a desperate financial squeeze when King Ludwig of Bavaria came to the rescue. The king gave him a stipend and a house in Munich, where Wagner readied for the first complete performance with orchestra on June 10, 1865.

Royal Residenz-Theatre was placed at our exclusive disposal. Everything has been carefully fitted up there for the requirements of an inward, clear, and snugly intelligible representation according to my directions. Here, almost daily, the magnificent Royal Court-Orchestra, Franz Lachner's model creation [44] is placed at our service for numerous rehearsals. My dear friend, Hans von Bülow has been given me to conduct the orchestra—he and no other, he who once effected the impossible when he compiled a playable pianoforte arrangement of this score, though no one can yet understand how he did it. With him, who is so well acquainted with the score, which still appears enigmatical to so many musicians, who knows by heart the very smallest fragments of it and has made himself master of my intentions down to their most delicate niceties—with this second self by my side, I can take into consideration every separate item of the musical and scenic representation in that quietly confidential artistic frame of mind rendered possible only by affectionate relations between myself and artists connected by the ties of the firmest friendship. The zeal displayed in providing beautiful scenery and highly characteristic costumes is such that it seems as if the question was no longer one of a mere theatrical performance, but of a monumental exhibition.

Transported thus from the desert of our ordinary tradesmanlike system of conducting theaters to the refreshing oasis of an art *atelier* [foreman], we prepare the work for a dramatic performance which, purely as such, must form an epoch for all who may witness it.

The performances, for the present—as announced—perhaps only three in number, are to be considered as art-festivals, to which I am permitted to invite the friends of my art from far and near. They are thus removed from the category of ordinary theatrical performances, and taken out of the usual relations existing between the theater and the public of our age. . . .

To any raillery to the effect that by such measure we appear to have taken into consideration an especially friendly public whom it would certainly require no great art to please, we quietly reply that on this occasion the question is not one of pleasing or not pleasing, that wonderful theatrical game of hazard of modern times, but exclusively one of deciding whether artistic problems, such as I have proposed in this work, are to be solved, in what way they are to be solved, and whether it is worth the trouble to solve them. That the last question does not mean that we wish to learn whether a great deal of money can be made by these performances (for this is the signification of anything pleasing or not pleasing in theaters nowadays), but, simply, whether by admirable performances, with works of this description, it is possible to produce the anticipated right influence generally upon the cultivated human mind, is something that must be emphatically stated. That, consequently, the first object in view is the solution of a purely artistic problem, and that, therefore, only those should be summoned to that solution who, by serious interest in the matter, are really prepared and able to cooperate in it. Should the problem be solved, the

44. Franz Lachner (1830–1890), a close friend of Schubert, orchestrated Schubert's *Song of Miriam*. Lachner had studied counterpoint and composition with Simon Sechter (1788–1867), the musician with whom Schubert had hoped to study just before he died (1828).

question will be widened, and it will then, too, be shown in what way we are ready to accord to and prepare for the people, properly so-called, a participation in the *highest* and the *profoundest* event of art, though, as yet we do not think we ought to take into consideration the actual theatrical public of the present day.

If you are now of opinion, my dear Uhl, that I have been treating of no unimportant event in art, and that it is worthwhile to do something for the announcement contained in what I have said, may I beg you to employ, as you may consider best, your connections as a publicist.

12

Musical Traditions
in Various Locations

12.1 ANTONIUS SEPP (b. 1655)

Musical composition from its earliest beginnings was dependent on the songs and customs of the people in the locale where the act of creation took place. The given melody of a work based on a cantus firmus, whether secular or sacred, was usually one which was so well known that nobody could tell who had first conceived it. The instrument used to reinforce or accompany a voice part came into being without exact information concerning its origin. As interchange became more prevalent between musicians of different institutions, different countries, and even different parts of the world, as exploration expanded and means of communication developed, musicians took their findings to remote regions and in return brought back to their countries the hitherto unrecorded musical practices of newly discovered territories. The musical explorers were interested in hearing the melodies and instruments specific to a locale, and in observing the people's musical sensitivity, whether innate or consciously developed. On the other hand, the inhabitants of a particular country might be oblivious to their heritage or they might be intent on preserving and developing a national style.

Antonius Sepp, a Jesuit missionary born at Kaltern in the Tyrol, sailed from Cadiz to Paraguay in 1689. Although his original purpose for going to South America was to help the native Indians to become economically self-sufficient, he was also interested in establishing a socially and culturally well rounded community. Sepp discovered that the natives already had instruments of their own, constructed before the arrival of the Europeans. To further foster their love for music, he founded a music school in Paraguay. His adventures in setting up a reduction or settlement for the natives provides us with information about the transmission of knowledge concerning musical instruments from the Old World to the New. The natives whom Sepp and his aides instructed in the construction and use of European art instruments were prepared, if they so desired, to mingle the musical impulses of their own heritage with those of others.

Building an Organ in South America*

I have already worked three whole years in the vineyard of the Three Holy Kings, helping the new Christian Indians to plow, plant, and graft. Toward this end, the Apostolic vineyardists sent me some boughs from many other distantly situated vineyards, which I myself mingled with my old and already fruitful vine plants so that in the future they might combine in producing good wine.

I wish to make known that I have established a music school in the aforementioned village, and took great pains to teach not only mine, but also the Indians of other reductions and villages. Also, the building Fathers of the mission sent their charges to me here so that I might teach them. This I did too, not only in voice or song, but I also gave them lessons in the instrumental art. One I taught to play the organ, another, the harp. Indeed, some learned to perform on the double-strung theorbo, the guitar, and the violin, others to blow on the shawm [1] and clarino.[2] I also brought the lovely psalterium to the attention of the Indians. I not only taught them how to play this aforementioned instrument, but also at the same time to make it in this shape. In various villages most of the Indians played a David's harp which they already knew how to make from resonant cedarwood.[3] They knew how to put together a clavichord, how to bore out shawms, bassoons, and flutes. And a few days ago I also had my smith make bores of this kind.

We still lacked the most important of all instruments, the fundament of string playing and of all music, namely, a good organ. When the ship from Spain arrived at Buenos Aires in the year 1700, bearing a large organ made in the Netherlands costing a thousand *Reichsthaler*,[4] but here worth five

From Antonius Sepp, Continuation oder Fortsetzung der Beschreibung, Deren denckwürdigeren Paraquarischen Sachen, selbiger Landschafft, Völckern, und Arbeit deren sich alldort befinden. (Continuation or Further Description of the More Memorable Paraguarian Matters, of Its Country, People, and Work; Ingelstatt, 1710), pp. 85–91.

1. The shawm was a double-reed instrument in use before the oboe became prominent.
2. For the clarin trumpet, see Altenburg, Section 9.5.
3. In the eighteenth century David's harp was considered to be a kind of psalterion, a harp without pedals whose shape might be triangular, square, rectangular, trapezoidal, wing-shaped, harp-shaped, etc.
4. A *Reichsthaler*, or rixdollar, was approximately the same value as our dollar.

thousand, it was not designed for our reductions or villages, but rather for the College at Buenos Aires, and thus we transported its crate there.

Now since, as has been said, we lacked a good organ with which the praise of God might be spread amongst these poor Indians, the most distinguished Father of the Province, Laurus Nunnez, gave me the order to construct a new mechanism and organ in the European system and manner. The work could not be instituted in my village of the Three Holy Kings because of the deficiency and lack of materials necessary for it. But on the other hand, since R. P. Franciscus de Azebedo, in his colony named Itapua, had lead, tin, and wire, it was best to make an organ by all of us working together. The situation demanded that I commit myself to starting this greatly needed work. This came to pass, for I placed myself at their disposal. And more from holy blind obedience than from my own knowledge, I became an organ maker. The reverend father Franciscus de Azebedo gave me many tin rowboats to melt, which he bought from the Spaniards of this country, for other tin was not at hand. But this would not resound for the large pipes, the principals and flutes, the so-called sub-bass.[5] And if this new organ of mine was not to exceed or be greater than the hall of the large congregation located at Ingolstadt, my rowboats would not resound to give the "foot" to the large pipes.[6] This exigency, however, turned into a virtue. Namely, from the best cedarwood, here in such great abundance and quantity, I had fine, thin sheets or veneers cut, fastened and glued them together well to delicate parchment, gave them the necessary height, depth, and thickness, opened and adjusted their mouth-pieces, and —listen to the surprise! The former barren, mute cedar began to rustle, to rumble, and to roar to such an extent that the fathers of the Mission and the reverend fathers of the Province, together with the Indians called out in astonishment, "Victor! Victor! Father Antonius."

This is a certain expression that the Spaniards use when they want to congratulate someone. And it means the same thing as "*Vivat, Vivat!*" does in the Latin language. But what surprised them all even more was that they now saw the previously mute cedarwood appearing as a stop in the organ and coming into conflict with the tin pipes clearly resounding, which between the two can rumble and roar more—a phenomenon not yet heard in Paraguay. Besides, they could not understand why people used their clumsy thick feet for playing the organ when nature had thoughtfully provided them with hands for real assistance. They were particularly astounded when with my hands and feet I made the cast metal and the hollowed-out cedar tree scream their heads off. Likewise they could not figure out how I animated the mechanism and made it speak with my feet. But when I had shown them the connection or inner relationship between the home-bred entangled iron wire and the wind-chamber, they praised and commended the interlocking mechanism which until that time had not been known in this country. Furthermore, the registers with whose projection I made the mechanism very soft, then loud, screaming with the

5. The "principals" and "flutes" are two types of flue pipe. The principals produce the first and second harmonics almost equally, while the flutes are characterized by the first harmonic or fundamental.
6. The flue pipe has a cylinder or "body" attached to a cone or "foot." There is a "mouth" or opening in the body near the foot.

fullest voice, seemed strange to them. Doubtless the best tuning for this organ was for the *cornet* to be high, with the *clarion, bassoon* and *schalmei* equal, so that it could be most useful.[7] The experienced European master organists knew only too well the harm that was caused by our lack of music. Now we have a good organ in the European system and manner, which I made at my village's expense. It is praised and commended to this day in the church of the Three Holy Kings.

12.2 BENJAMIN FRANKLIN (1706–1790)

In the 1760s music became the topic of a transatlantic correspondence between Benjamin Franklin, the American philosopher-statesman-scientist, and Henry Home (1696–1782), the Scottish philosopher-lawyer-agriculturist. Home, otherwise known as Lord Kames after the name of the town in Scotland where he was born, had written a book entitled *Elements of Criticism* (Edinburgh, 1762). It received immediate acclaim in the field of aesthetics for its consideration of beauty perceived through the senses of sight and hearing. Benjamin Franklin had a copy with him on one of his voyages to Europe. From London in 1765 he took the time to write a long letter to Lord Kames, mildly complaining that Kames did not devote enough attention to music, and then proceeding to lavish the care on music which he felt it deserved.

Franklin obviously liked his music natural and simple. In his letter to Kames he offers a hypothesis of the relationship of melody and harmony in folk song which fairly rivals that of Rameau.

Scotch Folk Tunes*

Letter To Lord Kames, at Edinburgh

London, 2 June, 1765

In my passage to America I read your excellent work, the *Elements of Criticism*, in which I found great entertainment. I only wished you had examined more fully the subject of music, and demonstrated that the pleasure artists feel in hearing much of that composed in the modern taste, is not the natural pleasure arising from melody or harmony of sounds, but of the same kind with the pleasure we feel on seeing the surprising feats of tumblers and rope-dancers, who execute difficult things. For my part I take this to be really the case, and suppose it to be the reason why those

---

*The Complete Works of Benjamin Franklin, *compiled & edited by John Bigelow* (*New York & London: G. P. Putnam's Sons, The Knickerbocker Press, 1887*), *III, 380–384.*

7. Here the terms *cornet, clarion, bassoon,* and *schalmei* refer to organ pipes, each with its distinctive tone quality or timbre.

who are unpractised in music, and therefore unacquainted with those difficulties, have little or no pleasure in hearing this music. Many pieces of it
are mere compositions of tricks. I have sometimes, at a concert, attended
by a common audience, placed myself so as to see all their faces, and observed no signs of pleasure in them during the performance of a great part
that was admired by the performers themselves; while a plain old Scotch
tune, which they disdained, and could scarcely be prevailed upon to play,
gave manifest and general delight.

Give me leave, on this occasion, to extend a little the sense of your position, that "melody and harmony are separately agreeable, and in union delightful," and to give it as my opinion, that the reason why the Scotch
tunes have lived so long, and will probably live forever (if they escape
being stifled in modern affected ornament), is merely this, that they are
really compositions of melody and harmony united, or rather that their
melody is harmony. I mean the simple tunes sung by a single voice. As this
will appear paradoxical, I must explain my meaning. In common acceptation,
indeed, only an agreeable *succession* of sounds is called *melody*, and only
the *coexistence* of agreeable sounds, *harmony*. But, since the memory is
capable of retaining for some moments a perfect idea of the pitch of a
past sound, so as to compare with it the pitch of a succeeding sound, and
judge truly of their agreement or disagreement, there may and does arise
from thence a sense of harmony between the present and past sounds,
equally pleasing with that between two present sounds.

Now the construction of the old Scotch tunes is this, that almost every
succeeding emphatical note is a third, a fifth, an octave, or, in short, some
note that is in concord with the preceding note. Thirds are chiefly used,
which are very pleasing concords. I use the word *emphatical* to distinguish
those notes which have a stress laid on them in singing the tune, from the
lighter connecting notes, that serve merely, like grammar articles in common
speech, to tack the whole together.

That we have a most perfect idea of a sound just past, I might appeal to
all acquainted with music, who know how easy it is to repeat a sound in the
same pitch with one just heard. In tuning an instrument, a good ear can
as easily determine that two strings are in unison by sounding them separately, as by sounding them together; their disagreement is also as easily,
I believe I may say more easily and better, distinguished, when sounded
separately; for when sounded together, though you know by the beating
that one is higher than the other, you cannot tell which it is. I have ascribed
to memory the ability of comparing the pitch of a present tone with that
of one past. But if there should be, as possibly there may be, something in
the ear, similar to what we find in the eye, that ability would not be entirely
owing to memory. Possibly the vibrations given to the auditory nerves by
a particular sound may actually continue some time after the cause of these
vibrations is past, and the agreement or disagreement of a subsequent sound
become by comparison with them more discernible. For the impression
made on the visual nerves by a luminous object will continue for twenty
or thirty seconds. Sitting in a room, look earnestly at the middle of a window a little while when the day is bright, and then shut your eyes; the
figure of the window will still remain in the eye, and so distinct that you
may count the panes.

A remarkable circumstance attending this experiment is, that the impression of forms is better retained than that of colors; for after the eyes

are shut, when you first discern the image of the window, the panes appear dark, and the cross bars of the sashes, with the window frames and walls, appear white or bright; but if you still add to the darkness in the eyes by covering them with your hand, the reverse instantly takes place, the panes appear luminous and the cross-bars dark. And by removing the hand they are again reversed. This I know not how to account for. Nor for the following: that, after looking long through green spectacles, the white paper of a book will on first taking them off appear to have a blush of red; and, after long looking through red glasses, a greenish cast; this seems to intimate a relation between green and red not yet explained.

Farther, when we consider by whom these ancient tunes were composed, and how they were first performed, we shall see that such harmonical successions of sounds were natural and even necessary in their construction. They were composed by the minstrels of those days to be played on the harp accompanied by the voice. The harp was strung with wire, which gives a sound of long continuance, and had no contrivance like that in the modern harpsichord, by which the sound of the preceding could be stopped, the moment a succeeding note began. To avoid actual discord, it was therefore necessary that the succeeding emphatic note should be a chord with the preceding, as their sounds must exist at the same time. Hence arose that beauty in those tunes that has so long pleased, and will please for ever, though men scarce know why. That they were originally composed for the harp, and of the most simple kind, I mean a harp without any half notes but those in the natural scale, and with no more than two octaves of strings, from C to c, I conjecture from another circumstance, which is, that not one of those tunes, really ancient, has a single artificial half tone in it, and that in tunes where it was most convenient for the voice to use the middle notes of the harp, and place the key in F, there the B, which if used should be a B flat, is always omitted, by passing over it with a third. The connoisseurs in modern music will say, I have no taste; but I cannot help adding, that I believe our ancestors, in hearing a good song, distinctly articulated, sung to one of those tunes, and accompanied by the harp, felt more real pleasure than is communicated by the generality of modern operas, exclusive of that arising from the scenery and dancing. Most tunes of late composition, not having this natural harmony united with their melody, have recourse to the artificial harmony of a bass, and other accompanying parts. This support, in my opinion, the old tunes do not need, and are rather confused than aided by it. Whoever has heard James Oswald play them on his violoncello, will be less inclined to dispute this with me. I have more than once seen tears of pleasure in the eyes of his auditors; and yet, I think, even *his* playing those tunes would please more, if he gave them less modern ornament.

12.3 WILLIAM BILLINGS (1746–1800)

Composers in the New World didn't need much encouragement to develop an individual style. The American musical genius, William Billings, a tanner by trade, studied music theory on his own, from the treatise of an English organist by the name of William Tan'sur. The book, originally entitled *The Royal Melody Compleat, or the New Harmony of Sion* (1760), was reissued as *The American Harmony* for consumption across the ocean. In addition to this means of gaining musical knowledge, Billings also studied music on the local scene first-hand. His opinions on such matters as the native music of North America and the effect of the settlers and slaves on American music were the result of direct observation.

A Good Musical Ear: *The Continental Harmony**

SCHOLAR: Sir, I should be glad to know which you think is to be preferred in a singer, a good voice or a good ear.

MASTER: A good ear is as much preferable to a good voice, as a good eye sight is to a good looking glass, for the ear is governor of the voice as much as the helm is governor of the ship. For when I attempt to strike a certain sound, my ear informs me whether I am right or wrong, and if wrong, whether I am too high or too low; Without this information I should not be able to sing one tune, nor strike one note correctly, but by mere chance, for anyone that does not have a musical ear [8] is no better judge of musical sounds than a blind man is of colors. And you may take it for granted that anyone who has a curious ear, with an indifferent voice, will harmonize much better in concert than one who has an excellent voice with an indifferent ear.

Sensitivity of the Afro-American to Music: *The Continental Harmony*

SCHOLAR: Have you ever heard it observed what part of this globe is most productive of musical performers?

MASTER: I have often heard it remarked by travellers that the people who live near the torrid zone are in general more musical than those who border on the frigid. I have made one observation which induces me to believe this remark to be just, viz. the blacks who are brought here from Africa are in general better constituted for music than the natives of North America. Indeed, nature seems to have lavishly bestowed on them all the mechanical powers requisite to constitute musical performers, for they have strong lungs, they

---

*From William Billings, The Continental Harmony, Containing a Number of Anthems, Fuges, and Chorusses, in Several Parts, *Composed by William Billings, Published according to Act of Congress (Boston: 1794), pp. xxxii f. The New-England Psalm-Singer: or American Chorister, Containing a Number of Psalm-Tunes, Anthems and Canons. In Four and Five Parts, *Composed by William Billings, a Native of Boston, in New England (Boston: 1797), Chap. 9.*

8. Billings' footnote here is: "I think we may with propriety make a distinction between those who (are said to) have a musical ear, and those who have an ear for music; for any who are pleased and entertained with musical sounds, may be said to have an ear for music, but before they can justly be said to have a musical ear, they must be able to make very nice distinctions.

are remarkably long winded, they have musical ears, and very melodious voices.

Importance of the Bass Part: *The New England Psalm-Singer*

In order to make good music, there is great judgment required in dividing the parts properly so that one shall not overpower the other. In most singing companies I ever heard, the greatest failure was in the bass, for, let the three upper parts be sung by the best voices on earth, and after the best manner, yet without a sufficient quantity of bass, they are no better than a scream, because the bass is the foundation, and if it be well laid, you may build upon it at pleasure. Therefore, in order to have good music there must be three basses to one of the upper parts. For instance, in a company of forty people, twenty of them should sing the bass. The other twenty should be divided, according to the discretion of the company, into the upper parts. Six or seven of the deepest voices should sing the ground bass, which I have set to most of the tunes in the following work, and have taken care to set it chiefly in the compass of the human voice, which if well sung together with the upper parts is most majestic, and so exceedingly grand as to cause the floor to tremble,[9] as I myself have often experienced.

Great care should also be taken to pitch a tune on or near the letter it is set, though sometimes it will bear to be set a little above and sometimes a little below the key, according to the discretion of the performer. But I would recommend a pitch pipe, which will give the sound even to the nicety of half a tone.

Much caution should be used in singing a solo. In my opinion two or three at most are enough to sing it well. It should be sung as soft as an echo in order to keep the hearers in an agreeable suspense till all the parts join together in a full chorus, as smart and strong as possible. Let all parts close in a proper key, and a full organ, which will yield great delight both to the performers and hearers.

12.4 WILLIAM LITTLE (fl.1798) AND WILLIAM SMITH (1754?–1821)

Several compositions by William Billings were included in "A Choice Collection of Psalm Tunes and Anthems, from the most celebrated Authors, with a number composed in Europe and America, entirely new;

9. Billings' note: All notes that descend below G Gamut in the bass, occasion an agreeable tremor. But in my opinion double D, viz. (an octave below the middle line of the bass) is the most commanding and majestic of any sound in nature. N. B. Blowing a note carries it an octave below itself, so as to make D blow'd as low as double D.

suited to all the Metres sung in the different Churches in the United States," printed at Albany in 1802. The psalm tunes and anthems, compiled by William Little and William Smith, were "Published for the Use of Singing Societies in general, but more particularly for those who have not the Advantage of an INSTRUCTOR." Accordingly, the overall title of the work was, *The Easy Instructor; or A New Method of Teaching Sacred Harmony*. Before the section containing the music, there was a section headed, "The Rudiments of Music on an improved Plan, wherein the Naming and Timing of the Notes are familiarized to the weakest Capacity."

Little and Smith give us a fine glimpse into the spirit of American psalmody at the beginning of the nineteenth century, as they discuss the topics of rhythm and how to manage the voice, with some general rules for interpretation.

Their special method for beginners learning to read music at sight is based on so-called "shape notes." Four shapes—namely, round (*sol*), square (*la*), diamond (*mi*), and triangle (*fa*)—were assigned to the notes of a diatonic tetrachord in the pattern of whole step, whole step, half step. As with the old Guidonian syllables (**Appendix 1**, Chart 2), the semitones came between *mi* and *fa* (diamond to triangle), or between *la* and *fa* (square to triangle).

American Psalmody*

Advertisement

As the authors are well aware, that whatever has the appearance of novelty is, from this very circumstance, in danger of meeting with an unfavorable reception; they request nothing more than a critical observation of the certificate annexed, and an impartial examination of the method proposed, being willing to submit the merit of the performance to the determination of the candid and judicious. As the introduction of the four singing syllables, by characters, showing at sight, the name of the notes, may perhaps be considered as subjecting those who are taught in this manner to difficulty in understanding other books without this assistance . . . the authors would just observe that, if pupils are made acquainted with the principle here laid down, the objection will be found, by experience, more specious than solid. To this it might be added, that in the old way, there are not less than seven different ways of applying the four singing syllables to the lines and spaces, which is attended with great difficulty. But this difficulty is entirely removed with the present plan. And we know of no objection to this plan, other than it is not in use. This objection is no

William Little and William Smith, The Easy Instructor; or a New Method of Teaching Sacred Harmony (Albany; Websters & Skinner and Daniel Steele, 1802), pp. 1, 6–8, 12, 25.

objection at all, or at least, cannot be decisive, as this would give currency to the entire rejection and exclusion of all improvements whatever. And it is the novelty of a singing book rendered so easy, from its improvements, that any person of a tolerable voice might actually learn the art of psalmody without an instructor, if they could but obtain the sounds of the eight notes, which has led its advocates to request a publication of the same. We have, therefore, the pleasure to inform the public, that since subscriptions have been in circulation for this book, we have been honored with upwards of three thousand subscribers; in consequence of which we flatter ourselves that this book will meet with a kind reception.

Time

The two first modes in Common Time have four beats in a bar, and may be performed in the following manner, viz. The first beat, strike the end of the fingers on what you beat upon. The second beat, bring down the heel of the hand. The third beat, raise the hand half way up. The fourth beat, raise the hand clear up. The third and fourth modes of Common, and the first and second of Compound Time, have but two beats in a bar, and the best method we know of measuring time in these four modes, is by beating with the hand, saying *one* with it down, and *two* with up.

To arrive at an exactness in this mode of calculating, the learner may beat by the motion of a pendulum vibrating in a second, without paying any regard to the notes. For by this method he will become habituated to regularity and exact proportion.

Beating of time should be attended to before any attempt to sounding the notes is made. Counting and beating frequently while learning the rules, will be of great service. A large motion of the hand is best at first, but as soon as the learner can beat with accuracy, a small motion is sufficient.

Of Managing the Voice

If directions, given by ancient and modern critics (for the modulating of the voice) to those who are desirous of excelling in public speaking are necessary, directions are particularly requisite to enable the student in music to sing with grace and energy. Therefore:

1. Above all things, affectation should be guarded against. For whilst it is contrary to that humility which ever ought to characterise the devout worshipper, it must be an enemy to the natural ease which always distinguishes the judicious performance.

2. Care should be taken to begin with a proper pitch of the voice, otherwise it is impossible to preserve the melodious connection of the notes, or the harmony of the parts. For if at the commencement of a tune the voice is too low, languor must prevail; if too high, an unnatural endeavor to maintain a proportioned elevation throughout the whole performance.

3. The articulation must be as distinct as the sound will possibly admit. For in this, vocal music has the preference of instrumental—that while the ear is delighted, the mind is informed.

4. Though it is the opinion of most writers, that the learners should take the parts best adapted to their respective voices; let them occasionally try the different parts; not only because it makes them better acquainted with the nature and degrees of sounds, but because it has a tendency to improve the voice, to file off what is too rough, and what is too effeminate to render more energetic; whereas monotony, is, otherwise, apt to take place. By attending to this direction the evil will be greatly guarded against.

5. Those who have but indifferent voices, will find great benefit, if after faithfully trying an easy tune themselves, they can get a good singer to sing with them. And by attending to his performance they will instantly perceive a difference. The ear will soon experience a pleasing superiority, and the learner, at every succeeding effort, will find that his mechanical sensibility, if we may be allowed the expression, is greatly improved.

General Observations

The high notes in all parts should be sung soft and clear, but not faint: The low notes full and bold, but not harsh. The best general rule of singing in concert is, for each individual to sing so soft as to hear distinctly the other parts. The practice of singing soft will be greatly to the advantage of the learner, not only from the opportunity it will give him of hearing and imitating his teacher, but it is the best, and most ready way of cultivating his own, and making it melodious.

When music is repeated, the sound should increase together with the emphasis. In tunes that repeat, the strength of voice should increase in the parts engaged, while the others are falling in with spirit, in which case the pronunciation should be as distinct and emphatic as possible.

When singing in concert, no one, except the teacher or leader, should attempt a solo which does not belong to the part which he is singing. It destroys the very intent of the composition, and intimates to the audience that the person, or persons, to whom the solo particularly belongs, was inadequate to the performance.

All solos should be sung softer than the parts when moving together.

Notes tied with each other, should be sung softer than when one note answers to a syllable, and should be swelled in the throat, with the teeth and lips a little asunder, and sung if possible to one breath, which should be taken previously, at the beginning of each slur which is continued to any considerable length.

To obtain the true sounds of the intervals, the learner will find great advantage by repeating the sound over and over from the last notes he is attempting to sound, until he can obtain the sounds he would wish to retain. Proceeding in this manner, an indifferent voice may be greatly cultivated, when a hasty performance would not only be to no advantage, but discouraging indeed.

Sol	La	Mi	Fa
○	□	◇	△
Round	Square	Diamond	Triangle

The Eight Notes

[Fa   sol   la   fa   sol   la   mi   fa]

Syncopation is when notes are so placed that the hand must rise and fall not always at the beginning of each note, but often in the middle.

Syncopation
Printed

[fa   solfa   mi   fa la   sol   lasol   fa   la   sol   fa   mi   fa]

Sung

These are called *driving notes* and are something difficult, but the above example shows both how sung and printed.

Bibliograhical Note

Frank J. Metcalf, "*The Easy Instructor*, A Bibliographical Study," *The Musical Quarterly*, XXIII, No. 1 (1937), 89–97.

12.5 ANTONIN DVOŘÁK (1841–1904)

In 1892 Antonin Dvořák, Czech by birth, came to New York to be director of the National Conservatory. In the following year the New York Philharmonic performed Dvořák's symphony *From the New World*. The composer expressed his views on the situation of music in the "New World" verbally, in an article published in *Harper's New Monthly Magazine*.

Prior to Dvořák's visit to America he had been living in Prague, eking out a living playing the violin and viola until 1873. In that year, after writing a large orchestral choral work that attracted attention, he became organist of St. Adalbert's Church in Prague. Two years later a symphony he composed, conducted by Smetana, won for Dvořák the Austrian State Prize, an award that was renewed for Dvořák again and again. Liszt,

Brahms, and Von Bülow also took an interest in his works, and Dvořák
became a professor in composition at the Prague Conservatory. In 1895,
the year that Dvořák's article entitled *Music in America* appeared, he returned to Prague to his old teaching position at the conservatory.

Before Dvořák was called upon to express his views on the possibility
of a national music in America, others had given the matter some thought.
However, it seemed easier to establish a negative response than a positive
one. If America was to have a national music, it must not be a direct copy
of European models. Nor should it be a "refinement" of traditional music
brought about by smoothing out the jagged rhythms and tempering the
pitches to suit the major and minor tunings. In for criticism were such
musical personalities as the composer Stephen Collins Foster (1826–1864)
and the pianist Louis Moreau Gottschalk (1829–1869). Up for scrutiny
was the music of the Creoles, the Blacks, the Indians, in both Americas.
How was the melting pot in the New World to handle such a wealth of
divergent possibilities?

Foster's melodies were often indistinguishable from folk songs. According to the *Albany State Register*, 1852, his *Old Folks at Home*, originally written for a minstrel group and published in 1851 was

> on everybody's tongue, and consequently in everybody's mouth. Pianos
> and guitars groan with it night and day; sentimental young ladies sing it;
> sentimental young gentlemen warble it in midnight serenades; volatile young
> "bucks" hum it in the midst of their business and pleasures; boatmen roar
> it out stentorially at all times; all the bands play it; amateur flute blowers
> agonize over it at every spare moment; the street organs grind it out at
> every hour; the "singing stars" carol it on the theatrical boards, and at con-
> certs; the chamber maid sweeps and dusts to the measured cadence of *Old
> Folks at Home;* the butcher's boy treats you to a strain or two of it as he
> hands in the steaks for dinner; the milkman mixes it up strangely with the
> harsh ding-dong accompaniment of his tireless bell. . . .[10]

While Foster was imitating the songs of the Blacks on one side of the
Atlantic, Gottschalk was playing Afro-Caribbean rhythms on the piano
across the ocean. In 1852 he made a highly successful tour of France,
Switzerland, and Spain, playing his compositions, many of which were
based on the chants of the Negroes and Creoles of Louisiana. Gottschalk,
born in New Orleans of an English father and a mother of French-Spanish
descent, had been sent to Paris to study the piano with Charles Hallé
(1819–1895), later founder of the Hallé Orchestra, and with Camille
Marie Stamaty (1811–1870), student of Kalkbrenner and Mendelssohn,

---

10. Reprinted in *Dwight's Journal of Music* (Boston: October 2, 1852), p. 202.

and teacher of Camille Saint-Saëns. Gottschalk also studied harmony with Pierre Maleden.

In 1853 Gottschalk made a grand tour of the United States. In contrast to the unstinted acclaim he had received in New York and New Orleans, the reviews of his concerts in Boston were disappointing, as is evident from this excerpt:

> The extravagant fame and the peculiar kind of enthusiasm which pre-ceded the arrival of the young New Orleans virtuoso, announced in the bills always as "the great American pianist," had forewarned us what to expect of him. We expected brilliant execution, together with perhaps some little touch of individuality, enough to lend a charm to pretty, but by no means deeply interesting or important compositions of his own. Some of the compositions we had heard from other players, and by their triviality were forced to feel that either these belied him, or that it was by sheer profes-sional puffery that he had been so long proclaimed the peer of Liszt and Thalberg [11] and even Chopin; all of whom, particularly the last, have been true tone poets, of decided individuality, which is stamped upon their writ-ten works, with which the Gottschalk *Bananiers* and *Dances Ossianiques* bear no more comparison than the slightest magazine verses with the in-spired lyrics of the great bards.
>
> Gottschalk's touch is the most clear and crisp and beautiful that we have ever known. His play is free and bold and sure and graceful in the extreme; his runs pure and liquid, his figures always clean and perfectly defined; his command of rapid octave passages prodigious; and so we might go through with all the technical points of masterly execution. It *was* great execution. But what is execution, without some thought and meaning in the combina-tions to be executed?
>
> Could a more trivial and insulting string of musical regmarole have been offered to an audience of earnest music-lovers than *American Reminiscences* to begin with! These consisted of a thin and feeble preluding, in which the right hand ran with exquisitely liquid evenness and brightness up and down the highest octaves, over and over, without any progress of ideas, as if it were mere scale exercise, followed at last by fragmentary and odd *allusions* to *Old Folks at Home*, and then by that homely tune (which seems to be a sort of catching, melodic *itch* of the times), fully developed, and then varied in divers difficult and astounding ways. Also *O Susanna* (if we re-member rightly) in the same fashion. There was an eruption of silly ap-plause here, and an encore which he answered with—*Yankee Doodle!* [12]

It was some forty years later that Dvořák set out to find the clue to an American national music.

---

11. Sigismond Thalberg (1812–1871) was a pianist adept at playing virtuoso pieces and salon music. Liszt said of him, "Thalberg is the only artist who can play the violin on the keyboard."
12. From "Gottschalk in Boston—Then and Now," in *Dwight's Journal of Music* (October 11, 1862), p. 222.

Music in America*

It is a difficult task at best for a foreigner to give a correct verdict of the affairs of another country. With the United States of America this is more than usually difficult, because they cover such a vast area of land that it would take many years to become properly acquainted with the various localities, separated by great distances, that would have to be considered when rendering a judgment concerning them all. It would ill become me, therefore, to express my views on so general and all-embracing a subject as music in America, were I not pressed to do so, for I have neither travelled extensively, nor have I been here long enough to gain an intimate knowledge of American affairs. I can only judge of it from what I have observed during my limited experience as a musician and teacher in America, and from what those whom I know here tell me about their own country. Many of my impressions therefore are those of a foreigner who has not been here long enough to overcome the feeling of strangeness, and bewildered astonishment which must fill all European visitors upon their first arrival.

The two American traits which most impress the foreign observer, I find, are the unbounded patriotism and capacity for enthusiasm of most Americans. Unlike the more diffident inhabitants of other countries, who do not "wear their hearts upon their sleeves," the citizens of America are always patriotic, and no occasion seems to be too serious or too slight for them to give expression to this feeling. Thus nothing better pleases the average American, especially the American youth, than to be able to say that this or that building, this or that new patent appliance, is the finest or grandest in the world. This, of course, is due to that other trait—enthusiasm. The enthusiasm of most Americans for all things new is apparently without limit. It is the essence of what is called "push"—American push. Every day I meet with this quality in my pupils. They are unwilling to stop at anything. In the matters relating to their art they are inquisitive to a degree that they want to go to the bottom of all things at once. It is as if a boy wished to dive before he could swim.

At first, when my American pupils were new to me, this trait annoyed me, and I wished them to give more attention to the one matter in hand rather than to everything at once. But now I like it; for I have come to the conclusion that this youthful enthusiasm and eagerness to take up everything is the best promise for music in America. The same opinion, I remember, was expressed by the director of the new conservatory in Berlin, who, from his experience with American students of music, predicted that America within twenty or thirty years would become the first musical country. . . .

A while ago I suggested that inspiration for truly national music might be derived from the negro melodies or Indian chants. I was led to take this view partly by the fact that the so-called plantation songs are indeed the most striking and appealing melodies that have yet been found on this side of the water, but largely by the observation that this seems to be recog-

*From Antonin Dvořák, "Music in America," Harper's New Monthly *Magazine*, XC, No. 537 (February 1895), 430–34.

nized, though often unconsciously, by most Americans. All races have their distinctively national songs, which they at once recognize as their own, even if they have never heard them before. When a Czech, a Pole, or a Magyar in this country suddenly hears one of his folk-songs or dances, no matter if it is for the first time in his life, his eye lights up at once, and his heart within him responds, and claims that music as its own. So it is with those of Teutonic or Celtic blood, or any other men, indeed, whose first lullaby mayhap was a song wrung from the heart of the people.

It is a proper question to ask, what songs, then, belong to the American and appeal more strongly to him than any others? What melody could stop him on the street if he were in a strange land and make the home feeling well up within him, no matter how hardened he might be or how wretchedly the tune were played? Their number, to be sure, seems to be limited. The most potent as well as the most beautiful among them, according to my estimation, are certain of the so-called plantation melodies and slave songs, all of which are distinguished by unusual and subtle harmonies, the like of which I have found in no other songs but those of old Scotland and Ireland. The point has been urged that many of these touching songs, like those of Foster, have not been composed by the negroes themselves, but are the work of white men, while others did not originate on the plantation, but were imported from Africa. It seems to me that this matters but little. One might as well condemn the Hungarian Rhapsody because Liszt could not speak Hungarian. . . .

If, as I have been informed they were, these songs were adopted by the negroes on the plantations, they thus became true negro songs. Whether the original songs which must have inspired the composers came from Africa or originated on the plantations matters as little as whether Shakespeare invented his own plots or borrowed them from others. The thing to rejoice over is that such lovely songs exist and are sung at the present day. I, for one, am delighted by them. Just so it matters little whether the inspiration for the coming folk-songs of America is derived from the negro melodies, the songs of the creoles, the red man's chant, or the plaintive ditties of the homesick German or Norwegian. Undoubtedly the germs for the best of music lie hidden among all the races that are commingled in this great country. The music of the people is like a rare and lovely flower growing amidst encroaching weeds. Thousands pass it, while others trample it under foot, and thus the chances are that it will perish before it is seen by the one discriminating spirit who will prize it above all else. The fact that no one has as yet arisen to make the most of it does not prove that nothing is there.

12.6 CÉSAR ANTONOVICH CUI (1835–1918)

Toward the end of the nineteenth century Russian music was torn between two camps. On one side were composers continuing to write in the European tradition; on the other were those who considered themselves direct representatives of the Russian folk. When Peter Ilyich Tchaikovsky (1840–1893) used Russian folk tunes in his symphonies, ballets, fantasies, marches, and piano pieces, the melodies became indistinguishable from his own. He was not trying to preserve their national character any more than he sought to make his symphonic fantasy *The Tempest* purely English or his *Italian Capriccio* purely Italian. Tchaikovsky had studied with Anton Rubinstein (1829–1894), who was European-trained before he established the Conservatory at St. Petersburg. In the other camp were the "young Petersburg composers," Nikolay Rimsky-Korsakov (1844–1908), César Cui, Alexander Borodin (1833–1887), Modest Moussorgsky (1839–1881), and Mily Balakirev (1837–1910), who came to be known as the Russian *Five*.

Tchaikovsky, in a letter to his patronness, Madame Nadezhda von Meck, dated December 24, 1877 wrote:

> The young Petersburg composers are very gifted, but they are all impregnated with the most horrible presumptuousness and a purely amateur conviction of their superiority to all other musicians in the universe. The one exception, in later days, has been Rimsky-Korsakov. . . . Five years ago he began to study with such zeal that the theory of the schools soon became to him an indispensable atmosphere. During one summer he completed innumerable exercises in counterpoint and sixty-four fugues, ten of which he sent me for inspection. From contempt for the schools, Rimsky-Korsakov suddenly went over to the cult of musical technique. . . . At present he appears to be passing through a crisis, and it is hard to predict how it will end. Either he will turn out a great master, or be lost in contrapuntal intricacies.
>
> Moussorgsky's gifts are perhaps the most remarkable of all, but his nature is narrow and he has no aspirations towards self-perfection. . . . He likes what is coarse, unpolished, and ugly. He is the exact opposite of the distinguished and elegant Cui.

Cui wrote the first book on Russian music that took into account its various aspects. *La Musique en Russie* (Music in Russia), dedicated to Franz Liszt, was published in Paris in 1880. It was natural for Cui to express himself in French, the native tongue of his father, who had served in Napoleon's army and had settled as a French teacher in Vilna.

Popular Russian Songs*

What is sung outside of Russia as Russian folk music, is most frequently nothing but dull and banale modern composition, attributable to some dilettante and adapted to a quasi-national text. These insignificant, antimusical trifles are generally propagated in Europe by certain Italian singers,

*César Cui, La Musique en Russie *(Paris, 1881), pp. 3–7, 11–17, 23–24, 31, 36–38, 70–79.*

partly because these songs do not exceed the level of their musical intelligence, but above all to express in some way their gratitude to a country which received them so well during the opera season. These pseudo-Russian *romances*, to tell the truth, are distinguished from the duller platitudes of certain Italian pieces only by their uneven division and the affectation of the minor mode in a continuous stream which is erroneously thought to be the most striking characteristic of the music of the Russian people. That is a gross error, because, besides the national songs tinged with a feeling of profound sadness, nothing is commoner than to find others filled with warmth and with true cheerfulness. It could even be that these are the most numerous. . . .

Russian folk songs are ordinarily restricted to a small compass within the octave, rarely exceeding the interval of a fifth or a sixth. And the older the song, the smaller is the extent of its compass. . . . These songs have evidently come down through the medium of a multitude of spokesmen and interpretations. After the original text had been altered or lost, that text which was so carefully accentuated in the prosody of the first composer, the tune remained in the memory of the people, who no longer took the trouble of adapting to it the original words.

Folk melodies are sung by a single voice or a chorus. In the latter case, the soloist starts and the song is taken up by the chorus. The harmony of these songs is preserved by tradition. It is very original. The different parts of the chorus converge or separate, coming to a unison or forming a chord. But often these chords are not complete. Ordinarily polyphonic melodies close on a unison.

The songs for a single voice are frequently accompanied by a small stringed instrument called a *balalaika* (a sort of theorbo, in a triangular shape, whose strings are plucked or caused to vibrate like a *glissando*). As for the choral compositions, they very rarely have an accompaniment. This part, when it exists, is performed by a sort of oboe, which improvises a variety of designs in counterpoint on the given melody, no doubt with little conformance to the strict rules of the art, but very picturesque.

One can classify Russian folk songs in the following manner: *rounds*, choruses sung on holidays, accompanied by certain games and dances; *songs for special occasions*, of which the wedding song is the most cultivated type; *street songs*, serenades for chorus, jovial or burlesque; *work songs* or *sailors' songs;* melodies for a single voice of every type and description.[13]

Glinka and His Predecessors

From Italy, its land of origin, opera spread progressively to all the other countries of Europe. It did not penetrate Russia until rather late, after it had already attained a certain development in occidental Europe.

In 1735, under the reign of Empress Anna Ivanovna, an Italian troupe, directed by the composer Francesco Araja was called to St. Petersburg and gave performances there in their own language. Russian opera was not established until Empress Elizabeth Petrovna. They succeeded in forming, at her request and after many difficulties, a troupe of Russian singers who performed, in 1755, the first opera written on a national text. But the actual

13. Balakirev made a collection of Russian folk songs, as did Rimsky-Korsakov.

work, *Cephalo and Procris*, of which Sumarokov was the librettist, was
not really set to music by Araja at all. A series of other operas was composed under the same conditions: the libretto, written in Russian, was offered to the Italians, mainly to the musical directors of the Italian troupe. . . .

The honor of creating Russian opera goes to Michael Glinka, one of the
greatest musical geniuses who ever lived, without limitation of time or place.

Glinka was born at Novosspaskoye in 1804. He was the descendent of a
rich family of landowners, members of the nobility in the government of
Smolensk. From earliest youth he had a passion for music. As a child he
attentively followed the carillon of the church bells and then reproduced
it very skillfully by tapping alternately on two copper basins. Later his
uncle's private orchestra inspired in him lively enthusiastic impulses, especially during the performance of fantasies on national Russian themes. . . .

In 1817 he was taken to St. Petersburg and placed in a boarding school
for the nobility. There he applied himself to the study of languages (he
knew 6), geography, zoology, etc. He left college in 1822, after having won
the first prize. He continued his piano lessons at St. Petersburg, especially
with Field and Charles Mayer, and acquired a real talent for playing, distinguished by neatness of execution and the charm of his touch. As for the
subject of harmony and theory, he studied either at St. Petersburg or
abroad, but never without following a complete and systematic course. It
was at Berlin, under the tutelage of Dehn that he worked in the most serious manner.[14] . . .

The work which established his reputation and set the date (1836) for
the new era of Russian music was the opera in four acts and an epilogue,
A Life for the Czar. The subject was recommended to him by the celebrated poet Zhukovski. The music for *A Life for the Czar* is all borrowed
from the Russian and Polish. In the whole opera there is probably not a
single musical phrase having more affinity with the music of western
Europe than with that of the Slavs. Such a marked degree of nationality,
united with the highest conditions of the art, is only found, it seems to us,
in the *Freischütz* [Section 11.1].

The subject of Glinka's second opera, *Russlan and Ludmila*, is borrowed
from one of the first poems of the great Pushkin, whose works lend themselves admirably to music, and have almost all served as themes for Russian
musicians. *Russlan* is a fantastic tale in which heroes, magicians, etc., figure.

The third act starts with a ravishing chorus of women, a Persian melody
with variations, of which one of the most intriguing is that which modulates
to minor, with triplets in the cellos establishing an organ point. Then follows a delightfully enchanting air sung by Gorislawa (an old favorite of

14. Siegfried Wilhelm Dehn (1799–1858) was the first musician to transcribe the
Penitential Psalms of Orlandus Lassus (Section 7.2) into modern notation. In his
book entitled *Theoretische-praktische Harmonielehre* (Berlin, 1840) Dehn differentiated the functions of thoroughbass and counterpoint as follows:

Thoroughbass is differentiated from counterpoint mainly in the fact that in
thoroughbass the main given voice to which the other voices are composed must
be a bass voice, which contains within itself the harmonic relationships of several voices to each other, and stipulates the conditions through the figures. In
counterpoint, on the other hand, the main voice to which the other voices are
compared may be either one of the two outer voices, the upper as well as the
lower voice, or any one of the middle voices.

the oriental prince, Ratmer), written in a very high range and demanding an exceptional voice. The *Adagio commodo assai* of Ratmer's air, in a poetic manner, conveys the feeling of tender dreaminess inspired by a night in the orient, calm, mild, fragrant, studded with stars. In the middle of the recitative joining the slow part to the *Allegro*, appears this oriental theme, in minor, adorned with a harmony full of charm, and made of it a piece where a frolicsome dream is intermingled with deep emotion.

Moderato
English horn

In the fourth act Glinka borrows another characteristic from oriental music. From the comic, from the bizarre (the march and the first part of the dances), he creates something with a fresh, piquant originality, which cannot be described in words. It is not less difficult to explain all the subtle, ingenious details of the instrumentation in that part of the opera (theme of the trio of the march), of the harmony and of the counterpoints which one finds there, for example a descending scale which runs through the whole orchestra, from high to low, on the theme of the dances. Liszt made a piano transcription of the march [1847]. The second part of the dances of the fourth act is a *lesguinka*, the most lively musical incarnation of oriental emotion, as wild as a desert steed.

The New Russian School

In 1856 two musicians, very young and deeply interested in their art, met at St. Petersburg. Since the capital of Russia was the principal musical and intellectual seat of the country, they definitely decided to establish residence there. One was Balakirev; the other, the author of these pages. Some time afterwards, Rimsky-Korsakov, Borodin, and Moussorgsky joined them, and, little by little, they formed a small circle of friends who shared the same lively passion for the art of music. What interesting and instructive discussions formed the basis for their meetings! They consciously reviewed almost all the existing musical literature. Criticism was the name of the game. Esthetic questions were deliberated; individual ideas on seeing and feeling were compared. Conferences thrived on lively analyses, on divers plans, on a thousand things that activate thought, nourish and develop taste, and seize the awakened artistic sense. It is thus that this small coterie succeeded in arriving at decisive tenets, by creating for itself a criterion applicable to a host of artistic questions, very often contrary to the current ideas of the press and the public. The ideal common to the members of that small society—with one reservation, the aptitude and the musical nature of each individual—soon began to take shape with clarity, and they strove to establish it in their works.

These artists justifiably thought that symphonic music had reached its complete development, thanks to Beethoven, Schumann, Liszt, and Berlioz who, exceeding all bounds, created masterpieces of variety and expression, free of all restraint. In this style of composition was revealed the depth of their genius, inspired emotion, the splendor of melodic language, paired with a harmony of inexhaustible wealth. The four traditional voice-parts of Haydn's style were no longer law. Beethoven introduced song and massive choruses into his Ninth Symphony. Schumann adds a fifth movement [in his Symphony No. 3 in E♭ major]. Liszt, in his series of symphonic poems, unites the separate episodes into a unified whole and courageously innovates the descriptive genre of *program music*. Likewise Berlioz, entirely on the principle of *expression* in music, paints while he writes. He too introduces vocal passages into his symphonies [*Romeo and Juliet*]. Besides, we see him give preponderant importance to certain orchestral instruments (the obbligato viola in *Harold in Italy*).

Haven't these powerful musicians done their best to deliver the symphonic work from all its shackles? Therefore one might reasonably suppose that henceforth there would be little that is new to add to what has already been done in this genre, and that the symphonic forms have all attained perfection.

It is otherwise with matters pertaining to opera. Dramatic music is still in a transitory state. The styles of the various genres of opera have not yet been immutably established. Neither the subject as a whole nor the text in all its parts are, in general, coordinated well enough in vocal music. Actually, opera is in a third evolution—which is probably not its last—on a direct route toward its ultimate goal, which consists of accentuation by enlivening, with musical sounds, the word which translates the thought. Wasn't this the idea that has possessed opera since its origin in the sixteenth century? . . .

The new Russian school endeavored to bring to light certain principles of the utmost importance, of which one of the first is this: *Dramatic music must always have intrinsic value as absolute music, apart from the text.* . . . What, with complete justification, would have been relegated to disdain in a symphonic composition, naturally found its place in opera. . . .

Vocal music must be in perfect agreement with the sense of the words. . . .

For music as well as for the libretto, *the structure of the scenes composing an opera must depend entirely on the relationship of the characters, as well as on the general movement of the piece.*

The new Russian school never rejects ensembles or choruses, but it wants the scenes in this genre to be seriously motivated. It is not necessary for the pace of the drama to slow down because of them. Thus, the choruses represent the crowds and the people, not only the choristers. They must offer a sense of determination, multitude, and tumult, and must not be interspersed between the other pieces for the sole purpose of creating a contrast, or for allowing the soloists to rest. . . .

Accordingly, as the musicians constituting the small circle mentioned at the beginning of this chapter saw the light, as stable, lucid, rational convictions took shape, they tried to put into practice the principles of their artistic creed, unshaken from that time on. In a little while they turned out a series of operas, conceived on these precepts. They appeared in the following order: *William Ratcliff* (on a subject by H. Heine), César Cui, 1869; *The Stone Guest*, Dargomyzhsky, 1872; *The Maid of Pskov*, Rimsky-

Korsakov, 1873; *Boris Godunov,* Moussorgsky, 1874; *Angelo* (drama by Victor Hugo), C. Cui, 1876.

12.7 EDVARD GRIEG (1843–1907)

Edvard Grieg, trained in the spirit of German Romanticism during his years of study at the Leipzig Conservatory, was soon caught up in plans to preserve the musical tradition of his own country. Grieg was encouraged in this direction by the Norwegian violinist Ole Bull (1810–1880), who had learned many of the old melodies from peasant fiddlers, and by the first modern composer with a distinctive Scandinavian style, Niels Gade (1817–1890), who taught the 20-year-old Grieg at Copenhagen.

Local melodies and harmonies penetrated Grieg's compositions consciously as well as intuitively. In Christiania, the town where Grieg's nephew lived, the organist Ludwig Lindeman had collected and published over 700 Norwegian mountain melodies and ballads before composing the *Chorale Book for the Norwegian Church* (1877). The trend toward preserving the folk music was well on its way when Knut Dale, a fiddler in Telemark, called on Grieg for help with the dance tunes he had assimilated. As indicated in the correspondence below, the intermediary between Dale and Grieg was Johan Halvorsen (1864–1935), a composer-conductor married to one of Grieg's nieces.

After Grieg had written his *Lyric Pieces,* Opus 71, he adapted for the piano the fiddle tunes that Halvorsen notated.[15] For this publication, his Opus 72, *Norwegian Bauerntänze (Slåtter),* Grieg wrote a highly informative preface, also quoted below.

Preservation and Adaptation of Norwegian Fiddle Tunes*

Letter from Halvorsen to Grieg

Christiania November 8, 1901

Knut Dale has come. Today we rescued two tunes from oblivion. It is not so easy to write them down. There are small turns and trills in them

The letters are from David Monrad-Johansen, Edvard Grieg, trans. Madge Robertson (Princeton, N.J.: Princeton University Press, 1938), pp. 345–347. Printed by permission of the American-Scandinavian Foundation. The Preface material is from Norwegische Bauerntänze (Slätter) für die Geige solo wie dieselben auf der norwegischen Bauernfiedel gespielt werden. Originalaufzeichnung von Johan Halvorsen. Freie Bearbeitung für Pianoforte solo von Edvard Grieg, *Opus 72; Preface. Reprint permission granted by C. F. Peters Corporation, New York.*

15. Ironically, aside from his orchestral suites on Norwegian themes, Halvorsen's name is remembered today for his arrangement of Handel's *Passacaglia* for violin, and viola or cello.

like a trout in a rapid—when you try to get hold of them they are off. Knut Dale is an intelligent and sound fiddler. Now and again he had some rhythmic turns, a blending of $\frac{2}{4}$ and $\frac{6}{8}$ time that made me laugh aloud with delight—and that does not happen often. He seems to have many dances in his storehouse. I must have him here for a fortnight or three weeks. He sends greetings and thanks for the money.

December 3, 1901

Dear Grieg!

I am sending with this the result of Knut Dale's stay in Christiania. I hope you will find something you like. I have tried to put everything down as carefully as possible. Repetitions there are in plenty, but that is very easy to put right. As regards the key, there is one curious feature—that G♯ is almost always used (at the beginning of the D major tunes). Not till towards the end (on the deeper strings) comes G. For myself, I find the G♯ fresh and delightful where G would have been insipid.[16] Then there were the trills and the grace notes. These trills are the soul and adornment of the fiddle dances together with the rhythm. They are produced often by only a vibration of the hand and give the effect of a kind of *quivering*. An exception is the trill on the open A which sounds out clear and fresh. I noticed that even the most complicated grace notes or trills did not take away in the slightest from the rhythmic lines of the tunes. I am practicing every day on the Haring fiddle [17] and have managed to achieve not a little of the *real thing*. A fiddle like that chuckles and chatters and whines and quivers. And how beautiful it can sound, for example, Möllarguten's wedding march.[18] Of the walking dances I think *Skuldalsbruri* takes the prize. I ought to get hold of Sjur Helgeland and Ole Moc and all the rest of them now that I have begun the job.

Grieg to Halvorsen

Troldhaugen December 6, 1901

This is what I call a real Saturday night, dear Halvorsen. Outside a storm from the south is thundering, shaking the house, and on top of it a proper deluge is pouring down from Heaven. But in the sitting room it is cosy.

16. In the D scale the note G♯ creates the interval of a tritone or augmented fourth with the tonic, a concept foreign to harmony based on perfect fourths and fifths. A traditional Arabian or Persian mode based on this pattern of steps had been noted by the Englishman William Jones in his treatise entitled *On the Musical Modes of the Hindus* (1784). Halvorsen, however, thinks of the pattern with an augmented fourth from the tonic as a deviation from the major mode rather than as an independent mode of the folk. The "trills and grace notes" of which he speaks are also deviations from the smoothed-out major-minor system. Greig knows otherwise, as he indicates in his response to Halvorsen.
17. Translator's footnote: The Haring fiddle. (Hardanger fiddle is a special sort of violin with two sets of strings, the lower set continuously sounding like the drone bass.)
18. Knut Dale had learned the melodies from the fiddler, Möllarguten.

I have just received your tunes for the fiddle and have this moment finished reading them through, chuckling inwardly with delight. But at the same time, I have been raging and burning over not being a player of the fiddle. How I do hate that Conservatory in Leipzig! But to business: Those *singularities* you speak of regarding G♯ in D major was what used to send the blood running wildly and madly in my veins in the year 1871. Naturally, I stole it at once in my folk-like pictures. That note is something for the research worker. The augmented fourth can also be heard in peasants' songs. They are revenants from some old scale or other. But which? Incomprehensible that no one among us takes up research in our national music, since in our folk music we have such rich well-springs for those who have ears to hear, hearts to feel, and understanding to write down. At present I am feeling as if it would be a sin to adapt the tunes for the piano. But that sin I shall come to commit sooner or later. It is too tempting. I send the heartiest thanks for your work, which has given me a very great happiness, and the future will show that you have done more than that. It won't be before summer that I can get down to them. Would you like me, when the time comes, to place both your work and mine with Peters?

Preface to *Norwegische Bauerntänze*

These Norwegian *Slåtter* (*Slåt* is the usual Norwegian name for the peasant's dance), now for the first time brought before the public in their original form for the violin (or for the so-called Hardanger-fiddle) and re-arranged for the piano, were written down after an old gleeman in Telemarken. Those who can appreciate such music, will be delighted at the originality, the blending of fine, soft gracefulness with sturdy almost uncouth power and untamed wildness as regards melody and more particularly rhythm, contained in them. This music—which is handed down to us from an age when the culture of the Norwegian peasant was isolated in its solitary mountain-valleys from the outer world, to which fact it owes its whole originality—bears the stamp of an imagination as daring in its flight as it is peculiar.

My object in arranging the music for the piano was to raise these works of the people to an artistic level, by giving them what I might call a style of musical concord, or bringing them under a system of harmony. Naturally, many of the little embellishments, characteristic of the peasant's fiddle and of their peculiar manner of bowing, cannot be reproduced on the piano, and had accordingly to be left out. On the other hand, by virtue of its manifold dynamic and rhythmic qualities, the piano affords the great advantage of enabling us to avoid a monotonous uniformity, by varying the harmony of repeated passages or parts. I have endeavored to make myself clear in the lines set forth, in fact, to obtain a definite form. The few passages in which I considered myself authorized as an artist, to add to, or work out the given motives, will easily be found, on comparing my arrangement with the original written down by Johan Halvorsen, in a manner reliable even for research-work, and published by the same firm.

The *Slåtter* sounds a minor third higher, when played on the peasant's fiddle; nevertheless, I have retained the key in which the original is written down, in order to obtain a fuller effect on the piano.

12.8 BÉLA BARTÓK (1881–1945)
THROUGH OTTO GOMBOSI

Grieg worked with Norwegian folk songs in his native land; Dvořák came to America imbued with the Czech spirit; Bartók brought Hungarian and Rumanian folk songs along with him when he came to America. The folk songs with which Grieg worked were authentic to the extent that he had someone take them down as played by a country fiddler. The songs which Dvořák heard as representative Americana did not come to him first-hand; Dvořák had no direct contact with Negro or Indian music, nor had he heard the songs of the Southern Appalachians and the folk ballads of New England.

Bartók used more sophisticated means for examining folk songs than did either of his predecessors. Working with Zoltán Kodály, Bartók went to the countryside and mechanically recorded the songs of the Hungarian and Rumanian peasants before transcribing them. They sought means to account for the minute differences between intervals; they were not content merely to regard every interval as some multiple of an equally tempered semitone. Alexander Ellis (1814–1890) had developed a system with 100 cents in a semitone, so that deviations down to the smallest microtone could be defined. Walter Fewkes had already recorded songs of the American Indians on Edison cylinders.[19] The time was ripe for Bartók and Kodály to listen past the rigid scales and rhythms to hear continuous pitch (*glissando*) as well as free rhythm (*parlando-rubato*).[20]

Bartók was also a brilliant pianist. He made a tour of the United States in 1927–28 and then returned in 1940, this time to settle here. Bartók had recently completed the 153 progressive pieces for piano entitled *Mikrokosmos* (1926–37), the *Contrasts* for violin, clarinet, and piano (1938), his Violin Concerto (1939), and his sixth String Quartet (1939). He was yet to write the Concerto for Orchestra commissioned by Serge Koussevitsky for the Boston Symphony Orchestra (1944). In an article written for the *New York Times* in 1940 the Hungarian musicologist Otto Gombosi (1902–1955) successfully entwines Bartók's love of folklore with his stylistic development as a composer of art music.

---

19. Bruno Nettl, *Theory and Method in Ethnomusicology* (London: The Free Press of Glencoe, Collier-Macmillan, 1964), pp. 16–17.
20. Bartók's collections include: *Rumanian Folksongs from the Bihor District* (Bucharest, 1913), *Transylvanian Folksongs*, with Kodály (Budapest, 1923), *Hungarian Folk Music* (London, 1931), *Serbo-Croatian Folk Songs*, with Albert B. Lord (New York, 1951).

The Art of the Hungarian Composer Bartók*

An Estimate of the Music of a Contemporary Who Is on a Visit Here

Béla Bartók is again among us, many years after his last visit to this country. The noted Hungarian composer is playing and lecturing at different places. . . .

Béla Bartók first became known as a brilliant concert pianist, while his faculty as a composer in the creation of a language of his own developed only step by step. Liszt and Richard Strauss gave him the first great impulses. In his early symphonic poem, *Kossuth,* which brought him his first harvest of international success, the future creator of a new style can be recognized. The Rhapsody for Piano and Orchestra, Op. 1 was the first masterpiece. It is perhaps the only composition which incarnated the ideal of a Hungarian music, created, but never brought to perfection, by Liszt. It is rather superfluous to discuss the artistic merits of such a stylistic trend. In this composition, however, its peak has been reached. It is the work of a genius who had not yet found his proper way.

A rather unique and fortunate constellation helped the young composer to develop his latent faculties. . . . With some other young composers, Bartók went through the country, collecting the songs of the farmer population and getting an intimate knowledge of this much more true and much less known Hungarian music. Gradually he extended the work to the folklore of the neighboring peoples, and eventually to Arabian and Turkish music.

Through this work, his first impressions of childhood and his musical heritage were awakened and the path of the peculiar possibilities of his artistic expression cleared. At once, the preliminaries for creating a new style were in his possession.

From this moment on, the two-fold activity of Bartók began: the creative and the scientific. The first again, has two aspects. On the one side there is a restless interest in all that is new, and an impulse to try and examine its possibilities. On the other side there is a gradual assimilation of his inspiration to the folklore, and the self-conscious building up of the artistic possibilities presented by this kind of melody.

The development of Bartók's style follows a straight line. He never broke with the past. His forms and problems often recall Beethoven and more recently, Bach. This solid background protected him against any colorful but superficial exoticism. His technical skill and his rich and peculiar ability of expression soon developed the interested observer and indefatigable experimenter into one of the most compelling and leading masters of modern music.

What has Bartók given to modern music? First, a richness of new harmonic possibilities. The influence of Debussy did not lead him into coloristic

* From Otto Gombosi, "The Art of the Hungarian Composer Bartók," The New York Times, *Music Section, May 5, 1940,* © *1940 by the New York Times Company. Reprinted by permission.*

effects, but to an ingenious and daring extension of tonality to the utmost limits. Then he gave to modern music a kind of rhythm which seems to incorporate the elemental powers of nature—a rhythm creating form. He gave to modern music a flourishing melody, which grew up from assimilated elements of folklore to a quite individual richness and originality. He gave examples of formal perfection, growing organically from the material. And finally, he gave to modern music a ripe polyphony that has very little to do with "neoclassicism" and which is formed with an iron consistency that reaches extreme possibilities. Works like the last string quartets, the Music for Strings, the Concerto for two pianos and percussion, are lasting value in modern music, both as regards formal perfection and expressive power.

Stylistic catchwords can hardly grasp this richness. In its deepest fundamentals, Bartók's music is of an elemental strength; it is orgiastic in its severity and its visionary poetry. Rhythm of extreme potency is one of its most characteristic features. This rhythm gives his music that Dionysian strain that produces its elemental effect, besides also giving it the strong backbone of the vision of sound. This is the reason for the pantomimic aptitude of this music, which found its strongest expression in Bartók's few stage works.

It is difficult to foretell the way of human meteors. Bartók, who is now 59, will certainly write many surprising works. The surprise will certainly not consist of capricious breaks in the stylistic line, but of the still increasing expansion of his horizon and of the growing lapidarity of his means of expression.

12.9 MANUEL DE FALLA (1876–1958)
THROUGH JOHN BRANDE TREND

In the twentieth century the guitar, which had been relegated to outdoor serenading or drawing-room entertainment when the violin family made its appearance, was again called into play by Spanish composers, notably, Manuel de Falla. In Madrid, de Falla studied with Felipe Pedrell (1841–1922), the composer and musicologist who edited Spanish music of the Renaissance (*Hispaniae Schola musica sacra*)[21] and collected Spanish folk songs (*Cancionero popular español*, 1919–29). From Madrid, de Falla went to Paris where he became acquainted with Debussy, Dukas, and Ravel.

John Brande Trend (1887–1958), who reminisced about de Falla in the excerpt quoted below, was an Englishman. After living in Spain, where he wrote *Manuel de Falla and Spanish Music*, Trend became professor of Spanish at Cambridge University.

21. Eight volumes of music containing the works of Morales, Victoria, Cabezón, and Ortiz, among others. Diego Ortiz is still remembered for his treatise on diminution and variation for the viola da gamba (1553).

The Spanish Guitar*

I was able to make closer acquaintance with the guitar in a house just outside the Alhambra. The player, whose father's house it was, Don Angel Barrios, is a composer of distinction and one of the best guitarists in Spain. On hot summer nights Falla and he would sit on the patio, where by means of a towel the fountain had been muffled, but not altogether silenced, and the guitar would be ingeniously transposed into a sharp key by the *cejuela* [or *capotasto*], screwed across the end of the fingerboard. As autumn came on, we took refuge in a small room hung with hams and sausages and lined with little kegs of *manzanilla;* and when Falla was confined to his bedroom with a cold, Barrios would come every evening with his guitar. I learned then that the guitar, as he played it, was not merely a part of the "National legend," or "one of the signs of national barbarity," as some Spaniards declare, but a thoroughly serious and admirable instrument. Falla has always treated the guitar seriously; and when the editor of the *Revue musicale* invited him to send something "*pour le tombeau de Claude Debussy*," he wrote his *Homenaje* for the guitar, and it was first tried over in his room at one of the meetings I have described.

Falla believes intensely in the future of the guitar. But at this point some reader may interrupt with a certain show of contempt: "Future? I should have thought it an instrument of the past: one *with* a past, at all events!" It is true that, with us, the idea of "playing on the Spanish guitar" has somehow acquired a curiously disreputable significance, while the instrument itself is—or was, until the arrival of Andrés Segovia [22]—regarded as a piece of romantic stage furniture. "No," says Falla. "Not at all! Romantic times were precisely those in which the guitar was at its worst; and then, of course, it spread all over Europe. It was made to play the sort of music that other instruments played, but it was not really suitable for nineteenth-century music, and so it dropped out. It is coming back again, because it is peculiarly adapted for modern music."

He went on to explain why. The six strings of the guitar are tuned in fourths, with a third in the middle: E, A, D, G, B, E. That instruments tuned in fifths are not particularly apt for modern music might be suspected from the fact that the technique of the violin has practically stood still since the days of Paganini.[23] By means of daring *scordature* Paganini was able to do what very few modern violinists would care to attempt now, for the violin is a "high-tension" instrument as it is, and the general tendency of modern orchestras is towards a further rise of pitch for the sake

From John Brande Trend, Manuel de Falla and Spanish Music *(New York: Alfred A. Knopf, Inc., 1929), pp. 38–43. Reprinted by permission of Alfred A. Knopf, Inc.*

22. Segovia gave his first public recital on the guitar in Granada in 1907, at the age of 14. Since then he has toured the world many times as a virtuoso guitarist.
23. Niccolò Paganini (1728–1840), one of the most famous violin virtuosos who ever lived, was known to have retuned his instrument to tones other than the customary tuning for the violin's open strings: G, D, A, E. This procedure, known as *scordatura,* was done in order to be able to play runs in double-stops and to perform other technical feats not otherwise feasible on the violin.

of brilliance. Moreover, in spite of the studies by Sor,[24] and the beautifully executed transcriptions with which Segovia has made us familiar, music of the later eighteenth and nineteenth centuries does not seem so apt for the guitar as music written since the time of Debussy. This is due partly to Debussy's harmonic scheme and to his widening of the range of harmonic and rhythmic expression (which came to him from the study of Spanish and oriental music), and partly also to the clearness of the texture of his music, which was necessary to bring out all its subtleties of rhythm and color. It is partly due also to the fact that modern composers have grown tired of the smoothness and fullness of massed strings supported by a rich round tone in the brass and are aiming at something clearer, in which bowed instruments have a comparatively small part.

Paganini also wrote for the guitar: but it is interesting to observe his elementary treatment of that instrument (a strange contrast to his treatment of the violin) as shown in the quartets for guitar and strings, written for drawing-room use and *dedicati alle amatrici* [dedicated to the amateur].

The guitar in Spain is not a drawing-room instrument; indeed, the circumstances under which it is often used are as remote from a drawing-room as anything in Europe, and in the hands of quite an ordinary player it can be made to do astonishing things. The effects of harmony produced unconsciously by guitarists in Andalucía are among the marvels of untutored art. There are two methods of playing. *Basguear*, "thrumming," consists of repeated chords in which all the five or six notes are seldom changed at once, and the notes which are held on—to steady the hand—produce an "internal pedal-point" such as we find in the sonatas of Domenico Scarlatti. *Puntear*, on the other hand, is the playing of different notes in succession. It is probable (Falla says) that the Spanish instrumentalists of the sixteenth century were among the first to play an accompaniment of repeated chords to a vocal or instrumental melody. Further, from the earliest times a distinction has been made in Spain between the *guitarra latina* [playing chords] and the *guitarra morisca* [playing melodies]; while to this day the popular *gembri* and other plucked instruments in Morocco play, not chords, but melodies, while in Andalucía the guitar prefers, not melodies, but chords. Barbarous chords, it used to be said. Falla soon convinced me that they were a marvellous revelation of harmonic possibilities hitherto unsuspected.

The different kinds of song and dance heard in the south of Spain have their own special preludes, with effects of rhythm and harmony (particularly cross-accent and false relation) peculiar to each; but a good player, while keeping within the limits proper to the song or dance he is accompanying, will employ considerable variation, and a master like Barrios can vary his preludes indefinitely. Though I heard him every day for weeks on end, I never grew tired of his playing; and Falla, though he can hear that kind of playing all the year round, can always find something in it to interest him. Even to Falla the guitar is still full of unsuspected possibilities; while to a mere traveller the prelude to a *fandango* is always an electrifying experience.

24. Fernando Sor (1778–1839) was a Spanish guitarist who emigrated to Paris, where he was encouraged to perform by Cherubini and Méhul.

The prelude lasts until the singer considers that the emotion of the audience (and the performer) has been sufficiently worked up; then the voice comes in with a long "*Ay!*" or "*Lelí, lelí,*" [25] followed by the characteristic wavering melody, punctuated at certain places by chords on the guitar and followed, at the end of each verse, by a recapitulation of the prelude.

The most striking feature of southern Spanish song of this kind is the characteristic cadence: la, sol, fa, mi. The melodies of the *fandango* and its derivatives, *malagueñas, rondeñas, granadinas,* etc., as well as the older *soleares, polos, seguidillas* and the rest—the chief exception (as far as I could determine) being the oldest of all, the *siguiriya gitana,* "gipsy *seguidilla*"—seem all to move in a harmonic atmosphere depending upon this "Phrygian" cadence, ending on what is apparently the dominant, which the guitar emphasizes in a way that leaves no doubt as to the effect intended. The *soleà* from Falla's opera *La Vida Breve* [*Life is Short*] is a good example, a movement entirely in the popular style.

Plenty of other instances may be found in Falla's music: in the ballet *El Amor Brujo,* for instance, in the first song; in the *polo* in the collection of *Seven Spanish Songs,* and in various dances in the *Three-Cornered Hat.* It is a cadence which has a long history, since it occurs in the earliest guitar versions of the Spanish (and Portuguese) *folías,* on which Corelli afterwards wrote his celebrated variations; in the accompaniment to *Las Vacas,* upon which lute-players and organists performed countless variations in the sixteenth century; and it was evidently a special favorite with Morales, who introduces it not infrequently into his church music. It occurs on several occasions also in the harpsichord music of Domenico Scarlatti.[26]

25. Trend's footnote: The singer begins by unconsciously reciting the Muslim creed, or a vague memory of it."
26. While Domenico Scarlatti (1685–1757) was maestro of the royal chapel at Lisbon (1719), he wrote *Esercizi for Harpsichord* for his pupil, the Princess Maria Barbara. When she married the Spanish crown prince in 1729, Scarlatti went with her to Madrid. He stayed there to become her maestro de cámara when Maria Barbara became queen in 1746.

13

Music Past, Present, and Future

13.1 CLAUDE DEBUSSY (1862–1918)

The Romantic world of dreams and the supernatural, of Oriental enchantment and traditional charm, were blended into French impressionism. Back in the mid-eighteenth century French scholars were trying to
fathom the musical mysteries of the Far East first-hand. They corresponded extensively with French Jesuit missionaries stationed in Peking and
got them to send two 19-year-old Chinese youths to Paris to study
the languages and sciences of Europe under the tutelage of two members
of the Académie Royale de Science, so that when they returned to China
the young men would have the common background necessary for trans-
mitting knowledge about their country to Europe. In the area of music,
the French missionary who made the main contribution in writing about
the venture was Joseph Marie Amiot (1718–1793)[1] Amiot compared the
Chinese with the French system and concluded,

> Rameau's system conforms to that of the Chinese only to the extent that
> one of the tones generated by the *basse fondamentale* becomes fundamental

1. Amiot, *Memoirs on the Music of the Chinese, Ancient as Well as Modern,* in
*Mémoires concernant l'Histoire, les Sciences, les Arts, les Moeurs, les Usages, Ec.
des Chinois, par les Missionaires de Pe-Kin* (Paris, 1780), VI, 130.

in its turn, thereby generating others. On the other hand, there is a perceptible difference between this system and that of the Chinese, in that a fundamental tone in the European system is supposed to support its third and its fifth; while in the Chinese system each fundamental tone is isolated and does not imply any harmonic, any attendant [*concomitant*] tone in its resonance, a phenomenon concerning which the Chinese happily have not the slightest idea. Here, indeed is the essential difference between the two systems.

A century later, for the Paris Exposition of 1889, the French actually imported the music from distant lands—instruments, performers, scenery, and all. Following is a contemporary description: [2]

Musical Promenades at the Exposition

Rome is no longer in Rome; Cairo is no longer in Egypt; nor is the Isle of Java in the East Indies. All this has come to the Champ de Mars, to the Esplanade des Invalides, and to the Trocadéro. Thus, without going out of Paris, for six months it will be possible for us to study the ways and customs of the most distant peoples, at least in their outward manifestations. And music being, among all these manifestations, one of the most striking, none of the exotic visitors at the Exposition will let you forget it. Not to mention the grand concerts for orchestra, vocal music, organ, etc., the series which is about to open at the Trocadéro—in the diverse sections of the universal Exposition may be found many an occasion to study the musical forms peculiar to the races whose art is composed in a fashion very different from ours. . . .

The music of the Arabs is not unknown to us. But it is so completely different from ours that one may always consider it as new, since it has not penetrated our minds sufficiently to engrave lasting memories. Also, this year we find at the Exposition specimens of music of the peoples from the whole of North Africa. . . . Besides, there are Algerian and Tunisian concerts where one sips hot mocha and smells the perfumed air while delighting in the sounds of the Kouitra [3] or the rebab. [4] Then, at the Champ de Mars we find musicians from Morocco, and in that picturesque street of Cairo, already famous, an Egyptian concert. On that subject, I read in a journal that it is absolutely impossible to notate the music which is played there. I would like to say that the word "impossible" is not French, as the readers of the *Ménestrel* will see. [5] Thanks to these music exhibits, we can

2. Julien Tiersot, "Promenades Musicales à l'Exposition," *Le Ménestrel* (May 26, 1889), p. 165.
3. A kouitra is a lute with four double gut strings.
4. A rebab is a fiddle with a tailpin like a cello. The body is flat and heart-shaped. Since there is no fingerboard, the pitch is altered by the pressure and the position of the fingers on the strings.
5. Tiersot does attempt to notate the music in subsequent articles.

capture live music which until now we could only study in books, which is insufficient, to say the least.

Into contact with this live dreamworld came Claude Debussy, whose student days almost read like a Romantic novel. One of Chopin's students, Mme. Mauté de Fleurville, trained Debussy for his entrance to the Paris Conservatory at the age of 11. A patroness of Tchaikovsky, Mme. Nadezhda von Meck, brought him to Switzerland, Italy, and Russia when he was 17, to instruct her children on the piano. While in Moscow, Debussy came to know the music of Borodin and Moussorgsky. Then, at the Paris Exposition Debussy became fascinated by Oriental music. Debussy's own particular blend of these influences resulted in the creation of French musical impressionism, with such works as the prelude *The Afternoon of a Faun* (1894) and the opera *Pelléas and Mélisande* (1902).

In 1901, Debussy—as music critic for the French periodical, *La Revue Blanche*—reviewed the performances of the virtuoso instrumentalists, singers, and conductors of his own day. The following excerpts from these reviews indicate Debussy's thoughts on the compositions played as well as on the players.

The Ornamentation of Counterpoint*

Ysaye [6] plays the Violin Concerto in G of J. S. Bach, as perhaps he alone is capable of doing without seeming to be an intruder. He has the freedom of expression and unaffected beauty of tone necessary for the interpretation of this music.

This concerto stands out from amongst many of the others previously inscribed in the notebooks of the great Bach.[7] One finds here, almost intact, that *musical arabesque*, or rather that principle of *ornamentation* which is the basis of all types of art. (The word *ornament* here has nothing whatever to do with the meaning given to it in the musical grammars.)

The early composers, Palestrina, Victoria, Orlando [di Lassus,] etc., made use of this divine *arabesque*. They discovered its principle in the Gregorian chant, and they supported the fragile interlacings with strong counterpoints. When Bach rediscovered the arabesque, he made it more supple, more fluid; and, in spite of the strict discipline which this great mas-

*Claude Debussy, Criticisms in La Revue Blanche (1901), XXV, [The Ornamentation of Counterpoint], pp. 67–68; [Beethoven's Choral Symphony], pp. 69–70; [Strauss' Till Eulenspiegel], pp. 229-230.

6. Eugène Ysaye (1858–1931) was a Belgian violinist to whom César Franck dedicated his violin sonata. Ysaye played the first violin part in Debussy's *String Quartet* at its premier public performance in Paris (1893).

7. This was probably Brandenburg Concerto No. 4.

ter imposed on beauty, it could move with that free fantasy, continuously renewed, which still astounds us to the present day.

In Bach's music it is not the character of the melody that affects us, but rather the curve of its line. Indeed, more often it is the simultaneous motion of several lines, whose meeting, whether by chance or design, incites the emotion. Through this concept of ornamentation music acquires the precision of a mechanism for impressing the audience by causing images to appear before it.[8]

Beethoven's *Choral Symphony*

The *Choral Symphony* has been enveloped in a mist of words and illustrious verbosity. It is a wonder that it has not remained buried under the mass of prose which it has stirred up. Wagner proposed completing the orchestration. Others imagined that they could explain the story with illustrative pictures. In short, they made a public horror of that powerful, clear work. In admitting that there is something mysterious about this symphony, one could perhaps clarify it. But is this really necessary?

Beethoven did not have two cents worth of the literary in him. (At least, not in the sense that is attributed to that word today.) He loved music proudly; it was for him the passion, the joy so consistently absent from his private life. Perhaps we ought to view the *Choral Symphony* as the most gigantic expression of musical pride, and let it go at that. A little notebook where more than 200 different versions of the leading theme of the Finale of this Symphony are sketched, is evidence of his persistent scrutiny and of the purely musical speculation which guided him. (Schiller's verses are really only of sonorous value.) Beethoven wanted this main idea to contain its virtual development: [9] if it is of extraordinary beauty in itself, it is superb for perfectly fulfilling his intention. There is no more magnificent plan for the development of a theme than the pattern which he proposes. On each successive plateau there is new joy. This is done without exhaustion, without the semblance of repetition, like the fantastic blossoming of a tree whose leaves sprout all at once. Nothing is useless in this work of enormous proportions, not even the *Andante* which recent critics accuse of being too long; is it not a subtly conceived pause after the rhythmic persistence of the *Scherzo*, an instrumental torrent invincibly rolling toward the voices and the glory of the *Finale*? Besides, Beethoven had already written eight symphonies and the number 9 seems to have possessed his fancy in an almost prophetic manner. Beethoven was determined to surpass himself. I hardly see how anyone can doubt that he succeeded.

As for the gushing humanity which overflows the usual symphonic bounds, it sprang from a man who, drunk with liberty, by an ironic turn

8. Debussy wrote two sets of piano solos entitled *Images* (1905, 1907), of which the first includes *Reflections in the Water, Homage to Rameau,* and *Motion.*
9. Kirnberger also conceived the idea that the potential for developing the theme is within the theme itself (Section 9.7).

of fate pitted himself against the gilded bars with which the inhuman friendship of the great surrounded him. Beethoven must have endured it with a heavy heart, and must have ardently hoped that humanity would communicate through him. This is the reason for this cry, uttered through the thousand voices of his genius toward his "brothers," the humblest and the poorest of them. Was he heard by them?—a troublesome question.

The *Choral Symphony* was conducted on Good Friday by Mr. Chevillard [10] with an understanding which elevated this masterpiece to the greatest heights. It was performed along with several of Richard Wagner's gamy masterpieces. Tannhäuser, Siegmund, and Lohengrin once again demanded the reclamation of the *leitmotiv!* [11] The pure, unadulterated mastery of the old Beethoven easily triumphed over this high-hatted quackery with no precise mandate.

Strauss' *Till Eulenspiegel*

The Berlin Philharmonic Orchestra, under the direction of Arthur Nikisch [12] gave its first concert. . . . Nikisch proved the uniqueness of his talents with *The Merry Pranks of Till Eulenspiegel* by Richard Strauss. This piece resembles "an hour of new music at a lunatic asylum." The clarinets play wild leaps, the trumpets keep on choking, and the horns, anticipating a latent sneeze, politely hasten to respond, "God bless you!" A bass drum sounds the *boom-booms* as if it were outlining the footwork of clowns. You want to roar with laughter or to howl with pain. Then you are astonished to discover that everything is in its customary place. For if the double basses blew across their bows, if the trombones rubbed their tubes with an imaginary bow, and if you found Mr. Nikisch seated on the knee of an usherette, there would be nothing unusual about it. Yet, none of this prevents the piece from being a work of genius in certain respects, above all in its unlimited orchestral certainty, and in its frenzied motion which carries us from the beginning to the end and forces us to take part in all the hero's merry pranks. Mr. Nikisch conducted this ordered tumult with astounding composure and the ovation which greeted both him and his orchestra was completely justified.

10. Camille Chevillard (1859–1923) was soon to conduct the first performance of Debussy's *La Mer* at the Lamoureux Concerts (1905). These concerts, initiated by Chevillard's father-in-law, Charles Lamoureux, were responsible for bringing Wagner's music to the attention of the French public.
11. *Leitmotiv* is the term assigned by one of Wagner's friends to a leading theme recurring throughout an opera. It might refer not only to a character, but also to an emotion (love in *Tristan and Isolde*), an object (Siegfried's sword), a location (the air through which the Valkyrie rode). During the course of the *Ring of the Nibelungen* Siegfried's leitmotiv is transformed from the sporting horn call of the youthful hunter to the syncopated march of manhood, to the full harmony of heroic stature, the latter depicted by a choir of horns supported by the rolling of drums.
12. Arthur Nikisch (1855–1922), born in Hungary, conducted the Boston Symphony Orchestra (1889–93), the Royal Opera in Budapest (1893–95), and the Gewandhaus Concerts in Leipzig (1895–97). As a visiting conductor in great demand, Nikisch went on several long tours with the Berlin Philharmonic.

13.2 LOUIS LALOY (1874–1944)

Louis Laloy, who had studied at Vincent d'Indy's Schola Cantorum in Paris from 1899 to 1905, was a devoted admirer of Debussy's compositions. In 1904 Laloy started his article entitled "Simplicity in Music" with the "sweet, expressive" opening theme of *The Afternoon of a Faun*, played by a solo flute.[13]

This theme, moving down through C♯, B, and A, to G, a tritone of the whole-tone scale, has come to symbolize the essence of musical impressionism. Whereas earlier critics had approached Debussy's music mainly from an aesthetic standpoint, Laloy dared to analyze the harmony of this illusory, magical music. It was in this spirit that Laloy wrote his article entitled "The Music of the Future," envisioning the use of tone produced through unconventional media as breaking all barriers.

The Music of the Future*

I have no intention of reopening here the dispute which for several years has been the cause of hostilities between the specialists of harmony and those of counterpoint. Those who uphold harmony will not allow the word *music* to be applied to anything but successions of chords, varied certainly and as rich and figured as possible. The partisans of counterpoint include only melodies which can be superposed; from their conjunction many chords are also derived but which are devoid of any meaning when separated from the melodies which accidentally gave them their existence. Rigid forms, which impose preconceived and conventional designs on an artist, are vindicated in this camp; while the harmonists claim a complete independence and the right of listening only to the dictates of their own feelings and fancies. It is all in the natural order of things: counterpoint implies a desire to construct, harmony infers a taste for freedom. In different ways and with varied success, the contest will continue as long as art is bounded on one side by logic and on the other by nature. Therefore, though one may have one's own personal preferences, one must not close the door of the future on either of these two styles. Besides, it is worth remarking that theory alone would try and make one believe them to be incompatible, while in the finest works they are in perfect agreement. M.

---

*Louis Laloy, "La Musique de l'Avenir," Mercure de France (Dec. 1, 1908), as trans. by Mrs. Franz Liebich.

13. Louis Laloy, "Claude Debussy: La Simplicité en Musique," *La Revue Musicale*, IV, No. 4 (1904), 106–11.

Claude Debussy, who is acknowledged a master of pure harmonies and of indefinitely supple forms, does not scruple, when it suits him, to employ the strictest figured counterpoint such as imitation or canon.[14] In order to find designs as solid and symmetrical as his, one would have to go back to Mozart. On the other hand, there is César Franck,[15] whose name is claimed by M. Vincent d'Indy and his disciples, and who wrote not only excellent fugues but had an intimate personal sense of harmony; it is even considered to be one of his most felicitous gifts.

It is therefore extremely probable that in the future counterpoint as well as harmony will each have their representatives. But these two words, it is certain, will be used to designate aggregations of notes altogether different from those we are accustomed to, and at first our ears will find them exceedingly bewildering. It is not at all likely that music will undergo less rapid modifications in the future than it has in the past. Far from it, for the movement which is impelling it onwards, together with the other arts and sciences, is one that has become more and more accelerated during the last ten centuries. Imagine Guido d'Arezzo listening to a thirteenth-century motet, Ockeghem coming to life again in the time of Roland de Lassus and Claude Le Jeune, Lully attending a performance of *Parsifal*, or Rameau one of *Pelléas and Mélisande*, and we have only a very faint notion of the state of perplexity we should find ourselves in after having entered a concert room or opera house in the beginning of the twenty-second century. We should perhaps experience some vague impression of grandeur and of force, or even of delicacy and sweetness; but we should be incapable of following the work and of attributing any meaning to it because we should be unable to disentangle or coördinate our perceptions. The universal laws of art vary as little as those of the human mind; it is their means of production which

14. Laloy's footnote: "A strict canon will be found at the octave between the violins, then the flutes and the bassoons in *Pelléas and Mélisande* in the third scene of the fourth act when Yniold tries to lift the heavy stone and fails (p. 309 of the orchestral score.)

    In one of the more recent works for piano, *Et la lune descend sur le temple qui fut*, the first idea is delineated with chords and the second is composed of two conjoined melodies, thus harmony and counterpoint respond to one another.
15. César Franck (1822–1890), born in Belgium, studied at the Paris Conservatoire, where he won numerous prizes for counterpoint, for such feats as transposing a fugue down a third at sight at the piano and composing fugues of his own. The last movement of Franck's Sonata in A major for violin and piano has a canon at the octave between the top voice part of the piano, and the violin which enters one measure later (*MSO*, Part II, 246 f.).

become modified, and to such a degree as to render the language of grand-children unintelligible to their grandparents. It is not, therefore, a discussion on aesthetics that will help us to prophesy anything concerning the music of the future, but it is to our advantage to study the progress which will be brought about in the production and perception of sound.

Moreover, production and perception are very closely allied. Imperfect instruments dull the sensibility of the ear and hinder the development of the hearing faculties; any improvement in their construction has almost immediately been followed by a consequent effect upon music. The ancient Greeks possessed only certain kinds of oboes of very rudimentary bore, and lyres whose strings were of equal length but of unequal tension. It was, therefore, extremely difficult for them to regulate the pitch of their notes and to make it conform to the very delicate experiments they were doing on the monochord. Only the fourth, the fifth and the octave had fixed sizes.[16] The smaller intervals were employed at will and the learned classifications of the theorists skilled in distinguishing the enharmonic quarter tones, the chromatic half tones, the third tones, and other "nuances" only indicate the uncertainty about their use. In the Alexandrian epoch the invention of organs finally helped to establish once and for all each note of a given scale. At the advent of the Middle Ages these instruments conferred a definite form on the musical modes, and one that might have been believed immutable: the diatonic genus which discreetly combines five tones and two semitones. But this series, established in one particular octave, could not be transposed indiscriminately to all the others. When the departure from the point of origin became too great, the proportions were no longer valid, because the intervals, first derived from the fifth and the fourth according to the Pythagorean system, then from the consonant third, could not be superposed exactly. In the meantime polyphony, that is to say, the art of combining the voices or the instrumental parts, had brought chord perception into being and, with it, the need for modulation. The eight or twelve ecclesiastical modes were reduced little by little into two scales, constructed on the two first chords of three tones, the major and the minor, and these two scales, so similar to each other, were seeking to regain diversity by their changes of position. Hence the multiplication of sharps and flats which divided each whole tone and the various attempts to equalize, at least among themselves, the great number of tones and semi-tones, by an ingenious alteration known as temperament. Keyed instruments, organs and ancestors of the harpsichord, alone were capable of providing the precision of a preliminary tuning. The others followed as best they could. The viols and lutes were tolerably accurate, because there were frets which marked the position of the fingers in advance. The tuning of wind instruments, sackbuts or cornets, remained exceedingly variable and imperfect. When these several instruments were combined either among themselves or with voices, there resulted a medley of sounds on either side of the required note; but the ear remained satisfied. Moreover, keys containing many accidentals always sounded false even on the organ and the harpsichord, neither of which had yet adopted equal temperament. It is

16. Laloy's footnote: "This is what theoretical treatises intended to convey when they named *immovable* the sounds which limited the intervals and *movable* those which were in between.

well-known that the system which divides the octave into twelve equal intervals, was advocated by Bach and Rameau at the same time, at the beginning of the eighteenth century, and was then promulgated in spite of the opposition of certain musicians who took pleasure in these discordances.[17] The wind instruments did not succeed in adapting themselves to it until towards the end of the nineteenth century. The flutes, oboes and clarinets did so thanks to Böhm's system,[18] and the horns and trumpets by means of the mechanism of their valves. Our present day music is based on a series extending for the length of six or seven octaves composed of equalized semitones. It is almost identical to the system of the twelve Chinese *liu*, defined by a wise emperor and his excellent minister thirty centuries before our era but which, lacking adequate means of production, could not be used in Chinese music. . . .

But in our day-dreams we can imagine other progress. Having imitated the old instruments, the organ will discover some new resources—here is the way. The timbre [tone color] of an instrument corresponds to a vibration of a certain configuration, which when analyzed is found to consist chiefly of a superposition of simple or pendular vibrations whose rapidity of motion increases in the ratio of a series of whole numbers. Another timbre would be represented by another union; and according to the law of combination the two combined would produce a certain number of different timbres. To what an extent this number could be increased if, instead of adding up amounts already existing, one were to work directly with the elements! Such and such a partial tone, which nature's vibrating bodies can only produce in one way, could be augmented or diminished or made audible or inaudible at will. One would be able to glide imperceptibly from one timbre to the other, and some entirely new tone colors would be produced: the series of colors would be simultaneously interpolated and extrapolated, almost without limit. An apparatus might be imagined consisting of a series of graduated tuning forks differing from one another at the ratio of a vibration a second or even less, and to which electricity would communicate a motion of determined amplitude and duration. It may even be possible to dispense with tuning-forks, which, being material bodies, are therefore somewhat inert and occasionally inaccurate. What would be the motive-power? Material particles? Gaseous molecules? By discarding the telephone's tiresome membrane should we be able to direct and transform the periods of an alternating current into vibrating air-columns? This is what the future will disclose. One may readily presume that pendular vibrations will be produced at will. By combining them every possible musical sound and the generality of noises will be obtained. Strictly speaking, musical sounds are produced by periodic vibrations whose maximum and minimum are equidistant; noises, by non-periodic vibrations. Every possible kind of periodic vibration can be obtained by a

17. Laloy's footnote: "One will find mention of this prejudice cited and refuted in D'Alembert's *Elements de Musique* (1752), p. 48."
18. Theobald Böhm (1794–1881), a goldsmith, and flutest at the Bavarian court, invented the modern flute with its holes proportioned to provide for accuracy of intonation and its keys covering the holes to cause the instrument to respond to the touch immediately. See *The Flute and Flute-Playing* (Munich, 1871) trans. Dayton C. Miller (New York, Dover Publications, 1964).

superposition of pendular vibrations whose velocity, as has already been said, is proportionate to a succession of whole numbers: these constitute what are known as harmonics. The generality of noises could very probably be produced by superposing pendular vibrations whose periods were not subservient to this rule. Music is composed of sounds and noises: the latter are more numerous than may be at first believed and our orchestras would seem quite different were the grating of bows, the tremor of reeds, and the blare of the brass suppressed. However, noise need not necessarily be proscribed or even discredited: many races, some, like the different African tribes, rougher, and others extremely discriminating, like the Chinese, the Javanese and the Hindus, find pleasurable artistic impressions in listening to a single note of a drum, a gong, a xylophone or a stringed instrument. We share their feeling when we listen to their music, and partly on account of their influence, partly by reason of natural evolution, we are trying to make a better use of percussion instruments, which are those that make the noises: kettledrums are becoming chromatic, the xylophone is already to be found in more serious works than Saint-Saëns' *Danse Macabre*, the celesta, according to announcements made by the Mustel Company, is "the only novelty that has been introduced into the orchestra for fifty years." How is it then, that from ancient times to the present day our music has scarcely paid attention to any sound other than tone? Because a tone is of simpler construction than a noise and therefore its pitch is more easily determined: everyone knows that a violin is easier to tune than a kettledrum. The Western mind, less given to contemplation than the Asiatic or the African, needs more especially a music that can be determined by fixed degrees.

13.3 MUSIC BY ELECTRICITY

The first use of electricity in connection with musical instruments came about in connection with the organ. The earliest electric action, however, was merely an aid toward producing musical sound; the actual tones of the organ still emanated from the columns of air vibrating in its pipes. After the invention of the pneumatic lever to lighten the touch required of the organist playing on a large organ (1832), an inventor by the name of Bryceson erected an organ with "an electric draw-stop-action and a cable of insulated wire through which it was played" in London, at Her Majesty's Opera, Theater–Royal Drury Lane (1867).[19]

In the preliminary experiments with electricity as the motive power in a musical instrument, inventors found those with keyboard the most suitable. In 1904 Thaddeus Cahill developed the Telharmonium. Cahill (1867–1934), who also invented the electric typewriter, was a graduate

19. Edward J. Hopkins and Edward F. Rimbault, *The Organ, its History and Construction* (London, 1870), p. 87.

of Oberlin College, with advanced degrees from George Washington University. He maintained a laboratory in Holyoke, Massachusetts.

In contrast to the technical articles about the Telharmonium which appeared in scientific journals at the time, *Musical America* ran a descriptive review of the instrument, from which the material below is quoted.

Dr. Cahill's Telharmonium, A Remarkable Invention*

Dr. Thaddeus Cahill's invention, the dynamophone, or telharmonium, is now ready for installation in New York City, writes Ray Stannard Baker in *McClure's Magazine* for August. No musical instrument ever departed further from the ordinary conception of what a musical instrument should be. Filling a large basement with steel machinery—shafts, dynamos, electric alternators, transformers and switch boards—it gives the impression of nothing so much as a busy machine shop.

Of all musical instruments ever constructed it is the largest and heaviest; none other probably ever cost so much money, more than $200,000 having been expended in building the first machine, and none ever required or gave opportunity for the use of more skill in playing.

Musicians located in a quiet room distant from the whir of the machine regulate the production of sound waves by playing upon keyboards similar to those of the pipe organ. Connecting with the central plant cables are laid in the streets, from which wires may be run into your home or mine or into restaurants, theaters, churches, schools or wherever music is desired. Upon our table or attached to the wall we have a telephone receiver with a funnel attached.

I recently heard an exhibition of the powers of the instrument at Holyoke, Mass. When the music began it seemed to fill the entire room with singularly clear, sweet, perfect tones. I listened especially for some evidence of the noisy dynamos which I had just seen, but without distinguishing a single jarring sound; nor was there any hollowness or strangeness traceable to the telephone or its horn attachment. It was pure music, conveying musical emotion without interference or diversion.

The music apparently comes out of nothingness, no players to be seen, no instrument, nothing but two wires running out of the wall; and in hundreds of different places widely separated—the present machine can supply more than a thousand subscribers—the same music may be heard at the same moment.

The first impression the music makes upon the listener is its singular difference from any music ever heard before; in the fullness, roundness, completeness of its tones. But, strangely enough, it possesses ranges of tones all its own. It can be made to imitate closely other musical instruments, the flute, oboe, bugle, French horn and cello best of all; the piano and violin not as yet so perfectly.

The musician sits on a high bench, like that of a pipe organ, with double-

From "Dr. Cahill's Telharmonium, A Remarkable Invention," Musical America *(August 25, 1906), p. 17.*

banked keyboard. Sixteen stops are used to regulate the harmonics, and there are other devices, pedals and expression levers for otherwise controling the tones. One telephone with a funnel is arranged behind the player so that by listening to his own music he may get the proper effects. The keys and stops build up the voices of flute or clarinet by combination.

The player uses one hand on the keys for giving the tones, and one at the stops for giving the tonality. In future instruments there may be many players with one great leader, as in an orchestra, having the whole performance under his control and interpreting his own musical genius.

Such players will not lack the stimulus of an audience, for it is the intention of the inventor to have the operating portion of the instrument located in a hall or opera house where the public may be admitted to hear the same music which is being rendered at the same moment in a thousand different places.

As in the case of most big inventions, the basic theory of the telharmonium is simple. Every schoolboy knows that a note consists of vibrations which produce sound waves, and that the difference in notes is the difference in the length and rapidity of these waves. A note is produced of many different tones, but the lowest or primary tone is more prominent than the others and is called the fundamental tone; the others, the overtones.

So long as you produce, by whatever means, this combination of aerial waves, you will secure a note. In the telharmonium this is done by means of electrical waves instead of aerial waves. A battery of alternators of different frequencies is used which answer to the strings of a piano. These alternators simply produce electric waves, and, by their construction, of any desired length and frequency.

Just what the result of this latest invention will be, no one can tell. To say the least, it is as startling as the manufacture of real paintings or genuinely beautiful statuary would be. It may open up an entirely new field in music.

13.4 ARNOLD SCHOENBERG (1874–1951)

The possibility of using all twelve tones of the diatonic genus as equals culminated in a system developed by Arnold Schoenberg. Born in Vienna, Schoenberg went to the Realschule there, where he learned how to play the violin and cello. At the age of 20 he studied counterpoint with Alexander von Zemlinsky (1872–1942) who subsequently became conductor of the Berlin State Opera. Schoenberg's *Verklärte Nacht*, a sextet for stringed instruments, was written in the Romantic style under the influence of Wagnerian harmonies. However, after his *String Quartet No. 2 with Soprano Solo* was completed in 1908, Schoenberg abandoned the use of key signatures and began to concentrate on the twelve-tone system.

Quoted below is a letter by Schoenberg to Josef Matthias Hauer (1883–1959), who independently arrived at the idea of basing the theory of music on twelve equal tones. Hauer, born in a suburb of Vienna, was a public school teacher with a great interest in music. Although Hauer's twelve-tone concept [20] was different from Schoenberg's, the latter attempted to establish congenial relations to avoid any possible conflict in the future. Since Schoenberg was an extremely active composer, putting his theory into practice and upholding it with vigor, the problem he anticipated did not develop.

The Twelve-Tone System*

Letter from Schoenberg to Hauer

Mödling   December 1, 1923

Your letter gave me very, very, great pleasure. And I can give you proof of this. The fact is that about one and a half or two years ago I saw from one of your publications that you were trying to do something similar to me, in a similar way. After coming to terms with the painful feeling that someone else, by also being engaged in something I had been thinking about for pretty well fifteen years, was jeopardizing my reputation for originality, which might cause me to renounce putting my ideas into practice if I do not want to pass for a plagiarist—a painful feeling, you will admit—after having come to terms with this feeling and having come to see wherein we differ from each other and that I was in a position to prove the independence of my ideas, I resolved to make the following suggestion to you:

Let us write a book together, a book in which one chapter will be written by one of us, the next by the other, and so on. In it let us state our ideas, exactly defining the distinctive elements, by means of objective (but courteous) arguments trying to collaborate a little bit in spite of these differences: because of what there is in common a basis can surely be found on which we can get along smoothly with each other.

And I meant to say also:

Let us show the world that *music*, if nothing else, would not have advanced if it had not been for the Austrians, and that *we* know what the next step must be.

---

* *From* Arnold Schoenberg Letters, *selected and edited by Erwin Stein, trans. Eithne Wilkins and Ernst Kaiser (New York: St. Martin's Press, Inc., 1964–65), pp. 103 ff. Reprinted by permission of St. Martin's Press, Inc.*

20. Hauer's system was based on establishing *tropes*, or patterns of tones. These specified series of tones lay the foundation for the compositions written in the system. In contrast, Schoenberg devised a special series of tones, a tone-row, for each individual composition. For a further discussion of Schoenberg's system, see Webern, Section 13.5.

Then, however, I had qualms (there are always mischief-makers and gossips) lest I would be exposing myself to a refusal and so the letter was never written. Perhaps, now, your suggestion of a school is even better. Above all, because in that way an exchange of ideas would come about spontaneously, more frequently, and without the agitatory contributions of a public maliciously looking on and provoking one to stubbornness. But the idea of the book, for the purpose of establishing the present point of view, should not be completely rejected either.

We are perhaps both in search of the same thing and have probably found related things. My point of departure was the attempt to replace the no longer applicable principle of tonality by a new principle relevant to the changed conditions: that is, in theory. I am definitely concerned with no other theories but the methods of "twelve-note composition" as—after many errors and deviations—I now (and I hope definitively) call it. I believe—for the first time again for fifteen years—that I have found a key. Probably the book to be entitled *The Theory of Musical Unity*, originally planned about ten years ago, often sketched out and just as often scrapped, time and again newly delimited and then again enlarged, will in the end have just the modest title, *Composition with Twelve Notes*. This is as far as I have got in the last approximately two years, and frankly, I have so far—for the first time—found no mistake and the system keeps on growing of its own accord, without my doing anything about it. This I consider a good sign. In this way I find myself positively enabled to compose as freely and fantastically as one otherwise does only in one's youth, and am nevertheless subject to a precisely definable aesthetic discipline. It is now more precise than it has ever been. For I can provide rules for almost everything. Admittedly I have not yet taught this method, because I must still test it in some more compositions and expand it in some directions. But in the introductory course for my pupils I have been using a great deal of it for some years in order to define forms and formal elements and in particular in order to explain musical technique.

Please do believe that my wish to reach an understanding with you springs above all from the urge to recognize achievement. This is something I have proved often enough; among other cases, also where you were concerned (I mention this in order to show you that the two occasions when you tried to find an approach to me were, after all, not wasted): in my *Theory of Harmony* I argue (on p. 488 of the new edition) against the concept *atonality* [21] and then continue with an appreciation of you personally: you will realize that I did that for no one's sake but my own, out of my own need to be fair: and this makes the value of my praise objectively even greater! My friends will be able to confirm, too, that although I have put my head down and charged like a bull at what I am opposed to in your ideas, in conversation I have acknowledged your achievements at least as much as I have done in my book.

It is a pleasure to be able to give you proof of all this, for your amicable advance is of a kind that should remove all misunderstandings and all grudges; and so I shall gladly contribute a share as large as yours. I should be very pleased if we could now soon also have a personal discussion about further details. It is in particular the project of the school that I have a

21. Schoenberg's footnote: "Against the term, I mean, not against the thing itself!"

good deal to say about, having long been turning over the idea of starting a school for the development of style. Perhaps you will yourself name some afternoon next week when you would care to visit me (excepting Tuesday and Friday). Although I may be in Vienna next week, I do not know whether I shall then have time.

I am looking forward very much to the further development of our understanding and remain, with kindest regards, yours sincerely,

Arnold Schoenberg

N.B. This letter was not dictated, but written by me personally on the typewriter, thus respecting your wish that for the present I should not mention our discussions to any third person.

13.5 ANTON WEBERN (1883–1945)

Anton Webern's knowledge of musical composition through the ages enabled him to view the theoretical system of Schoenberg, the composer to whom he was thoroughly devoted, in its broadest aspects. Born in Vienna, Webern studied musicology with Guido Adler and composition with Arnold Schoenberg.[22] Webern wrote his doctoral dissertation for the University of Vienna on the *Choralis Constantinus*, a setting of all the Propers of the Mass throughout the church year by Heinrich Isaac (1508).

Webern worked closely with the Society for Private Musical Performances, a group organized by Schoenberg to meet in private homes, away from the opposition of public criticism. When Webern gave sixteen lectures in a private house in Vienna from 1932 to 1933, one of the auditors, a Viennese lawyer, recorded the lectures in shorthand. This lecture series, whence the excerpts below originated, was edited posthumously by Willi Reich, who himself had studied with another famous Schoenberg student, Alban Berg.

Webern's own compositions, despite their individual brevity, have been very influential. A measure of Webern's talent lies in his ability to unify his thoughts to the exclusion of extraneous material, aided by a skilful manipulation of tone color.

22. Guido Adler (1855–1941) studied under Bruckner at the Vienna Conservatory. In 1884, with Friedrich Chrysander, the editor of the complete works of Handel, and Philipp Spitta, the author of an outstanding work on J. S. Bach, Adler founded a quarterly periodical in whose first issue modern musicology was defined.

Extension of the Overtone Series*

Concretely: notes are natural law as related to the sense of hearing. . . . A note is a complex of fundamental and overtones. There has been a gradual process in which music has gone on to exploit each successive stage of this complex material. This is the one path: the way in which what lay at hand was first of all drawn upon, then what lay farther off. So, nothing could be more incorrect than the view that keeps cropping up even today, as it always has; "They ought to compose as they used to, not with all these dissonances you get nowadays!" For we find an ever growing appropriation of nature's gifts! The overtone series must be regarded as, practically speaking, infinite. Ever subtler differentiations can be imagined, and from this point of view there's nothing against attempts at quarter-tone music and the like; the only question is whether the present time is yet ripe for them. But the path is wholly valid, laid down by the nature of sound. So we should be clear that what is attacked today is just as much a gift of nature as what was practiced earlier.[23] . . .

The diatonic scale wasn't invented, it was discovered. So it's given, and its corollary was very simple and clear: the overtones from the "parallelo-gram of focus" of the three adjoining, related notes form the notes of the scale. So it's just the most important overtones, those that are in the closest relationship—something natural, not thought up—that form the diatonic scale. But what about the notes that lie between? Here a new epoch begins, and we shall deal with it later.

The triad, the disappearance of which so provokes people, and which has played such a role in music up to now: what, then, is this triad? The first overtone different from the fundamental, plus the second one—that's to say a reconstruction of these overtones, and an imitation of nature, of the first primitive relationships that are given as part of the structure of a note. That's why it sounds so agreeable to our ear and was used at an early stage.

Yet another thing which, so far as I know, Schoenberg was the first to put into words: these simple complexes of notes are called consonances, but it was soon found that the more distant overtone relationships, which were considered as dissonances, could be felt as a spice. But we must understand that consonance and dissonance are not essentially different—that there is no essential difference between them, only one of degree. Dissonance is only another step up the scale, which goes on developing further. We do not know what will be the end of the battle against Schoenberg, which starts with accusations that he uses dissonances too much. Naturally that's nonsense; that's the battle music has waged since time immemorial. It's an accusation levelled at everyone who has dared to take a step forward. How-

*From *Anton Webern*, The Path to the New Music, *ed. Will Reich (Bryn Mawr, Pa.: Theodore Presser Co., 1963)*, pp. 15–16, 32, 36, 38–41. © 1960, Universal Edition, © 1963, Theodore Presser Company. Used by permission.

23. The intervals between successive tones of the overtone series become successively smaller (see Chart 3).

agreeable. Ambiguous chords were produced, such as the augmented triad, which plays a great role in Wagner but isn't really anything so terrible—it happens in any minor key as a diatonic chord on the mediant. The augmented $\frac{6}{5}$ chord belongs here, too.[31] With these wandering chords one could get to every possible region. Even the so-called "Tristan chord" occurred before Wagner, but only in passing, and not with the significance and the kind of resolution it has in Wagner.[32] Then there came the chords built on fourths, and others built out of superimposed thirds. Later this happened faster; the new chords were themselves altered, and so we got to a stage where these new chords were almost the only ones used. But we still related them to the tonic, so we could still rejoin the key.

But ultimately, because of the use of these dissonant chords—through ever-increasing conquest of the tonal field and introduction of the more distant overtones—there might be no consonances for whole stretches at a time, and finally we came to a situation where the ear no longer found it indispensable to refer to a tonic. When is one keenest to return to the tonic? At the end, of course. Then one can say, "The piece is in this or that key." But there came a time when one returned at the last moment, and where for long stretches it was not clear what key was meant. "Suspended tonality." Before long it was possible to do without the relationship to the tonic, for there was nothing consonant there any more. The ear was satisfied with this suspended state; nothing was missing when one had ended "in the air"—one still felt that the flow of the complex as a whole was sufficient and satisfying.

Is all this clear? That moment—I can speak from personal experience—that moment, in which we all took part, happened in about the year 1908. Now it's 1933—so it's twenty-five years ago— a jubilee, no less!

31. Following is the augmented triad as the III chord in A minor with a raised leading tone:

A minor: III

The augmented $\frac{6}{5}$ chord is produced by raising the fourth and lowering the third and sixth steps of the scale in the IV ^{7} chord in its first inversion, as follows:

key of C: IV^7 IV$\frac{6}{5}$+   V

32. Following is the beginning of the Prelude to *Tristan:*

"Tristan chord"

Arnold Schoenberg was the man responsible. Now I must carry on the tale from my own experience. You mustn't imagine it was a sudden moment. The links with the past were most intense. One can also take the view that even with us there is still a tonic present—I certainly think so—but over the course of the whole piece this didn't interest us any more. So there came to be music that had no key-signature; to put it in a more popular way, it used not only the white notes in C major but the black ones as well. But it was soon clear that hidden laws were there, bound up with the twelve notes; the ear found it very satisfying when the course of the melody went from semitone to semitone, or by intervals connected with chromatic progression. That's to say, on the basis of chromaticism, not of the seven-note scale. The chromatic scale came to dominate more and more: twelve notes instead of seven.

Next was a stage that's hard to explain; the dominance of the chromatic scale, of chromatic progressions, brought up a particularly tricky point. What happens when I try to express a key strongly? The tonic must be over-emphasized—so that listeners notice; otherwise it won't be enough to give satisfaction. In Beethoven the tonic was constantly reiterated, especially toward the end, in order to make it stand out enough. . . . *Now*, however, the exact opposite becomes a necessity; since there is no tonic any more, or rather, since matters have gone so far that the tonic is no longer necessary, we feel the need to *prevent* one note being over-emphasized, to prevent any note's "taking advantage" of being repeated.

Of course composition can't go on without note-repetition; the work would have to end when all twelve notes had occurred. What does one make of it? How are we not to repeat? When is a repetition not disturbing? I said the composition would have to be over when all twelve notes had been there. So no note must be repeated during a round of all twelve! But a hundred "rounds" could happen at once! That's all right; but when *one* has started, then the other notes of the row must follow it, without any of them being repeated. . . .

The basic shape, the course of the twelve notes, can give rise to variants. We also use the twelve notes back to front—that's cancrizans—then inverted —as if we were looking in a mirror—and also in the cancrizans of the inversion. That makes four forms. But then what can one do with these? We can base them on every degree of the scale. Twelve times four makes forty-eight forms. Enough to choose from! Until now we've found these forty-eight forms sufficient, these forty-eight forms that are the same thing throughout. Just as earlier composition was in C major, we write in these forty-eight forms.

We've reached the end! Ever more complete comprehension of the tonal field and clearer presentation of ideas! I've followed it through the centuries and I've shown here the wholly natural outcome of the ages, that's to say, composition with twelve notes related only to each other.

13.6 PAUL WHITEMAN (1890–1967)

Paul Whiteman, the conductor, was among the first to recognize the qualities of American jazz as being suitable for the concert hall. Whiteman, the son of the supervisor of music for the Denver public schools, was a violist with the Denver Symphony Orchestra before conducting a band for the U.S. Navy (1917–18).

Whiteman's concert at Aeolian Hall in New York City, where he conducted the *Rhapsody in Blue* by George Gershwin with the young composer at the piano, is recounted in the excerpt below. The article from which this material is taken was simply entitled "Jazz." It was written for *The Saturday Evening Post* by Whiteman in collaboration with Mary Margaret McBride, a feature writer and radio broadcaster, then in her twenties, who recognized the importance of Whiteman's undertaking.

Jazz*

   Visions of playing a jazz concert in what a critic has called the "perfumed purlieus" of Aeolian Hall, used to rouse me up at night in a cold perspiration. Sometimes a nightmare depicted me being borne out of the place on a rail, and again I dreamed the doors were all but clattering down with the applause.

   That's the way I lived during waking hours, too, all the time I was planning the Aeolian Hall experiment—alternating between extremes of dire fear and exultant confidence. We began to rehearse for the concert as soon as we came back from England. The idea struck nearly everybody as preposterous at the start. Some hold to the same opinion still. But the list of pessimists was a little shorter, I believe, when at 5:30, on the afternoon of February 12, 1924, we took our fifth curtain call.

   "What! an all-jazz concert?" one of my best friends, a musician, shouted when I confided my plan to him in strictest secrecy. "Why, my boy, it simply can't be done. You mustn't try it. It would ruin you! You have your future and your reputation to think of. So far you've been getting on splendidly with your dance music and if you watch your step you will be able to put away a good smart sum while the vogue lasts. But a jazz concert! Honestly, my boy, I'm afraid you've got softening of the brain. Be guided by me in this and you will never regret it."

   Such expressions were naturally depressing, especially since I myself realized that I was gambling with public favor. There were plenty of similar warnings from other friends, and those who weren't in that category said even worse things. I was called "fresh," "publicity-hungry," "money-mad" —and some of the musicians I most admired, who had until then regarded me with a slightly amused but tolerant air, now talked themselves red in the face about the insolence of jazz boys who want to force their ridiculous efforts upon the world—by the world meaning, I suppose, their own little coterie, the final court of critical appeal in their opinion. Here's something I have never been able to understand. Why should it be supposed that all the good taste in the world is monopolized by a few people? Isn't it possible that the so-called masses have considerable instinctive good judgment in matters of beauty that they never get credit for? . . .

My idea for the concert was to show these skeptical people the advance which had been made in popular music from the day of discordant early jazz to the melodious form of the present. I believed that most of them had grown so accustomed to condemning the *Livery Stable Blues* sort of thing, that they went on flaying modern jazz without realizing that it was different from the crude early attempts—that it had taken a turn for the better.

My task was to reveal the change and try to show that jazz had come to stay and deserved recognition. It was not a light undertaking, but setting Aeolian Hall as the stage of the experiment was probably a wise move. It started the talk going, at least, and aroused curiosity. "Jazz in Aeolian Hall!" the conservatives cried incredulously. "What is the world coming to?"

Fifteen minutes before the concert was to begin, I yielded to a nervous longing to see for myself what was happening out front, and putting an overcoat over my concert clothes, I slipped around to the entrance of Aeolian Hall. There I gazed upon a picture that should have imparted new vigor to my wilting confidence. It was snowing, but men and women were fighting to get into the door, pulling and mauling each other as they do sometimes at a baseball game, or a prize fight, or in the subway. Such was my humility by this time, that I wondered if I had come to the right entrance. And then I saw Victor Herbert going in. It was the right entrance all right, and the next day the ticket-office officials said they could have sold the house out ten times over.

It was a strange medley out there in front; society women, vaudevillians, concert managers come to have a look at the novelty; Tin Pan Alleyites, composers, symphony and opera stars, flappers and cake-eaters, all mixed higgledy-piggledy. Beginning with the earliest jazz composition, *Livery Stable Blues*, we played twenty-six selections designed to exhibit legitimate scores as contrasted with the former hit-and-miss effects which were also called jazz. At that time I argued that all was not jazz that was so named. I still believe that *Livery Stable Blues* and *A Rhapsody in Blue*, played at the concert by its talented composer, George Gershwin, are so many millions of miles apart that to speak of them both as jazz needlessly confuses the person who is trying to understand modern American music. At the same time, in the course of a recent tour of the United States, I have become convinced that people as a whole like the word "jazz." So it is improbable that they will give it up. Recently they have been tried with all sorts of substitutes—syncopep, and the like—but will have none of them. So I am resigned to "jazz" and have ceased trying to reform our language.

This is the program we played that day:

TRUE FORM OF JAZZ: Ten years ago—*Livery Stable Blues*, La Rocca; With Modern Embellishment—*Mama Loves Papa*, Baer

COMEDY SELECTIONS: Origin of *Yes, We Have No Bananas*, Silver; Instrumental Comedy—*So This Is Venice*, Thomas (Adapted from *The Carnival of Venice*)

CONTRAST—LEGITIMATE vs. JAZZING: Selection in True Form—

Whispering, Schonberger; Same Selection with Jazz Treatment

RECENT COMPOSITIONS WITH MODERN SCORE: *Limehouse Blues*, Braham; *I Love You*, Archer; *Raggedy Ann*, Kern

ZEZ CONFREY (Piano): *Medley Popular Airs; Kitten on the Keys; Ice Cream and Art; Nickel in the Slot;* Confrey (Accompanied by the Orchestra)

FLAVORING A SELECTION WITH BORROWED THEMES: *Russian Rose*, Grofe (Based on the Song of the Volga Boatmen)

SEMI-SYMPHONIC ARRANGEMENT OF POPULAR MELODIES: *Alexander's Ragtime Band, A Pretty Girl Is Like a Melody, Orange Blossom in California*, Berlin

A SUITE OF SERENADES: *Spanish, Chinese, Cuban, Oriental,* Herbert

ADAPTATION OF STANDARD SELECTIONS TO DANCE RHYTHM: *Pale Moon*, Logan; *To a Wild Rose*, McDowell; *Chansonette*, Friml

GEORGE GERSHWIN (Piano): *A Rhapsody in Blue*, Gershwin (Accompanied by the Orchestra)

IN THE FIELD OF CLASSICS: *Pomp and Circumstance*, Elgar

I was very proud of the suite the late Victor Herbert wrote especially for that occasion. He was a great-souled, wonderful musician and my friend. His encouragement during the weeks we were rehearsing meant a great deal to all of us. . . . He complained a little about the doubling in a jazz orchestra, which he said hampered him when he wanted an oboe, say, and found the gentleman who should play the oboe busy with the bass clarinet. . . .

A Rhapsody in Blue was regarded by critics as the most significant number of the program. It was the first rhapsody written for a solo instrument and a jazz orchestra. The orchestral treatment was developed by Mr. Grofe. Mr. Gershwin's manuscript was complete for the piano. It was a successful attempt to build a rhapsody out of the rhythms of popular American music. None of the thematic material had been used before. Its structure was simple and its popularity has been remarkable since we have put it on the records. It is music conceived for the jazz orchestra, and I do not believe any other could do it justice, though there has been talk of orchestrating it for a symphony.

The audience listened attentively to everything and applauded wholeheartedly from the first moment. When they laughed and seemed pleased with *Livery Stable Blues*, the crude jazz of the past, I had for a moment the panicky feeling that they hadn't realized the attempt at burlesque— that they were ignorantly applauding the thing on its merits. I experienced all sorts of qualms as the program went on, most of them unjustified.

A few of the men had accidents with their instruments, picking up one when they wanted another, but nobody noticed. This happens sometimes when one man plays five or six instruments. My twenty-three boys that day played thirty-six instruments.

It seemed as if people would never let us go. We played all the encores we knew and still they applauded. My heart was so full I could hardly speak as I bowed again and again. The spark that a responsive audience can always kindle in the performers had been glowing all afternoon and as a result we played better than I had ever hoped.

W. C. Handy [Section 13.7] was asked once as witness in a dispute over a blues copyright, what was the difference between jazz and blues. He was plumb amazed at the question.

"Why," said he, "any fool knows that—jazz is jazz and blues is blues!"

I feel a good deal the same way, because to anybody who knows them jazz and blues explain themselves. And if you don't know them, words fail when it comes to describing them.

I have heard some folks refer to jazz as "an obnoxious disease," "musical profanity," and others call it "the true voice of the age," and "the only American art." You can readily see why I keep hedging. Jazz seems to me to be, as nearly as I can express it, a musical treatment consisting largely of question and answer, sound and echo. It is what I call unacademic counterpoint. It includes rhythmic, harmonic and melodic invention.

To rag a melody, one throws the rhythm out of joint, making syncopation. Jazz goes further, marking the broken rhythm unmistakably. The great art in any orchestra is a counterbalancing of the instrumentation, a realization of tone values and their placement.

With a very few but important exceptions, jazz is not as yet the thing said; it is the manner of saying it. Some critics think this fact establishes the unimportance or even the vulgarity of jazz. I believe it is true that if jazz does not develop its own themes, its own distinctive messages, it will fail to be musically valuable. . . .

Jazz is today a method of saying the old things with a twist, with a bang, with a rhythm that make them seem new. A large part of its technic consists of mutes being put in the brass.

The first beat in any bar, which normally is accented, is passed over and the second, third or even fourth beat is accented. Or any normally accented beat can be slighted and the accent be placed on a normally unaccented beat.

This can be illustrated roughly with a familiar bar of music. Suppose we take *Home Sweet Home* in its original form, jazzed up as a waltz, and as a fox trot:

The normal accents (1 and 2) falling on the first beat of the bar in the original are shifted to the third beat of the preceding bar in the jazz waltz arrangement, and to the fourth beat of the preceding bar in the jazz fox-trot arrangement.

That won't be quite the real thing though. The jazz treatment is hard to put into written music. Follow the notes as carefully as you like, and you will merely be as a person trying to imitate, for instance, a Southern accent—unless jazz is in your blood. If it is, you'll add to the notes that indefinable thing, that spontaneous jazzing, that will make the music talk jazz as a native tongue.

13.7 WILLIAM CHRISTOPHER HANDY (1873–1958)

The "Father of the Blues," William Christopher Handy, was born in Florence, Alabama, in a log cabin built by his grandfather. The teacher in the district school he attended as a boy liked to start the day's lessons with singing. Indoors, in the classroom, with no guide other than the teacher's pitch-pipe and the tonic sol-fa system, the pupils learned how to sing hymns and passages from Wagner and Verdi. Outdoors, Handy liked to test his skill at identifying the sounds of the riverboats and the chirping of the birds, even to the point of notating them.

Handy had a many-faceted musical career as cornetist, bandmaster, composer, and publisher. As he assimilated the spirit of the blues, and preserved the folk idiom, he also developed his own inimitable style of composition.

Origin and Form of the Blues*

The primitive tone or a correlated note of the blues was born in my brain when a boy. In the valley of the Tennessee River was McFarland's Bottoms, which our school overlooked. In the spring, when doors and windows were thrown open, the song of a Negro plowman half a mile away fell on my ears. This is what he sang:

A - o,   Oo   A - o,   I   would-n't   live   in
Cai - ro - oo;   A - o,   Oo   A - o,   Oo.

*From *W. C. Handy*, Father of the Blues (*New York: The Macmillan Company,* 1941), pp. 143–144, 147–149, 155–156. © 1941 by *W. C. Handy*, renewed 1969 by Irma L. Handy, W. C. Handy Jr., Katherine Handy Lewis and *Wyer Owens Handy.* Reprinted by permission of Macmillan Publishing Co., Inc.

All through the years this snatch of song had been ringing in my ears. Many times I wondered what was in the singer's mind. What was wrong with Cairo? Was Cairo too far south in Illinois to be "up North," or too far north to be considered "down South?"

In any event, such bits of music or snatches of song generated the motif for my blues and with an imagination stimulated by such lines as "I wouldn't live in Cairo," I wrote my lyrics.

If I had published at that time a composition called *The Cairo Blues*, and this simple four-bar theme had been developed into a four-page musical classic, every grown-up who had then heard that four-bar wail would now claim that Handy didn't write this number. And you would hear them say, "I heard it when I was knee-high to a grasshopper." Politely put, this would be a misstatement of fact; bluntly written, it would be a falsehood. That two-line snatch couldn't form a four-page composition any more than the two letters *i-n* could spell the word *information*. Some of the hot jazz I've heard on the radio in recent years, jazz played by sophisticated bands, is simply expanded treatment of little four-bar rhythms similar to that played by Uncle Whit Walker on his fiddle back in the days when I stood behind him, leaned over his shoulder and went to town with a pair of knitting needles. Today the cats have ten or twelve instruments to replace the single fiddle of those old sundown days, but the rhythmic themes remain much the same. Play Uncle Whit's *Little Lady Goin' to the Country* on your piano and you can imagine what the saxes and brasses would do to it today, yet it was a stomp popular in the days of the five-string banjo.

Uncle Whit's Song   Arr. by W.C. Handy*

Uncle Whit had a tune called *Sail Away, Ladies*. To the same tune my wife and her school chums patted, danced and sang *Oh, di-di-de-O*. Likewise, Cab Calloway's *Hi-de-ho* is an evolution from music that Negroes made with their mouths, hands and feet in the days when no instruments were available, naked rhythm replacing musical strains. . . .

While sleeping on the cobblestones in St. Louis ('92), I heard shabby guitarists picking out a tune called *East St. Louis*. It had numerous one-line verses and they would sing it all night.

I walked all the way from old East St. Louis,
And I didn't have but one po' measly dime.

That one line was an entire stanza. The impression made upon me by
hearing this phrase and by the tonality of these men's singing may well
have contributed to my writing the *St. Louis Blues,* but it should be clear
by now that my blues are built around or suggested by, rather than constructed of, the snatches, phrases, cries and idioms such as I have illustrated.

The three-line structure I employed in my lyric was suggested by a song
I heard Phil Jones sing in Evansville during my sojourn there.

Ain't got no friend nowhere, Lawd,
Ain't got no friend nowhere, Lawd,
Ain't got no friend nowhere.

Got no more home than a dog, Lawd,
Got no more home than a dog, Lawd,
Got no more home than a dog.

Phil Jones called the song *Got No More Home Than a Dog.* It was a
blues, but the word formed no part of its title. What we now call blues,
to the folk musicians meant a *kind* of song; individually they bore no such
designation. They were known by simple titles like *Stack O'Lee, Brady,
Frankie and Johnnie, John Henry, Stavin' Chain, Lost John, Joe Turner,*
and the like.

While I took the three-line stanza as a model for my lyric, I found its
repetition too monotonous. I figure it would have taken too long to tell
my story if I had repeated every thought three times. Consequently I
adopted the style of making a statement, repeating the statement in the
second line, and then telling in the third line why the statement was made.
Thus I said in *St. Louis Blues:*

I hate to see de eve'nin sun go down,
Hate to see de eve'nin' sun go down,
'Cause my baby, he done lef' dis town.

Feelin' tomorrow lak Ah feel today,
Feel tomorrow lak Ah feel today,
I'll pack my trunk and make ma get-away.

To vary the pattern still further, and to avoid monotony in the music,
I used a four-line unit in the next part of the lyric.

Saint Louis woman wid her diamon' rings
Pulls dat man roun' by her apron strings.
'Twant for powder an' for store-bought hair
De man I love would not gone nowhere.[33]

33. From *St. Louis Blues,* copyright, 1914, by W. C. Handy. Published by Handy
Brothers Music Co., Inc., New York.

Here, as in most of my other blues, three distinct musical strains are carried as a means of avoiding the monotony that always resulted in the three-line folk blues.

The question of language was a very real problem at the time I wrote *St. Louis Blues*. Negro intellectuals were turning from dialect in poetry as employed by Paul Lawrence Dunbar. I couldn't follow them, for I felt then, as I feel now, that certain words of Negro dialect are more musical and more expressive than pure English. Take the expression "Gonna walk all over God's Heaven." When Negro singers say "Heab'm" with their large nasal cavities serving as resonators and top it off by prolonging the *m*, they produce an effect that it is impossible for any other singers to match. Imagine sacrificing this pure magic for the sake of a properly enunciated "Heaven"!

Glissando on the Clarinet

I have taught beginners who taught themselves wrong on the clarinet and cornet. One on the clarinet had fingering that had never been written into diagrams. These notes he made by false fingering and incorrect lipping. He taught me something. This technique was made use of by musicians who liked to clown and finally a new technique was acquired by outstanding composers and instrumentalists. Theory once had it that no instruments other than the violin family and slide trombone family are capable of perfect legato or glissando. Had it not been for the mistakes of the ignorant and illiterate, Gershwin would not have been able to write a two-octave chromatic glissando clarinet passage for his *Rhapsody in Blue*. Edison made a mistake and discovered the electric light. Columbus made a mistake and discovered America. Theory made a mistake and had to be rewritten. Perfect glissandos now are made on clarinet, sax and trumpets.

13.8 PAUL HINDEMITH (1895–1963)

Not willing to sacrifice the natural force of tone to equal temperament, Paul Hindemith developed his own theory of music; and he composed with his theory in mind. Hindemith was a consummate musician who immersed himself in music of the past and yet was an integral part of the contemporary scene.[34] He played the violin and viola professionally; at various times in his career he was concertmaster of an opera orchestra or performer in a string quartet which he organized.

34. For Hindemith's association of the music of the late Middle Ages to the problems of modern music, see his preface to *French Secular Music of the Late Fourteenth Century*, ed. Willi Apel (Cambridge, Mass.: Mediaeval Academy of America, 1950).

  For Hindemith's musical philosophy, see his book entitled *A Composer's World* (New York: Doubleday & Co., 1961), a compilation of the Charles Eliot Norton Lectures which Hindemith gave at Harvard College (1949–1950).

Hindemith taught at the Berlin Hochschule für Musik (1927–1935), at the Ankara Conservatory in Turkey, and, from 1940 on, in the United States. That year, during the summer, he was in residence at the Berkshire Music Center at Tanglewood, and in the fall he joined the faculty of Yale University. In 1946 he became an American citizen.

Atonality and Polytonality*

We have seen that tonal relations are founded in Nature, in the characteristics of sounding materials and of the ear, as well as in the pure relations of abstract numerical groups.[35] We cannot escape the relationship of tones. Whenever two tones sound, either simultaneously or successively, they create a certain interval-value; whenever chords or intervals are connected, they enter into a more or less close relationship. And whenever the relationships of tones are played off one against another, tonal coherence appears. It is thus quite impossible to devise groups of tones without tonal coherence. Tonality is a natural force, like gravity. Indeed, when we consider that the root of a chord, because of its most favorable vibration-ratio to the other tones, and the lowest tone of a chord, because of the actually greater dimension and weight of its wave, have greater importance than the other tones, we recognize at once that it is gravitation itself that draws the tones towards their roots and towards the bass line, and that relates a multiplicity of chords to the strongest among them. If we omit from consideration the widely held notion that everything in which the ear and the understanding are not at once completely at home is atonal (a poor excuse for a lack of musical training and for following the path of least resistance), we may assert that there are but two kinds of music: good music, in which the tonal relations are handled intelligently and skilfully, and bad music, which disregards them and consequently mixes them in aimless fashion. There are many varieties between these two extremes, and of course it does not follow that all music in which the tonal relations are beautifully worked out is good music. But in all good music account is taken of them, and no music which disregards them can be satisfying, any more than could a building in which the most elementary laws of the vertical and horizontal disposition of masses were disregarded. For the creation of tonality it is all the same, being a matter of style and period, or of the manner in which a composer works, what kind of chord material is employed. A piece that consists primarily of very harsh and grating chords need not be atonal; and, on the other hand, limitation to the purest triads is no guarantee of clean tonal relationships.

The only music which can really be called atonal, therefore, is the work of a composer who is motivated perhaps by a consciousness of the inadequacy of old styles to the musical needs of our day, perhaps by a search for an idiom that will express his own feelings, perhaps by sheer perversity, to invent tonal combinations which do not obey the laws of the medium and cannot be tested by the simplest means of reckoning. Such a

*From Paul Hindemith, Craft of Musical Composition (New York: Associated Music Publishers, Inc.), I, 152–156. Printed by permission of B. Schott's Soehne.
35. For the overtone series, to which Hindemith is referring, see Chart 3.

man is not impelled by the instinct of the musician, who even in what seems his blindest groping never loses the true path entirely from view. But even among the music which can be completely analyzed there are two types which, although they cannot be called atonal, yet by the accumulation of harmonic means of expression place too great a burden on the listening ear for it to be able to follow them completely. One of these types, although it starts from diatonic premises, works with the material of the chromatic scale, and packs in so closely a multitude of dominant relations, alterations, and enharmonic changes, that the key is bursting with harmonic groups of short duration. The ear may succumb to an excess of harmonic procedures each reasonable in itself. The other type, by a continuous use of chords containing seconds or sevenths, produces an opaque kind of harmony which in its avoidance of any chord resembling a triad seems to fly in the face of Nature. Neither of these types can be made reasonable by the logic of its degree-progression; both are too crowded with material to be enjoyed. The development of music has left far behind the style of accumulated dominant relationships within short spaces of time, in favor of more important things. This style was developed by the German post-Wagnerian school. About 1900 it dominated the entire technique of composition, and it was still throwing up sizable waves as recently as the second decade of the present century, after which it quickly disappeared. The other style, which as a reaction to the outmoded diatonic style and the exaggerated technique of over-subtle harmonic relations and enharmonic changes, made great use of the sharpest chords, is still widely cultivated. We may assume that it will give way to a quieter and more enlightened style as soon as the quite praiseworthy joy of discovery on the part of composers and their pre-occupation with technical speculation become less important, and the accumulated knowledge of the expanded tonal materials and their laws prepares the way for a fuller and higher craft of composition.

Anyone to whom a tone is more than a note on paper or a key pressed down, anyone who has ever experienced the intervals in singing, especially with others, as manifestations of bodily tension, of the conquest of space, and of the consumption of energy, anyone who has ever tasted the delights of pure intonation by the continual displacement of the comma in string-quartet playing; must come to the conclusion that there can be no such thing as atonal music, in which the existence of tone-relationships is denied. The decline in the value placed upon tonality is based on the system of equal temperament, a compromise which is presented to us by the keyboard as an aid in mastering the tonal world, and then pretends to be that world itself. One needs only to have seen how the most fanatical lover of the piano will close his ears in horror at the falseness of the tempered chords of his instrument, once he has compared them a few times with those produced by a harmonium in pure intonation, to realize that with the blessing of equal temperament there entered into the world of music—lest the bliss of musical mortals be complete—a curse as well: the curse of too easy achievement of tone-connections. The tremendous growth of piano music in the last century is attributable to it, and in the "atonal" style I see its final fulfillment—the uncritical idolatry of tempered tuning.

The concept of atonality arose at the end of the first World War. . . . Today we know that there can be no such thing as atonality, unless we are to apply that term to harmonic disorder. The vagueness of the conception, arising from its negative origin—here even less fruitful than in other fields of creation—cause it to grow from a technical term into a popular catchword, used by some to praise to the skies any music they did not understand, and by others to condemn whatever they did not like, whether it consisted of strange harmonies, muted trumpets, *fortissimo* outbursts, or new experiments in structure.

There is another catchword that dates from the post-War period: polytonality. The game of letting two or more tonalities run along side by side and so achieving new harmonic effects, is, to be sure, very entertaining for the composer, but the listener cannot follow the separate tonalities, for he relates every simultaneous combination of sounds to a root—and thus we see the futility of the game. Every simultaneous combination of sounds must have one root, and only one; one cannot conceive of additional roots somewhere above, belonging to other tonal spheres. Even the craziest harmonic combinations can result in only one degree-progression. The ear judges the total sound, and does not ask with what intentions it was produced.

13.9 IGOR STRAVINSKY (1882–1971)

Whether tinged with ideas from Russian folklore, American jazz, Webern's technique of serial composition, or whatever else appealed to him as he went along, Igor Stravinsky's compositions were inevitably the work of the master. Stravinsky was born near St. Petersburg, the son of a bass singer at the Imperial Opera. Igor, however, did not decide to pursue a musical career until at the age of 19 he met Rimsky-Korsakov, (Section 12.6) with whom he studied privately starting in 1907.

Stravinsky's ballets, orchestral works, operas, and large choral compositions have had an inestimable impact on twentieth-century music. During his long, productive period of creative activity, he went from Russia, to France, to the United States. As he expressed himself musically, various styles emerged.

The Polar Attraction of Sound*

All of you know that the range of audible sounds constitutes the physical basis of the art of music. You also know that the scale is formed by means of the tones of the harmonic series arranged in diatonic order in a succession different from the one that nature offers us.

*From *Igor Stravinsky*, Poetics of Music in the Form of Six Lessons, *trans. Arthur Knodel and Ingolf Dahl (New York: Alfred A. Knopf, Inc.), pp. 35–40. Reprinted by permission of the publishers from Igor Stravinsky*, Poetics of Music in the Form of Six Lessons, *Cambridge, Mass.: Harvard University Press, Copyright © 1942, 1947, 1970 by the President and Fellows of Harvard College.*

You likewise know that the pitch relationship between two tones is called an interval, and that a chord is the sound-complex that results from the simultaneous sounding of at least three tones of different pitches.

All is well up to this point, and all this is clear to us. But the concepts of consonance and dissonance have given rise to tendentious interpretations that should definitely be set aright.

Consonance, says the dictionary, is the combination of several tones into a harmonic unit. Dissonance results from the deranging of this harmony by the addition of tones foreign to it. One must admit that all this is not clear. Ever since it appeared in our vocabulary, the word dissonance has carried with it a certain odor of sinfulness.

Let us light our lantern: in textbook language, dissonance is an element of transition, a complex or interval of tones which is not complete in itself and which must be resolved to the ear's satisfaction into a perfect consonance.

But just as the eye completes the lines of a drawing which the painter has knowingly left incomplete, just so the ear may be called upon to complete a chord and cooperate in the resolution, which has not actually been realized in the work. Dissonance, in this instance, plays the part of an allusion.

Either case applies to a style where the use of dissonance demands the necessity of a resolution. But nothing forces us to be looking constantly for satisfaction that resides only in repose. And for over a century music has provided repeated examples of a style in which dissonance has emancipated itself. It is no longer tied down to its former function. Having become an entity in itself, it frequently happens that dissonance is thus no more an agent of disorder than consonance is a guarantee of security. The music of yesterday and of today unhesitatingly unites parallel dissonant chords that thereby lose their functional value, and our ear quite naturally accepts their juxtaposition.

Of course, the instruction and education of the public have not kept pace with the evolution of technique. The use of dissonance, for ears ill-prepared to accept it, has not failed to confuse their reaction, bringing about a state of debility in which the dissonant is no longer distinguished from the consonant.

We thus no longer find ourselves in the framework of classic tonality in the scholastic sense of the work. It is not we who have created this state of affairs, and it is not our fault if we find ourselves confronted with a new logic of music that would have appeared unthinkable to the masters of the past. And this new logic has opened our eyes to riches whose existence we never suspected.

Having reached this point, it is no less indispensable to obey, not new idols, but the eternal necessity of affirming the axis of our music and to recognize the existence of certain poles of attraction. Diatonic tonality is only one means of orienting music toward these poles. The function of tonality is completely subordinated to the force of attraction of the pole of sonority. All music is nothing more than a succession of impulses that converge toward a definite point of repose. That is as true of Gregorian chant as of a Bach fugue, as true of Brahms's music as of Debussy's.

This general law of attraction is satisfied in only a limited way by the traditional diatonic system, for that system possesses no absolute value.

Few present-day musicians are not aware of this state of affairs. But the fact remains that it is still impossible to lay down the rules that govern this new technique. Nor is this at all surprising. Harmony as it is taught today in the schools dictates rules that were not fixed until long after the publication of the works upon which they were based, rules which were unknown to the composers of these works. In this manner our harmonic treatises take as their point of departure Mozart and Haydn, neither of whom ever heard of harmonic treatises.

So our chief concern is not so much what is known as tonality as what one might term the polar attraction of sound, of an interval, or even of a complex of tones. The sounding tone constitutes in a way the essential axis of music. Musical form would be unimaginable in the absence of elements of attraction which make up every musical organism and which are bound up with its psychology. The articulations of musical discourse betray a hidden correlation between the *tempo* and the interplay of tones. All music being nothing but a succession of impulses and repose, it is easy to see that the drawing together and separation of poles of attraction in a way determine the respiration of music.

In view of the fact that our poles of attraction are no longer within the close system which was the diatonic system, we can bring the poles together without being compelled to conform to the exigencies of tonality. For we no longer believe in the absolute value of the major-minor system based on the entity which musicologists call the *c*-scale.

The tuning of an instrument, of a piano for example, requires that the entire musical range available to the instrument should be ordered according to chromatic steps. Such tuning prompts us to observe that all these sounds converge toward a center which is the *a* above middle *c*. Composing, for me, is putting into an order a certain number of these sounds according to certain interval-relationships. This activity leads to a search for the center upon which the series of sounds involved in my undertaking should converge. Thus, if a center is given, I shall have to find a combination that converges upon it. If, on the other hand, an as yet unoriented combination has been found, I shall have to determine the center toward which it should lead. The discovery of this center suggests to me the solution of my problem. It is thus that I satisfy my very marked taste for such a kind of musical topography.

13.10 OTTO LUENING (b. 1900)

Through electronic means the musical synthesizer made available to composers every possible attribute of sound, including pitch, duration, intensity, and decay. In 1959 the synthesizer for the Columbia-Princeton Electronic Music Center was completed in New York City. One of the guiding forces of this project, the composer Otto Luening, describes the establishment of the synthesizer in its historical context.

Luening, born in Milwaukee, Wisconsin, studied flute and composition at the Royal Academy of Music in Munich and at the Zürich Conservatory. After touring Europe for five years as a flutist and conductor, he returned to the United States in 1920, at which time he founded the American Grand Opera Company in Chicago. As a composer Luening has mingled the sounds of nineteenth-century instruments with those of the twentieth-century electronic media in such works as *Sonority Canon* for four solo flutes accompanied by thirty-three flutes on tape (1962).

Electronic Music*

Electronic music is music which uses electronically generated sound or sound modified by electronic means, with or without voices or musical instruments, live or over speakers. My effort here is to highlight events from the past that have a bearing on the present or point to the future. . . .

Preoccupation with acoustics is not new. I Ching and Chinese acoustical studies both stem from approximately 2800 B.C., and King Fang tried a fifty-three-tone scale within an octave over fifteen centuries before the West got around to it. The work of the Sanskrit grammarian Panini of the third or fourth century B.C. has survived. In addition to making purely linguistic studies, he found the relationship between language sounds and physical positions of the mouth. Ptolemy and Pythagoras are so well advertised that they need only brief mention. As we move forward in time a number of interesting experiments come to mind. Don Nicola Vicentino's *Archicembalo* was a harpsichordlike instrument with thirty-one steps within an octave [Section 7.1]. With it he hoped to revive the ancient Greek modes. Athanasius Kircher [Section 8.5, fn. 15] constructed a composing machine with the fine name *Arca Musarithmica* (1660). Scale, rhythm, and tempo relations were represented by numbers and number relations, indeed arithmetic, from which the machine got its name. A hundred years after Kircher had built his composing machine the drive toward machine music had produced not only instruments like the mechanical organs, trumpets, musical clocks, and glass harmonicas that interested Mozart, Kirnberger, Haydn, and Handel, but also those practical and playing instruments, the perfected organ and pianoforte. The *Electric Harpsichord*, invented by J. B. Delaborde in Paris (1761), Hipp's *Electromechanical Piano* in Neuchatel (1867), Elisha Gray's *Electroharmonic Piano* demonstrated in Chicago in 1876, the same year that Koenig's *Tonametric* apparatus (which divided four octaves into 670 equal parts) was demonstrated in Philadelphia, and Julian Carrillo's theories of microtones and preoccupation with a 96-tone scale (Mexico, 1895) bring us to the threshold of the twentieth century.

Edison's patent for the phonograph (1878), the Emile Berliner telephone transmitter and disc record (1877), the development of various acoustical principles by Alexander Melville Bell (1867), Helmholtz's *Sensations of Tone* (1885), and the work of W. C. Sabin, P. M. Morse, Lord Rayleigh,

From Otto Luening, "Some Random Remarks about Electronic Music," Journal of Music Theory, VIII, No. 1 (1964), 89–98. Reprinted by permission of the Journal of Music Theory.

Dayton Miller, Harvey Fletcher, and other scientists gave focus to experiments of the past and influence us to this day.

On March 10, 1906, an editorial in the professional electrotechnical journal, *Electrical World*, published in New York, described a demonstration that took place in Mount Holyoke, Massachusetts on that date. A machine, the *Dynamophone*, produced music made by a group of dynamos run by alternating current. The editorial was signed L. Stokowski. Other reporters wrote that the machine, also called *Telharmonium*, was the largest musical instrument in the world [Section 13.3]. It weighed 200 tons. The electrically generated music was transmitted over telephone wire systems, but these proved to be too fragile to carry such an array of signals. Upon the complaint of the regular telephone subscribers this "extraordinary electrical invention for the production of scientifically perfect music" stopped functioning.

The experiments of Thaddeus Cahill, who invented this instrument, were presented first in 1900. They came to the attention of Ferruccio Busoni when he read the July, 1906, article in McClure's Magazine, "New Music for an Old World," by R. S. Baker. At that time Busoni was writing his *Sketch of a New Esthetic of Music* which was published in 1907.[36] In this remarkable collection of "notes," as he called the booklet, he questioned much of the prevailing music practice and pointed out some new possibilities. He wrote that art forms last longer if they stay close to the essence of each individual species. He suggested that music is almost incorporeal (he called it "sonorous air"), almost like Nature herself. He opposed formalism, systems, and routine, but asserted that each musical motive contains within itself its "life germ," the embryo of its fully developed form, each one different from all the others. He proclaimed that the creative artist did not follow laws already made; he made laws. Busoni decried a too rigid adherence to existing notation and said that the terms *consonance* and *dissonance* were too confining. He suggested an expansion of the major-minor-chromatic scale and assembled 113 other scale formations within the octave C-C. (Ernst Bacon expanded this number by using algebraic permutations. Using intervals no larger than a major third he found 1,490 possibilities. See "Our Musical Idiom," *The Monist*, 1917, about this and other interesting matters.) Busoni predicted a revolution in the field of harmony. He was convinced that instrumental music had come to a dead end and that new instruments were needed, and he suggested a scale of 36 divisions within the octave as an interesting possibility for new music.

In Cahill's instrument Busoni saw a way out of the impasse which instrumental music had reached. However, he warned that a lengthy and careful series of experiments and further ear training was necessary to make the unfamiliar material plastic and useful for coming generations. Two

---

36. Ferruccio Busoni (1866–1924), famous composer and pianist, taught at the Helsingfors Conservatory in Moscow (1888), the New England Conservatory in Boston (1891), and the Vienna Conservatory. In 1913 Busoni became director of the Liceo Musicale in Bologna. He is known for his piano transcriptions of Bach's keyboard works. Busoni tried to achieve orchestral effects by such means as doubling the voice parts in octaves, and extending the range as he worked out the arpeggios. Otto Luening studied with Busoni. Busoni's *Sketch of a New Esthetic of Music* has been reprinted together with Debussy's *Monsieur Croche the Dilettante Hater* and Ives' *Essays before a Sonata* under the title, *Three Classics in the Aesthetic of Music* (New York: Dover Publications, Inc.)

years after Busoni made these statements the Italian Marinetti published in *Le Figaro* in Paris his *Futurist Manifesto* which called for a world-wide artists' revolt against the ossified values of the past. The movement spread rapidly to Germany, Russia, and Switzerland.

The Art of Noises, compiled in 1913 by Luigi Russolo, a painter, is still of interest. He suggested fixing the pitch of noise sounds and classified them as follows:

Group 1	*Group 2*	*Group 3*
Booms	Whistles	Whispers
Thunder claps	Hisses	Murmers
Explosions	Snorts	Mutterings
Crashes		Bustling noises
Splashes		Gurgles
Roars		

Group 4	*Group 5*	*Group 6*
Screams	Noises obtained by	Voices of animals, men
Screeches	percussion on	Shouts
Rustlings	metals, wood,	Shrieks
Buzzes	stone, and terracotta	Groans
Cracklings		Howls
Sounds by friction		Laughs
		Wheezes
		Sobs

In his diary about *Concrete Music* Pierre Schaeffer names Russolo as the precursor of the noise montage as it developed at the Centre d'Etude of the Radiodiffusion-Télévision Française by mid-century. Russolo implemented his catalogue of noises by building a whole collection of noise-making instruments. Futurism became Dadaism when Tristan Tzara coined the term in 1916 in Zurich. His recipe for making a poem still has a bearing on some of today's artistic manifestations: ". . . cut out the single words of a newspaper article, shake well in a bag, take them out one by one and copy down in the order in which you picked them."

Between Busoni's booklet and the advent of Dadaism Schoenberg wrote his *Harmonielehre* (1911). In this important book triadic harmony evolved systematically and logically to a system of chords built on perfect fourths. The work ends with a prophetic statement about timbre melodies. And in 1913 the Paris premiere of Stravinsky's *Rite of Spring* took place [Section 13.9]. Orchestral rhythm and timbre were given a new dimension and the work had a profound effect on composers, indeed, on the art world in general.

When I met Busoni in Zürich in 1917, his views about composition had changed since 1907. On tour he had seen the German-American theorist Bernhard Ziehn in Chicago. Ziehn had published in 1887 a remarkable harmony text which developed a system of symmetrical inversion based on the old *Contrarium Reversum*.[37] When Busoni met him in 1910, he was engaged in developing a system of canonical techniques.

In his Zurich years Busoni assumed that composers who showed him

---

37. *Contrarium Reversum* is inverted and backwards. See Webern's description of *Composition with Twelve Notes*, Section 13.5. The postlude of Hindemith's *Ludus tonalis* is the retrograde inversion of the prelude.

scores would have mastered technical problems more or less by themselves. He expected experimentation and analysis; novelty for its own sake interested him no longer. He talked of form, not formula, and spoke, as he had written in the past, of taste, style, economy, temperament (human, not musical!), intelligence, and equipoise.

Edgar Varèse,[38] friend and protégé of Busoni, and precursor of much that has happened, suggested in the early 1920's that greater cooperation between engineers and composers would be both desirable and necessary if the art were to reach new heights. Curiously enough, Carlos Chavez in his *Toward a New Music* [W. W. Norton, 1937] also expressed the hope that a collaboration between engineers and musicians would take place. Some of the results of this kind of cooperation have been and still are far-reaching.

Joerg Mager built an electronic *Spharaophon* in Germany which was presented at the Donaueschingen Festival in 1926. Supported by the city of Darmstadt he later developed a *Partiturophon* and a *Kaleidophon*. All these useful electronic instruments had been tried in theatrical productions, and although all were destroyed in World War II, Mager's example animated others to explore the field. It was Friedrich Trautwein who introduced his *Trautonium* a few years later. It became a practical instrument that was used by a number of composers including Hindemith,[39] Richard Strauss, and Werner Egk. Hindemith, in his *Craft of Musical Composition*, acknowledges his debt to Trautwein and his instrument for providing the foundation for many of the theses that he expresses in his book. The Hindemith-Trautwein research team was discontinued because of the war and was never active again, but improvements of the *Trautonium* by Oscar Sala resulted in the *Mixtur-Trautonium*, a very brilliant instrument which Sala plays and for which he composes with skill. The German composers Henze, Orff, Erbse, and others have also composed for this instrument.

Leon Theremin introduced to Russia in 1923 the instrument bearing his name. A number of composers have used it in their compositions, among them Paschtschenko, Schillinger,[40] Slonimski, Varèse, Grainger,[41] Martinu,[42]

38. Edgar Varèse (1885–1965) studied at the Schola Cantorum in Paris with Vincent d'Indy and Albert Roussel. After composing works in the Romantic and Impressionistic styles, he turned to innovative techniques. Varèse came to the United States in 1915, where he organized the Pan American Society to further the music of the Americas. His first major work was fittingly entitled *Amériques* (1918–21). Rejecting consonant harmony and thematic development, he concentrated on timbre, subtle dynamics, and intricate rhythms. His *Ionization* for percussion and two sirens (1931) exploits sound without definite pitch. *Density 21.5* is for unaccompanied (platinum) flute (1936, 1946). *Ecouatorial*, for baritone, theremin, organ, brasses, and percussion (1933–34) was revised to replace the theremin with the Ondes Martenot (1961). *Nuit* is a symphonic poem with electronic sound (1965).

39. In 1927 Hindemith composed music for a mechanical organ to accompany *Felix the Cat*, a cartoon film.

40. Joseph Schillinger (1895–1943), who wrote his *First Airphonic Suite* for theremin and orchestra in 1929, developed a mathematical system of composition that was a boon to the arrangers of radio and film music.

41. Percy Aldridge Grainger (1882–1961), born in Australia, came to the U.S. in 1914. After meeting Grieg in 1906, Grainger consistently included Grieg's Piano Concerto in his successful concert tours. Grainger was deeply interested in the gliding intervals inherent in scales derived from folk melodies, as well as in traditional rhythms.

42. Bohuslav Martinu (1890–1959), Czech composer who spent much time in America,

and Fuleihan.[43] The Theremin-Cowell Rhythmicon, for which Cowell composed several pieces in 1932, could perform the most complicated kinds of polyrhythmic formations with clarity. Henry Cowell's tone-clusters, introduced to the wider public in the early 1920's, became the starting point for further extensions of piano resonance, for other preparations of the piano useful as sound sources for experimental music.[44]

Just before and during the 1920's various kinds of research were brought into focus. For example, in the field of theory Ernst Kurth published his *Grundlagen des linearen Kontrapunkts* (1917) and other works that dealt with musical form in Busoni's sense of the term, and in 1926 Josef Mathias Hauer presented his theory of tropes [see Section 13.4]. In France, Maurice Martenot demonstrated his Ondes Martenot in the Paris Opera on April 20, 1928. Nineteen years later he was Professor at the Paris Conservatoire, instructing classes in Ondes playing. A long list of composers have used the Ondes Martenot. They include Honegger,[45] Milhaud,[46] Messiaen,[47] Jolivet,

---

wrote almost 400 compositions, many of which have conventional titles such as *Symphony, Concerto, String Quartet, Quintet, Ricercar,* and *Fantasy.* He had a special talent for writing music that achieved powerful effects after short periods of rehearsal, and as a result was in demand for radio-opera and television music.

43. Anis Fuleihan (1900–1970), born in Cyprus, came to the U.S. in 1915. Under the auspices of the U.S. State Department, he went to Tunis in 1962, where he founded and conducted the Orchestre Classique de Tunis. His compositions reflect his wide acquaintance with musical styles in the vicinity of the Mediterranean.

44. Henry Dixon Cowell (1897–1960), composer and pianist, studied in California, where he was born, and in Berlin with Erich von Hornbostel. The distinguished musicologist, von Hornbostel, had come to the United States in 1906 to record and transcribe the music of the American Indians; he also worked with the native music of Japan, Madagascar. Indonesia, and Africa. Cowell's wide interest in the pitch systems and rhythms of other lands as well as his own is reflected in the titles of some of his works, such as the *Gaelic Symphony,* the *Madras Symphony,* the *Icelandic Symphony,* the *Old American Country Set,* the *Celtic Set,* the *Irish Set, American Muse, To America,* etc. Cowell was interested not only in developing himself as an American composer but also in promoting the works of others, such as Charles Ives and Walter Piston. From 1927 to 1936 Cowell published and edited new music in the *New Music Quarterly* which he founded.

Cowell's technique of striking several keys on the piano at once with his palm, fist, or forearm *(tone clusters)* and reaching inside the piano to pluck the strings instead of producing the tone via the keyboard, were among the areas of innovation pursued further by John Cage (b. 1912), one of Cowell's talented students. Cage, particularly interested in tone, noise, and silence, composed *Imaginary Landscape* for twenty-four radios, combining aleatory (chance) music with mechanics.

45. Arthur Honegger (1892–1955), along with Milhaud, Poulenc, Auric, Durey, and Germaine Tailleferre, was dubbed a member of *Les Six* by the Parisian critic Henri Collet. In an article in the periodical *Comoedia* Collet compared these six young French composers with the *Russian 5* (Section 12.6). In 1924 Honegger wrote *Pacific 231,* a symphonic movement describing a powerful American locomotive gaining speed and then slowing down to a full stop, a veritable symbol of the machine age.

46. Darius Milhaud (b. 1892), trained in Paris, emigrated to the United States in 1940 alternately spending one year as a professor at Mills College in California and the next year in Paris. His compositional prowess is revealed in works with polytonality and simultaneous fugues. His double string quartet of 1948 may be played as a whole or as two separate quartets. In the electronic vein, the *Etude poétique* combines seven different tapes into one performance montage.

47. Olivier Messiaen (b. 1908), together with Jolivet, Baudrier, and Lesur, hoped to

Koechlin, and Varèse. The inventor built a special model of the instrument in 1938 following specifications of Rabindranath Tagore and Alain Daniélou for the purpose of reproducing the microtonal refinements of Hindu music.[48] Another invention of far-reaching importance must be mentioned here. Lee DeForest, with inspired vision, thought first of the Audion (1906), now called the Triode. This and his 300 other patents had a deciding influence on modern communications.

At the 1926 Chamber Music Festival in Donaueschingen in Germany it was suggested that recordings might be used as creative tools for musical composition. Two years later a research program was established at the Hochschule für Musik in Berlin to examine this and related problems. By 1930 Paul Hindemith and Ernst Toch had produced short montages based on phonographic speed-up and slow-down, sound transposition and mixing, as well as polyrhythmic experiments. Toch produced his *Fuge aus der Geographie*, a work based on four-part vocal choral writing. Hindemith used instruments and solo voice as his sound sources. Robert Beyer, in the article "Das Problem der Kommender Musik" (*Die Musik*, Vol. 19, 1928), had expressed new ideas on space or room music but without having gained significant reactions from professionals and the public.

From the 1930's until after World War II much attention was given to producing electric instruments that could imitate existing instruments. At the same time the tape recorder was perfected and seemed destined to be used for creative purposes. Research and development took place, in part, at great institutions like the Bell Telephone Laboratories, the Brookhaven National Laboratories, the University of California, and the Institutes of Physics in Berlin and Moscow.

Pierre Schaeffer, an engineer in Paris, had presented a "Concert of Noises" over the French Radio in 1948. He had arranged sounds from natural and instrumental sources into a series of montages, somewhat like the experiments by Hindemith and Toch in Berlin but with much greater freedom in sound and noise selection. The sounds were treated, manipulated, and presented from phonograph records. By 1952 Schaeffer was director of the research center of Radio-Diffusion Française and had associated himself with the engineer Poulin and, among others, the composers Jolivet, Messiaen, Pierre Henry, and Boulez.[49] This group presented two concerts of

promote contemporary French music in an organization called *La jeune France*. Messiaen has described his theories, embracing resources such as the Gregorian chant and Eastern rhythms, in *The Technique of My Musical Language* (1944, trans. 1957). His gigantic symphony, the ten-movement *Turangalila*, includes three Talas for piano and orchestra. After its performance in Paris (1948), Leonard Bernstein conducted this work with the Boston Symphony Orchestra in 1949. Messiaen's *Mode de valeurs et d'intensité* for piano (1949) was an important influence on the development of Stockhausen and Boulez.

48. Rabindranath Tagore (1861–1941), famous Indian poet born in Calcutta, founded an experimental school nearby. His wide travels through Europe, Japan, and the United States brought Tagore into contact with ideas which he endeavored to combine with the Indian tradition, steeped in improvisatory practices. See William W. Austin, *Music in the Twentieth Century* (New York: W. W. Norton, 1966), p. 65.

49. Pierre Boulez (b. 1925) studied composition with Olivier Messiaen and René Leibowitz. Boulez's cantata *Le Marteau sans Maître* (1956) is scored for contralto, flute, viola, guitar, vibraphone, and percussion.

Musique Concrète in the hall of the Conservatoire in May, 1952. A year later Schaeffer's *Orpheus* was first performed at the Donaueschingen Festival. The resulting scandal focused international attention on the new music. Since then the Paris Radio has organized study groups, produced much music over the air and in concert, and built a concert hall to perform the music. Schaeffer has taken out many patents, notably those for the Phonogène and Morphophone, both used in the Paris center.

Vladimir Ussachevsky, born in China of Russian parents and educated in the United States, first experimented with tape in 1951, independent of the Paris group. His experiments were presented at Columbia University in May, 1952. At the Bennington Composers Conference in the fall of 1952 some short compositions by Ussachevsky and the present writer were performed. On October 28, 1952, in a concert at the Museum of Modern Art in New York, Leopold Stokowski introduced a work by Ussachevsky and three by this writer. Both composers used tape techniques, with flute and piano as sound sources. Thus, the pieces were called tape music. (For a description of the techniques see Vladimir Ussachevsky, "The Processes of Experimental Music," *Journal of the Audio Engineering Society*, July, 1958.)

The first public performance of a work for tape recorder and symphony orchestra was *Rhapsodic Variations* by the present writer and Vladimir Ussachevsky, a work commissioned by the Louisville Orchestra and programmed there March 20, 1954. It was during these years that the Columbia Studio was first established and the earlier works by Ussachevsky and Luening were produced with Peter Mauzey as consulting engineer. In 1959 with the help of a Rockefeller grant the Columbia-Princeton Electronic Music Center was established under the direction of Milton Babbitt [50] and Roger Sessions [51] from Princeton and Vladimir Ussachevsky and the present writer from Columbia. The Center has been active in advising other institutions about establishing studios. There are now seven in the United States and more are planned.

In 1955 the Radio Corporation of America demonstrated the Olson-Belar *Electronic Music Synthesizer* for the American Institute of Electrical Engineers in New York. The concept of almost limitless possibilities of tonal synthesis was impressive. In 1958 Babbitt, Ussachevsky, and this author did research with the Synthesizer at RCA. A second model, Mark II, was lent to the Columbia-Princeton Center in 1959. My work, *Dynamophonic Suite*, based on material from the Synthesizer manipulated on tape, was presented at the American Academy in Rome in 1958. Babbitt, who has been concerned with electronic music since the late 1930's, presented the first extended work for this medium, entitled *Composition for Synthesizer*, on May

50. Milton Babbitt, born in Philadelphia in 1916, is a professor of music and mathematics at Princeton University. Babbitt adopted the number 12 not only for the series of tones in a row, in the manner of Schoenberg, but also for the twelve time values in a theme, and for the twelve different instruments successively playing the theme.

51. Roger Sessions, born in Brooklyn, N.Y. in 1896, studied at Harvard University (B.A. 1915), at the Yale School of Music with Horatio Parker (B.M. 1917), and with Ernest Bloch in Cleveland. From 1928 to 1931 Sessions and another notable American composer, Aaron Copland, presented a series of outstanding concerts featuring modern music.

9, 1961, at Columbia University. The output of the Synthesizer provided the sole material for the piece and it was not subjected to any further modifications.

On the same program my composition entitled *Gargoyles*, for violin and synthesized sound, was performed. The violin is played live; the sounds from the Synthesizer have been manipulated on tape. Appearing also on this program was Ussachevsky's *Creation*, a work which combines a live chorus and solo voice with electronic sounds. The voices sing a tri-lingual text.

In Germany in 1948 H. W. Dudley from the Bell Telephone Laboratories demonstrated the *Vocoder*, a composite device consisting of an analyzer and an artificial talker. This instrument and the Mathematical Theory of Communication (1949) by Claude Shannon and Warren Weaver made a strong impression on Dr. Werner Meyer-Eppler at the Phonetic Institute of Bonn University. Meyer-Eppler presented the *Vocoder* at the Northwest German Music Academy in Detmold where he gave a lecture, "Developmental Possibilities of Sound," in 1949.

In 1950 Beyer, who had been present at Meyer-Eppler's lecture in Detmold, gave two lectures and Meyer-Eppler gave one lecture on "The World of Sound of Electronic Music." Varèse and Herbert Eimert attended. The next year Meyer-Eppler produced models of synthetic sounds at Bonn University and presented them at Darmstadt. On October 18 these experiments were broadcast over the Cologne Radio station and the staff recommended . . . "to follow the process suggested by Dr. Meyer-Eppler to compose directly onto magnetic tape." These events led to the creation of the *Electronic Studio* at the Northwest German Radio in Cologne. In 1952 Bruno Maderna composed his *Music su due Dimensioni* for live instruments and electronic sounds. The preparation of the tape was made with the help of Meyer-Eppler. Pierre Boulez and Karlheinz Stockhausen heard the work in Darmstadt.

May 26, 1953, saw the first performance of works from the Cologne studio, works by Eimert and Beyer. Then in 1954 the studio gave a concert of purely electronic works by Goeyvaerts, Pousseur, Gredinger, Eimert, and Stockhausen. The compositions used a strict serial technique. The Cologne studio has had a study group for some time and last year appointed Stockhausen Artistic Director.[52]

Luciano Berio and Bruno Maderna founded the electronic Studio di Fonologia Musicale at the Italian Radio in Milan (RAI). Berio's *Mutazioni* and Maderna's *Sequenzi a Strutture* were performed there in 1958, and since that time the studio has been opened to a number of composers from various countries.[53]

52. Karlheinz Stockhausen (b. 1928), German composer, studied in Cologne and then with Messiaen and Milhaud in Paris. Stockhausen has worked out the means of manipulating snatches of pretaped sounds which he then incorporates into his compositions, and has devised ways of letting the performer choose the succession of themes or their simultaneous presentation in a composition.

53. Luciano Berio (b. 1925) attended the Music Academy in Milan. After graduating in 1951, Berio came to Tanglewood, the summer location of the Boston Symphony Orchestra, where he studied serial techniques with Luigi Dallapiccola. Berio stayed at the Milan studio for tape manipulation and electronic music until 1961. The following year he started to teach composition at the Juilliard School in New York City.

The present state of electronic studio facilities has fairly complete documentation from 1948 through 1962 in the publication *Répértoire International des Musiques Expérimentales* which lists twenty-one studios in 1962. Since then another dozen have come to my attention including those at Brandeis, Yale, Wayne State, Pennsylvania, Michigan, San Francisco Conservatory of Music, and Bennington College.

Bibliography

DICTIONARIES AND CATALOGS

APEL, WILLI, *Harvard Dictionary of Music*. Cambridge, Mass.: Harvard University Press.

Baker's Biographical Dictionary of Musicians. New York: G. Schirmer.

Grove's Dictionary of Music and Musicians. London: Macmillan Publishers Ltd. and New York: St. Martin's Press, Inc.

HEYER, ANNA H., *Historical Sets, Collected Editions and Monuments of Music, A Guide to their Contents*. Chicago: American Library Association.

RIEMANN, HUGO, *Dictionary of Music*, trans. J. S. Shedlock (London, 1908). Reprint New York: Da Capo Press.

ANTHOLOGIES OF MUSIC

DAVISON, ARCHIBALD T., and WILLI APEL, *Historical Anthology of Music*. Cambridge, Mass.: Harvard University Press.

The History of Music in Sound, Gerald Abraham, gen. ed. New York: Oxford University Press.

PARRISH, CARL, *A Treasury of Early Music*. New York: W. W. Norton & Company, Inc.

—— and JOHN F. OHL, *Masterpieces of Music Before 1750*. New York: W. W. Norton & Company, Inc.

STARR, WILLIAM J., and GEORGE F. DEVINE, *Music Scores Omnibus*. Englewood Cliffs, N.J.: Prentice-Hall, Inc.

MUSIC HISTORIES

BURNEY, CHARLES, *A General History of Music* (1776–1789). Reprint New York: Dover Publications, Inc.

HAWKINS, JOHN, *A General History of the Science and Practice of Music* (1776). Reprint New York: Dover Publications, Inc.

The New Oxford History of Music.

The W. W. Norton & Company History of Music.

The Prentice-Hall History of Music Series, including Music in the Medieval World, Renaissance, Baroque, Classic Period, Nineteenth-Century Romanticism, Twentieth-Century Music, Folk and Traditional Music of the Western Continents, Music Cultures of the Pacific, the Near East and Asia, Music of Latin America, Music in the United States.

Appendixes

APPENDIX I

Chart 1.

The Pythagorean Proportions Related to the Central Octave of the Greek System

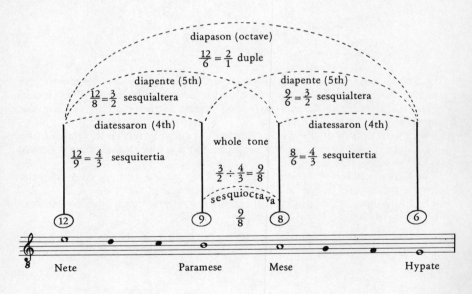

To add intervals, multiply their ratios. To subtract one interval from another, divide the ratio of the larger interval by the ratio of the smaller.

Chart 2.

Relationship of the Greek Systems to the Guidonian Gamut

GREEK SYSTEMS IN THE DIATONIC GENUS   GUIDONIAN GAMUT
  Tetrachords   *Hexachords*

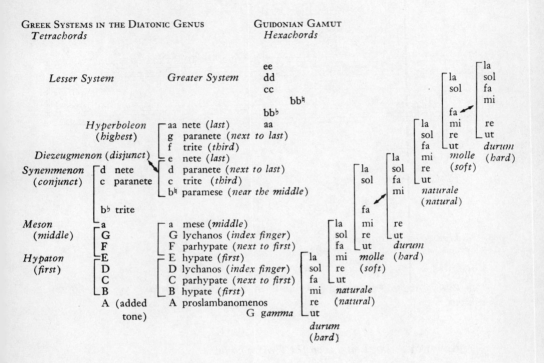

Indicated here is the Greek instrumental notation, which designated the pitches according to the placement of the finger on a string. The Greeks also had a vocal notation which used letters rather than names for the pitches.

The lowest octave of the scale is written in capital letters A through G, the next octave is in lower case a through g, and the highest incomplete octave is aa through ee.

The Greek central octave was E to e. They added a tone, A, below the lowest tetrachord to complete a two-octave range.

The Guidonian hexachord system extended one tone below and the interval of a fifth above the Greek systems.

Chart 3.

The Harmonic Series from Numbers 1 through 16

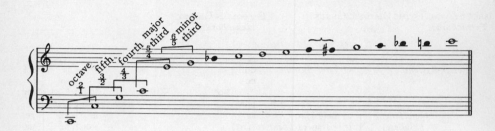

Fundamental:

1

Harmonic Numbers:

1   2   3   4   5   6   7   8   9   10   11   12   13   14   15   16

Ratios of String Lengths to the Fundamental:

1   $\frac{1}{2}$ $\frac{1}{3}$ $\frac{1}{4}$ $\frac{1}{5}$ $\frac{1}{6}$

Ratios of Vibrations to the Fundamental:

1   $\frac{2}{1}$ $\frac{3}{1}$ $\frac{4}{1}$ $\frac{5}{1}$ $\frac{6}{1}$

Numbers 1 through 6 were designated as the basic harmonics through the Renaissance era. Numbers 7, 11, 13, and 14 are not in tune with the fundamental in an equally tempered system.

Chart 4.

Proportions Implicit in the Greek Tetrachords

Tetrachord: Four pitches in descending motion.
Diesis: An interval smaller than a whole tone.
There were varying sizes of half-tones and quarter-tones, depending on how they were derived.

Diatonic tetrachord (whole tone, whole tone, semitone)

A perfect fourth minus two whole tones equals a minor semitone (limma)

$$\frac{4}{3} \quad \div \quad \left(\frac{9}{8} \times \frac{9}{8}\right) \quad = \quad \frac{256}{243} \quad \text{or} \quad \frac{25}{24}$$

Enharmonic tetrachord (major third, quarter-tone, quarter-tone)

A perfect fourth minus a ditone (major third) equals a major semitone

$$\frac{4}{3} \quad \div \quad \frac{5}{4} \quad = \quad \frac{16}{15}$$

| ditone | major tone | minor tone | major semitone | chromatic diesis | enharmonic diesis |

$$\frac{5}{4} = \frac{9}{8} \times \frac{10}{9} \qquad \frac{16}{15} = \frac{128}{125} \times \frac{5}{8}$$

Chromatic tetrachord (minor third, semitone, semitone)

A perfect fourth minus a semiditone equals a minor whole tone.
(minor third)

$$\frac{4}{3} \quad \div \quad \frac{6}{5} \quad = \quad \frac{10}{9}$$

Minor whole tone equals major semitone plus minor semitone

$$\frac{10}{9} \quad = \quad \frac{16}{15} \quad + \quad \frac{25}{24}$$

Chromatic diesis equals major semitone minus minor semitone

$$\frac{128}{125} \quad = \quad \frac{16}{15} \quad \div \quad \frac{25}{24}$$

Syntonic comma equals $\begin{cases} \text{major whole tone minus minor whole tone} \\ \\ \text{major third minus Pythagorean third} \end{cases}$

$$\frac{81}{80} \quad = \quad \frac{9}{8} \quad \div \quad \frac{10}{9}$$

or

$$\frac{5}{4} \quad \div \quad \frac{81}{64}$$

Chart 5.

The Eight Church Modes or Psalm Tones

There are four authentic modes within the octaves of D, E, F, and G, and four plagal modes outlined by the octaves a fourth below.

The finalis for each set of authentic and plagal modes is the same.
Except where the note B is involved,
  The confinalis of the authentic modes is a fifth above the finalis.
  The confinalis of a plagal mode is a third below that of the corresponding authentic mode.

Trends in Musical Thought, Style, and Performance Practice

1. REASON (*Ratio*), HEARING (*Audio*), AND MUSICAL MEMORY: Aristoxenus, Ptolemy, Boethius, St. Augustine, Isidore, Notker, Guido, Al Fārābi, Salinas, Billings

   SENSE OF THE WORDS: Plato, Priscian, Erasmus
   REAL AND ARTIFICIAL RHYTHMS AND MOTIONS: Berardi

2. PITCH (Vibrations produced by motion of a sounding body): Euclid, Aristides

   CONTINUOUS AND DISTINCT PITCH: Aristoxenus, Cicero, Bartók

   Medial motion or chant: Aristides
   Tone (pitch with steady vibrations): Gaudentius, Rameau
   Noise (irregular vibrations): Laloy, Luening
   Liquescence (fading away of tone): Guido, Corelli, Luening
   Glissando: Bartók

   PITCH AND SYLLABLE: Hindu, Priscian, Hucbald, Guido, Waelrant, Puteanus

   A AS CENTRAL NOTE OF SYSTEM: Aristotle, Absolute pitch at Paris Academy, Stravinsky

3. INTERVAL (Ratio of pitches) AND MODE (Pattern of steps)

   FIFTH: Chinese pentatonic modes as spiral of fifths
   FOURTH: Tetrachords

Fixed and mobile tones in the diatonic, chromatic, and enharmonic genera: Aristoxenus, Aristides, Gaudentius, Vitruvius, Vicentino

Disjunct and conjunct tetrachords: Gaudentius, Hucbald
Dasien tetrachords: Priscian, *Musica Enchiriadis*

OCTAVE: Pythagoras, Aristotle, Gaudentius, Prosdocimus, *Musica Enchiriadis*

Discrete intervals within the octave: Euclid, Aristides, Gaudentius, Boethius

Division of the octave into fifth plus fourth (Authentic mode with fifth below, plagal mode with fourth below): Gaudentius, Aurelian, Odo, Glareanus, Zarlino

HEXACHORD SYSTEM (Six-tone pattern with half step in middle): Guido, de Vitry

OCTAVE SYSTEM (Solmization with seven syllables through successive octaves): Puteanus

COMPOUND INTERVALS: Gaudentius, *Musica Enchiriadis*, Koch

MICROTONES

Perceptible and imperceptible intervals: Hindu, Aristoxenus, Aristides

Division of a whole tone into half, third, and quarter tones: Aristoxenus, Aristides

CONSONANCE AND DISSONANCE: Hindu, Arabic, *Musica Enchiriadis*, Guido

The six sonorous numbers: Zarlino
Tritone: Gaudentius, *Musica Enchiriadis*, Byrd, Koch
Augmented second

4. RHYTHM

PULSE OR BEAT: Cicero, Gafurius, Praetorius, Frescobaldi, Corelli, Couperin

ACCENT

Upbeat and downbeat: Cicero, Guido
Short and long (poetic feet): Cicero, Anonymous IV, Salinas, Morley, Praetorius

DURATION OR TIME VALUE: (Ratio of beats): Gaudentius, Bacchius, Guido, rhythmic modes, Paumann, Zarlino

CADENCE OR RHYTHMIC MOTION: Guido, Couperin

METER

> Perfect and imperfect meters: de Vitry, Marchettus, Paumann, Salinas
>
> Syncopation and suspension: Tinctoris, Morley, Berardi, rag and jazz
>
> Compound meter and hemiola (combination of duple and triple): Praetorius
>
> Proportions (augmentation and diminution): Tinctoris, Praetorius

5. MEDIUM OF PERFORMANCE (Tone color, tone quality, timbre): Aristides, Gaudentius, Rousseau, Laloy, Webern

VOCAL (*cantare*)

> Chant: monophonic, antiphonal, responsorial
> Folk song and popular influence
> Accentuation of the text according to the language

INSTRUMENTAL (*sonare*)

> Folk dance and popular influence
> Expressive effects
>> *String* (tremolo, pizzicato, staccato, smorzando, vibrato): Monteverdi, Corelli, Brossard, Cui, Grieg, de Falla
>>
>> *Wind* (tonguing, glissando): Artusi, Handy
>> *Keyboard:* Frescobaldi, Couperin, J. S. Bach, Mozart, Liszt, Field, Gottschalk
>>
>> *Orchestra:* Mannheim dynamics, Kirnberger, Haydn, Weber, Wagner, Rimsky-Korsakov, jazz
>>
>> *Chamber music:* Brossard, Koch, Brahms
> Solo performance: Athenaeus
> Concerted performance on wind and string instruments: Athenaeus, Artusi, Schütz
> Soloists (*concertino*) and orchestra (*ripieno*): Berardi, Vivaldi

VOICES AND INSTRUMENTS COMBINED

> Thoroughbass accompaniment (basso continuo)
> Improvised performance

ADJUSTMENT OF TONE AND RHYTHM IN PERFORMANCE

> Intonation: St. Augustine, John the Deacon, Byrd, Praetorius, Billings, Rossini, Cui

Musica ficta: de Vitry, Marchettus, Prosdocimus, Aron

Tempo: tempo rubato, parlando rubato

Dynamics: Cicero, Isidore, Artusi, Rousseau, Haydn

Expression (affect): Cicero, Charlemagne, Guido, Artusi, Praetorius, Rousseau, Koch

Conducting

NOTATED PERFORMANCE

Literate and illiterate sound: Priscian

Neumes, tablature, score

DRAMATIC OR THEATRICAL PERFORMANCE

Song as the medium of imitation in acting: Aristotle, Cicero, Zarlino, Galilei, Rousseau

The chorus as an actor: Plato, Aristotle, Athenaeus, Isidore

OPERA: Italian, French, German, Russian, English

EFFECT OF LOCATION ON PERFORMANCE: Vitruvius, Isidore, Artusi

6. COMPOSITION (Organizing the elements of music with inventive genius)

MELODY: Melodic modulation, phrasing, period, cadence, repetition, double period with open and closed endings, mutation, motion by step and by leap, retrograde motion

MUSICO-POETIC FORMS: *Chanson de geste;* Italian ballata, madrigal; French virelai, ballade, rondeau; blues

SAME MELODY IN DIFFERENT VOICE-PARTS: Magadizing, parallel organum, fauxbourdon, round, exchange of voices

DIFFERENT MELODIES (polyphonic texture): Contrary motion, clausula, interaction of rhythm (*talea*) and pitch (*color*) in isorhythmic motet, prohibition of parallel fifths and octaves, order of composing parts, cadence, the modes of different parts, composing for more than four voices

THEME OR SUBJECT: As a cantus firmus in one voice through the work, as a point of imitation in a motet

ORNAMENTATION, DIMINUTION, VARIATION

CONTRAPUNTAL TECHNIQUES (strict or learned style in contrast to the free or gallant style)

Imitation: canon, subject and answer, real and artificial rhythms and motions, fugue

Combining several melodies into one: Paumann, Mattheson, Rousseau

HARMONIC MOTION IN THE CYCLE OF FIFTHS: China, Paumann, Bull, Kircher, Rameau

THE MAIN IDEA AND ITS DEVELOPMENT

Form of sonata as a whole: Czerny, Webern
Form of first movement of a sonata: Czerny
Balance between homophony and polyphony: Koch, Webern
Recurrence of an idea as a cyclic element: Berlioz, Wagner

PROGRAM MUSIC: Berlioz, Mendelssohn, Cui, Debussy

TONALITY AND BEYOND (chromaticism, ambiguous chords): Wagner, Verdi, Handy, Webern, Debussy, Schoenberg, Bartók, Hindemith, Stravinsky

COMPOSITION WITH INFINITE SONANT AND RHYTHMIC POSSIBILITIES: Laloy, Luening

Index

Passing tones, 199, 214–215
  chromatic (*see* Foreign tones)
  connecting notes, 286
Passion in music, 1, 21, 67, 69, 167, 195
Pastoral, 150, 181, 263
Paumann, 96–97, 104, 367, 369
Pavan, 139–140, 147, 173
Pedal-point, 310
Pendulum for beating time, 291, 320–321
Pentachord, 99, 339
Pentameter, 63
Pentatonic series, 4, 365
Perception of sound, 15, 17–18, 21, 36, 58, 318–
  321
Percussion, 12, 38, 235, 321, 349, 352
Perfect and imperfect time, 89
Perfect intervals, 68, 74, 190–191, 345
  fifth, combining major and minor third, 127,
    212
  most perfect interval, 122
  unison, fifth, octave, 90
Perfection (three beats), 80, 85, 89
Performance of melody, 17, 21, 55
  by human voice, 230–231
  by instruments, 200, 204, 232
Performance practice, 133–138, 173, 190, 218–
  220, 223–225, 265–266, 365–369
  adjustment of tone and rhythm, 367–368
  concerted music for voices with instruments,
    169
  distance of performers, 134, 253
  dramatic or theatrical, 22, 326, 368
  electronic, 322
  guitar, 309–311
  improvised, 59, 179, 202, 210, 367
  instrumental:
    ensemble, 177
    orchestral, 134, 253
    solo, 252
    string quartet, 229, 270, 341, 343
    trio sonata, 174–176
  keyboard, 171, 204, 228, 271
    clavichord, 100, 277
    left hand beat, 228
    organ, 153, 228
    varying the reprise, 210
    with or without, 159–160
  liquescence, 63–64, 81, 176
  location, effect of, 134
  medium of, 273, 367
  minute time values, 176
  opera, 182–186, 272, 274, 278–281, 368
  ornaments, 145, 171, 187, 188
  piano, 244, 258, 263–264, 268–271, 295, 300,
    306–307
  recitative, 197–198
  trumpet, 206–209
  violin, 227, 309, 314
    arpeggiating chords on, 202
    conducting with, 251–252, 341
  vocal:
    acting while singing, 69
    antiphonal and responsorial, 51
    articulation, 47
    choral, 10, 27, 42
    chromatic alterations during, 83–84
    difficult leaps, 108
    directions to singers, 101
    fauxbourdon, 108
    live instruction, 145
    solo, 10, 41, 79, 95, 344
    use of solmization syllables, 110
Pergolesi, Giovanni Battista, 267
Peri, Jacopo, 126, 153, 157
Period, 31, 61–62, 216, 243–244, 277
  eight bar, 328–330
Periodic vibration, 320–321

Perotin, 78–83
Petrarch, 70
Petrus de Cruce, 81
Phalèse, Pierre, 168
Philosophy and music, 112, 169, 195, 285
Phonograph, 347, 352
Phrase, 368
  melodic, 57, 60–63, 65, 216, 300
  poetic, 61
  rhythmic, 80
  word, 56, 272
Phrygian mode, 110–11, 122, 124, 213
Physical and metaphysical speculation, 190
Pianissimo, 224
Piano (Pianoforte), 226, 249, 263, 305, 322
  arrangement for, 268, 280, 305
  composition for, 264, 294, 298
  construction of, 226–228
  electro-, 347
  tuning and temperament of, 343, 346
Piano (soft), 177, 220, 224
Piccolo flute, 249
Pieces, musical, 187–188
Pipe, 2–5, 15, 26, 73, 111, 131, 137, 142
  organ, 284
  vocal, 138
Pitch, 346, 365
  absolute and relative, 3, 273
  choir, chamber, and cornett, 273
  continuous, medial, discrete, 17–18, 21
  fixed and variable, 24, 33, 52, 319–321
  indefinite, indeterminate, 36, 110
  inflection from language, 1, 35
  raise or lower, 88
  stationary position, 23
  tension and relaxation, 12, 18, 21, 49, 123, 319
Pitch pipe, 3–4, 289, 338
Pizzicato, 154, 367
Places where music is performed:
  chamber, 73
  church, 156
  concert hall, 134–136, 218, 248, 270, 318, 323,
    333–337, 353
  opera house, 183
  theater, 33–35, 184
Plainchant, 71, 82, 86, 88, 140
Plato, 9–11, 14, 17, 35, 40, 112, 150
  elements of melody or song, 9–10, 156
Plectrum, 28, 57
Pleyel, Ignaz Joseph, 233, 249
Plica, 81
Plucked instruments, 73, 98, 310
Poetic feet, 7–8, 62–63, 80, 107, 119–120
  iamb, 28, 29, 31
  relation to dance, 141
  spondee, 148
  trochee, 31, 139, 148
Poetics (Aristotle), 14, 16–17
Poetry and music, 16, 29, 69, 131, 184
  phrase, 61
  stanza, 68, 70, 85, 94–96, 154, 340–341
  verse, 1, 50, 61–63, 70, 107, 142, 184, 272, 339–
    340
    double, 77, 94–95
Poets as musicians, 40, 69, 71–73, 132 (*see also*
  Rhapsodists)
Point, 139 (*see also* Punctum, Theme)
Points of voluntary, 140
Polar attraction of sound, 344–346
Polarization of treble and bass, 186
Polonaise, 264
Polos, 311
Polyphony, 74, 78, 111, 154, 319, 368
  balance with homophony, 369
  fourteenth-century, 92
  modern, 308
  rhythmic proportions in, 103–106